M000267487

WAMPUM

ALSO BY DONALD CRAIG MITCHELL

Sold American:
The Story of Alaska Natives and Their Land, 1867-1959
(1997 and 2003)

Take My Land Take My Life:
The Story of Congress's Historic Settlement of
Alaska Native Land Claims, 1960-1971
(2001)

WAMPUM

HOW INDIAN TRIBES, THE MAFIA, AND AN INATTENTIVE CONGRESS INVENTED INDIAN GAMING AND CREATED A $28 BILLION GAMBLING EMPIRE

DONALD CRAIG MITCHELL

THE OVERLOOK PRESS
NEW YORK, NY

Henderson County Public Library

This edition first published in hardcover in the United States in 2016
by The Overlook Press, Peter Mayer Publishers, Inc.

141 Wooster Street
New York, NY 10012
www.overlookpress.com

For bulk and special sales, please contact sales@overlookny.com,
or write us at the address above.

Copyright © 2016 by Donald Craig Mitchell

All rights reserved. No part of this publication may be reproduced
or transmitted in any form or by any means, electronic or mechanical,
including photocopy, recording, or any information storage and
retrieval system now known or to be invented, without permission
in writing from the publisher, except by a reviewer who wishes to quote
brief passages in connection with a review written for inclusion
in a magazine, newspaper, or broadcast.

Cataloging-in-Publication Data is available from the Library of Congress

Book design and type formatting by Bernard Schleifer
Manufactured in the United States of America
ISBN: 978-1-4683-0993-5

FIRST EDITION
1 3 5 7 9 10 8 6 4 2

Henderson County Public Library

For Myles Anderberg and Osley Saunooke

CONTENTS

INTRODUCTION

> Indians are no different from anybody else.
> They've shown that if they have the oppor-
> tunity to make a buck, they'll act on it.
>
> DISTRICT JUDGE LAUGHLIN WATERS

O N FEBRUARY 8, 2007 THE BUXOM TABLOID CELEBRITY ANNA NICOLE
Smith died of a prescription drug overdose in her suite on the sixth
floor of Anna Nicole's favorite venue: the Hard Rock Hotel & Casino
in Hollywood, Florida.

A twenty-minute drive west from Fort Lauderdale, the Hard Rock
Hotel & Casino, which opened in 2004, is bounded on the east by Route
441, a stop-and-go commuter artery lined with used car lots, fast food
restaurants, X-rated video stores, and pawn shops, and on the west by the
Florida Turnpike.

The twelve-story hotel commands the skyline. On the west side of
the hotel is a faux-Polynesian swimming lagoon. On the east side is an
open-air shopping mall. Between the two, the casino is the anchor.

When Anna Nicole died the casino's gaming floor was jammed with
rows of video gaming machines whose software had been programmed
to allow players to play bingo, but whose blinking lights and beeping
sound effects fostered the illusion that the bingo machines were video
slot machines. Today, the fake slot machines are gone, having been replaced with more than 2,200 real ones, as well as with blackjack and
baccarat tables.

In keeping with the Hard Rock motif, the casino's walls are covered
with rock-and-roll memorabilia ranging from guitars once used by Duff
McKagan of Guns N' Roses and Richie Sambora of Bon Jovi to three jack-
ets with modish purple collars that Eric Clapton, Jeff Beck, and Jimmy
Page wore onstage when they played with the Yardbirds.

What is a sprawling Las Vegas–style casino complex doing in the
midst of the working-class detritus of suburban south Florida? The answer

is posted on a sign on the shoulder of the Florida Turnpike west of the hotel that notifies southbound drivers they are: "Entering Seminole Indian Reservation."

In 1911, President William Howard Taft signed an executive order that withdrew 480 acres of federal land west of Fort Lauderdale "as a reservation for the Seminole Indians in southern Florida." At the time, the reservation was part of the Everglades, a saw-grass swamp whose only dry ground was a hammock known as Big City Island. The reservation also was deserted, since the fewer than four hundred Seminoles in Florida lived deeper in the Everglades or near Miami, where they wrestled alligators for tourists and sold handicrafts. But by 1927, the New River Canal, which Florida governor Napoleon Bonaparte Broward had begun dredging in 1906, had dried out the swamp around Big City Island.

That year, the Bureau of Indian Affairs (BIA) constructed an administration building and a schoolhouse on the reservation, as well as a row of cottages into which Ivy Stranahan, the chairwoman of the Seminole Indian Committee of the Florida Federation of Women's Clubs, whose husband operated a trading post at Fort Lauderdale that Seminole alligator hunters frequented, persuaded three Seminole families to move.

Today, several hundred descendants of the Seminoles who lived in Florida in 1911 live on the Hollywood Reservation in a single-family housing tract across the street from the Hard Rock Hotel & Casino and directly south of the tribal headquarters, a gated and guarded office building that has a helicopter pad on the roof.

Most other members of the 4,000-member Seminole Tribe live on the bucolic Big Cypress Reservation in the Everglades west of Hollywood and on the Brighton Reservation west of Lake Okeechobee. At Brighton, the tribe operates a casino, as it does on small parcels of land in Immokalee, Coconut Creek, and Tampa. Like the hotel and casino on the Hollywood Reservation, the hotel and casino in Tampa is a Hard Rock.

Only the Seminole Tribe and the National Indian Gaming Commission, the federal agency Congress created in 1988, know how much money the tribe now earns annually from its video slot machines and card games. A conservative estimate is $2.1 billion, and that does not include the money the tribe earns from its hotels and restaurants and from its other businesses, including Hard Rock Cafe International, which the tribe purchased in 2007 for $965 million and which operates restaurants, hotels, and casinos in sixty countries.

And the Seminole Tribe is not alone. In 2015, 239 other groups the BIA says are Indian tribes operated 478 casinos, bingo halls, and other types of gambling facilities in twenty-eight states. In 2014, those facilities collectively earned $28.5 billion in gross gaming revenue.

The amount of money the tribes are making is astronomical because the demand for what they are selling is insatiable.

In all cultures throughout all epochs of human history, human beings have loved to gamble. Six-sided dice called *astragali*, fashioned from the knuckle bones of sheep, have been found at archaeological sites in Iraq. The ancient Egyptians believed the god Thoth invented gambling, and hieroglyphics that decorate the walls of their tombs include depictions of the activity. According to the New Testament, at the foot of the cross on which Jesus was crucified, Roman soldiers cast lots to determine who would win his cloak. In 1530, the city of Florence began La Lotto de Firenze, the world's first municipal lottery. In 1949, Mao Zedong abolished gambling in China, but in 2009 the China Center for Lottery Studies estimated that revenue from illegal gambling in the country totaled $146 billion in 2008.

In the United States in 2010, nearly one-third of all Americans twenty-one years of age or older—60 million people—visited a casino. Visitors who lived less than a two-hour drive from a casino made an average of nine trips. In 2008, when the Seminole Tribe began offering blackjack and baccarat at the Hard Rock Casino, patrons lined up three- and four-deep around each table waiting for a chance to play, and a tribal spokesman estimated that "in the first two weeks of play there was approximately—as close as we can figure—about 40,000 players."

Several million people live within a two-hour drive of the Hard Rock Casino. But the month after the Seminole Tribe began offering blackjack and baccarat, the Quapaw Tribe opened a casino in a farm town in northeastern Oklahoma that in 2000 had 984 residents. Less than an hour after the doors opened, 10,000 players had crowded onto the gaming floor to compete for a chance to give their money to one of the 2,000 video gaming machines. That December, when the Shingle Springs Band of Miwok Indians opened a casino in the foothills northeast of Sacramento, California, within an hour of the opening traffic was backed up bumper-to-bumper for a mile west of the freeway exit leading to the casino.

When they press the button on a video slot machine or place a bet at a blackjack or craps table, every gambler knows that, because the house sets the odds, the house wins. So why do men and women the world over think they can beat the house odds?

The first reason is that once in a while someone does. In 2007, at the Wind River Casino the Northern Arapaho Tribe operates in Wyoming, a patron put $2 into a video slot machine and won $454,716. In 2010, a retired firefighter won $8.4 million playing a video slot machine at the Twin Pine Casino that the Middletown Rancheria of Pomo Indians operates in California. When they hear that such wondrous lightening has struck, everyone, including me, fantasizes, if only for a moment, that next time it just might strike them.

A second reason people gamble is because they enjoy the factitious comradery that being part of the crowd on a gaming floor can create. Several years ago, I met that segment of the market at B.J.'s Bingo, a 584-seat bingo hall a Puyallup Indian woman named Bertha Jane Turnipseed operates on the Pacific Coast Highway north of Tacoma, Washington. On the Wednesday evening I visited, most of the patrons, the majority of whom were middle-aged to elderly women, were wearing red. When I asked two silver-haired women why, they explained that Wednesday is Red Rageous Night, and every player who wears red receives $25 worth of bingo cards. They also told me they and their friends play bingo at B.J.'s at least three evenings a week.

A third reason people gamble is because, over thousands of years, risk-taking has been hardwired into the human brain. When a risk is taken and the risk pays off, winning triggers a neurotransmitter called dopamine, and the level of dopamine swirling through the brain increases. When the level comes down, the brain wants to experience the pleasure of the swirl again. A snort of cocaine up the nose pulls the same trigger.

Because, like other drug highs, the dopamine high that making a bet and winning produces can be manipulated, International Game Technology and the other companies that manufacture video gaming machines have spent millions of dollars perfecting the ability of their machines to intensify the dopamine high in order to keep a gambler gambling until he or she has nothing left to gamble with.

But that puts us ahead of the story.

In 2003, by which time gambling casinos on Indian reservations had become commonplace in a majority of states, the thought crossed my mind: How had Indian gaming happened? I now know the answer to that question, and this book tells the story.

The story begins in the eighteenth century, when newspapers in colonial America regularly published the betting odds for cockfights. Over the more than two hundred years since, from Wild Bill Hickok holding a pair of aces and a pair of eights when he was shot in the back while playing poker in a Dakota Territory saloon in 1876, to the carpet joint casinos organized crime figure Meyer Lansky operated in New York and Florida, to the slot machines Mafia don Frank Costello operated under police protection in New York and Louisiana, to street-corner craps games and penny-ante poker games, to today's Super Bowl and March Madness office betting pools, in every state and in all its guises, gambling has been and continues to be ubiquitous. By 1910, however, every state legislature had prohibited casino gambling.

Nevada's experience to 1931 was typical. In 1860, the principal leisure activities of the mostly male residents of Virginia City, the raucous mining camp at the site of the Comstock silver strike, were drinking, whoring, and gambling. According to geologist Eliot Lord, when he visited Virginia City's saloons: "Little stacks of gold and silver fringed the monte tables" and "The rattle of dice, coin, balls, and spinning-markers, the flapping of greasy cards and the chorus of calls and interjections went on day and night."

In 1861, President Abraham Lincoln appointed James Nye, the commissioner of the New York City Police Department, governor of the Nevada Territory. When he assumed office, Nye urged the Nevada legislature to prohibit gambling because "of all the seductive vices extant, I regard that of gambling as the worst." To the undoubted amusement of the pick-and-shovel-wielding libertines in Virginia City, in 1863, the Nevada legislature followed Governor Nye's lead and made operating a game of chance a felony.

In 1864, when Nevada became a state, Nye's successor shared his predecessor's low opinion of the activity. In 1869, Nevada governor Henry Blasdel admonished the legislature that gambling was "the root of all evils" and "the highway that leads to immorality and crime."

This time, however, the legislature found the condemnatory rhetoric unpersuasive, and, over the governor's veto, enacted a statute that regulated, rather than prohibited, gambling. In 1909, the pendulum swung again when the Reno Women's Civic Reform Club and the Reno Anti-Gambling League convinced the legislature to reenact a blanket prohibition on gambling, the only consequence of which, according to historians Barbara and Myrick Land, was to move the activity into the shadows. In the only town in Nevada large enough to call itself a city, gamblers "found their way to the new clubs of Reno—half-hidden, dimly lighted, and without identifying signs. There the high-stakes games were usually played at night, with a tough man with a rasping voice and a two-day beard keeping close watch at the door."

But then Nevada broke the mold. In 1931, a member of the Nevada State Assembly, Philip Tobin, introduced a legalization bill because he thought gambling establishments should pay their fair share of state and municipal taxes. George Wingfield, the richest man in Nevada, whose political machine controlled the legislature, also supported legalization. And a year earlier, a real estate developer in Las Vegas had placed advertisements in the local newspapers in which he opined that the solution to the economic doldrums the state was experiencing was for the legislature to transform Nevada into the "playground of the United States" by legalizing "wide-open gambling."

In March 1931, the Nevada legislature passed Tobin's bill. The morning after Gov. Fred Balzar signed the bill into law, a *New York Times* reporter described the stentorious scene at the Bank Club in Reno:

> At 10:00 a.m. the principal gambling hall in the heart of the city was thronged with hundreds who played or strolled about the roulette wheels, faro tables, mechanical dice throwing and other gambling games. The hum and hubbub of gambling, the click-clack of machines and the clatter of poker chips were partly drowned by the staccato noise of a compressed air drill operated by a construction crew engaged in cutting through massive walls to enlarge the gaming room.

Two days later, the same reporter described for *Times* readers what the laws of probability produce when a gambler on a dopamine high stays high trying to beat the house odds:

In a downtown gambling hall a man who kept about $3,000 in front of him has played faro for thirty-three hours without leaving his seat. He still was at the table late today. Although his fortunes had varied, at that hour he was reported two or three thousand dollars behind.

Legalized gambling transformed Reno into a cacophonous hodge-podge of storefront casinos that operated twenty-four–seven in a town that began celebrating itself as the "Biggest Little City in the World," which it was until 1941, when neon-lit marquees even more garish than those on the casinos in Reno began lighting up the night along the section of highway west of Las Vegas that the world soon would know as The Strip.

The first hotel-casino to open on the Las Vegas Strip was the El Rancho in 1941. Five years later, Meyer Lansky's boyhood friend Bugsy Siegel opened the Flamingo, the construction of which Siegel financed with money from Mafia families in New York, Cleveland, Kansas City, Minneapolis, and Chicago. By 1960, the Desert Inn, the Sahara, the Riviera, the Dunes, the Hacienda, the Tropicana, the Stardust, and other hotel-casinos, most Mafia-financed and controlled, had transformed the Las Vegas Strip into a resort destination.

In 1941, when the El Rancho opened, 16,000 people lived in Las Vegas's Clark County. In 2015, more than 2.1 million people did, and twenty-six of the fifty largest hotels in the world, which collectively rent out more than 90,000 rooms, are located on The Strip or within a few blocks of it.

After watching gambling transform Las Vegas, in 1954 Paul "Skinny" D'Amato, the owner of the 500 Club, the mob hangout in Atlantic City where the Dean Martin and Jerry Lewis comedy act got its start, pitched New Jersey political bosses on the idea that the state legislature should allow casinos to open in Atlantic City, which since its heyday in the 1920s had deteriorated into a trash-strewn slum.

The idea found no takers. But in 1968, when many of the same bosses attended a surprise birthday party for Skinny, he pitched it again. This time the idea whetted imaginations and, according to Skinny's biographer, transformed the birthday party into "a miniconference of influential Atlantic City and Philadelphia businessmen and politicians to discuss legalization."

Of the politicians at the party, the most influential was Hap Farley, a state senator who had been sent to the New Jersey legislature in 1937 by Enoch "Nucky" Johnson, the Republican boss of southern New Jersey. In 1941, when Johnson was convicted of income tax evasion, Farley took control of the political machine Nucky had built. In 1968, he still controlled it and, according to historians George Sternlieb and James Hughes, in 1970

> Farley attempted to force through the New Jersey Senate enabling legislation for a statewide referendum that would legalize gambling in Atlantic City. Fearing a potential backlash if he were to introduce the bill himself, Farley allowed one of his long-time political cronies, Union County Senator Frank McDermott, to act as its sponsor.

McDermott's public rationale for Farley's bill was that gambling would generate enough tax revenue to stave off the need for the legislature to impose an income tax. But in 1971, the bill died in the Senate Judiciary Committee when the former chairman of the New Jersey State Commission on Investigation told the committee he had been informed by the U.S. Department of Justice that as early as 1969 "rumors began flying" that organized crime figures from as far west as Chicago had begun meeting "to whack up casino gambling in Atlantic City."

In 1972, members of the New Jersey legislature who supported legalization regrouped and persuaded the legislature to create a Gambling Study Commission. The next year, the commission recommended that the state constitution be amended to give the legislature authority to own and operate as many casinos as it wished at any locations in the state it wished as long as voters in the affected municipalities approved.

New Jersey governor Brendan Byrne was agreeable to giving Atlantic City "a shot in the arm," but he opposed the commission's more expansive recommendation. Nevertheless, the legislature put the constitutional amendment the commission recommended on the ballot.

In 1974, when the votes in the November election were counted, the amendment lost by more than 500,000 votes., many of which had been cast by voters who had been lobbied from the pulpit on the Sunday before the election by the more than 3,000 pastors and priests the New Jersey Council of Churches recruited to do so.

Undeterred by the defeat, two years later, the pro-gambling members of the New Jersey legislature again regrouped, this time around a constitutional amendment that authorized the legislature to license private companies to operate casinos only in Atlantic City.

According to Jack Davis, the president of Resorts International, which operated several casinos in the Bahamas, "For the Catholic Church, we made a deal that we wouldn't have bingo, so they were neutralized." The amendment's supporters also raised $1 million to finance a professionally managed campaign,. This time the constitutional amendment passed by more than 300,000 votes.

Two months before the 1976 election, Jack Davis bet on a victory by having Resorts International buy the Chalfonte-Haddon Hall Hotel, one of the decrepit grand dames along the Atlantic City boardwalk. The hotel was repainted and renamed the Resorts International Hotel & Casino. During its first year of operation, the casino's 30,000-square-foot gaming floor generated $134 million in gross gaming revenue.

Since 1978, there have been as many as fourteen casinos in Atlantic City that, until recently when their revenues began plummeting, made their owners hundreds of millions of dollars.

Prior to the 1974 election, Hugh Hefner, the publisher of *Playboy* magazine, who hoped to open a casino in New Jersey, predicted that if New Jersey voters voted to allow casinos "that will speed up what I think is inevitable in some other states." Contrary to Hefner's prediction, the passage by New Jersey voters in 1976 of the constitutional amendment that authorized casinos in Atlantic City did not open the flood-gates to casino gambling in other states. Although at the time no one appreciated that it would, the event that did open the flood-gates occurred three years later when in 1979 the Seminole Tribe opened a bingo hall on the tribe's reservation in Hollywood, Florida.

How the Seminole Tribe was able to open its bingo hall is a story that begins, not in Florida in 1979, but in Washington, D.C., in 1934.

1: SOVEREIGNTY AND CIGARETTES

> That state laws have no force within the ter-
> ritory of an Indian tribe in matters affecting
> Indians is a general proposition that has not
> been successfully challenged.
>
> —FELIX S. COHEN

BROWARD COUNTY—IN WHICH THE SEMINOLE RESERVATION IN HOLLY-
wood, Florida, is located—is 1,200 square miles of housing tracts,
condominium developments, strip malls, and office buildings that are
part of the suburban sprawl that runs down the east side of south Florida.
One million eight hundred thousand people live in Broward County, fewer
than a thousand of whom are members of the Seminole Tribe. All Broward
County residents, including members of the Seminole Tribe, are required
to comply with the state of Florida's civil and criminal laws.

In 1967, the Florida legislature passed a law that authorized charitable,
nonprofit, and veterans organizations to operate bingo games. The law prohibited an organization from holding bingo games more than two days a
week, limited jackpots to no more than $100, required the games to be con-
ducted by unpaid volunteers, and required each organization to spend the
money it earned on the organization's charitable and nonprofit endeavors.
Nevertheless, in 1979, when the Seminole Tribe opened its bingo hall on the
Hollywood Reservation, bingo games were held seven nights a week, jackpots
ranged from $200 to $2,000, paid employees operated the games, and the
tribe did what it wanted with its share of the profits.

The Seminole Tribe ignored Florida's bingo law because, on the
morning of the day the hall opened, in the U.S. District Court in Fort Lauderdale District Judge Norman Roettger issued an injunction that prohibited
Bob Butterworth, the sheriff of Broward County, from enforcing the state's
bingo law inside the boundaries of the Hollywood Reservation. Judge
Roettger decided as he did based on his understanding of the agglomeration

of federal treaties and statutes, Department of the Interior regulations and legal opinions, and judicial decisions that attorneys who practice in the subject area call "Indian law," a swirl of analytical confusion whose core principle is the doctrine of inherent tribal sovereignty.

According to the doctrine, every Indian tribe possesses inherent sovereign powers that predate the founding of the United States in 1776. As a consequence, the state in which a tribe's reservation is located has no authority to enforce its laws inside the boundaries of the reservation except to the extent the U.S. Congress has delegated the state that authority. Since 1979, when the Seminole Tribe successfully invoked the doctrine of inherent tribal sovereignty in Judge Roettger's courtroom, the doctrine has provided the legal underpinning for the Indian gaming industry. And today, for the 240 tribes that operate casinos, bingo halls, and other types of gambling facilities, the doctrine is a sacrosanct legal principle whose validity is beyond question.

But the doctrine of inherent tribal sovereignty is a sophistry.

In 1607, when European colonists began settling along the Eastern Seaboard, two million people lived on the North American continent, divided into hundreds of groups that anthropologists call "tribes," whose members occupied demarcated territories.

In 1776, when the thirteen colonies declared their independence from Britain and joined to create the United States, the fact that thousands of Indians were living west and south of the new nation's borders and were resisting the intrusion of white settlers into their territories was a serious problem. But operating under the Articles of Confederation that took effect in 1781, the federal government had neither the legal authority nor the military capability to do much about it. By 1788, the situation was so out of control on the North Carolina frontier that Secretary of War Henry Knox reported to Congress that "an actual although informal war" was raging between white settlers and Cherokee Indians that Knox blamed on the settlers' "avaricious desire" for the land the Cherokees occupied. The situation northwest of the Ohio River was the same.

To bolster the federal government's legal authority to deal with the Indian problem, the delegates who attended the Constitutional Convention of 1787 included a clause in the U.S. Constitution that grants Congress authority "To regulate Commerce" with "the Indian Tribes." When he assumed the presidency, George Washington persuaded Congress to exercise its Indian Commerce Clause authority by authorizing the War Department to open trading posts, called factories, across the frontier. The factories were not in business to make money. Rather, their purpose was to encourage Indians to consider iron kettles, wool blankets, and similar trade goods necessities; the theory being that when trade goods became necessities, to maintain their access to the factories' inventories, Indians would cede their right to occupy land on which whites wanted to settle.

Washington prohibited factory managers from extending credit. However, when he became president, Thomas Jefferson directed the managers to encourage Indians to go as deeply into debt as the managers could persuade them to go, because, as he explained in 1803, "[W]hen these debts get beyond what the individuals can pay, they become willing to lop them off by a cession of lands."

Trying to transform Indians into consumers who would voluntarily cede their right to occupy large tracts of land to settle their debts was an interesting experiment in human psychology. But the experiment was derailed by John Jacob Astor, whose American Fur Company competed with the factories for Indian furs. When Congress abolished the factory system in 1822 at Astor's instigation, the federal government was left with only two ways to quiet Indian objections to white settlement. The first was removal; the second, military force.

Jefferson first advocated removal in 1803, when he predicted that Indians "will in time either incorporate with us as citizens of the United States, or remove beyond the Mississippi." In 1825, President James Monroe recommended that Congress adopt removal as the nation's official Indian policy because, as a consequence of the Louisiana Purchase, there was a "vast territory" between "the limits of our present States and Territories, and the Rocky Mountains and Mexico" into which the "tribes now within our limits might gradually be drawn."

Congress took no action on Monroe's recommendation. Then, in 1828, Andrew Jackson was elected president.

In 1783, the Treaty of Peace that ended the Revolutionary War established the Mississippi River as the western boundary of the United States, even though the thirteen states that had formed the new nation were clustered along the Eastern Seaboard. But by 1829 when Jackson assumed office, the public domain east of the river had been divided into the states of Mississippi,

Alabama, Tennessee, Illinois, Indiana, Kentucky, Michigan, and Ohio. Indians who lived east of the river now lived inside the jurisdiction of a state government; a situation Jackson considered ripe for more interracial conflict.

To prevent such conflict, in his first Annual Message to Congress, Old Hickory recommended that Congress set "apart an ample district west of the Mississippi, and without the limits of any State or Territory now formed, to be guaranteed to the Indian tribes as long as they shall occupy it." Congress accepted the recommendation, and in 1830 authorized the president to designate land west of the river as districts "for the reception of such tribes or nations of Indians as may choose to exchange lands where they now reside, and remove there."

Jackson had recommended that removal be voluntary because "it would be as cruel as unjust to compel the aborigines to abandon the graves of their fathers and seek a home in a distant land." But that is not how removal was carried out.

Here is how Alexis de Tocqueville, who traveled through America in 1831, described the "negotiations" in which the headmen of Indian tribes whose members occupied land east of the river agreed to move west:

> The expulsion of the Indians often takes place at the present day in a regular and, as it were, a legal manner. When the European population begins to approach the limit of the desert inhabited by a savage tribe, the government of the United States usually sends forward envoys who assemble the Indians in a large plain and, having first eaten and drunk with them, [explain why they must move. The envoys then] spread before the eyes of the Indians firearms, woolen garments, kegs of brandy, glass necklaces, bracelets of tinsel, ear-rings, and looking glasses. If, when they have beheld all these riches, they still hesitate, it is insinuated that they cannot refuse the required consent and that the government itself will not long have the power of protecting them in their rights. What are they to do? Half convinced and half compelled, they go to inhabit new deserts, where the importunate whites will not let them remain ten years in peace.

By 1850, thousands of Indians who lived east of the Mississippi River had been relocated. By then, gold had been discovered in California, and it was not long before thousands, and soon tens of thousands, of white settlers wanted to plant crops, graze cattle, and mine gold, silver, and copper west of the river. To clear that land of Indians, Commissioner of Indian Affairs Luke Lea* recommended that tracts of land with "well-defined boundaries" be designated as reservations within which the members of tribes who lived west of the Mississippi River would "be compelled to remain until such time as their general improvement and good conduct may supercede the necessity of such restrictions."

When thousands of Indians refused to be confined on the reservations to which they had been assigned, their recalcitrance provoked a guerrilla war that raged across the frontier for more than twenty years. According to historian Robert Utley, "Virtually every major war of the two decades after Appomattox was fought to force Indians on to newly created reservations or to make them go back to reservations from which they had fled."

To maintain the fiction that the confinement of Indians on reservations was voluntary, the federal government "negotiated" treaties in which tribal leaders agreed to their own confinement. Today, tribal leaders are adamant that their tribes and the United States government are, and have always been, co-equal sovereigns. But that is mythology masquerading as history.

In 1854, for example, Isaac Stevens, the superintendent of Indian affairs for the territory of Washington, met with sixty-two headmen, representing nine tribes, at Medicine Creek, fifteen miles east of Olympia, Washington. When the meeting convened, Stevens's interpreter, Benjamin Shaw, explained the terms of a treaty that had been written before the meeting: in exchange for a cash payment, the members of the tribes the headmen represented would cede their right to occupy 2.5 million acres of land east and south of Puget Sound and agree to move on to three small reservations.

After reviewing the record of the negotiation of the Treaty of Medicine Creek in 1974, District Judge George Boldt concluded that

> the treaty provisions and the remarks of the treaty commissioners were interpreted by Colonel Shaw to the Indians in the Chinook jargon and then translated into native languages by Indian interpreters. Chinook jargon, a trade medium of limited vocabulary and simple grammar,

---

*In 1824, Secretary of War John C. Calhoun established the Bureau of Indian Affairs (BIA) inside the War Department and appointed the commissioner of Indian affairs as the supervisor of the BIA bureaucracy. In 1849, Congress transferred the BIA to the Department of the Interior.

was inadequate to express precisely the legal effects of the treaties, although the general meaning of treaty language could be explained. Many of those present, however, did not understand Chinook jargon.

Nevertheless, when Shaw finished explaining the treaty in a patois many could not understand, the headmen, all illiterate, signed the Treaty of Medicine Creek with their marks. They did so because, as Shaw explained in 1903,

> there was not a man of note among all the Indians at that council who did not know that they had not a single right that could be maintained by either force of arms or by law. Every one of them recognized that there was no power that could protect them from the encroachment of the white settlers, save and except the Government of the United States . . . [which] had possession of the whole country and could do as they [sic] pleased with it.

Neither Congress nor the secretary of the interior recognized tribal sovereignty inside the boundaries of the reservations. Instead, each reservation was administered by a BIA agent whose word quite literally was the law.

In 1877, Commissioner of Indian Affairs Ezra Hayt asked for authority to write a code of laws for Indian reservations. Bills granting that authority were introduced in Congress, but none were enacted. In 1882 when Commissioner of Indian Affairs Hiram Price again asked for authority to write a code of laws for Indian reservations, Secretary of the Interior Henry Teller told Price to write a code without continuing to wait for Congress to authorize him to do so.

Price wrote a code, and in 1883 he directed BIA agents who had organized an Indian police force on the reservations they supervised to each appoint three members of their police force to serve as judges of a Court of Indian Offenses that would have jurisdiction over "Indian offenses" that included polygamous marriages, drunkenness and whiskey peddling, and unspecified misdemeanors. In 1892, Commissioner of Indian Affairs Thomas Jefferson Morgan amended Price's code to clarify that "misdemeanors" meant misdemeanors "as defined in the laws of the State or Territory within which the reservation may be located."

As late as 1928, after a comprehensive investigation of conditions on Indian reservations, the Institute of Government Research at the Brookings

Institution reported to Secretary of the Interior Hubert Work that

> The charge is frequently made that the Indian judges are dominated by the superintendents [as BIA agents by then had been renamed]. At some reservations where the superintendent conducts the prosecution of the case or even acts as one of the judges, this is undoubtedly true. In fact, at ten reservations the regular Court of Indian Offenses has been abandoned and the superintendent himself has assumed the role of judge. At many other places, however, the decision of the Indian judges is untrammeled, and the only interference by the superintendent is an occasional diminution of punishment. Although the superintendent should not attempt to control the action of the court, and certainly should not himself act as judge, it is extremely desirable that he advise the court when requested, veto its actions when arbitrary and unjust, and assist in enforcing its judgments.

That was the situation on Indian reservations in 1933 when President Franklin Roosevelt appointed John Collier, a dour former social worker, commissioner of Indian affairs.

When he had visited New Mexico in 1920, Collier attended several events at Taos Pueblo and had been struck by what he considered the Pueblo Indians' mystical connection to nature. Profoundly affected by that experience, in 1922 Collier quit his job as a sociology professor in California and moved to Washington, D.C., to lobby against a bill whose enactment would have compromised Pueblo land rights. By 1933 when he was appointed commissioner, Collier was executive secretary of the American Indian Defense Association, an organization dedicated to protecting Indian rights that Collier and other white "friends of the Indian" had organized.

Since the end of the Indian wars more than forty years earlier, there had been a consensus among the members of the Senate and House Committees on Indian Affairs that Congress should encourage Indians living on reservations to abandon what remained of their tribal relations and, like the Italians, Irish, and other immigrant minorities, assimilate into the national economy and popular culture. John Collier, however, romanticized life on the reservations. And when he became commissioner he set about writing a bill whose enactment would, without saying so explicitly, have Congress abandon assimilation as the objective of its Indian policy.

To help Collier write his bill, the Department of the Interior hired a twenty-six-year-old attorney from New York City named Felix Cohen. A tall, thin man with wavy hair and wire glasses, Cohen had an easy style and a wry sense of humor. But according to a colleague, he was a "romantic" who, like John Collier, had a "rose-colored picture of Indians." In February 1934 Commissioner Collier sent his bill to Congress.

Because Indians had never had any legal authority to govern themselves on their reservations, section 2 of Title I of the bill authorized the secretary of the interior to issue Indians living on a reservation a charter that granted "such powers of government . . . as may seem fitting in the light of the experience, capacities, and desires of the Indians concerned." To that end, section 3 of Title I authorized the charter to "prescribe a form of government adapted to the [Indians'] needs, traditions, and experience," "specify the powers of self-government to be exercised by the chartered community," and "provide for the planned extension of these powers as the community offers evidence of capacity to administer them."

When the Senate Committee on Indian Affairs held its first hearings on Collier's bill, Sen. Burton Wheeler, the chairman of the committee, objected to many of the bill's provisions, including the authority in sections 2 and 3 of Title I to organize reservation governments. So Collier had no choice but to work with Wheeler to write a new bill the chairman would support. Wheeler's bill passed the Senate, after which its text was blended with the text of a companion bill the members of the House Committee on Indian Affairs had written into the version of the bill that in June 1934 President Roosevelt signed into law as the Indian Reorganization Act (IRA).

According to Indian historian Vine Deloria, a former executive director of the National Congress of American Indians, the preeminent national Indian rights organization, for John Collier the IRA was a "solid defeat" because it "bore little if any resemblance to what he had originally suggested." So to get back what Collier had lost, Felix Cohen set about cooking the law books.

Section 16 of the IRA authorized an Indian tribe to "organize for its common welfare" by adopting a constitution. It also stated: "In addition to all powers vested in any Indian tribe or tribal council by *existing law*, the constitution adopted by said tribe shall also vest in such tribe or its tribal council the following rights and powers," (emphasis added) after which section 16 described three inconsequential governmental powers.

Four months after President Roosevelt signed the IRA into law, in October 1934 the Department of the Interior published a legal opinion Felix Cohen had written entitled "Powers of Indian Tribes," in which Cohen purported to analyze the intent of Congress embodied in the words "existing law" in section 16. According to the opinion:

> Perhaps the most basic principle of all Indian law, supported by a host of decisions hereinafter analyzed, is the principle that *those powers which are lawfully vested in an Indian tribe are not, in general delegated powers granted by express acts of Congress, but rather inherent powers of a limited sovereignty which has never been extinguished.* . . . What is not expressly limited remains within the domain of tribal sovereignty, and therefore properly falls within the statutory category, "powers vested in any Indian tribe or tribal council by existing law." (emphasis in original)

In other words, every Indian tribe possesses "inherent sovereignty," except to the extent Congress has enacted a statute that has taken an attribute of that sovereignty away. But as Vine Deloria notes, "Since Congress had never presumed that tribes had this astounding set of powers, it was unlikely that they [sic] would have thought to limit them specifically." Deloria goes on to say:

> Had Collier's original legislative package been approved without amendment, tribes would have been able to exercise these same powers, except that they would have been *delegated* powers, and delegated by Congress in an experiment in social engineering. . . . With the opinion as the basis of authority, tribal governments could exercise powers of self-government, but these powers were regarded as *inherent* powers, powers that could only be surrendered on the initiative of the tribe or changed, but not abolished, by the Congress. . . . Modern tribal sovereignty thus begins with this opinion. (emphases in original)

In other words, to give Indian tribes the legal authority to govern themselves on their reservations that Senator Wheeler and the other members of the Senate and House Committees on Indian Affairs intentionally withheld, Felix Cohen intentionally misconstrued Wheeler's and the other members' intent.

But that was not Cohen's only prestidigitation. At the U.S. Department of Justice, attorneys who worked in the Lands Division represented the Department of the Interior in lawsuits that involved Indian-related legal issues. Because the federal treaties and statutes, Department of the Interior regulations and legal opinions, and judicial decisions that formed the corpus of "Indian law" were a disorganized muddle, in 1938 Assistant Attorney General Carl McFarland, the head of the Lands Division, decided that the attorneys he supervised needed a manual on Indian law. By 1938 Felix Cohen, who by then had worked at the Department of the Interior for five years, was considered the department's Indian law expert. So McFarland borrowed Cohen to supervise the writing of an Indian law manual. Cohen arrived at the Lands Division in January 1939 and by April had assembled a staff of eight attorneys, two law clerks, and eleven file clerks and secretaries. That same month Norman Littell, a politically connected attorney from Seattle, replaced McFarland as the head of the Lands Division.

Littell initially thought that developing a manual on Indian law was worth the expense because, as he advised Attorney General Frank Murphy, "[T]he present confusion of the law invites litigation, and a clarifying manual currently maintained would seem to be an essential instrument in discharging our legal responsibilities." But he soon began to question whether a manual would have any "practical value," so he appointed an attorney in the Lands Division named Robert Fabian to chair an advisory committee to monitor the project.

Felix Cohen later conjectured that Fabian's private agenda was to discredit Cohen and his work. But rather than Fabian, Cohen's actual problem was Assistant Attorney General Littell. Because, as Carl McFarland had, what Littell wanted was a manual on Indian law that would be of practical value to Lands Division attorneys. But what Cohen told Littell he was writing was a book that "would primarily fulfill for Indian law the function of a text book in other branches of law, such as evidence or contracts." Even more important, rather than describing what Indian law was, Cohen wanted his book to describe what he thought Indian law should be.

When he read the first draft chapters Cohen and his staff had written, Robert Fabian advised Assistant Attorney General Littell that

All of the material submitted gives evidence of inadequate research and lack of experience in the preparation of a law book designed to serve as a complete and accurate handbook for lawyers engaged in actual litigation. Difficult and complex problems are casually answered in the handbook by cursory paragraphs. General propositions of law are stated repeatedly without citation of authority. Citations that are made do not support the propositions for which they are cited.

Littell agreed and terminated the project. Cohen then returned to the Department of the Interior with the draft chapters and the boxes of research material his staff had assembled. Nathan Margold, the solicitor of the Department of the Interior, then allowed Cohen to continue writing the book he wanted to write, which in 1941 the Department of the Interior published as the *Handbook of Federal Indian Law*.

Charles Wilkinson, the Moses Lasky Professor of Law at the University of Colorado Law School and a dean of the Indian law bar, has celebrated the *Handbook* as "one of the greatest treatises in all of the law." Perhaps without appreciating the import of the admission, Professor Wilkinson has also praised the *Handbook* as "one of the more voluminous lawyer's briefs ever produced for the revival of tribal sovereignty."

And it was, because beneath its veneer of erudition, the *Handbook of Federal Indian Law* was a polemic. Nowhere is that fact more apparent than in the chapter entitled "The Scope of Tribal Self-Government." The chapter begins with Cohen's assertion that the powers to govern themselves that Indian tribes possess are not "delegated powers granted by express acts of Congress, but rather inherent powers of a limited sovereignty which has never been extinguished." The *Handbook* then opines that "Each tribe begins its relationship with the Federal government as a sovereign power, recognized as such in treaty and legislation." What was the legal authority the *Handbook* cited for those statements of purported law? The sole footnote cites two: "Powers of Indian Tribes," the legal opinion Felix Cohen wrote in 1934, and an article Cohen wrote in 1940 for the *Minnesota Law Review*.

The Department of the Interior published the *Handbook of Federal Indian Law* in August 1941. In September, Cohen sent a copy to each justice of the U.S. Supreme Court. Several days later, he received a letter from Doris Williamson, a friend who worked at the Court, who reported that she had "showed the book around generally, and it was borrowed almost immediately for reference." Miss Williamson also predicted that the *Handbook* "will probably be cited before long in some opinion."

Less than three months later that prediction proved prescient when in the opinion he wrote in *United States v. Santa Fe Pacific Railway Company*, Justice William O. Douglas cited the *Handbook of Federal Indian Law* in a footnote as legal authority for a principle of law. For the next forty years, the U.S. Supreme Court and the lower federal courts would cite the *Handbook* in hundreds of judicial decisions. The influence the *Handbook* had in persuading the U.S. Supreme Court to accept Felix Cohen's assertion that inside the boundaries of their reservations Indian tribes possess inherent sovereign powers and the state in which a reservation is located has no authority to enforce its laws inside reservation boundaries except to the extent Congress has delegated the state that authority cannot be overstated.

In 1959, Felix Cohen's invention of the doctrine of inherent tribal sovereignty accomplished Cohen's intended objective when the U.S. Supreme Court issued its decision in *Williams v. Lee*.

After destroying their villages and burning their crops, in 1864 the army marched 8,000 Navajos 300 miles from Arizona to New Mexico where they were confined under military guard. In 1868, when the army decided to move the Navajos back to Arizona, Gen. William T. Sherman negotiated a treaty with twelve Navajo headmen the army selected for that purpose. The treaty created a 3.5-million-acre reservation that today straddles the border between Arizona and New Mexico. As he was on all reservations, on the Navajo reservation the BIA agent was the law.

After a series of executive orders added additional land to the reservation, between 1901 and 1908 the BIA divided the Navajo Reservation into five subreservations and appointed an agent for each. Several agents appointed a business council for their subreservations. According to historians Garrick Bailey and Roberta Glenn Bailey:

> The councils did not function as a tribal government. . . . Where councils did exist, they did not really govern or even advise, but merely served the interests of the superintendents [as BIA agents would be renamed]. For example, the early Leupp business council

met to "report violations" of policy and to "control" other Navajos. Consequently, superintendents had a relatively free hand in implementing policy within their jurisdictions. Navajos resisted this usurpation of power only to a limited degree and on a local level. In some cases they were forcibly suppressed when they did.

In the 1920s when oil companies wanted to obtain leases that would allow them to explore the Navajo reservation, in January 1923 the secretary of the interior appointed Herbert Hagerman, who in 1906 had served a brief tenure as governor of the territory of New Mexico, as special commissioner for the Navajos. Commissioner of Indian Affairs Charles Burke then directed each BIA agent to hold an election in his subreservation for the election of a delegate to a Navajo Tribal Council. If Navajos living on a subreservation refused to participate in the election, the secretary of the interior would appoint a delegate to represent that subreservation. The secretary also could remove any delegate, and the council was prohibited from meeting except when Commissioner Hagerman was present. In June 1923 at the first meeting of the Navajo Tribal Council, which Professor Peter Iverson would characterize as "little more than a paper organization," the members of the council unanimously approved a resolution that had been written at BIA headquarters in Washington, D.C. The resolution authorized Special Commissioner Hagerman to sign whatever oil leases he wished "on behalf of the Navajo Indians."

Thirty-six years later in its decision in *Williams v. Lee,* the U.S. Supreme Court made only cursory mention of that history when it decided that the state of Arizona and its courts had no authority to enforce state law within the boundaries of the Navajo Reservation because "implicit" in the terms of the treaty General Sherman had imposed on the army's handpicked Navajo negotiators in 1868 "was the understanding that the internal affairs of the Indians remained exclusively within the jurisdiction of whatever tribal government existed." In a footnote, the Court cited as legal authority, not only the *Handbook of Federal Indian Law*, but also "Powers of Indian Tribes," the legal opinion Felix Cohen had written in 1934.

Felix Cohen invented the doctrine of inherent tribal sovereignty because he believed Native Americans who live on reservations should have autonomy to govern themselves. But whether granting that autonomy is a good policy result or a bad one, the U.S. Supreme Court's acceptance of the doctrine of inherent tribal sovereignty in *Williams v. Lee* and the decisions that have followed it created locations inside the boundaries of states within which, absent congressional authorization, the states had no authority to enforce their laws.

Leonard Tonasket, who lived on the Colville Reservation in northeastern Washington state, was one of the first Indians to understand how that jurisdictional situation could be exploited for financial gain. In 1935, the Washington legislature began requiring cigarette wholesalers and retailers to attach a tax stamp to each pack of cigarettes they sold. In 1964, in a building located just east of the western boundary of the Colville Reservation, Tonasket began selling unstamped, and therefore untaxed, cigarettes to non-Indians who lived in Omak, the farm town a short distance west of the reservation. The Stogie Shop, as Tonasket named his business, was an immediate success. As the BIA superintendent of the Colville Reservation explained when Tonasket and his wife applied for a loan, "The Tonaskets have operated this business for five weeks and have shown a good profit but they have run out of cigarettes each week because they are not able to stock a sufficient quantity to meet the demand."

The next summer, the Washington legislature raised the price of a tax stamp from seven to eleven cents a pack, and business at the Stogie Shop and at the smoke shop another Indian entrepreneur had opened on the Colville Reservation spiked. When the owners of food markets and liquor stores in Omak complained about the unfair competition, in July 1965 the Washington State Tax Commission directed the commission's secretary "to prepare a bulletin advising all cigarette distributors that stamps must be hereafter affixed to cigarettes held for sale to Indians."

When the wholesalers then refused to sell Tonasket and the other Indian owners of smoke shops any more unstamped packs of cigarettes, the twelve tribes whose members jointly occupy the Colville Reservation, as well as other tribes in Washington state whose members by then were selling untaxed cigarettes, filed lawsuits against the commission in which the tribes alleged that the state of Washington had no authority to enforce the legislature's cigarette tax statute inside the boundaries of the tribes' reservations.

In December 1965, Superior Court Judge Hewitt Henry dismissed the first lawsuit because, as the Washington Supreme Court would affirm, since the state was collecting its cigarette tax from wholesalers whose inventories were stored in warehouses located outside the boundaries of the reservations, the incidence of the tax occurred "prior to the entry of the cigarettes into Indian commerce." Judge Henry's decision began fifteen years of jurisdictional confusion regarding the sale of untaxed cigarettes on Indian reservations that the U.S. Supreme Court would not straighten out until 1980.

During the interregnum, in 1967, Washington Department of Revenue agents raided the Stogie Shop and seized 848 cartons of unstamped cigarettes that Leonard Tonasket apparently had acquired from an out-of-state wholesaler. Tonasket then hired an attorney in Omak who filed *Tonasket v. State of Washington*, a lawsuit in which Tonasket contended that the state had no authority within the boundaries of the Colville Reservation to require him to collect its cigarette tax.

When the state Superior Court dismissed the lawsuit, a Seattle attorney named Robert Pirtle took over Tonasket's representation. He appealed the dismissal to the Washington Supreme Court, lost there, and then appealed to the U.S. Supreme Court, which in 1973 sent the case back to the Washington Supreme Court. According to Pirtle, "It was in the Tonasket case that I got my first inkling of what was needed to win lawsuits involving tribal sovereignty: the case would have to be 'sexy,' that is, it would have to incorporate substantial elements of tribal involvement." So while *Tonasket v. State of Washington* was making its way to the U.S. Supreme Court, Pirtle had the tribal councils for the Confederated Tribes of the Colville Reservation, the Makah Tribe, and the Lummi Nation pass ordinances that established a system for licensing smoke shops and taxing their inventories.

Representing the three tribes, the month after the U.S. Supreme Court sent *Tonasket v. State of Washington* back to the Washington Supreme Court, Pirtle filed a new lawsuit, *Confederated Tribes of the Colville Indian Reservation v. State of Washington*, in the U.S. District Court in which he argued that the regulation of the sale of cigarettes on the Colville, Makah, and Lummi Reservations was the tribes' prerogative as sovereign governments. Six months later, District Judge Charles Powell issued, first a temporary restraining order, and then a preliminary injunction, that prohibited the state "from enforcing its cigarette and tobacco products taxes against the Tribes" until the merits of the lawsuit were decided.

In February 1978, a three-judge panel of the U.S. District Court made Judge Powell's preliminary injunction permanent in a decision in which the panel announced that "as applied to non-Indians as a result of their on-reservation purchases from [the Stogie Shop and the other smoke shops], the State's cigarette taxing scheme constitutes an interference with tribal self-government." As authority for that conclusion of law, the panel cited *Williams v. Lee,* in which the U.S. Supreme Court had instructed that "absent governing Acts of Congress, the question has always been whether the state action infringed on the right of reservation Indians to make their own laws and be ruled by them."

Like the Colville Reservation, most Indian reservations in the state of Washington are located distant from the non-Indian population centers. The Puyallup Reservation is an exception. The reservation was established in 1855 at the mouth of the Puyallup River, which empties into Commencement Bay on the shore of Puget Sound south of Seattle. By 1873, when the Northern Pacific Railroad extended its track to Tacoma, on the shore of the bay, the reservation had been expanded to encompass 18,050 acres on both sides of the river.

When the railroad arrived, Tacoma's population boomed, and the new residents quickly became frustrated that land inside the boundaries of the Puyallup Reservation was off-limits. As Washington senator John B. Allen complained to the U.S. Senate in 1890, "The Indian reservation at Tacoma . . . is as much in the way of the growth and the progress of that thrifty and expanding city as a permanent Indian reservation two miles from the national Capital would be in the way of the growth of the city of Washington."

Six years earlier, the BIA had divided 17,663 of the reservation's 18,050 acres into individual parcels, called allotments, that were given to the Indians who lived on the reservation. By 1950, the Indian owners had sold all but ten of their allotments to non-Indians. By 1960, Tacoma's city limits had expanded to include one-fifth of the land within the boundaries of the reservation. And most of the remaining land had been included within the city limits of Fife, the town next door to Tacoma.

When Leonard Tonasket opened the Stogie Shop on the Colville Reservation in 1964, more than 25,000 people, almost all non-Indians, lived inside the boundaries of the Puyallup Reservation. Another 321,000 lived in Pierce County, in which the reservation is located. So a smoke shop on the Puyallup Reservation had tens of thousands of potential customers.

In 1966 a Puyallup Indian named Bob Satiacum opened the first smoke shop on the Puyallup Reservation. By 1974, the Satiacum Smoke Shop was selling almost a million cartons of untaxed cigarettes a year and annually earning its owner $1.2 million.

After Satiacum pioneered the business model, other Puyallup Indians opened smoke shops. One of those individuals was Bertha Jane Turnipseed, whose nickname is B.J., who opened B.J.'s Cigarettes with her Caucasian husband Pernelle, who everyone called Ray. In 1976, the Turnipseeds decided to expand their business by opening a smoke shop on a reservation in another state that, like Washington, had a high cigarette tax. The state they chose was Florida, whose cigarette tax was seventeen cents a pack. The reservation they chose was the Seminole Reservation in Hollywood.

When the Turnipseeds mentioned to a Lummi Indian friend of theirs named Freddie Lane that they were interested in opening a smoke shop on the Seminole Reservation in Hollywood, Lane telephoned Osley Saunooke, with whom Lane was acquainted because both men were active in the National Congress of American Indians.

2: SEMINOLE CIGARETTES

They are just exercising the same rights of
any other Americans to go into business and
make money. If they have an advantage, that
is just the way it is. Why not? The Indians
certainly have not had all the advantages in
a lot of other ways in this country.

VINCENT LOVETT
Bureau of Indian Affairs

OSLEY SAUNOOKE WAS THE RIGHT MAN FOR FREDDIE LANE TO CALL. THE
son of a former chief of the Eastern Band of Cherokees, after having
been raised through high school on the band's reservation in North
Carolina and then attending Brigham Young University in Utah, Saunooke
enrolled at the University of New Mexico Law School.

After graduating from law school in 1972, Saunooke became executive director of United Southeastern Tribes (USET), which the Eastern
Band, the Mississippi Choctaws, and the Seminole and Miccosukee Tribes
in Florida* had organized four years earlier to address issues of common
concern. USET was headquartered in Sarasota, Florida. In 1973 when the
USET board of directors decided to relocate the organization's headquarters to Nashville, Saunooke decided not to make the move. Howard Tommie, the chairman of the Seminole Tribe, and Buffalo Tiger, the chairman
of the Miccosukee Tribe, then hired Saunooke to commute from Sarasota
to the state capital in Tallahassee to lobby Florida governor Reuben Askew
to create a Council on Indian Affairs. By 1974, when Askew established
the council, after having worked together for three years, Saunooke and
Howard Tommie had become friends.

---

*Miccosukees are Seminoles who lived in camps scattered along the Tamiami Trail,
the two-lane highway that runs west from Miami across the Everglades. In 1962, the
Bureau of Indian Affairs (BIA) allowed the Miccosukees to organize as a tribe separate from the Seminole Tribe.

Born in 1938, Tommie lived in the swamps north of Fort Lauderdale until he was eight years old. "My Dad was an alligator hunter," Tommie would recall years later. "There were a bunch of ponds west of Palm Beach. He'd go out to each pond and call those alligators in, shoot them in the head with a twenty-two, and skin them right there. Then we'd roll them up. We'd have stacks and stacks of them. When I was four or five, the first time I saw a white man he came to pick up alligator skins."

In the 1940s, Howard Tommie's father, Sam Tommie, moved his family out of the swamps and onto the Hollywood Reservation. A Baptist missionary persuaded Sam to send his son to school. So when Howard, who had grown up speaking the Muskogee and Miccosukee Creek dialects, learned enough English to do so, he began attending a grade school four miles east of the reservation and later South Broward High School. When his parents decided to move to the Brighton Reservation west of Lake Okeechobee, Howard went along, enrolled in high school there, dropped out, and eventually graduated from Chilocco Indian Agricultural School in Oklahoma.

In 1964, President Lyndon Johnson declared war on poverty. Congress responded by enacting the Economic Opportunity Act. One of the programs the act created was the Neighborhood Youth Corps (NYC), which paid teenagers a stipend to work in their local communities. When the Office of Economic Opportunity started a NYC program on the Seminole Reservations, Howard Tommie, who by then had married and was supporting his wife and two young children driving a truck, applied to the NYC program and was hired as the assistant director.

Until the war on poverty, the BIA had provided almost all government programs, services, and employment on the Hollywood, Brighton, and Big Cypress Reservations. Working for the NYC program educated Howard Tommie that obtaining contracts from federal agencies other than the BIA was a way to bring more money and jobs onto the reservations. To make that happen, Tommie, then thirty-three years old, ran in the 1971 election for chairman of the Seminole Tribal Council.

The incumbent, Betty May Jumper, an observant Baptist who was fifteen years Tommie's senior, was the candidate of the status quo. By contrast, according to Jumper's biographer, Howard Tommie campaigned on a platform "more aggressive than Betty's" that advocated "bucking the establishment to promote tribal self-help and sovereignty issues."

"Tribal self-help" was a euphemism for challenging BIA hegemony by obtaining money from federal agencies other than the BIA. And according to his biographer, when Tommie won the election, he "hit the ground running" by embarking "on a furious cycle of grant writing, and money began to pour in." Yet despite the new federal dollars and the new jobs those dollars created, most Seminoles continued to live impecunious lives. As a BIA employee familiar with the situation reported at the time, "Out of 1,200 Seminoles, somewhat more than 1,000 are receiving some kind of aid, whether it's food stamps, unemployment, or whatever." Selling tax-free cigarettes to non-Indians was hardly free-market capitalism. But as Bob Satiacum and B.J. and Ray Turnipseed were demonstrating on the Puyallup Reservation, it was a way to make money that every Seminole needed more of.

In 1976, when Osley Saunooke told Howard Tommie that B.J. and Ray Turnipseed were interested in opening a smoke shop on the Hollywood Reservation, a Seminole named Marcellus Osceola already was well along to opening his own shop. Osceola had a job working on the Hollywood Reservation as the administrator of Indian Action, a federal job training program. But when he read about the money Indians "out west" were making selling tax-free cigarettes, he decided to get into the business.

Osceloa found a partner, a Las Vegas resident named Don Kitchens. In 1976, he signed a contract with Kitchens pursuant to which Osceola agreed to secure a location on the Hollywood Reservation for a smoke shop and obtain the tribal council's approval, and Kitchens agreed to finance and manage the business.

Since his father was chairman of Seminole Tribe of Florida, Inc. (STFI), the BIA-chartered corporation that handled the tribe's business dealings, Osceola had no difficulty leasing a vacant lot on Route 441 and obtaining the exclusive right to operate a smoke shop on the reservation for five years. It was at that point that Bob Satiacum, who like B.J. and Ray Turnipseed had realized there was money to be made operating a smoke shop on the Hollywood Reservation, flew to Florida. According to Osceola, "Bob went to the council, and the council told him that we already have a tribal member who's getting ready to do cigarettes. So he came to see me. But I didn't care for the way he talked to me. So I didn't do business with him."

When Satiacum departed, the Turnipseeds arrived. When he learned that Marcellus Osceola had the exclusive right to operate a smoke shop on the Hollywood Reservation and that Osceola had gone into business with Don Kitchens who had agreed to pay Osceola ten cents a carton as compensation for being the shop's figurehead owner, Ray Turnipseed told Osceola that he and B.J. were willing to pay more than ten cents a carton. "I told Ray that I had made a fair deal with Don, and I wasn't going to break my contract," Osceola recalled years later. "So he and B.J. were going to have to buy Kitchens out. Then I talked to Don, and he said he was willing to be bought out for ten thousand dollars. I went back to Ray, and Ray gave me the ten thousand."

Before they could open for business, Osceola and the Turnipseeds needed legal advice because the legal theory that had made the sale of tax-free cigarettes on Indian reservations in Washington state possible was untested in Florida. In addition to being a friend of Howard Tommie's, Osley Saunooke was a friend of Marcellus Osceola's. He also was a friend of an attorney in Tallahassee named Jack Madigan.

When he went to Tallahassee to arrange for Madigan's law firm to represent Osceola and the Turnipseeds, Saunooke met Jack Skelding, one of the firm's junior partners. "Osley and I hit it off immediately," Skelding would recall years later. "He asked me to come down to Hollywood to help develop a plan to sell tax-free cigarettes in light of this case that somebody was familiar with that said that the state can't collect the taxes." The plan Skelding developed was to buy cigarettes from an out-of-state wholesaler and then have the cigarettes transported through Florida to the Hollywood Reservation by truck in a sealed container; the legal theory being that since the container would be moving in interstate commerce, the state would have no authority to confiscate its contents.

With inventory transported by truck from a warehouse in Alabama, in April 1977, B.J. and Ray Turnipseed opened Osceola's Trading Post in a trailer on the vacant lot Marcellus Osceola had leased. Almost immediately, the trailer was robbed by burglars who shot the guard dog and stole three hundred cartons of cigarettes. Nevertheless, in its first year Osceola's Trading Post sold more than two million cartons of cigarettes for $4.25 a carton without collecting Florida's $2.10 a carton cigarette tax. The Turnipseeds cleared $1 per carton and paid Marcellus Osceola more than

$300,000. "That was more money than I'd ever made in my life," Osceola would recall of his amazement at the time. "I bought six pickup trucks in one month. I bought my dad one. My brother. Kept a couple for myself."

When Osceola's Trading Post opened and six days a week automobiles backed up in long lines down Route 441, Ed Stack, the sheriff of Broward County, launched an investigation he named "Operation Sitting Bull." In July, he announced that Operation Sitting Bull had revealed that during its first three months of operation, Osceola's Trading Post had cost the state of Florida $476,502 in lost cigarette taxes. Sheriff Stack also announced that, because the Florida Department of Business Regulation was refusing to take action to require Osceloa's Trading Post to collect the state's cigarette tax, Stack, acting as a private citizen, had filed a lawsuit against the department in the circuit court in Fort Lauderdale to obtain a court order that would require the department to take action.

Because Jack Madigan's law firm represented the Florida Sheriff's Association, Jack Skelding knew Ed Stack. So he arranged a meeting. During the meeting, when Skelding asked Stack, "Why are you suing my Indians?," the sheriff responded, "They're my Indians, too. I love them."

Then why a lawsuit? Because Ed Stack was a politician. In 1966, he had run unsuccessfully in the Republican primary election for Broward County's seat in Congress. Two years later, he ran for sheriff and won. In 1976, when he was easily reelected to a third term as sheriff, Stack decided that in 1978 he would run again for Congress. So when Jack Skelding asked him why he had filed a lawsuit, Sheriff Stack explained that he had filed it because candidate Stack needed the publicity.

Represented by Jack Skelding, in October, Marcellus Osceola intervened in Stack's lawsuit, which, at the request of the Florida Department of Business Regulation, had been moved to Tallahassee and consolidated by Circuit Court Judge Charles Miner with a similar lawsuit a vending machine company had filed against the department.

Stack and the vending machine company seemingly had a strong case because in April 1976 the U.S. Supreme Court had issued a decision called *Moe v. Confederated Salish and Kootenai Tribes*. In *Moe*, the Court said that the state of Montana could require smoke shops on Indian reservations in Montana to collect Montana's cigarette tax because the Montana law that imposed the tax had been carefully written to impose the tax on the smoke shops' non-Indian customers, rather than on the shops' Indian owners.

But a few days before Judge Miner heard oral argument in the consolidated lawsuits, Jack Skelding caught a break: in the U.S. District Court in Washington, the three-judge panel released its decision in *Confederated Tribes of the Colville Indian Reservation v. State of Washington*, the lawsuit Robert Pirtle had filed. Citing *Williams v. Lee*, rather than the *Moe* decision, as the controlling legal authority, the panel announced that "the state [of Washington]'s cigarette taxing scheme constitutes an interference with tribal self-government." The panel's decision allowed Skelding to argue to Judge Miner that Florida's cigarette tax collection scheme was more like the cigarette tax collection scheme that in *Confederated Tribes* the three-judge panel had held that the state of Washington had no authority to enforce on Indian reservations in Washington than it was like the cigarette tax collection scheme in Montana that the U.S. Supreme Court had upheld in *Moe*.

Skelding later said he thought the case "could have gone either way." But in March 1978, it went his way when he received a call from Judge Miner who said, "I'm not sure I am right, but I'm ruling with you and your Indian friends. So draw up the order." In November the Florida District Court of Appeal brought the legal dispute between Sheriff Stack and the Florida Department of Business Regulation and Marcellus Osceola and B.J. and Ray Turnipseed to an end when it issued a decision in which that court upheld Judge Miner's decision.

Once the legal principle was established that Florida had no authority to enforce its cigarette tax law on the Hollywood Reservation, it was an easy leap of logic to conclude that other items that non-Indian customers wanted to buy could be sold tax-free on the reservation. The *Alligator Times*, the Seminole Tribe's newspaper, soon reported that Marcellus Osceola "had been approached by many non-Indians anxious to cash in on the idea of a tax-free business," and quoted Osceola saying, "If I was running the tribe, I would definitely put out a liquor store or a gas station to some kind of management contract, where the Indians own a majority of the business."

Selling tax-free alcohol and gasoline was a sensible, although not a particularly imaginative, business plan. Osley Saunooke, an entrepreneur by temperament, soon hatched a more ambitious one.

In 1922, Owen Patrick Smith, who had invented an artificial lure for dogs to chase instead of rabbits, opened the first greyhound race track in Florida. In 1978, the sixteen dog tracks operating in Florida still were attracting crowds, and a crowd of 14,500 set an attendance record at the Hollywood Kennel Club in Hallandale a few miles south of the Hollywood Reservation.

Florida law allowed a dog track to hold races only during a designated racing season for that particular track. But a dog track on the Hollywood Reservation could ignore Florida law the same way Osceola's Trading Post could ignore Florida law. "We could have dog races twelve months a year instead of just for a season," Osley Saunooke recalled years later. "That's the reason I suggested a dog track. Plus, my mom loved the dogs. She loved to go to the dog tracks." Teaming up with Marcellus Osceola, Saunooke found a location for a dog track: an eighteen-acre parcel of vacant land on the Hollywood Reservation across Route 441 from Osceola's Trading Post.

Unlike a smoke shop, which consisted of a trailer, a sales clerk, and inventory, a dog track would cost hundreds of thousands of dollars to construct. To find the money, Saunooke approached Charles Stover, president of the American Indian National Bank in Washington, D.C. With an introduction from Stover, Saunooke pitched the project to Leon Greenberg, the owner of Monticello Raceway, a harness-racing track in the Catskill Mountains northwest of New York City. He also pitched the project to Neal Amdur who, since the death of his father-in-law, Isadore Hecht, two years earlier, had been managing the Flagler Dog Track in Miami for the Hecht family.

It was then that Duane Moxon, the BIA superintendent of the Seminole Agency, suggested another idea.

Moxon had worked for the BIA on Indian reservations in North and South Dakota. According to Saunooke, when he mentioned to Moxon that he and Marcellus Osceola wanted to build a dog track on the Hollywood Reservation, the superintendent said, "When I was at the Pine Ridge Agency in South Dakota, I used to run a bingo game. What you need to do is you need to start bingo here."

When he attended Brigham Young University, Saunooke and his roommate would take road trips to Las Vegas. According to Saunooke,

"There was a place in Las Vegas called the Hacienda. It had the best buffet I've ever been to in my entire life. Me and my roommate, we would go there, and we would play bingo at midnight because they would give out free meal tickets. So the second Duane Moxon said have a bingo parlor, I thought, 'Las Vegas–style bingo! Of course!' I told Duane, 'You know what? You're an absolute genius.'"

3: SEMINOLE BINGO

> People always say there's criminal activity
> and I continue to say, "If there is, prove it."
>
> JAMES BILLIE,
> *Chairman, Seminole Tribe*

WHEN DUANE MOXON SUGGESTED TO OSLEY SAUNOOKE THAT HE AND Marcellus Osceola open a bingo hall, bingo had been played lawfully in Florida for eleven years.

IN 1929 A TRAVELING toy salesman from New York named Edwin Lowe stopped one evening at a carnival in rural Georgia and saw a crowd gathered around a table playing a game called Beano. To play Beano, a player purchased a card on which rows of numbers had been printed. When the carney called out a number, the player marked the number on the card. The first player to fill in a vertical or horizontal row of numbers won a prize. "I watched the people playing Beano," Lowe recalled years later, "and I noticed that they were practically addicted to it. The pitchman wanted to close up, but every time he said, 'This is the last game,' it did no good. The players simply wouldn't budge."

Lowe returned to New York, made his own Beano game, and invited friends to play. When he began calling out numbers, the players in Lowe's living room became as excited as the players at the carnival had been. During one of the games, a player filled in her last number, and, rather than saying "Beano," she shouted "Bingo!" "I cannot describe the strange sense of elation which that girl's shriek brought to me," said Lowe. "All I could think of was that I was going to come out with this game—and it was going to be called Bingo!"

In 1930 when the E.S. Lowe Toy and Game Company began selling bingo games, Lowe hired a Columbia University mathematics professor named Carl Leffler to produce 6,000 bingo cards, each with a different set of numbers. According to bingo legend, Leffler drove himself insane doing so. Also according to bingo legend, the man who turned bingo into a national craze was a Catholic priest in Wilkes-Barre, Pennsylvania, who began holding bingo games to raise money for his parish. The idea caught on, and by 1934 ten thousand bingo games a week were being played in church basements.

THE LAW THE FLORIDA legislature passed in 1967 to regulate bingo allowed charitable, nonprofit, and veterans organizations to operate bingo games. The games could be offered no more than two days a week, jackpots were limited to no more than $100, the individuals who operated the games had to be unpaid volunteers, and an organization was required to spend the money it earned on the organization's charitable and nonprofit endeavors.

But why would a bingo game operated on the Seminole Tribe's reservation in Hollywood have to comply with Florida's bingo law any more than Osceola's Trading Post had to comply with Florida's law that required retailers to collect the state's cigarette tax? While the legal situation seemed similar, the practicalities were closer to a dog track's than to a smoke shop's, because to hold bingo games that would pay out thousand-dollar jackpots required a building large enough to hold a crowd, a professional manager, and trained employees. While Osley Saunooke and Marcellus Osceola had not been able to raise the money they needed to build a dog track, the money and the management needed to open a bingo hall soon appeared.

In 1977, the Catholic Services Bureau gave the Seminole Tribe a grant to hire an attorney. In August of that year, the attorney Howard Tommie, the tribal chairman, hired was a thirty-seven-year-old lawyer from Washington, D.C., named Steve Whilden. Seven months after Whilden became the tribe's general counsel, in March 1978, Circuit Court Judge Charles Miner issued his decision in the consolidated lawsuits Sheriff Stack and the vending machine company had filed the previous summer.

A month later, the Florida legislature opened its legislative session in Tallahassee. According to Howard Tommie, "There were a lot of innuendos going around that we were going to put smoke shops in Pensacola and Jacksonville. And the legislature got all upset. So I went up there and told them that we can't open a smoke shop except on a federal Indian reservation."

By then, Osley Saunooke had been talking up the idea of building a dog track or opening a bingo hall. In Tallahassee, when Howard Tommie mentioned that the Seminole Tribe was considering building a dog track or opening a bingo hall, one of the legislators suggested to Tommie that he needed talk to Barry Horeinbein, the lobbyist who represented the horse and dog tracks. But rather than Tommie, the individual who sought out Horenbein was Steve Whilden. As Hornbein told the story years later:

> A young attorney came up to me and introduced himself as Steve Whilden. Steve said he was the attorney for the Seminole Tribe of Florida, and he had been told that I was the lobbyist the tribe needed to hire. He told me the tribe wanted to get into tax-frees, wanted to start with cigarettes, wanted to get into high-stakes bingo, eventually get into big-time gaming. I said, "That's very aggressive. I hope you have a lot of money." To which Steve replied, "We don't have any money. We would like you to help us find investors."

When Horenbein told his wife about meeting Steve Whilden and mentioned that he was pondering who he knew who might be willing to invest $1 million—the amount Whilden said the tribe needed—in such high-risk, high-reward ventures as a dog track or a bingo hall, according to Horenbein, "My wife said, 'Why don't you ask Mr. Cooper?'"

BORN JACOB COOPER IN 1915 in Brooklyn to Yiddish-speaking parents who had emigrated from Russia five years earlier, Jack Cooper was raised in New Haven, Connecticut. Two years after graduating from Commercial High School, in 1935 he married a local girl named Gertrude Blodinger. In 1939 the couple moved to Miami Beach, where Cooper began selling fruit.

Next to their photographs in the Commercial High School yearbook, each member of the class of 1933 listed his or her future vocation. Most listed bookkeeper, secretary, teacher, or collegiate. Jack Cooper listed financier.

Consistent with that expression of entrepreneurial ambition, during the Second World War when the Cuba Libre (rum, coke, and a lime) was a popular drink, Cooper bought limes from farmers for a penny and resold them to Miami Beach hotels for ten cents a lime. He bought watermelons in Georgia that he trucked to Miami Beach. He also began importing bananas. In 1951, by which time he had come to the attention of the FBI, the special agent in charge of the Miami field office reported: "Jack Cooper has been engaged in the banana importing business since 1940 or 1942. He is regarded as the type of individual who will 'bank roll' anything that will produce a good return on his money."

By then Jack Cooper's business career also had taken several curious twists. Cooper told Barry Horenbein that when he and Gertrude moved to Miami Beach, they occasionally had to sneak in and out the back door of their apartment when they did not have enough money to pay their rent. But in 1967, the FBI reported that Cooper became a partner in the Southern Produce Company in 1940, "and at that time also became part owner of the Child's Hotel and the Imperial Hotel, both located in Miami, Florida." The FBI also reported that, according to a January 1953 credit report, in 1951 Cooper sold his interest in the Cromwell Hotel in Miami Beach for more than a million dollars and also had sold his interests in the Child's and Imperial Hotels. The credit report also related that as of January 1953 "Cooper had a net worth of over one million dollars and an annual income in excess of $30,000." Less than a year after the credit report listed his assets, Cooper and a business associate named Isadore Hecht purchased the West Flagler Kennel Club, the major dog track in Miami, for $2 million.

How did a son of immigrant parents who, when he arrived in Miami Beach, did not have enough money to regularly pay his rent, acquire interests in three hotels and become a millionaire by age thirty-eight? A talented hard-working businessman? Maybe. But there also is another possibility.

Cooper told Barry Horenbein that when he was working in a fruit store across the street from the Roney Plaza Hotel in Miami Beach "a man came in one day and ordered fresh fruit to be sent to New York and Chicago and paid him in cash. He didn't know who the man was. This happened over a period of five or six months. The guy would come in almost every week. It was Meyer Lansky."

One of the most legendary of all organized crime figures, Lansky was the son of Russian Jews who, after emigrating through Ellis Island in 1911, settled on the Lower East Side of Manhattan. By the time he was a teenager, Lansky, who had a perspicacious intellect and a fearless nature that belied his diminutive physical stature, was the leader of a gang of Jewish hoodlums-in-the-making that included his boyhood friend Benjamin "Bugsy" Siegel.

The Jewish ghetto on the Lower East Side bordered Little Italy. One day when he was walking down a street along the border, Lansky was accosted by a group of Italian teenagers. When Salvatore Luciana, the curly-haired Sicilian boy who was the leader of the group, told the short, slight Jewish boy to turn out his pockets and give over his money, Lansky told Luciana to "Go fuck yourself." That stand-his-ground defiance impressed Luciana and began a lifelong friendship between Meyer Lansky and the man the world would come to know as Charlie "Lucky" Luciano.

During Prohibition, Lansky and Luciano worked for Arnold Rothstein, who by 1928, when he was shot to death, had organized the distribution of bootleg whiskey throughout the northeastern United States into what was tantamount to a corporate business. In 1931, when Luciano became the *di tutti capi* (boss of bosses) of the Mafia families that controlled organized crime in New York, Meyer Lansky became Luciano's unofficial (because he was Jewish, rather than Sicilian) consigliere. As Bugsy Siegel described their relationship:

> Charlie was tough and ruthless in an open way. Meyer was just as tough, just as ruthless, but he never showed it. Charlie was the brains of the organization and he knew how to handle the gunmen and the soldiers who worked for us. Lansky was the financial genius and could keep in his head how to move from one business to another, what to do with the money and where the future prospects lay. They were an unbeatable team.

When Prohibition ended, Lansky turned to gambling, and by the 1940s, he owned casinos that operated under paid police protection in Saratoga Springs, New York, and Hallandale, Florida, a few miles north of Miami Beach. According to his daughter, when Lansky and his family wintered in Miami Beach, they frequently stayed at the Roney Plaza Hotel.

Meyer Lansky avoided putting down on paper evidence of his ownership of many of the businesses in which he had interests. In 1969, Florida's attorney general filed a series of lawsuits to expose the hidden ownership of eighteen

Miami Beach motels that *Life* magazine reported were "controlled by Lansky through a group of associates known as the Minneapolis Combination."

So did Jack Cooper get his start in Miami Beach as a strawman owner of the Child's, Imperial, and Cromwell Hotels whose real owners were Meyer Lansky and members of the Combination? And could some of the $2 million Cooper and Isadore Hecht used to buy the West Flagler Kennel Club have been Lansky's money?

In February 1962, in Miami, Judge Emett Clay Choate convicted Cooper of income tax evasion for having failed to report $744,000 he had earned in 1952 and 1953. Cooper's defense was that the money belonged to Ramfis Trujillo, the son of the Dominican Republic dictator Rafael Trujillo. The story, which Judge Choate did not believe, was that when he became acquainted with the Trujillos through his banana import business, Ramfis Trujillo, who was the head of the Dominican Republic's air force, asked Cooper to broker the purchase of P-51 fighter aircraft from Sweden with money the United States had given to the Trujillo government. According to Cooper, the $744,000 was Ramfis Trujillo's kickback from the inflated purchase price of the aircraft, which was how business was done in the Dominican Republic during the Trujillo era.

For the West Flagler Kennel Club, having a felon as an owner was not good for a pari-mutuel betting business that the state of Florida regulated. Which may be why, according to an FBI report:

> Information was received from a confidential source of information that a meeting was held on July 26, 1962, at the Miami International Airport Hotel, Miami, Florida. The purpose of the meeting was to discuss the desire of Cooper to sell the West Flagler Dog Track. Among other persons at the meeting was Meyer Lansky.

Was Lansky at the meeting because he owned some of what Cooper needed to sell?*

---

*If, in 1962, Jack Cooper sold his interest in the West Flagler Kennel Club, he did not sell all of it, because in 1974 the state of Florida tried "to take away the West Flagler dog track's racing permit because one of its major stockholders, Jack B. Cooper, had been photographed with underworld financial wizard Meyer Lansky." In 1977, Cooper still owned 19 percent. In 1981 the *Miami Herald* reported that "because of earlier questions about his reputation" Cooper held his interest in the West Flagler Kennel Club in a blind trust.

Here is what else the FBI report has to say:

In July 1960, information was received that Cooper and Isadore Hecht, co-owners of the West Flagler Dog Track in Miami, indicated they would like to obtain a connection in a Las Vegas, Nevada, gambling casino.

. . .

In 1962 and 1963, information was received from two separate individuals that Cooper held an interest in the gambling casino at the Flamingo Hotel, Las Vegas, Nevada. One of these sources expressed his personal opinion that Meyer Lansky has an interest in a Las Vegas casino, possibly the one at the Flamingo Hotel, utilizing someone else to "front" for him.

In May 1965, information was received that Jack Cooper was spending a substantial portion of his time at the Bayshore Golf Club, Miami Beach, Florida. This is a city-owned establishment which has been described as a "hang-out" for various gamblers and racket figures.

In 1965, information was received that Cooper, Benjamin Sigelbaum and Edward Levinson were reportedly interested in obtaining a gambling concession in London, England. During the same year, information was received from three sources that Cooper had, in fact, acquired an interest in a London gambling establishment.

. . .

It is noted that Edward Levinson, mentioned above, is owner of record of the Fremont Hotel, Las Vegas, Nevada, and is operator of the gambling casino in that hotel.

In Las Vegas, Levinson's principal responsibility was to collect the "skim"* from the Fremont, the Flamingo, and the other casinos Meyer Lansky and various Mafia families controlled. Couriers transported the cash to Miami Beach, where Lansky distributed the money to the men to whom it was owed.

---

*The "skim" is the cash from the gaming tables and slot machines that was diverted before it reached a casino's counting room or after it reached the counting room but before the money was recorded as income on the casino's books.

In 1964, the FBI's Las Vegas field office wrote a report on the Nevada gambling industry that identified eleven individuals Levinson used as couriers. According to the report, a confidential informant

> advised during January and February, 1963, that Edward Levinson had, on two occasions, discussed the utilization of one Jack Cooper as a courier of skimmed funds. According to the source, Levinson intimated that Cooper had been used in the past but was not considered reliable.

And, in 1974, Dougald McMillan, the head of the U.S. Department of Justice's Organized Crime Strike Force in Miami, concluded that Jack Cooper "without question was a courier of Las Vegas skim money for Lansky in the early 60s."

Barry Horenbein, who had been a star athlete at Miami Beach High School, first met Jack Cooper in the early 1950s. "Mr. Cooper was a big sports fan and used to come to the games," Horenbein would remember years later. "He met my father, and they became friends at sporting events." Jack and Gertrude Cooper did not have children, and over the years Cooper came to consider Horenbein a surrogate son.

In 1964, when the U.S. Supreme Court refused to review his conviction for income tax evasion, Cooper reported to a minimum security federal prison camp west of Tallahassee. One afternoon during the seventy-nine days Cooper was incarcerated, Barry Horenbein drove out for a visit. According to Horenbein:

> I asked for Mr. Cooper and they said, "He's out hitting golf balls." So I went out there, and Jack is hitting golf balls. Wearing a pair of shorts with his golf shoes on. He's got some guards retrieving the balls. We went back to Mr. Cooper's cell, where he had a stack of Cuban cigars and his own TV.

If Cooper's accommodations during his stay in prison were comfortable, in Miami Beach they were opulent. In addition to the condominium in which he lived with his wife, Cooper owned a compound on North Bay Road that had two tennis courts, a houseboat dock, and a house Cooper used as an office. "When I came down from Tallahassee, I would stay there," Horenbein recalled. "Mr. Cooper would give me the bedroom. He made sure I had fresh fruit in the morning. He treated me like a son."

So when his wife suggested that he ask Jack Cooper if he might be interested in going into business with the Seminole Indians, Barry Horenbein did so. And according to Horenbein, when he finished explaining why the tribe needed $1 million, "The first remark out of Mr. Cooper's mouth was 'When can I sign up?'" and "probably within the next thirty days a contract was signed." But the contract was not with the Seminole Tribe. It was with Howard Tommie, who had decided that Marcellus Osceola was not the only Seminole who should be getting rich.

THE SEMINOLE TRIBAL COUNCIL had given Osceola an exclusive franchise to sell cigarettes on the Hollywood Reservation. But when Osceola's Trading Post was an immediate success, other members of the Seminole Tribe who wanted to open a smoke shop persuaded the council to renege. By 1978, when Jack Cooper went into business with Howard Tommie, in addition to Osceola's Trading Post, there were several other smoke shops on the Hollywood Reservation, two of which Marcellus Osceola had opened.

When Osceola had realized how much money B.J. and Ray Turnipseed were making, he asked Ray to increase the number of cents per carton he was being paid to serve as Osceola's Trading Post's figurehead owner. According to Osceola, Ray told him, "You signed a contract. So you have to live with it."

"When you make money you start to get smarter. And I got smarter," Osceola would recall with a grin years later. So instead of living with it, Osceola opened two smoke shops on Route 441, one north of Osceola's Trading Post, the other south. He did so because "most customers don't scout around. The first shop they see is where they pull in." When Osceola's smoke shops began stealing their customers, B.J. and Ray Turnipseed decided to sell Osceola's Trading Post to Osceola and return to Tacoma, where they used the money they made in Florida to open B.J.'s Bingo.

When the Turnipseeds departed, Osceola sold Osceola's Trading Post and his other smoke shops to Howard Tommie, who used Jack Cooper's money to pay the rumored $500,000 purchase price. In 2013, when I asked Osceola why he sold his shops, he had no forthright answer. But according to historian Harry A. Kersey Jr., "It was a joke on the reservation that

Howard Tommie, like Marlon Brando's movie character in *The Godfather*, had made Marcellus 'an offer that he couldn't refuse.'"

In 2009, when I asked B.J. Turnipseed why she and Ray sold Osceola's Trading Post, she told me that Howard Tommie first bought out Marcellus Osceola, after which the "Mafia" explained to Ray and her that it was time for them to go. And in 2014, George Simon, Jack Cooper's partner in the smoke shops venture told me that he and Cooper had bought out both Marcellus Osceola and the Turnipseeds and that they spent $800,000 to do so.

But Jack Cooper had bigger plans than selling tax-free cigarettes.

In December 1978, Marcellus Osceola's father, Bill Osceola—on behalf of the Seminole Tribe of Florida, Inc. (STFI)—and Howard Tommie—on behalf of Howard Tommie—signed an agreement that gave Tommie a fifty-five-year lease on the eighteen-acre parcel of vacant land on Route 441 on which Osley Saunooke had wanted to build a dog track. The agreement authorized Tommie to open a smoke shop on the property and build a bingo hall and a shopping center that would be called Seminole Indian Plaza. In return, Tommie agreed to pay STFI 15 percent of the profit from the smoke shop and 20 percent of the profit from the bingo hall, plus an annual rent of $350,000. He also agreed that his businesses would pay the Seminole Tribe a sales tax.

Tommie later said Jack Cooper planned to spend $3 million to build Seminole Indian Plaza. But the project died before ground could be broken when the Bureau of Indian Affairs (BIA), which had to approve leases of federal land located inside the boundaries of Indian reservations, refused to approve Tommie's lease because someone in the Washington, D.C., office decided the lease did not give the Seminole Tribe a large enough share of the profit.

Jack Cooper then came up with a new plan: he organized a partnership called Seminole Management Associates (SMA) that would contract with the Seminole Tribe to build and manage a bingo hall on the land on which he had planned to build Seminole Indian Plaza. Since the tribe would own the building and the business, no lease and no BIA approval were needed.

SMA HAD FIFTEEN LIMITED partners and two general partners. One of the general partners was Eugene "Butch" Weisman.

In late 1978, Jack Cooper met with two Miami Beach bookmakers named Benny Husick and Abe Roth at his compound on North Bay Road. When Cooper mentioned during the meeting that he was looking for someone to manage a bingo hall he was planning to open on the Hollywood Reservation, Roth said he knew a professional manager in Pittsburgh named Weisman.

At the time, Steve Paskind, who pioneered "charitable" bingo in south Florida,* and a Miami Beach bookmaker named Red Silber were operating a bingo hall in North Miami Beach. Silber knew Benny Husick. When Husick told Silber that Abe Roth had suggested to Jack Cooper that he bring in Weisman to manage the bingo hall Cooper was planning to open on the Hollywood Reservation, Silber told Husick, "Are you nuts? Steve and I should have that deal."

When Silber told Steve Paskind about his conversation with Husick, Paskind was livid that, "like the moron he was," Benny had not told Jack Cooper that the managers he needed were Paskind and Silber. So Paskind had Silber call "a gentlemen he was involved with named Eddie Coco." Why call Eddie Coco? Because Coco, a high-ranking member of the Lucchese Mafia family, could reach out to Meyer Lansky.

And why did Steve Paskind need Eddie Coco to reach out to Meyer Lansky? In 1992, the Pennsylvania Crime Commission reported that the bingo hall SMA was managing on the Hollywood Reservation had been "set up with the help of . . . the late Meyer Lansky." The commission didn't say what help Lansky provided. But according to Lansky biographer Robert Lacey, "It was with his friends—Benny Sigelbaum, Hymie Siegel, Harry Stromberg, Yiddy Bloom, Jimmy Blue Eyes, Jack Cooper, and brother Jake—that [Lansky, who died in Miami Beach in 1983] spent his retirement days . . . Jack Cooper lived in a grand mansion on the water with a tennis court, where the group often gathered on Sunday mornings. Meyer said that he was no longer fit enough to go out on the court. But he

---

*In 1970, Paskind came up with the business plan that has made the septuagenarian the wealthy man he is today. The plan was to rent a building, remodel it into a bingo hall, and then lease the hall to charities as tenants in common. According to Paskind: "I came up with the idea of getting four charities. Three could play two days a week, and one could play one. We supplied everything, kept all the money, paid all the bills, and gave each charity a set amount of money. They were tickled to death to get $100 or $200 a week for nothing."

liked to bring foil carryout dishes of deli snacks on Sundays to sustain spectators and players."

Since Jack Cooper and Meyer Lansky had been friends and business associates for more than thirty years, it is reasonable to assume that Cooper discussed with Lansky both Abe Roth's suggestion that he bring in Butch Weisman from Pittsburgh and the consequences if he did so. Because when Eddie Coco explained Steve Paskind and Red Silber's situation to Lansky, Lansky told Coco to tell Silber to get in touch with Kelly Mannarino.

In Pittsburgh, Gabriel "Kelly" Mannarino, who had been an associate of Lansky's since the 1950s when both men operated casinos in Havana, was a capo in the LaRocca Mafia family. According to the Pennsylvania Crime Commission:

> Eugene Weisman operated bingo games at 346 Electric Avenue, East Pittsburgh, a bingo hall which he owned. Weisman conducted these bingo games from the mid-1970s to the mid-1980s and was required to pay tribute to a number of Pittsburgh LCN [Mafia] members, including Gabriel Mannarino.

According to Steve Paskind: "Red went to Pittsburgh and met with Kelly Mannarino, who told him, 'You're right. Florida is your area. So we'll give you 25 percent of our 40 percent. But you'll have to put up your share of the money.'" Paskind was willing to buy the share of the LaRocca family's share of the SMA partnership that Mannarino offered. But what he wanted was to manage the bingo hall. So when the final word came from Pittsburgh that "We're committed to Weisman," Paskind let the matter drop.

SMA's OTHER GENERAL PARTNER was George Simon. Simon first met Jack Cooper in 1939 when Simon was sixteen and Cooper, who was twenty-four and had only recently moved to Miami Beach, was unloading oranges from the back of a truck at Simon's father's store. But the two men did not become business associates until 1948 when Simon, an accountant, took over Cooper's account at the CPA firm at which Simon was working. Cooper and his new accountant quickly became such close friends that Cooper began giving Simon 25 percent of the business investments in which he was involved; particularlly investments that required the investor to have no criminal record and no public relationship with Meyer Lansky.

George Simon's most interesting business dealing with Jack Cooper involved Serv-U Corporation.

FROM 1955 TO 1963, Bobby Baker, the secretary of the U.S. Senate, was the most powerful congressional employee on Capitol Hill. Baker's mentors were Texas senator Lyndon B. Johnson, the majority leader for whom Baker worked, and, after Johnson left the Senate to become vice president, Oklahoma senator Robert Kerr.

In 1963, Baker brokered a quid pro quo in which Kerr told the administrator of NASA to have NASA award North American Aviation, a California aerospace company, a $400 million contract in exchange for North American Aviation agreeing to build a new manufacturing plant in Oklahoma. To reward Baker for his service, Kerr told Fred Black, the lobbyist who represented North American Aviation, to tell his client to "take care of Bobby." Black then incorporated Serv-U Corporation, whose principal stockholders were Black and Bobby Baker, and North American Aviation gave Serv-U Corporation a contract to operate the vending machines in the company's manufacturing plants, which employed 40,000 workers.

What do Bobby Baker and Serv-U Corporation have to do with Jack Cooper and George Simon? According to Baker, "Fred Black owed a lot of money in Las Vegas." So Black settled his markers by giving Eddie Levinson stock in Serv-U Corporation. Levinson then spread his Serv-U Corporation stock around to friends, including Jack Cooper.

In 1964, when his ownership of Serv-U Corporation landed Bobby Baker, first on the cover of *Time* magazine, and then in jail, the Senate Committee on Rules and Administration held hearings on Baker's influence-peddling. One of the witnesses was Jack Cooper, who, each time he was asked a question, invoked the Fifth Amendment and refused to answer. The committee also subpoenaed George Simon, who the committee's investigators described as an "original stockholder of Serv-U-Corp." Years later when he was asked, the only thing Bobby Baker could remember about Simon was that he was an accountant.

The reason Baker had next to no recollection of George Simon was that Simon's involvement with Serv-U Corporation had been to serve as a front for the owners of the stock Eddie Levinson had made available. Here is what Simon told the committee:

SIMON: There were moneys put up, and we invested approximately $91,000.

COMMITTEE COUNSEL: You mean you and Cooper jointly?

SIMON: Me and Cooper and a few others; some of my partners in my accounting practice, and a couple of friends of ours.

COMMITTEE COUNSEL: Your name appears as a stockholder on the records of the Serv-U Corp. But Mr. Cooper's does not.

SIMON: I represented his interest and all the others, sir.

COMMITTEE COUNSEL: You represented his interest and also these other individuals that you speak of?

SIMON: That is correct?

ACCORDING TO THE SMA partnership agreement, Butch Weisman and George Simon each invested $100,000, and then each loaned the partnership $100,000. But in 1994, when he was deposed regarding his involvement in SMA, after admitting that he didn't "know the first thing about operating a bingo hall" and that he visited the hall no more than once or twice a year, Simon explained that, insofar as his $200,000 was concerned, "I contributed as a trustee." For whom was Simon the trustee? The attorney who deposed Simon didn't ask.

In September 1979, Butch Weisman and George Simon—on behalf of SMA—and James Billie, who four months earlier had been elected to succeed Howard Tommie as chairman of the Seminole Tribal Council—on behalf of the Seminole Tribe—signed a management agreement. In exchange for a fee "equal to forty-five percent of the net operating profits for each fiscal year," SMA agreed, for a term of twenty-five years, to manage a bingo hall on the Hollywood Reservation that SMA would build but the tribe would own.

The Seminole Tribe then borrowed $900,000 from City National Bank of Miami to finance construction of a 20,000-square-foot building on the land on Route 441 that Howard Tommie had tried to lease. The president of City National Bank of Miami told the *Miami Herald* that the bank had given the Seminole Tribe the loan on James Billie's signature because "we have confidence in the tribe" and "their word is their bond." But Steve Whilden more candidly told the *Fort Lauderdale News* that "friends of the tribe" guaranteed the loan. And in 1994, George Simon said that he and other SMA partners "personally signed notes with City National Bank in order for them to lend the tribe money to build the bingo hall."

If Simon and other SMA partners did sign notes, Jack Cooper told Howard Tommie that Tommie needed to pledge the revenue from the smoke shops of which he was the figurehead owner as collateral for the loan. While the money that had been used to buy out Marcellus Osceola and B.J. and Ray Turnipseed had been Cooper's and George Simon's, with truly brazen chutzpah, Tommie refused to agree to pledge the smoke shops' revenue unless Cooper would agree to give Tommie half of SMA. According to Tommie, "We finally agreed on 25 percent." Tommie astutely got that agreement in writing.

In November 1978, the publicity Sheriff Stack generated when he sued the Florida Department of Business Regulation paid its dividend when candidate Stack was elected to Congress. In December, Florida governor Reubin Askew appointed Bob Butterworth, an attorney from Fort Lauderdale who had been serving as a circuit court judge, to replace Stack as sheriff.

Several years earlier, Steve Paskind sold a bingo hall he had been operating on Oak Park Boulevard in Broward County to a professional operator named Chuck Bogus. Bogus subsequently transferred his interest in the Oak Park hall and several other halls in Broward County to Anthony Accetturo, a capo in the Lucchese Mafia family, and an associate of Accetturo's named James Williams.

Upon taking office, Sheriff Butterworth ordered his deputies to begin raiding Accetturo and Williams's bingo halls, much to the outrage of the mostly middle-aged-to-elderly female patrons. "When we went in, it was all retirees," Butterworth would remember of one of the raids. "We're not going to arrest them. But they stick around. They started singing 'God Bless

America.' There was not much sympathy for our position. We tried to say, 'This guy's organized crime.' But they didn't care. They just wanted to play bingo."

When the Seminole Tribe began advertising that it soon would begin holding bingo games seven nights a week in its new 1,200-seat bingo hall, and would pay out jackpots of as much as $1,000, Butterworth and Nick Navarro, the head of the Broward County Sheriff's Office's organized crime division, investigated the situation. According to Butterworth,

> What got our attention was—if the Seminoles' bingo hall is going to be unregulated—who's involved? The people we found out were involved were Jack Cooper and Eugene Weisman. So the reason I got involved was because of the wise guys on Collins Avenue [in Miami Beach] and in Pittsburgh.

When Butterworth told James Billie, the chairman of the Seminole Tribal Council, "These guys are Mafia," and Billie's unperturbed response was, "Prove it," Butterworth asked Phil Shailer, whose law firm handled the Sheriff's Office's legal work, whether, when the Seminole bingo hall opened, he had the legal authority to shut it down. According to Shailer, "My people and I researched it, and we concluded that it was a close question, but under Florida law and federal law, for the Seminole Tribe to operate bingo with no jackpot limits was going to be a violation of Florida's bingo statute, and the Sheriff's Office had the right to enforce the statute against them."

With Phil Shailer's legal opinion in hand, Butterworth told James Billie that if, when the hall opened, the bingo games SMA conducted violated Florida's bingo law, his deputies would raid the hall. To try to prevent that from happening, at SMA's expense the Seminole Tribe hired prominent Miami Beach attorney Marion Sibley. Sibley then filed a lawsuit—*Seminole Tribe of Florida v. Butterworth*—in the U.S. District Court in Fort Lauderdale. The lawsuit requested District Judge Norman Roettger to prohibit Sheriff Butterworth from enforcing Florida's bingo law inside the boundaries of the Hollywood Reservation.

On the morning of December 14, 1979, just hours before the bingo hall was set to open, and after a hearing at which Sheriff Butterworth was the only witness, Judge Roettger issued a temporary injunction that allowed the hall to open as planned. (In May 1980, Roettger made his temporary injunction permanent. In October 1981 a three-judge panel of the U.S. Court of Appeals for the Fifth Circuit affirmed Roettger's action.)*

That evening a thousand patrons, most middle-aged-to-elderly women, paid a $15 admission to sit at long rows of tables and play bingo for jackpots that ranged from $200 to $1,000. Seven nights a week the players kept coming, on average more than seven hundred players every evening. In October 1980, when the admission price was raised to $100 for a chance to win $90,000 in prizes, including a $20,000 jackpot and a new Cadillac, all 1,200 seats sold out in less than forty-eight hours.

The bingo hall was such an immediate success that the Seminole Tribe paid City National Bank of Miami back the entire $900,000 construction loan six months after the doors opened. In January 1982, the admission price again was raised to $100 for a chance to win another $90,000 in prizes, including another new Cadillac. When the doors opened at 5:00 p.m., the line for entry, which had begun forming at noon, circled twice around the building. After all 1,200 seats were taken, a hundred wannabe players stood outside in a rainstorm still hoping to be admitted.

SMA ran advertisements in the *Alligator Times* that encouraged tribal members to apply for jobs working at the refreshment stand and as bingo card sales clerks ("It is preferred that housewives 35 years and older apply for this position."), bingo number callers, security guards, parking lot attendants, and janitors. But Butch Weisman brought in his brother, James "Skip" Weisman, to manage the hall day-to-day, and Skip brought in associates from Pittsburgh as assistant managers. Eugene Kubitz, an SMA limited

---

*In their decisions, Judge Roettger and the court of appeals both cited *Bryan v. Itasca County*, a 1976 decision of the U.S. Supreme Court in which the Court assumed that a state has no authority to enforce its laws on Indian reservations within the state's borders except to the extent that Congress has delegated the state that authority. As precedent for that conclusion of law, the Court cited *Williams v. Lee* for the proposition that "Congress has . . . acted consistently upon the assumption that the States have no power to regulate the affairs of Indians on a reservation," and the court cited the Department of the Interior's 1958 edition of the *Handbook of Federal Indian Law* for the proposition that "State laws generally are not applicable to tribal Indians on an Indian reservation except where Congress has expressly provided that State laws shall apply," which was a near verbatim republication of the same sentence as it appears in Felix Cohen's 1941 edition of the *Handbook*.

partner from Pittsburgh, was given the concession to provide the buses that transported players to the bingo hall from locations as distant as Orlando, Tampa, and Fort Myers.

In 1983, SMA paid the Seminole Tribe $2.5 million as its 55 percent share of the profit and kept $2.04 million. When he was deposed in 1994, George Simon said that in 1992 the split had been $4 million to the tribe and $3.27 million to SMA, and in 1993 the split had been $11 million to the tribe and $9 million to SMA.

Howard Tommie's agreement with Jack Cooper gave Tommie 25 percent of SMA's 45 percent share of the profit. When the *Miami Herald* reported in 1987 that SMA was paying Tommie $150,000 to $200,000 a year, Tommie conceded that some members of the Seminole Tribe thought he had cut a "sweetheart deal" while chairman of the tribal council. "I don't look at it that way," he protested, because he had to take a risk "I thought was worth taking."

The risk was that, if Sheriff Butterworth shut down the hall, the revenue from the smoke shops Tommie owned would have been used to pay off the $900,000 construction loan. George Simon told the *Miami Herald*, however, that Tommie had taken no risk, and SMA was paying him only because SMA had needed a Seminole Indian figurehead in order to smooth the way with the BIA. When the *Miami Herald* asked how much SMA was paying Tommie, Simon answered, "He gets more than [$200,000 a year], but we'll let it go at that."

How much more? In 1992, Simon, who kept SMA's books, sent the Internal Revenue Service 1099 forms reporting that SMA had paid Tommie and his ex-wife $2.4 million during that tax year. So, rather than the $3.27 million Simon later would testify to in his deposition, in 1992, SMA's 45 percent share of the profits from the Seminole bingo hall had been $9.6 million.

That was the on-the-books profit.

WHEN HE WAS ASKED in 1997 if SMA had skimmed any money, James Billie responded, "That I can't answer, 'cause I don't know." That profession of ignorance was, at best, disingenuous.

The management agreement James Billie signed in 1979 on behalf of the Seminole Tribe, and a supplemental agreement he signed the day after he signed the management agreement, gave SMA control of the tens of thousands of dollars that flowed through the bingo hall seven nights a week and into a bank account to which George Simon and the Weisman brothers had the only access. In 1990, Daniel Lane, the special agent in charge of the eastern region of the United States for the inspector general of the Department of the Interior, reported that "a confidential informant had disclosed that the two management firms responsible for managing the bingo games at Hollywood and Tampa, Florida, were skimming profits from both operations."* Lane also reported that

> a preliminary investigation of the bingo operations revealed a relationship between the management personnel, [name redacted], a known former organized crime boss in southern Florida, and the [name redacted] organized crime family. The relationship was corroborated by reviewing a case file concerning Seminole bingo operations in the FBI office in Miami, Florida.

After conducting its own investigation, the Pennsylvania Crime Commission reached a similar conclusion in 1992, which, in 1994, Butch Weisman and George Simon confirmed when they settled a lawsuit that had been filed by a security guard at the bingo hall on the Hollywood Reservation.

The guard was a non-Indian named Bruce Wheeland. When his supervisor discovered that Wheeland was HIV positive because he had been infected by his wife whose first husband had died of AIDS, Wheeland was fired. Wheeland hired an attorney named Marc Sarnoff who in November 1993 in the U.S. District Court in Fort Lauderdale filed a lawsuit—*Wheeland v. Seminole Management Associates*—in which Wheeland alleged that his firing had been unlawful.

The district court appointed a mediator who, on May 20, 1994, conducted a mediation that failed, after which the mediator reported to the court that a trial would have to be held because there was no possibility the parties could agree on a settlement. Then, on June 1, 1994, Marc Sarnoff informed the court that a settlement had been reached.

---

*In 1982, the Seminole Tribe opened a bingo hall in Tampa.

What happened between May 20 and June 1?

A month earlier, Sarnoff had sent an investigator to the Hollywood Reservation to find and interview employees who had worked with Wheeland. One of the employees the investigator found was Sharon Lyons, a bingo card seller. Lyons told the investigator that she had walked into a back room at the hall when she should not have and seen Skip Weisman packing bundles of cash into cardboard boxes that then were mailed to a casino in which the Weisman brothers owned interests on the Caribbean island of St. Maarten. Lyons also said she was told that "if she wanted to keep her legs," she should "keep her mouth shut."

On April 26, 1994, Marc Sarnoff deposed Skip Weisman. During the deposition, he asked, "Was any cash transported in cardboard boxes to the casino in St. Maarten?" Weisman answered under oath, "Absolutely not."

Three weeks later, when the mediation failed to produce a settlement, Sarnoff sent SMA's attorney an affidavit in which Sharon Lyons described what she had seen, as well as a chart Sarnoff had prepared that diagramed his theory of how the skim at the bingo hall worked. Several days later, SMA's attorney asked Sarnoff to come to his office.

When Sarnoff was seated in SMA's attorney's conference room, Butch Weisman and George Simon walked in, dropped a duffel bag on the table, and told Sarnoff the lawsuit was over. Inside the duffel bag was more than half a million dollars in cash. And as he was leaving, Weisman and Simon paid Sarnoff the compliment of telling him that he had come as close as anyone had to figuring out how the skim worked.

IN 2014 I SPENT a morning with George Simon at his apartment on the twelfth floor of the condominium tower in which he lives on a private island north of Miami Beach. Simon, who was ninety-one years old and appeared to still have every last one of his marbles, professed to have no recollection of the *Wheeland v. Seminole Management Associates* lawsuit. But after telling me that for seventeen years he had simply accepted as accurate the financial statements Skip Weisman sent him, Simon begrudgingly conceded that "Butch probably made a lot of money we didn't know about." He also volunteered that after Jack Cooper died of cancer in 1983 an individual, who Simon claimed he did not know, came to him and said,

"I expect the money I've been getting to continue." According to Simon, when he told Butch Weisman about that conversation, Butch said he had no idea what that individual could have been talking about.

There also is a codicil. In 1988, Congress enacted the Indian Gaming Regulatory Act (IGRA), the statute that sets out the framework for the regulation of gambling on Indian reservations. One of the IGRA's provisions directed the chairman of the National Indian Gaming Commission (NIGC), the new federal agency the act created, to review the management agreements Indian tribes had entered into prior to 1988. Another provision required the secretary of the interior to perform that function until the NIGC was up and running.

In 1992, when he reviewed the Seminole Tribe's management agreement with SMA, B.D. Ott, the director of the BIA's eastern area office, informed James Billie that the agreement was invalid because it had never been approved by the secretary of the interior.* In response, Billie told Lott that the "Seminole Tribe has honored SMA's contract all these years, and we have no problem with them."

When Ott remained adamant that the management agreement was invalid, in December 1992 James Billie and Butch Weisman and George Simon signed a new agreement that, as the IGRA required, reduced SMA's management fee from 45 percent to 30 percent of the profit. But the chairman of the NIGC refused to approve the agreement.

Four years later, Butch Weisman concluded that the chairman of the NIGC would never approve the new management agreement. So he proposed to James Billie that the Seminole Tribe buy SMA out of the eight years that remained of the twenty-five-year term in the original agreement. Even though that agreement was invalid, Billie agreed. When Weisman suggested $60 million, "Without bickering with him, I said, 'Sure,'" Billie recalled years later. "Sixty million was really nothing, given the things they had done for us. We were making $40 million a year. So we came up with

---

*In 1983, attorneys at the Department of the Interior advised the BIA that, as had been the situation since 1979, the secretary of the interior did not have to approve management agreements. After several contrary court decisions, in 1986, Assistant Secretary of the Interior for Indian Affairs Ross Swimmer reversed course and announced that "It is now the Department's policy to exercise its authority to review tribal bingo management contracts in all cases."

the money, because I needed to honor these Mafia guys here in Florida so they'd know the Seminoles are honorable people."

The Seminole Tribe paid the $60 million in installments. After Howard Tommie was given his 25 percent, the remainder of the money was distributed to SMA's partners and to anyone else who had a claim on it, if anyone else did.

Several years earlier, Butch Weisman—who had changed his last name to Moriarty—had purchased an estate on a bucolic country road in Fairfield, Connecticut, that today would be the envy of Martha Stewart and which Moriarty later sold to the president of the Mobil Oil Company.

At 11:00 a.m. on October 14, 1998, a Jeep Cherokee drove into the driveway of the estate. A white male dressed as a deliveryman—later described as "6 feet tall, average build, 25 to 28 years old, clean shaven, with short, dark brown hair"—got out of the vehicle and knocked at the door. Butch Moriarty was not home. But his wife, Jane, and her eighty-year-old mother, Helen Kennedy, were.

When he looked through a window near the door and saw that Mrs. Kennedy was responding to his knock the deliveryman went to the Cherokee and returned with a wicker gift basket whose contents were wrapped in cellophane. Then in front of the window he displayed a receipt for the basket from the gift shop at Foxwoods, the casino the Mashantucket Pequot Tribe operated several miles up the freeway.

When Mrs. Kennedy opened the door, the deliveryman brandished a handgun, jammed a scarf into her mouth that he secured with tape, and bound her hands behind her back with plastic handcuffs. He then pushed her up the stairs to the second floor, where Jane Moriarty was standing in the hallway talking on the telephone.

After Jane hung up the phone, the gunman told her to give him the money or he would shoot her mother. While professing that she did not know what money he was talking about, Jane walked backward from the hallway into her bedroom until she got close enough to press an alarm button. According to the police report,

> When the subject heard the sound, he got very angry . . . [and] started
> punching Moriarty with his fists. Somehow Moriarty was able to run
> from the bedroom, but he caught her in the hall, where he started

punching her in the face. Somehow she got away from him, ran downstairs through the kitchen, and through the side door of the house. She ran down the driveway, across the street to her neighbor's lawn and fell down.

A moment later, the Cherokee careened out of the driveway and vanished down the road.

When he returned from Florida, where he said he had been playing golf, Butch Moriarty was interviewed at the Fairfield Police Department. Moriarty, who was "cooperative but reserved," told the police he was a general partner in SMA and had been receiving quarterly payments from the Seminole Tribe as his share of the tribe's buyout of SMA's management agreement. He also said he would be receiving fifteen more payments that would total 2.5 to 3 million dollars.

When asked who he thought might have sent the gunman who assaulted his wife, Moriarty suggested Willard Shiner. Shiner was one of SMA's limited partners who, Moriarty said, had a "strong hate for him" as a consequence of a falling out the two men had had over their ownership of a bar in the Shadyside neighborhood of Pittsburgh. When he was interviewed, Shiner said he had "no love" for Moriarty, but denied having anything to do with the home invasion. And there the investigation ended. The Fairfield Police Department's file remains open, and the case remains unsolved.

Today, Butch Moriarty lives in Southport, a wealthy enclave on Connecticut's Gold Coast south of Fairfield, apparently without fear of further retribution for what may (or may not) have been his failure to make a proper accounting for the distribution of money to which the individuals who sent him to Florida in 1979 considered themselves entitled. And on the Hollywood Reservation the bingo hall SMA opened in 1979 still operates across the street from the Seminole Hard Rock Hotel & Casino.

4: BARONA BINGO

A rat ran away with the cheese here.

SUSAN OSUNA
Member, Barona Group of the Capitan
Grande Band of Mission Indians

IN 1982, MYLES ANDERBERG HAD A GOOD LIFE. A FIFTY-FOUR-YEAR-OLD aerospace engineer, Anderberg worked for Hughes Helicopters and lived with his wife on a sixty-foot sailboat they moored at Marina del Rey south of Los Angeles.

Harrison "Harry" Hertzberg, a Los Angeles attorney, and his trophy wife Jeanne, a former Miss California, moored their boat in an adjoining slip, and the Hertzbergs and the Anderbergs became friends. "Harry was a very sociable fellow," Anderberg would remember how it all began. "Everybody liked Harry."

One day in December 1982, Harry Hertzberg pitched Myles Anderberg on a seemingly preposterous idea: Anderberg should quit his job at Hughes Helicopters and go to work for Hertzberg as the manager of a bingo hall on an Indian reservation.

HERTZBERG WAS ACQUAINTED with a stand-up comedian named Allan Drake. Drake, who lived in the San Fernando Valley, performed occasionally on the *Ed Sullivan* and *Johnny Carson* shows and had bit parts in television series such as *Sanford and Son*. But he earned most of his money on the road, performing as the warm-up act for such singers as Bobby Darin and Engelbert Humperdick. Drake also performed on the Playboy Club circuit, which is where he met his second wife, Wanda, when she was working as a bunny at the Chicago club.

In 1980, when Allan Drake was performing in Miami, an acquaintance suggested that he and Wanda might enjoy visiting the bingo hall on the Seminole Reservation west of Fort Lauderdale. According to

Wanda Drake, her husband was an "idea man" who was always on the lookout for a new one. So when Allan visited the Seminole bingo hall and saw hundreds of people spending tens of thousands of dollars, he conceived the idea of opening a bingo hall on an Indian reservation in southern California.

Harry Hertzberg told Myles Anderberg that when Drake returned to Los Angeles, he proposed the idea of opening a bingo hall to Hertzberg. And after flying to Florida and visiting the Seminole bingo hall, Hertzberg agreed that a bingo hall could be a lucrative business.

To replicate the Seminole business model Hertzberg needed an Indian tribe whose reservation was located within a reasonable automobile drive from a large number of non-Indian customers. And fortuitously, Hertzberg owned a vacation home at just such a location.

IN 1875 PRESIDENT ULYSSES S. Grant withdrew several sections of federal land around a hot springs in the Coachella Valley east of Los Angeles as a reservation for the Agua Caliente Band of Cahuilla Indians. Between 1877 and 1907 additional land was withdrawn, and by 1938, when the town that had grown up around the hot springs was incorporated as Palm Springs, the Agua Caliente Band was the city's largest landowner.

Hertzberg proposed to the chairwoman of the band's tribal council that the band contract with American Amusement & Management, Inc. (AAMI), a company Hertzberg had incorporated, to build, and then manage, a bingo hall on a parcel of the band's land in Palm Springs. While the chairwoman passed on the idea, she told Hertzberg there was a group of Indians living on a reservation east of San Diego whose members, because they were "starving to death," might be receptive to the idea.

IN 1542 WHEN THE Portuguese navigator Juan Cabrillo, sailing in the service of the Spanish crown, sailed into the harbor at what today is San Diego, as many as 275,000 Indians lived in California, most in villages scattered along the coast and in the inland river valleys. In 1769 the Franciscan Junipero Serra disrupted that arrangement when he established San Diego de Alcala, the first of the missions the Franciscans built along the El

Camino Real (King's Highway), the wagon road that ran from San Diego to Sonoma, north of San Francisco.

Having come to California to save Indian souls and needing Indian labor to till the fields and tend herds on the land around the missions, the Franciscans gave colored cloth and trinkets to Indians who agreed to settle around the missions and be baptized. But, as it is with most things that seem too good to be true, there was a catch: the missions were a police state theocracy. As the French explorer Jean-Francois de Galaup la Pérouse reported after visiting the mission near Monterey in 1786:

[A]t the moment an Indian is baptized, the effect is the same as if he had pronounced a vow for life. If he escape, to reside with his relations in the independent villages, he is summoned three times to return, and if he refuse, the missionaries apply to the governor, who sends soldiers to seize him in the midst of his family, and conduct him to the mission, where he is condemned to receive a certain number of lashes, with the whip.

In 1821, Mexico, of which California was a part, won its independence from Spain. In 1833, when the Mexican Congress ended the Franciscans' theocratic rule, more than 1,300 Indians lived at San Diego de Alcala. Now free to stay or go, most Indians went, and by 1848, when the United States acquired California from Mexico, San Diego de Alcala had deteriorated into a "mournful state of decay," and its rooms were "dirty and full of fleas."

In 1853 the few Indians who still lived at San Diego de Alcala moved to an old village site located on federal land in the Capitan Grande Valley in the foothills east of San Diego. In 1875 President Ulysses S. Grant made the relocation official when he withdrew 12,800 acres in the valley as a reservation for the Indians who occupied it.

By 1916, fewer than 150 Indians lived on the reservation in two villages, Capitan Grande and Los Conejos. Unfortunately for the Indians, by that date San Diego needed more water if the city was going to continue to grow. So Rep. William "Brother Bill" Kettner, who represented San Diego in the U.S. House of Representatives, introduced a bill whose enactment would authorize the city to acquire whatever land inside the Capitan

Grande Reservation it needed to construct a dam and reservoir to divert the San Diego River, which flowed through the reservation, into the city's water system.

After visiting the reservation, in 1918 Commissioner of Indian Affairs Cato Sells urged Congress to pass the Kettner bill and authorize the Bureau of Indian Affairs (BIA) to relocate the Indians. Sells told Congress that the Indians had agreed to make the move, which was not true. But in 1919 Congress enacted a version of the Kettner bill that authorized the city to condemn the land it needed in exchange for paying the secretary of the interior an amount of money adequate to purchase land for the Indians elsewhere.

After more than a decade of delay, in 1931 the city paid the secretary $361,428.

After looking at available properties, Ramon Curo Ames, one of Capitan Grande's "captains," as the headmen of southern California Indian villages were called, persuaded twelve of the families who lived at Capitan Grande to ask the BIA to spend $75,000 to purchase Barona Ranch. The ranch was a 5,000-acre tract of land in a boulder-strewn valley west of the Capitan Grande Reservation through which a creek flowed that was adequate, although just barely, for irrigation and stock-watering. In 1932, fifty-seven Indians, almost half of whom were children, loaded their possessions into horse-drawn wagons and several Model A automobiles and rode and drove up Wildcat Canyon Road to their new reservation.

At the Barona Reservation, the BIA built each family a concrete-block house and paid Ramon Curo Ames $7.75 a body to return to Capitan Grande before the village was flooded and relocate the graveyard. The BIA hoped to build a model community on the Barona Reservation whose residents would be able to earn enough money raising crops, grazing cattle, and working for wages on the surrounding farms to support themselves. But by 1981, when Harry Hertzberg proposed to the tribal council of the Barona Group of the Capitan Grande Band of Mission Indians that AAMI open a bingo hall on the reservation, the BIA's utopian experiment had proven an abject failure. The houses were ramshackle and in disrepair, most Barona Indians of working age were unemployed, and the reservation was riven with alcohol abuse and disputes between families that occasionally erupted into violence.

Two years earlier, the council had tried to earn extra money by holding bingo games that were conducted pursuant to California's bingo law whose provisions were similar to those in Florida's bingo law. But the games failed to attract many players because at Lakeside, the town down Wildcat Canyon Road from the reservation, the VFW and the local Catholic church sponsored bingo games that paid the same jackpots.

Since the council members knew something about bingo, they were receptive to Hertzberg's proposal. On April 4, 1981, at a meeting in which all adult residents of the reservation participated who wished to do so, by a vote of 22 to 0, the Barona Indians agreed to contract with AAIA. Two weeks later, Harry Hertzberg and tribal chairman Edward "Joe" Welch and the other council members signed a management agreement that gave AAMI the right to operate bingo games on the Barona Reservation for twenty years in exchange for paying the Barona Group 55 percent of the profit.

WHILE HE NOW HAD an Indian tribe and a reservation, Harry Hertzberg understood that opening a bingo hall in which games would be played that violated California's bingo law might provoke the same reaction from San Diego County Sheriff John Duffy that Broward County Sheriff Bob Butterworth had had. To find out whether it would, in June, Hertzberg met with Under Sheriff William Shope. When he told Shope that AAMI intended to open a bingo hall on the Barona Reservation that would offer games that would pay out jackpots of more than $250 (the limit California's bingo law allowed), Shope told Hertzberg that if AAMI did so, Sheriff Duffy's deputies would arrest everyone involved.

In response to Shope's threat, Hertzberg did what Jack Cooper, Butch Weisman, and George Simon paid Marion Sibley to do eighteen months earlier—he filed a lawsuit. In July 1981, in the U.S. District Court in San Diego, Hertzberg filed *Barona Group of the Capitan Grande Band of Mission Indians v. Duffy,* in which he sought an injunction that would prohibit Sheriff Duffy from "interfering with the plaintiff's operation of its bingo business on the Barona Indian Reservation."

Hertzberg knew about the decision District Judge Norman Roettger had issued in *Seminole Tribe of Florida v. Butterworth* because the West Publishing Company had published the decision in its "advance sheets," which most attorneys routinely read. So in his lawsuit, Hertzberg made the two-part legal argument that Judge Roettger had found persuasive.

Part one was that, in 1976, in *Bryan v. Itasca County*, the U.S. Supreme Court had held that in states such as Florida (and California) the state did not have authority to enforce its civil regulatory laws on Indian reservations. Part two was that Florida's (and California's) bingo law was a civil regulatory law because the law regulated, rather than prohibited, bingo.

Unfortunately for Hertzberg, District Judge Judith Keep, to whom his lawsuit was assigned, had a different view of California's bingo law. She dismissed the lawsuit on the on the ground that "the California gambling laws in issue are criminal/prohibitory." Hertzberg appealed the dismissal, and on December 20, 1982, a three-judge panel of the U.S. Court of Appeals for the Ninth Circuit reversed Judge Keep because, in the panel's view, California's bingo law was "regulatory and of a civil nature."

It was when the panel settled the legal situation in his favor that Hertzberg proposed to Myles Anderberg that he quit his job at Hughes Helicopters and go to work for AAMI.

BY CHANCE, ANDERBERG was flying to Florida to attend a meeting at the aerospace company Martin Marietta, so he agreed to visit the Seminole bingo hall. As Anderberg later told the story:

> I went there to get Harry off my back. To be able to tell him, "Ok. I've seen it, and I'm not interested." I rented a car in Miami and drove up to Hollywood. The Seminole bingo hall was a prefabricated Butler building. Inside, there was standing room only. The aisles were crammed. People were holding up green cash trying to buy bingo cards and using overturned trash cans as tables. I was astonished by the whole scene. I went back to my motel and called my wife and told her that I couldn't believe there was so much money involved.

When he returned to California, Anderberg told Hertzberg that, while he now found his proposition intriguing, he still was not interested in quitting his job. But Hertzberg continued to pester him, and Anderberg finally agreed that he and his wife would accompany Hertzberg on his next visit to the Barona Reservation.

TWO MONTHS EARLIER, Anderberg's younger brother, a Catholic priest who was a member of the Marist Order, had died of a heart attack. Since 1968 Eric Anderberg, who was known as Brother Vincent, had lived on the Pine Ridge Reservation in South Dakota were he had dedicated his life to working among the Oglala Sioux, the most impoverished Indian tribe in the nation. Profoundly affected by his brother's death, Anderberg was moved by his visit to the Barona Reservation. As he would recall years later:

> There were cattle guards on both ends of the highway leading in and out of the reservation, and range cattle roamed everywhere. The housing was substandard, but most houses had running water and indoor toilets. A lot of the houses had been HUD built. But a lot of them were shacks. Squalor was widespread. We talked to Joe Welch and met several of the tribal council members. They were very enthusiastic about bringing some kind of money-making scheme onto the reservation. Everything on the reservation was abject poverty, and I was touched by it. When we discussed it, my wife agreed with me that my brother would be very pleased if we could help.

Which is how Myles Anderberg became executive vice president of AAMI and how, on April 15, 1983, Barona Bonus Bingo opened in the community center on the reservation that Anderberg had spent AAMI's money to remodel into a 500-seat bingo hall.

BARONA BONUS BINGO was an immediate success. The first evening, the first game did not begin until 6:30 p.m. But by 5:30 p.m., every seat in the hall had been taken, and players were being turned away at the door. At that point, according to Anderberg,

> I had to station people at the bottom of Wildcat Canyon Road with big signs that said, 'Barona Bonus Bingo Closed.' When asked why, the guys with the signs would tell people, 'Don't go up there. The

parking lot's full. The canyon is clogged. Just turn around and go back.' And it was that way on many other nights.

Four evenings a week, and during the afternoons on weekends, so many people were driving up Wildcat Canyon Road to play bingo for jackpots that ranged from $300 to $1,500 that Anderberg built an addition onto the community hall that added another 200 seats.

In May, Anderberg told the *San Diego Union* that Barona Bonus Bingo was "running close to capacity almost every night we play." By September, Barona Bonus Bingo was operating five nights a week. In October, Anderberg contracted with Aztec Bus Lines to transport players from throughout San Diego County to the Barona Reservation.By November, Barona Bonus Bingo was operating six nights a week, and as a promotion, lured players with a bingo game that paid the winner $33,000.

During its first twelve months of operation, Barona Bonus Bingo netted $1 million, $550,000 of which AAMI paid to the Barona Band, the other $450,000 went to AAMI's owners and to Anderberg, whose employment contract, in addition to his $4,000 a month salary, paid him 5 percent of AAMI's share of the profit. And every Barona Indian who wanted a job had one working as a bingo card seller, restaurant worker, cashier, parking lot attendant, or security guard.

HARRY HERTZBERG'S BUSINESS plan was to start out holding bingo games in the community center. If the games made money, AAMI would build a bingo hall similar to the hall Seminole Management Associates had built in Florida.

The success of Barona Bonus Bingo so quickly exceeded expectations that two weeks after the bingo hall in the community center opened, AAMI announced that it had contracted with a San Diego construction company to build a 54,400-square-foot bingo hall down the road from the community center. In August, Harry Hertzberg and Joe Welch broke ground for construction. That November, the *San Diego Union* reported that

> construction of a $2.5 million, 2,000-seat bingo palace is now under way on the reservation, and arrangements have been made with a local transportation company to start bringing in busloads of players

from Los Angeles, Orange and Riverside Counties. There was some delay in finding financing for the bingo palace project (a New Year's Day completion date had been set, but now is doubtful), and there was talk that investors did not want any part of it. But, as it turns out, a single anonymous investor has decided to bankroll the entire project, according to Harrison Hertzberg.

The anonymous investor was Mel Garb, a corpulent fast-food entrepreneur who had sold twenty-seven McDonald's hamburger stands he had been operating as a franchisee to the McDonald's Corporation for $29 million.

When the new bingo hall—which Myles Anderberg touted as the "MGM Grand of Southern California bingo"—opened on the evening of August 3, 1984, not only were all 2,000 seats occupied, but Anderberg had to turn away more than eight hundred wannabe players who had made the drive up Wildcat Canyon Road for a chance to win the Ford Thunderbird that was given away as a door prize and the $1 million "blackout" bingo game Anderberg had advertised to promote the opening.

In addition to Harry Hertzberg, Allan Drake, and Mel Garb, AAMI's other owner was Eddie Drasin, who Hertzberg told Anderberg was an acquaintance who owned a clothing factory in Los Angeles. Under Myles Anderberg's management, AAMI's owners were making money. Which is why Anderberg was dumbstruck when—two months after the new bingo hall opened—Bobby Hertzberg, Harry Hertzberg's lawyer son, told him he was fired.

THE NEXT DAY a balding and bespectacled forty-six-year-old resident of Las Vegas named Steward Siegel replaced Myles Anderberg as manager of Barona Bonus Bingo. Unlike Anderberg, Siegel had spent thirteen years in the gaming industry. However, between October 1984 when Siegel replaced Anderberg and September 1985 when he left AAMI's employ, Barona Bonus Bingo lost money. How did such a profitable business so quickly become unprofitable?

In July 1985, FBI agents appeared on the Barona Reservation and served a subpoena for Barona Bonus Bingo's books. Two months later,

Siegel resigned and returned to Las Vegas. Three months after that, deputies from the San Diego County Sheriff's Office executed search warrants at the offices of Barona Bonus Bingo, while other law enforcement officers did the same at Siegel's townhouse in Las Vegas.

In March 1986, a grand jury in San Diego indicted Siegel on six felony counts. The indictment alleged that, between January and August 1985, Siegel had used "shills" (as the individuals he recruited for the work were called) to rig bingo games that skimmed $139,000. Before the indictment was unsealed, Siegel's attorney negotiated a plea agreement in which Siegel pled guilty to four felony counts and agreed to cooperate with the investigation by giving up Joe Catania, the Barona Bonus Bingo employee who, at Siegel's direction, had handled the shills.

When they were given immunity, the shills told the grand jury they had turned over the money they had won in the rigged games to Siegel. Did Siegel pocket the $139,000? And was that the only money he or anyone else skimmed?

Before he was fired, Myles Anderberg had become suspicious that Catania was rigging games by weighting the "wheel of fortune" that was spun to select the numbers players marked on their bingo cards. So is it possible that before Siegel arrived at Barona Bonus Bingo money was being skimmed? If it was, who ordered the skim, how did it work, and who got the money? Investigating the answers to those questions begins with who Steward Siegel was.

STEWARD SIEGEL WAS born in 1938 in Queens, New York. After graduating from high school and serving a stint in the army, in 1961 Siegel married. He and his wife settled in Lakewood, New Jersey, where Siegel began his career as a grifter who would compile an FBI file that is three inches thick.

After running up a string of bad debts and then being arrested in 1968 in Puerto Rico for car theft (case dismissed for lack of evidence), in 1970 Siegel and his wife began spending their summers in the Catskill Mountains northwest of New York City where, at the Monticello Raceway, Siegel reinvented himself as a harness horse trainer. He also became associated with Tommy "Corky" Vastola, a capo in the DeCavalcante Mafia family based in northern New Jersey.

In 1971, Vastola and Siegel tried to work a con on Sammy Davis, Jr., with whom Vastola was acquainted socially. They attempted to persuade Davis to be the figurehead owner of Sammy Davis, Jr., Farms, Inc., a corporation that would purchase a horse farm in New Jersey and then trade on Davis's name to induce other investors to buy worthless stock. As part of the hustle, Siegel arranged for a racing magazine to publish a photograph of him and Davis below a caption advertising that, in addition to Sammy Davis, Jr., "other famous names of the entertainment world are expected to join the newly formed stable." Siegel also arranged for another racing magazine to publish a news blurb reporting that

> Sammy Davis, Jr., one of the premier stars of the entertainment world, has entered the harness-racing world—he and his associates have purchased 20 acres in Lakewood, N.J., including a five-eighths mile training track. Davis made the announcement while visiting the barn area at Northfield Park recently. The farm, "Sammy Davis, Jr., Farms, Inc.", will be managed by long time harness racing enthusiast Steward Siegel of New York.

Siegel also went to Kentucky and bought four horses at a yearling sale that the auctioneers allowed him to transport to New Jersey without paying for because he said he represented Sammy Davis, Jr.

When the con was exposed, Siegel left his wife and two children in New Jersey and moved to Miami, where he lived for a year under an assumed name. Between 1971 and 1975, Siegel worked at casinos in Santo Domingo in the Dominican Republic; Bled, Yugoslavia; and Santa Marta, Columbia. Years later, he told the FBI that the DeCavalcante family and Josip Tito, the president of Yugoslavia, jointly owned the casino in Bled.

Siegel also spent time in Las Vegas. In 1974, he was indicted there for wire fraud for using stolen identification to obtain a $20,000 line of credit that he used to write $12,000 worth of bad checks. While the wire fraud case was pending, he returned to New Jersey where he scammed a bank for $23,000 and began organizing gambling junkets to the casino in Santa Marta.

Convicted in November 1974 in Las Vegas on the wire fraud charge, Siegel was given a suspended sentence. Until he pled guilty twelve years later for rigging bingo games at Barona Bonus Bingo and then violated his probation, Siegel never spent a day in jail because throughout his career as a grifter he worked on the side as a confidential informant for the FBI.

IN 1976 NEW JERSEY voters amended their state constitution to authorize casinos to open in Atlantic City. In 1977, the Atlantis Casino, owned by a corporation and a partnership that likely had mob connections, hired Siegel as its director of operations. Siegel also opened a school to train dealers. Throughout that time, he provided the FBI with information regarding "individuals or groups who were attempting to 'move into' Atlantic City."

The FBI assigned Siegel a handler and the code name "Crap Shooter."

By 1981, Siegel was back in Las Vegas, where he was employed at the Aladdin Casino. The FBI knew it was dealing with "a consummate 'con artist' who will, if given the opportunity through being placed in a position of trust steal money through any scam conceivable." But Crap Shooter's information was useful. A December 1983 FBI memorandum summarized Siegel's value as an informant:

> A review of the source's accomplishments for the past year determined that he furnished information regarding 93 individuals who were either organized crime members or were associating with same. His information directly resulted in 8 arrests in the Buffalo and Los Angeles Divisions, the seizure of 2.2 kilos of cocaine, the identification and arrest of a corrupt Customs official, as well as the individual who was bribing him.

STEWARD SIEGEL WAS psychologically incapable of telling the truth. So anything he said about anything must be carefully vetted. However, in December 1986 when he testified during his sentencing hearing after he pled guilty to rigging bingo games at Barona Bonus Bingo, Siegel said he had been recruited in Las Vegas by Allan Drake to orchestrate a skim. The reason, according to Siegel, was that AAMI was in "financial trouble," and Mel Garb "was fed up with being the only one putting money into the bingo hall." Siegel also told the court that he had given Garb and Eddie Drasin most of the money the shills had given to him.

At the hearing, three Barona Indians testified that they had been present at a Barona Tribal Council meeting at which Harry Hertzberg admitted that he and AAMI's other owners had hired Siegel to rig bingo games because "they had to have the money to keep the business going." By the time the hearing was held Allan Drake was dead, and Hertzberg was on his deathbed (and would die of cancer a month later). But Siegel's attorney subpoenaed Eddie Drasin and Mel Garb. But when he called them as witnesses to substantiate Siegel's story, Drasin and Garb both invoked the Fifth Amendment and refused to testify.

In the end, none of the four owners of AAMI were prosecuted for conspiring with Siegel to steal from the Barona Indians and the IRS. However, unbeknownst to Myles Anderberg, there also was a fifth owner.

THROUGHOUT HIS CAREER as a nightclub comedian and television actor, Allan Drake was an organized crime associate. Originally from Boston, in 1944, Drake was driving a taxi in Miami and earning money on the side competing as a semiprofessional prizefighter, when a man who had seen Drake fight got into his cab. During the ride, Drake's fare said, "You're pretty handy with your mitts, kid. Maybe I could use you."

The fare was Anthony Carfano, also known as Little Augie Pisano. In the 1920s, Carfano had worked as muscle for Frankie Yale, the Mafia boss who controlled Brooklyn. In the 1930s, Little Augie began spending time in Miami, overseeing the interests there of the Mafia family that, after being led by Lucky Luciano and Frank Costello, since 1957 has been known as the Genovese.

Carfano hired Drake as his driver, and when Drake decided to try telling jokes for a living, Carfano became his manager. After performing on the circuit of mob-controlled nightclubs that stretched as far west as Covington, Kentucky, Drake became the warm-up act for the singer Tony Martin, and Carfano, who was connected in New York City, arranged for Drake to make his first appearance on *The Ed Sullivan Show*.

Through Carfano, Allan Drake knew Albert Anastasia, the leader of Murder, Incorporated; Mafia enforcer James Plumeri; and Anthony "Tony the Jack" Giacalone, a capo in the Mafia family in Detroit. In 1983, the FBI reported that, prior to Johnny Roselli's murder in 1976, Drake had been associated with Roselli, who in Los Angeles and Las Vegas represented the Outfit (as the Mafia family in Chicago is called), and that other Mafia members with whom Drake was associated included: "[name redacted] member of the DeCavalcante Family; [name redacted] Gambino Family member in Los Angeles; [name redacted] capo Los Angeles Family; [name redacted] Lucchese Family member in Miami; and [name redacted] boss, Bufalino Family (Philadelphia)."

Allan Drake also was acquainted with Rocco Passanante.

In 1978, the California Attorney General's Organized Crime Control Commission identified 292 individuals "who from testimony or other evidence are linked to organized crime activity in California." One of those individuals was Rocco Passanante.

Born in Brooklyn in 1925, in 1951 when he was twenty-six-years-old Passanante was convicted in New York of felonious assault. After apparently serving time for that offense, he moved to Los Angeles. In 1964, Passanante and a partner, Louis Stern, were arrested for writing $250,000 worth of bad checks and then, when they were asked for payment, threatening the individuals they had defrauded with a hatchet. Passanante pled no contest. Before he was sentenced, he was with Stern in Palm Springs when Stern shot three men with whom he and Passanante had gotten into a bar fight.

After serving five years in state prison on the charges to which he had pleaded no contest, Passanante was paroled in 1970. He returned to Los Angeles, where he became an associate of Michael Rizzitello, a capo in the Los Angeles Mafia family, whose acquaintance Passanante may have made when both men were incarcerated.

In 1977 the FBI reported that "Passanante is associated with the Los Angeles family of the LCN [Mafia] and that in the past has been a robber, jewel thief, and extortionist," and that "Passanante is suspected in trafficking in stolen gold bullion."

In 1982, Passanante was suspected of conspiring with a grifter named Joseph Levy to defraud cash-strapped businessmen who hired Levy to collect their past-due receivables. Also in 1982, Passanante was arrested for car theft and receiving stolen property. His attorney in that case was Harry Hertzberg.

IN 2009 I HAD lunch with Rocco Passanante and Allan Drake's widow, Wanda Drake, with whom Passanante was living. Passanante told me that—contrary to what Harry Hertzberg told Myles Anderberg—when Allan Drake returned to Los Angeles after visiting the Seminole bingo hall, the man to whom he took the idea of opening a bingo hall on an Indian reservation in southern California was Passanante. Passanante then took the idea to Hertzberg. The two men formed AAMI, Passanante investing $60,000, Hertzberg $30,000. Then Passanante allowed Eddie Drasin, whose father was an acquaintance, to invest $30,000, which Passanante pocketed so that Passanante, Hertzberg, and Drasin each made the same $30,000 contribution. Passanante also gave Allan Drake an ownership interest in AAMI as a finder's fee.

When Barona Bonus Bingo was an immediate success, Passanante decided to open AAMI to new investors by selling 20 "points" at $100,000 per point. Comedian Milton Berle considered buying a point, as did a local bookmaker.

Then one morning, when Eddie Drasin was having breakfast at the La Costa Resort north of San Diego, Mel Garb, who lived at the resort, came to Drasin's table and said he had heard that points in AAMI were for sale. When Drasin said twenty points were available at $100,000 a point, Garb bought them all.

The next August, the 2,000-seat bingo hall, whose construction Mel Garb financed, opened. The first evening, the net profit was $57,000, and Passanante remembers thinking that "everybody was on easy street." Then Wanda Drake, who had been quietly listening to my conversation with Passanante, volunteered, "Everybody got greedy."

When Myles Anderberg became the manager of Barona Bonus Bingo, he knew nothing about managing a bingo hall. But he had no criminal record and, because of his work in the aerospace industry, he had a security clearance. So, insofar as the San Diego County Sheriff's Department was concerned, he was beyond reproach. For AAMI's owners, however, Anderberg's probity may have had a downside.

To prevent players and floor workers from colluding, he installed television cameras throughout the bingo hall. According to Anderberg,

Floor workers sold bingo cards to the players. Then they took the cash back to the office and bought more cards. But they had to pay dollar-for-dollar for what they took out. All that money went into cash boxes. Each morning, the counters would bring in the boxes that had been locked up the night before. Before they unlocked the boxes, they had to call the security office upstairs, and the security office had to tell them that the cameras were on. When the cameras were recording, the counters would start unlocking boxes and taking the money out. It was as foolproof as you could get handling that much cash.

Anderberg's security system may have been one of the problems at Barona Bonus Bingo that Steward Siegel was brought in to fix.

EVEN WHEN THE $139,000 Siegel skimmed from the bingo games he and Joe Catania rigged is deducted, Barona Bonus Bingo, which made money when Myles Anderberg was manager, should have made money during Siegel's tenure. But under Siegel's management, the operation, which according to Passanante should have been grossing $12 to $15 million a year, was not profitable. The reason, according to Passanante, was that Siegel, who had been hired to steal from the Barona Indians and the IRS, also stole from the men who employed him.

When Passanante heard that Siegel had been bragging that he was skimming $14,000 a week, according to Passanante, he went to Las Vegas and met with "some people." When he returned to Los Angeles, Passanante met at the Beverly Wilshire Hotel with Siegel and a New York bookmaker named Georgie Forest. Before the meeting, Forest gave Passanante an envelope that contained $5,000 and told Passanante to take the money and let Siegel be. But Passanante told Siegel he was fired. According to Passanante, Siegel responded, "Rocco, give me thirty days, and I'll turn the place around." But Passanante was finished with him.

That is the story Rocco Passanante told me. However, Robert Dwyer, who was the assistant manager of Barona Bonus Bingo at the time, told me that Eddie Drasin fired Siegel after Dwyer discovered that Siegel had twice rigged raffles to allow his girlfriend to win automobiles. But Dwyer was not present when Drasin purportedly did the firing.

Whatever the truth, when Siegel was indicted, he avoided jail by providing the FBI with information that led to the arrest of an associate of Siegel's in Las Vegas named Steve Homick for a double murder-for-hire Homick had committed in Los Angeles. In *Family Blood*, his book about the Homick murders, author Marvin Wolf reported: "In late 1985, San Diego Sheriff's police pounced on the Barona Reservation bingo operation Stewart [sic] Siegel was supervising for the Chicago-based Mafia crime family run by Sam Carlisi." Wolf's source for that information was the FBI, which would have gotten its information from Siegel, who cannot be believed about anything without corroboration.

When I asked Steve Homick, who from 1989 until his death in 2014 was incarcerated on Death Row at San Quentin and who spent time with Siegel on the Barona Reservation, he was adamant that the Chicago Outfit had no involvement. But if Rocco Passanante, Harry Hertzberg, Allan Drake, Eddie Drasin, and Mel Garb were the only individuals who were taking money out of Barona Bonus Bingo, why did Georgie Forest offer Passanante $5,000 to let Siegel keep his job? And who were the "some people" Passanante talked to in Las Vegas before he fired Siegel? And why did they need to be talked to?

Whatever the true facts are, in 1986 when he was waiting to be sentenced, Steward Siegel was diagnosed with colon cancer. In 1989, he died in Minnesota while incarcerated in the federal witness protection program because, after receiving a suspended sentence, he had violated his probation.

Before he died, in February 1989 the U.S. Department of Justice flew Siegel to Washington, D.C., to testify before the Senate Select Committee on Indian Affairs on organized crime infiltration of bingo halls on Indian reservations. Sitting behind a screen to hide his identity, Siegel, who during the hearing was referred to as "Marty," told the senators he had personal knowledge that the Mafia controlled bingo halls on twelve reservations. When asked to name the families, Siegel answered, "The Lucchese family, the Buttalino family, and the Meyer Lansky organization." He did not name the Chicago Outfit.

Nothing Steward Siegel said about anything can be believed without collaboration. On the other hand, by 1989, Siegel had been associated with Corky Vastola, the capo in the DeCavalcante family, and members of other Mafia families for almost twenty years. Most intriguing of all, when we had lunch, Wanda Drake mentioned in passing that "the mustache guys tried to get into the Barona casino." "Mustache Pete" is a slang term for a traditional Mafia boss.

So what is the truth? All that can be said for certain is that, as we shall see, by 1983, attorneys in the Criminal Division of the U.S. Department of Justice were aware of what Steward Siegel later would tell the Select Committee on Indian Affairs: there were bingo halls on Indian reservations in Florida, California, and elsewhere that were riven with mob influence.

5: STEVE WHILDEN AND PAN AMERICAN MANAGEMENT COMPANY

Steve Whilden is a self-styled national figure on Indian bingo but nobody knows quite how he got there.

Department of the Interior Official

EVERAL MONTHS AFTER THE BINGO HALL ON THE SEMINOLE TRIBE'S RESERvation in Hollywood, Florida, opened, James Billie, the chairman of the tribe, received a telephone call from an anonymous caller. The next morning, when Billie told Steve Whilden, the tribe's general counsel, about the call, according to Billie, "Steve grabbed my arm and said, 'Come on, James.'"

Whilden took Billie to Tampa, the city on the eastern shore of the Gulf of Mexico that is the center of the second largest metropolitan area in Florida. They went to Tampa because the anonymous caller had told Billie that a work crew excavating a vacant city block in downtown Tampa to construct a municipal parking garage had inadvertently unearthed the cemetery at Fort Brooke, the stockade the U.S. Army had built on the shore of Tampa Bay in 1824. What grabbed Whilden's attention was that the caller had told Billie that archaeologists who investigated the site had unearthed 126 skeletons, 42 of which were of Seminole origin.

In Tampa, at Whilden's instigation, Billie demanded that the city relinquish the bones of its members' ancestors to the Seminole Tribe for reburial. Whilden later said James Billie considered the skeletons a gift his ancestors had "tossed in his lap." And that is how the fortuity played out.

Whilden negotiated an agreement with the city of Tampa in which the city agreed to give the Seminole skeletons and Seminole-related artifacts the archaeologists had discovered at the construction site to the Seminole Tribe. In return, the tribe agreed to relocate the skeletons and artifacts to a "site to be chosen, acquired and developed by the Tribe at no expense to the City."

On July 11, 1980, Bob Martinez, the mayor of Tampa, and James Billie signed the agreement. That same day, the Seminole Tribe mailed Secretary of the Interior Cecil Andrus a deed that conveyed to the United States the title to an 8.5-acre parcel of land the tribe had acquired next to the Interstate 4 freeway east of downtown Tampa. The tribe also requested that Secretary Andrus accept the deed pursuant to section 5 of the Indian Reorganization Act (IRA), which authorizes the secretary of the interior to acquire land for Indian tribes "in trust."

Deputy Assistant Secretary of the Interior for Indian Affairs William Hallett told James Billie that he would not advise Secretary Andrus to accept the deed unless the Seminole Tribe could "demonstrate that trust status is necessary for the intended use of the site, which we understand is as a cemetery and nonprofit museum." To circumvent Hallett's recalcitrance, Whilden and Billie lobbied Sam Gibbons, Tampa's representative in the U.S. House of Representatives. Representative Gibbons then told Andrus that he supported the United States taking the title to the parcel into trust because it was his "understanding that the land acquired by the Tribe would be used only as a site for a cemetery for the recovered Seminole remains and a small non-profit museum to house the other recovered Seminole artifacts and relics."

That also was the understanding of Assistant Secretary of the Interior for Indian Affairs Tom Fredericks. On Secretary Andrus's behalf, on January 16, 1981, Fredericks accepted the deed. When he did so, Fredericks explained, "This tract will be used to preserve remains of Seminole Indians and artifacts of Seminole culture recently discovered during excavations of a site in Tampa."

But instead of a cemetery and a museum, the Seminole Tribe built a concrete block building with six drive-thru windows. And in July 1981, the tribe opened a smoke shop in the building that by October was selling 40,000 cartons of untaxed cigarettes a month, which Florida's Secretary of Business Regulation complained would cost the state $1 million a year in lost cigarette taxes. When Mayor Martinez expressed outrage that the city of Tampa had been duped, James Billie, with a semi-straight face, pointed out that the agreement Steve Whilden had negotiated with the city did not prohibit the tribe from developing the land on which the skeletons would be interred.

The smoke shop was just the beginning. On June 1, 1982, the Seminole Tribe opened a 1,300-seat bingo hall on the land. When the doors opened, an hour before the first game began, every seat was taken. Players, many of whom had been bused in from as far away as Fort Myers and Orlando, each hoped to win a $4,000 jackpot. The hall was such a success that in 1986 the Seminole Tribe's share of that year's profit was $4.6 million. And according to his son, Steve Whilden always was "particularly proud" of the bait-and-switch he and James Billie had pulled off in Tampa.

When Whilden and Billie hatched their scheme, they decided not to involve Seminole Management Associates (SMA). The reason was that, by the spring of 1980, the U.S. Department of Justice's Organized Crime Strike Force in Miami knew Jack Cooper and Butch Weisman had organized crime connections and had subpoenaed SMA's financial records.*

So instead of SMA, on May 27, 1980, James Billie signed a management agreement with a company called Pan American & Associates (PA&A). The agreement gave PA&A the right to "operate all business activities related to the sale of cigarettes, sale of beverages and bingo" in Tampa for twelve years. In exchange, PA&A agreed to give the Seminole Tribe 53 percent of the profit from those enterprises.

PA&A was owned by three chemical engineers from Houston— James Clare, Donald Valverde, and Cuban immigrant Alfred "Fred" Estrada. James Billie had become acquainted with the Texans because they

---

*SMA's attorney persuaded District Judge Alcee Hastings to issue an order quashing the subpoena. The strike force intended to appeal the order, but before an appeal was filed, an informant told the strike force that Hastings was dirty. The strike force's attorneys then set up a sting that resulted in Hastings being arrested in 1981 for taking a $150,000 bribe. At his trial, Hastings was acquitted when his co-conspirator to whom the FBI had delivered the $150,000 refused to testify. However, in 1989, Hastings was impeached by the U.S. House of Representatives, convicted by the Senate, and removed from the bench. According to Fred Schwartz, the deputy attorney in charge of the strike force, because the strike force got sidetracked by the Hastings bribery investigation, the appeal of the order in which Hastings quashed the subpoena for SMA's financial records was not filed. The *Miami Herald* summarized the outcome as follows: "Members of the federal Organized Crime Strike Force involved in the probe [of SMA] said profit-skimming was a specific concern, but without the financial records, nothing was resolved, no action taken." In 1992, Alcee Hastings was elected to represent Fort Lauderdale in the U.S. House of Representatives, where he continues to serve.

had been working with the Seminole Tribe to determine the feasibility of manufacturing ethanol from sugar cane that would be grown on the tribe's Big Cypress Reservation. Clare, Valverde, and Estrada knew nothing about managing a bingo hall. But according to Estrada, "[T]he Seminoles were looking for someone who was cleaner than Mr. Clean. We had nothing to do with gambling before. But we said we'd give it a try."

After James Billie signed the management agreement, PA&A purchased the 8.5-acre parcel of land in Tampa. PA&A then built the building in which the smoke shop was opened, which James Clare moved from Houston to manage. PA&A then spent $1.2 million to build the bingo hall, which Clare also managed.

According to Barry Horenbein, when Jack Cooper learned that the Seminole Tribe had signed a management agreement with PA&A, rather than with SMA, he was "upset with Steve Whilden." But according to James Billie, Cooper and Butch Weisman and George Simon had not been upset because "if they were part of any kind of organized crime Trafficante was in that area." Which raises the question: How could PA&A have operated a bingo hall in Tampa during the 1980s without the permission and participation of Santo Trafficante, Jr.?

THE ARRIVAL OF the railroad at Tampa in 1884 transformed what had been a quiet beach town into a bustling port. By 1930, the city had a polyglot population of more than 100,000, many of whom were Cuban immigrants who worked in factories in a neighborhood called Ybor City, hand-rolling Cuban tobacco leaf into cigars. Many of those immigrants played bolita, a lottery that had originated in Cuba.

By the 1930s, Santo Trafficante, Sr., who had emigrated from Sicily in 1901, was the boss of the Mafia family in Tampa. The family controlled the bolita lottery, narcotics trafficking, loan-sharking, prostitution, and the other cash-generating activities that organized crime had been organized to exploit. When Trafficante Senior died in 1954, leadership of the Tampa family passed to his son.

Ten months before PA&A opened the Seminole Tribe's bingo hall in Tampa, a 600-seat bingo hall that Steve Paskind had been operating in Tampa was destroyed when a disgruntled employee set the hall on fire.

Until the fire, Paskind had been able to operate because one of his partners was Benny Husick, the Miami Beach bookmaker who handled Trafficante's involvement in bingo.

"I only met Santo one time," Paskind recalled years later.

Benny introduced me. Opening in Tampa was discussed. But I didn't ask for his permission, because I had permission because I was partners with Benny. If there was a profit, I would meet Benny once a week and give him his money. He was affiliated with Trafficante. So I assumed Trafficante was getting a piece of it.

In 2012, when I had lunch in Miami with Fred Estrada and Buddy Levy, who had been PA&A's attorney, Levy was adamant that "We never had a meeting with Trafficante or any of his people. There were never any phone calls or any attempts to contact us. Ever." But when I asked Michael Fisten, a retired veteran of the Miami-Dade Police Department whose beat had included organized crime, he was just as adamant that from Tampa to Orlando and then north to the Alabama-Georgia border "nothing happened in Florida without cutting in Trafficante," and anyone who refused to give Trafficante his percentage "would have ended up in a dumpster."

Santo Trafficante, Jr., Benny Husick, and James Clare are dead. So the men who would have known for sure what arrangement, if there was one, there might have been are not available to ask. But according to Barry Horenbein, one day when he was staying in the house at Jack Cooper's compound on North Bay Road, the telephone rang, and Cooper took the call. Cooper's side of the conversation was: "That's a bad idea. The FBI would investigate. You don't want to do that." When he hung up, Cooper told Horenbein that the caller was Santo Trafficante, who had called to tell Cooper that he had decided to set fire to the Seminole bingo hall. Since no fire was set, Trafficante apparently took Cooper's advice.

Here is what else is known.

In 1990, an inspector general of the Department of the Interior who investigated the Seminole Tribe's bingo halls reported that

a confidential informant had disclosed that the two management firms responsible for managing the bingo games at Hollywood and

Tampa, Florida, were skimming profits from both operations. The management firms were: Seminole Management Associate Ltd. [sic], and Pan American Management Associates [sic], respectively.

The following year, an assistant manager of the bingo hall in Tampa, the manager's son, and a floor worker named Anthony Piazza were arrested for using shills to rig bingo games. The conspirators stole more than $288,000. When two of the shills, Brian Peterson and Patrick O'Leary, had misgivings and told James Clare about the scheme, according to Peterson and O'Leary, Clare "did not come across as being shocked." And when Peterson was deposed in a civil suit, he said under oath that Anthony Piazza told him that Clare knew bingo games were being rigged and had "been taken care of." Piazza also told Peterson that there were "many hands in the pot."

STEVE WHILDEN, WHO died in 1995, is someone else who may have known what the situation was in Tampa. Two weeks before PA&A opened the bingo hall in Tampa, the Seminole Tribal Council fired Whilden as the tribe's general counsel. Marcellus Osceloa, the council member who orchestrated the firing, said he did so because a Seminole named James Shore was available to replace Whilden.* But Osceola, who bad-mouthed Whilden as the Seminole Tribe's self-appointed "white chief" and a "snake," may also have had a personal reason.

Less than a year earlier, Whilden had told officials in Fort Lauderdale that the Seminole Tribe wanted to purchase the Oak Ridge Country Club—whose golf course was the largest tract of undeveloped land in Broward County east of the Florida Turnpike, and then ask the secretary of the interior to take the title to the land into trust to enable the tribe to build housing for its members. In fact, purchasing the country club was a scheme

---

*In 1970 when he was twenty-five-years-old James Shore lost his eyesight in an automobile accident. Overcoming that handicap, in 1981 he graduated from law school and in 1982 replaced Whilden as the Seminole Tribe's general counsel. In 2002 while Shore was sitting in his house he was shot three times by a gunman who fired through the home's plate glass patio door. Shore survived and today remains general counsel. The gunman and the motive for the attempt on Shore's life have never been publicly identified.

Marcellus Osceola and two felons named Joel Kline and Bernard Green-berg had cooked up to turn the golf course into an Indian reservation in order to build 7,000 condominiums on the property in violation of Broward County's zoning ordinance.

The *Miami Herald* reported that Whilden, the Seminole Tribe's general counsel, had "demanded a cut" before he would lobby the secretary of the interior to take the title to the land on which the golf course was located into trust. When Whilden denied the accusation, Joel Kline gave the *Herald* canceled checks totaling $10,000 that Osceola and his partners had written to Whilden. The *Herald* also reported that Whilden had an agreement with Osceola that gave him 10 percent of whatever Osceloa earned from real estate ventures that involved "federal trust tribal land."

Within days of being fired, Steve Whilden reinvented himself by becoming vice president of Pan American Management Company (PAMC, not to be confused with PA&A), a new company James Clare, Donald Valverde, and Fred Estrada created. Whilden's job was to identify "Indian reservations which had the potential for being valuable locations for bingo parlors" and then "negotiate and sign contracts on behalf of [PAMC] with the tribe or tribes involved." The first contract Whilden negotiated on PAMC's behalf was not with an Indian tribe, however, it was with the New England Entertainment Company (NEEC), a company two Massachusetts residents, Michael Frechette and Allen Arbogast, had created and with which Whilden had been involved while he was still the Seminole Tribe's general counsel.

FRECHETTE AND ARBOGAST became friends in 1968 when they were convalescing at a naval hospital in Massachusetts. Frechette, who was in the U.S. Navy, had been injured in a helicopter crash; Arbogast, a corporal in the marines, had been wounded in Vietnam.

When he left the Marine Corps in 1973, Arbogast moved to Las Vegas, where he dealt cards for three years until he moved back to Massachusetts. He settled in Revere, five miles north of Boston, and five miles east of Medford, his hometown.

Massachusetts had a "Las Vegas Night" law that allowed charitable organizations to sponsor fund-raising events at which games such as blackjack, roulette, and craps could be played. In Revere, Medford, and the other small towns on Boston's north side, Arbogast operated Las Vegas Night events for Jerry Angiulo, the capo who ran North Boston for Raymond Patriarca, the boss of the Mafia family that controlled organized crime in New England. Frechette, whose day job was working as an officer in the Medford Police Department, provided security for Arbogast.

In July 1980, *Time* magazine published an article on the bingo hall the Seminole Tribe had opened on its reservation in Hollywood. Frechette and Arbogast read the article and decided to fly to Florida to try to get a meeting with James Billie to pitch him on the idea of allowing them to host Las Vegas Night events in the bingo hall.

The trip to Florida did not happen because Frechette was indicted for filing false federal income tax refund claims in the names of individuals whose identities had been stolen from the Massachusetts Department of Motor Vehicles. Arborgast was indicted on lesser charges related to the same crime. Both men were convicted. Arborgast received a suspended sentence, and Frechette spent nine months in the federal prison camp west of Tallahassee in which Jack Cooper had been incarcerated seventeen years earlier.

When Frechette was released in December 1981, the terms of his parole prohibited him from leaving Massachusetts without permission and from consorting with felons. Allen Arbogast was a felon. Nevertheless, Frechette and Arborgast flew to Florida and met with James Billie.

According to Frechette,

> We pitched Jim Billie on holding casino nights on the reservation. At the time, the *Seminole Tribe v. Butterworth* lawsuit still was in the courts, so he wasn't interested. But Billie said, 'We're going to win. So you guys, if you're smart, go set up some tribes.' So Allen and I began looking for tribes.

Which is how Michael Freschette and Allen Arborgast met Norman Crooks.

IN 1851, THE HEADMEN of the bands of Dakota (also known as Santee) Sioux Indians whose members lived in the Minnesota Territory, signed their marks on a treaty in which the headmen agreed that the members of their bands would move onto a reservation whose boundaries ran along both sides of the Minnesota River. In 1850 the territory had a population of 6,000. By 1858, when it entered the Union, the population of the new state of Minnesota had exploded to 172,000. So another treaty was "negotiated" in which, to make more land available for white settlement, the Sioux gave up the portion of their reservation on the north side of the Minnesota River.

In 1862, the situation on the south side of the river became untenable for the Sioux when their crops failed and the Bureau of Indian Affairs (BIA) failed to make annuity payments that an earlier treaty guaranteed. Little Crow, the headman of the Mdewakanton Band, met to discuss the situation with the local Indian agent and Andrew Myrick, a trader whose storage sheds were full of foodstuffs. When Little Crow explained that unless Myrick would extend credit the Sioux would starve, the trader famously replied: "If they are hungry, let them eat grass or their own dung."

Several days later an incident that began with four Sioux stealing chicken eggs from a farmer and then escalated to the murder of the farmer and his family was the spark that set off a rampage born of desperation during which the Sioux attacked farms and towns along the Minnesota River, killed 500 whites, and took 269 others, most women and children, captive.

After the Sixth Minnesota Infantry, commanded by Col. Henry Sibley, quelled the violence, Sibley convened a military commission that sentenced 307 Sioux to be executed. President Lincoln commuted the sentences of all but thirty-nine. On December 26, 1862, thirty-eight of the thirty-nine were hanged in the largest mass execution in U.S. history. The army then removed most of the remaining Sioux to Nebraska and South Dakota.

A few Sioux did not participate in the uprising. As a reward, they were allowed to stay in Minnesota.

In 1884, Minnesota representative Horace Strait persuaded Congress to appropriate $10,000 to enable the secretary of the interior to purchase articles for the "civilization and education" of the "Medewakan band of Sioux Indians." In 1888, Congress appropriated $20,000 to enable the secretary to purchase land for "full-blood" Sioux Indians who "belong[ed] to the Mdewakanton band" and who had "severed their tribal relations" and had been living in Minnesota in 1886 when the BIA made a roll of band members. In succeeding years, Congress appropriated additional moneys for that purpose.

In 1890 and 1891, the BIA spent $4,700 to purchase three parcels of land, totaling 258 acres, at Prior Lake, a small town thirty miles southwest of Minneapolis. According to historian Roy Meyer, when Congress appropriated the money for land purchases, it had "no intention to provide reservations for the Minnesota Mdewakantons or to return them to a wardship status." And consistent with that view, while the United States owned the 258 acres, the land did not have the legal status of being an "Indian reservation." Instead, the BIA divided the land into parcels that it "assigned" to "full-blood" members of the Mdewakanton Band who had "severed their tribal relations" and had been living in Minnesota in 1886. When an assignee died, the BIA reassigned the land to "some other Indian who was a resident of Minnesota on May 20, 1886, or a legal descendant of such a resident Indian."

In 1967, the BIA area director in Minneapolis gave Mdewakanton descendant Norman Crooks an assignment onto which Crooks moved with his wife and children. Crooks would recall that, in 1967, he and the three other families that had been given assignments "couldn't get any help from the Bureau because we weren't organized." So, in January 1969, Crooks and the other assignees sent the area director a petition in which they "request[ed] to be separately identified for the purpose of improving construction of homes, general improvement of living conditions, and on overall Indian betterment."

In 1935, Felix Cohen, the attorney in the Department of the Interior who in 1934 had been a principal author of the IRA and who that same year had invented the doctrine of inherent tribal sovereignty, advised Commissioner of Indian Affairs John Collier that the Mdewakanton Sioux "cannot be recognized as a tribe, since the statutes providing for land purchases for these Indians expressly restrict the use of these funds to Indians who have abandoned tribal relations." Nevertheless, in response to Crooks' petition, Daniel Boos, the BIA attorney in Minneapolis, advised the area director that "the Indians residing on the so-called 'Mdewakanton lands' near Prior Lake, Scott County, Minnesota, do reside on a reservation and are eligible to organize [pursuant to section 16 of the IRA, which authorizes an 'Indian tribe' to 'organize for its common welfare' by 'adopt[ing] an appropriate constitution and bylaws.']"

When the area director sent a draft constitution for the "Shakopee Mdewakanton Sioux Tribe" to the BIA in Washington, D.C., for review, he was told that "all references to Shakopee Mdewakanton Sioux 'Tribe' must be changed to 'Community,'" because "the group does not possess the inherent powers of a tribe" and "[i]t should be understood that since the group does not constitute a tribe it would not possess all the powers generally considered as 'inherent in a tribe.'"

When that legally consequential modification was made, in November 1969 Norman Crooks hosted an election in his living room at which, by a vote of 13 to 0, he and his neighbors approved a constitution for the Shakopee Mdewakanton Sioux Community. Secretary of the Interior Walter Hickel then approved the constitution, even though the 258 acres at Prior Lake were not an Indian reservation, and even though Norman Crooks and the other assignees were descendants of Sioux who had "severed their tribal relations."

Now that living on the 258 acres at Prior Lake gave the residents better access to BIA services, other Mdewakanton descendants began moving trailer homes onto the land. By 1972, fifteen families had moved to Prior Lake. As Norman Crooks explained, "This is a good locale for them, because they can jump on the freeway, and they're downtown [in Minneapolis] in half an hour."

In 1980, Minnesota representative Richard Nolan introduced a bill in the U.S. House of Representatives whose enactment would designate the 258 acres at Prior Lake as an Indian reservation. First the House, then the Senate, passed the bill with no hearings, no explanation or debate, and no recorded votes.

The Shakopee Mdewakanton Sioux Community council, which Norman Crooks chaired, had no money other than the few dollars the council occasionally received from the BIA. So Crooks investigated what Indians elsewhere were doing to earn money. After visiting reservations in Nevada and Wisconsin on which smoke shops were operating, in January 1982 Crooks began selling untaxed cigarettes out of a trailer that fronted the county road that bordered the Prior Lake Reservation.

SEVERAL WEEKS LATER, when they were transiting through the Minneapolis airport on their way home to Boston, Michael Frechette and Allen Arbogast bought a newspaper to read during their flight. According to Frechette,

"We saw an article that said the Shakopee Mdewakanton Sioux were selling tax-free cigarettes. Allen and I looked at each other and said, 'Let's go back.'" So when they landed in Boston, they turned around and flew back to Minneapolis, drove to Prior Lake, and introduced themselves to Norman Crooks.

As an outcome of that meeting, Frechette and Arborgast "put some money" into Crooks' smoke shop, which Crooks allowed Arborgast to begin managing. Frechette and Aborgast then began meeting with Crooks to work out a management agreement for a bingo hall. According to Frechette, "We'd be putting papers in front of Norm, but we didn't know he couldn't read, and he didn't tell us." The negotiations concluded when Frechette and Arborgast brought in Steve Whilden, with whom they had become acquainted when they pitched James Billie on the idea of holding Las Vegas Night events.

In April 1982, Whilden and Norman Crooks spent four days at a motel near the Minneapolis airport negotiating the terms of a management agreement between the Shakopee Mdewakanton Sioux Community and NEEC, whose owners, in addition to Frechette and Arbogast, were Arbogast's brother; Dennis Courtney, with whom Arbogast had worked dealing cards in Las Vegas; and John Panetta, a Canadian Arbogast had met in Fort Lauderdale. While Steve Whilden had no equity interest in NEEC, according to Frechette, "We had an understanding that we would take care of Steve."

When Norman Crooks, Mariana Shulstad (the BIA attorney in Minneapolis who was advising Crooks), and Steve Whilden concluded their negotiations, Crooks and Dennis Courtney (who because he had no criminal record Frechette and Arbogast had appointed president of NEEC) signed a management agreement that obligated NEEC to build a bingo hall on the Prior Lake Reservation. But according to Frechette, "Allen and I didn't have any money. We had my American Express card and a lot of hopes. So we needed to find financing."

When Frechette failed to find any, Steve Whilden introduced Frechette and Arbogast to James Clare, Donald Valverde, and Fred Estrada who agreed to have PAMC buy 60 percent of NEEC's management agreement. PAMC and NEEC formed a joint venture called Little Six Enterprises. Clare, Valverde, and Estrada then borrowed $1 million to get the project underway, and Estrada moved to Prior Lake to supervise construction of the 1,300-seat Little Six Bingo Palace, which opened on October 16, 1982.

For a $12 ticket, players were transported to the Little Six Bingo Palace by bus from pick-up stops throughout Minneapolis. Its first year of operation, the hall averaged 750 players a night and grossed $9 million. The cash flow allowed Little Six Enterprises to pay off the $1 million construction loan in seven months. After paying other expenses, Little Six Enterprises earned $900,000 and paid the Shakopee Mdewakanton Sioux Community $1.1 million.

ONE OF WHILDEN'S next projects was in Massachusetts where, undoubtedly through Frechette and Arbogast, he worked out an agreement with Earl "Flying Eagle" Mills. Mills was a high school physical education teacher and titular chief of a group whose members said they were descendants of the Mashpee Wampanoag Indians who lived in New England when the *Mayflower* arrived. Whilden agreed to lobby Congress to enact a statute that would create the Mashpee Wampanoag Tribe and designate a parcel of land as the tribe's reservation. The land was on an air force base west of Cape Cod that had been declared surplus federal property. Mills agreed that, if the scheme worked—which it did not—PAMC would build and manage a bingo hall on the reservation.

Whilden had better luck in Arizona.

BEGINNING IN THE seventeenth century, the Yaqui Indians who lived along the Yaqui River, which flows into the Gulf of California in northern Mexico, resisted, first Spanish, then Mexican encroachments on the land they had occupied for generations. To end further resistance, in 1885 Mexican president Porfino Diaz sent the Mexican army to clear the Yaqui River Valley of Yaquis. In a series of military engagements that lasted into the 1920s, thousands of Yaquis were killed. Thousands more were captured and transported to the Yucatán Peninsula, where they were worked as slaves on plantations that grew hemp for export.

Several thousand other Yaquis fled north across the border. By 1930, Yaqui refugees had established seven settlements in Arizona, one of which was Old Pascua, a thirty-two-acre parcel of desert on the outskirts of Tucson. In 1930 Tucson had a population of 32,000. By 1960 the population was 213,000 and the city limits had encircled Old Pasqua. The overcrowded neighborhood was home to more than four hundred Yaquis who lived in shacks they had constructed from railroad ties, rusted panels of discarded corrugated sheet metal, and cardboard.

In 1964, Rep. Morris Udall, who represented Tucson in the U.S. House of Representatives, persuaded Congress to enact a statute that gave the Pascua Yaqui Association, a nonprofit corporation the Yaquis at Old Pascua created, title to a 202-acre parcel of federal land ten miles south of Tucson. However, because the Yaquis were from Mexico, the statute made clear that "none of the statutes of the United States which affect Indians because of their status as Indians shall be applicable to the Yaqui Indians."

Half of Old Pasqua's residents moved onto the 202-acre parcel, which the Yaquis named Pascua Pueblo. Fourteen years later, by which time no members of Congress remembered, or if they did remember, cared, that the Yaquis were not American Indians, Representative Udall sponsored a new statute. Enacted in 1978, the statute announced that the members of the Pascua Yaqui Association now would have the same legal status as members of American Indian tribes. The statute also transformed Pascua Pueblo into an Indian reservation.

Three years later, PAMC signed a management agreement with the Pascua Yaqui Tribe to build and manage a bingo hall on the reservation. In December 1982, the *Tucson Citizen* reported:

> An ambitious bingo operation will begin next month at the village southwest of Tucson, tribal officials said. A Florida firm, Pan American Management Co., Inc., of Tampa, has already provided $1 million in start-up money, said Steven Whilden, consultant for the firm.

In January 1983 when the doors of the bingo hall opened 1,600 players jostled for the 1,400 seats and a chance to win the $10,000 jackpot PAMC advertised. PAMC's take that night is estimated to have been $25,000.

By then Steve Whilden had moved on.

IN 1855, ISAAC STEVENS, the superintendent of Indian affairs for the Territory of Washington, assembled the headmen of tribes whose members occupied land in the northeastern portion of Puget Sound. Fourteen of the headmen represented the Lummi Tribe whose members migrated seasonally between mainland locations and the San Juan Islands. In the Treaty of Point Elliott, which they signed with their marks, the headmen agreed that the Lummi would stop migrating and settle on a reservation on a peninsula that extends into Bellingham Bay twenty miles south of the Canadian border.

By 1982, the city of Bellingham, ten miles south of the reservation, had 46,000 residents. Fifty miles north, the metropolitan area around Vancouver, British Columbia, had more than a million. Given the reservation's "good location," Steve Whilden contacted the Lummi Tribal Council, most likely through Freddie Lane, the council member who had introduced B.J. and Ray Turnipseed to Osley Saunooke. But rather than bingo, the management agreement Whilden negotiated with the Lummi Nation (as the tribe today is called) authorized PAMC to open a blackjack casino in a gymnasium on the reservation.

Back at Prior Lake, because NEEC was a minority owner of the Little Six Enterprises joint venture, Michael Frechette and Allen Arbogast increasingly found themselves at loggerheads with Fred Estrada and PAMC's other owners in disputes relating to the construction and, once the hall opened, the management of the Little Six Bingo Palace. To end the discord, an accommodation was reached: PAMC would manage the Little Six Bingo Palace without further interference, and Frechette and Arborgast would take over the blackjack casino on the Lummi Reservation.

When the casino opened in January 1983, the *Bellingham Herald* described the scene:

> Plush new carpeting provided a red backdrop to the 24 spotless blackjack tables, each with tribal markings. Minutes before the scheduled noon start, the excitement of a Broadway opening was in the air as final touches were added. Dealers checked the fit of their white shirts, bow ties and crisp black vests. Cards were sorted and counted and shuffled. . . . Twenty minutes past noon, the first customers swarmed to a half-dozen tables. Dealers dealt. Gamblers won. Gamblers lost. But no one complained of having a poor time.

According to Michael Frechette, "The business was absolutely incredible. We didn't know there was a large Asian population in Vancouver. And come to find out, they like to gamble."

Like Massachusetts, Washington state had a Las Vegas Night law that allowed charitable organizations to sponsor fund-raising events at which blackjack could be played. So the legal theory that made playing blackjack on the Lummi Reservation possible was the same one the three-judge panel of the U.S. Court of Appeals for the Ninth Circuit (whose jurisdiction included Washington) had accepted in the decision the panel had issued a month earlier in *Barona Group of the Capitan Grande Band of Mission Indians v. Duffy*, the lawsuit Harry Hertzberg had filed. The theory was that, because Washington's law regulated, rather than prohibited, blackjack, the state had no authority to enforce its other gambling laws that prohibited blackjack inside the boundaries of the Lummi Reservation.

Nine days after the panel issued its decision in the *Barona Group* lawsuit, the attorney representing the Lummi Nation notified the U.S. attorney in Seattle that the tribe was opening a blackjack casino. In response, the U.S. attorney told the tribe's attorney that he needed to discuss the situation with Keith Kisor, the director of the Washington State Gambling Commission. The week after the blackjack casino opened, tribal representatives met with Kisor. The meeting ended in discord because Kisor was adamant that Washington's Las Vegas Night law was "prohibitory," rather than "regulatory."

The U.S. attorney then told Michael Frechette and Allen Arbogast they had two choices: be indicted in a RICCO criminal prosecution, or PAMC could be sued civilly. When they picked choice number two, the U.S. attorney filed a lawsuit in the U.S. District Court in Seattle against PAMC and the Lummi Nation.

Three weeks later, District Judge John Coughenour ordered the Lummi Nation to close the casino because it was "a professional gambling operation that is prohibited as a matter of public policy by state law." But as the *Bellingham Herald* reported: "In making his ruling, the judge noted that two people involved in one of the gambling firms, New England Entertainment Co., were convicted felons."

• • •

BY THE TIME JUDGE Coughenour announced his ruling, Steve Whilden was in California. There he negotiated a management agreement with Anne Prieto Sandoval, the chairwoman of the Sycuan Band of Diegueno Mission Indians. The band's fewer than fifty members lived on a 640-acre reservation President Ulysses S. Grant created in 1875 in the foothills east of San Diego and south of the Capitan Grande Valley.

In 1883, when the writer Helen Hunt Jackson visited the reservation, she found the few Indians living there "much dispirited and demoralized and wretchedly poor." A hundred years later, the situation was no better. But whereas in 1883 few non-Indians lived near the reservation, by 1983 El Cajon, population 74,000, was only a few miles to the west. And for the many bingo players living in San Diego, the drive to the Sycuan Reservation was more convenient than the drive up Wildcat Canyon Road to the Barona Reservation. Donald Valverde moved to California to manage the 1,350-seat bingo hall PAMC opened on the Sycuan Reservation in November 1983, to which players were bused from locations as distant as Los Angeles and Tijuana, Mexico.

Several months earlier, Valverde, James Clare, and Fred Estrada had discovered that Steve Whilden, who was supposed to be negotiating management agreements for PAMC, not only had been negotiating his own deals, but he had tried to persuade Anne Prieto Sandoval to terminate the Sycuan Band's management agreement with PAMC and sign an agreement with another group of investors. When those transgressions came to light, in June 1983 Whilden resigned as PAMC's vice president. Five months later, at his instigation, the leaders of the Pascua Yaqui Tribe, who had soured on PAMC because the management company said the bingo hall at Pascua Pueblo was losing money but refused to provide an accounting, threatened to lock out PAMC's manager.

So, in February 1984, PAMC filed a lawsuit against Whilden in San Diego. The complaint alleged that, throughout his tenure as vice president of PAMC, Whilden had repeatedly breached the fiduciary duty he owed to the company. Whilden's attorney filed a cross-complaint, after which PAMC and Whilden both agreed to walk away. Years later, Buddy Levy, PAMC's attorney, said, "[T]he idea of the litigation wasn't to get money from Steve. It was to disassociate Pan American Management Company from him. We wanted to make sure everybody in the business knew that we had nothing to do with the guy." But if James Clare, Donald Valverde, and Fred Estrada wanted to be done with Whilden, what Whilden wanted was to settle a score.

By 1984, several members of the Shakopee Mdewakanton Sioux Community had become suspicious of Norman Crooks' rumored self-dealing and of Little Six Enterprises' management of the Little Six Bingo Palace. At their urging, in February 1984 the Minneapolis field office of the FBI opened an investigation of both. That August, Steve Whilden telephoned the U.S. attorney in Minneapolis to report that he had "information about criminal violations, including 'racketeering,' perpetuated by the management company, Pan American Management, in their operation of the [Shakopee Mdewakanton Sioux Community's] bingo operation." But each time the FBI scheduled an interview with Whilden in Minneapolis, he failed to appear.

Only Steve Whilden knows why he did not, but the month before he telephoned the FBI, Whilden went to San Francisco to be on hand for the 1984 Democratic National Convention. According to his son, who accompanied Whilden on that trip, when they were in San Francisco, his father told him that, while he had never had life insurance, he recently had bought a $1 million term life policy because he thought he "could end up dead."

IN APRIL 1982, WHEN Steve Whilden began traveling the country negotiating management agreements, he was not alone in doing so. Three months earlier, Butch Weisman had flown Bob Santiacum, who at that time was chairman of the Puyallup Tribal Council, and the other members of the council to Fort Lauderdale to tour the bingo hall SMA was managing on the Seminole Reservation in Hollywood. The trip was part of Weisman's effort to persuade Santiacum to sign a management agreement that would allow SMA to operate a bingo hall on the Puyallup Reservation. When the *Tacoma News Tribune* reported that the Broward County Sheriff's Office had been investigating whether "there were links between the men who operated the Seminole games and Meyer Lansky, an underworld financier," and asked Satiacum whether SMA had "links to organized crime," Satiacum replied that SMA looked to him like "a real clean-cut operation." Then Joseph Bowen, the Puyallup Tribe's attorney, told the *News Tribune* that the "Weisman group" had told him "it was investigated by the FBI when it first went into the bingo business and was given a 'clean bill of health.'" While the opposite was true, when no deal was struck between Butch Weisman and Bob Satiacum, the *News Tribune* lost interest in investigating SMA's ties to organized crime.

HOWARD TOMMIE TRIED to get into the bingo management business with Don and Bill Whittington, brothers from Texas with whom Tommie had become acquainted through their mutual interest in automobile racing. In 1981, Tommie began negotiating with the Papago Tribe (now the Tohono O'odam Nation) whose reservation south of Tucson is only a few miles from Pascua Pueblo. According to Tommie, "I put over seventy grand into the Papagos. We chartered Lears for lawyers and accountants. I even brought five people back here [to the Hollywood Reservation], including two councilmen and the Bureau of Indian Affairs superintendent."

While Tommie almost had a deal, in February 1983 the leaders of the Papago Tribe terminated their negotiations with Tommie after the local press reported that Steve Whilden had said the Seminole Tribe had hired PA&A to manage its bingo hall in Tampa because Jack Cooper and George Simon were associates of Meyer Lansky's. And then, according to Tommie, Osley Saunooke, who had created his own management company and wanted to sign up the Papago Tribe, "went out there [to Tucson] with newspaper articles about organized crime and Seminole bingo and threw them in the face of the Papago lawyers."

In the end, the Papago Tribe signed a management agreement with Bingo Partnership, a company whose owners included two Tucson businessmen: Louis Cohn, who owned a chain of liquor stores, and Gary Triano, a local real estate developer.

OSLEY SAUNOOKE HAD no better luck back home in Cherokee, the tourist town on the Eastern Band of Cherokee's reservation in North Carolina. Two years earlier, Saunooke and his mother, who was a member of the band's tribal council, had convinced the council to approve a bingo ordinance Saunooke had written based on the ordinance the Seminole Tribal Council had adopted. Saunooke then acquired a partner, an associate of Butch Weisman's named Morris Levine.

In February 1982, Saunooke presented the tribal council with a proposal to allow Saunooke and Levine to open a bingo hall. The council rejected that proposal. Then six months later it accepted one that had been submitted by McCoy, Young & Associates, a company council member Dan McCoy had created with John Young, a member of the Eastern Band. McCoy and Young were fronts for two non-Indians, Sherman Lichty and Leonard Morrison, who managed "charitable" bingo halls in Norfolk and Newport News, Virginia.

In December 1982, Cherokee Bingo, as the business was named, began holding bingo games in Cherokee in a former factory Lichty and Morrison spent $200,000 that they had raised from forty-eight investors to remodel. When the first bingo number was called, 5,000 players, were on hand to try to win jackpots totaling $200,000. Many of those in attendance had been transported to Cherokee from as far north as Canada in one of eighty-three buses Cherokee Bingo chartered.

Cherokee Bingo hosted bingo games every other weekend. And four times a year, for a $500 admission, more than 3,000 players competed to win $250,000 jackpots in what Cherokee Bingo advertised as "The World's Largest Bingo Game."

Between December 1982 and April 1986, Cherokee Bingo grossed $35 million. Of that amount, McCoy, Young & Associates paid the Eastern Band a pittance: $150,000 a year, $3,500 a month rent for the building, a $2 per player head tax, and 1 percent of the gross. Sherman Lichty and Leonard Morrison kept the books, which Dan McCoy refused to allow the band's accountants to audit.

In 1985, a grand jury began investigating Cherokee Bingo. In 1987, John Young, Sherman Lichty, and Leonard Morrison were indicted for skimming $425,682. They pled guilty, and the three men went to prison.

IN ADDITION TO Steve Whilden, Butch Weisman, Howard Tommie, and Osley Saunooke, James Billie put the Seminole Tribe into the bingo management business by mailing more than 1,400 solicitation letters to members of the tribal councils of the 263 Indian tribes the BIA had recognized to be such. He did so because, by 1983, senior officials at the BIA in Washington, D.C., had decided that bingo halls could provide a new source of funding to make up for the money President Reagan had asked Congress to cut from the BIA's budget. As a consequence, the BIA began both making and guaranteeing construction loans for tribes that did not have financing arrangements with PAMC or one of the other management companies whose non-Indian owners had the ability to borrow the money needed to build a bingo hall.

For example, in Washington state, the BIA arranged a $945,000 loan to enable the tribes whose members reside on the Tulalip Reservation north of Seattle to construct a 1,400-seat bingo hall. With the BIA's encouragement, by June 1983 when the hall on the Tulalip Reservation opened, fifty-nine Indian tribes, principally in Florida, Washington, Oklahoma, Minnesota, Wisconsin, Michigan, New York, North Carolina, and California, had opened bingo halls.

But if in Washington, D.C., the BIA considered bingo halls an innovative new form of "economic development" for Indian reservations, at the U.S. Department of Justice, attorneys in the Criminal Division understood that bingo was an all-cash business and that several tens of millions of dollars were now flowing annually through bingo halls on Indian reservations whose counting rooms had few controls to prevent money from being skimmed. And the attorneys knew there was evidence that, from Florida to Minnesota to California, individuals who had organized crime connections were involved in managing a number of the halls.

In February 1983, D. Lowell Jensen, the head of the Criminal Division, persuaded Attorney General William French Smith that the president should include a provision in a new crime bill, which the U.S. Department of Justice was writing, whose enactment by Congress would reverse *Seminole Tribe of Florida v. Butterworth*, *Barona Group of the Capitan Grande Band of Mission Indians v. Duffy*, and the several other federal court decisions that prohibited states from enforcing their gambling laws within the boundaries of Indian reservations. But the vagaries of the dance of legislation are such that, rather than granting states authority to enforce their gambling laws on Indian reservations, five years later, Congress would prohibit states from enforcing their gambling laws on the reservations.

How that happened is a story that demonstrates the influence members of the staffs of congressional committees wield over the content of seemingly minor bills that few members of Congress care about enough to read.

6: NINETY-EIGHTH CONGRESS

> There hasn't been, to my knowledge, one instance of organized crime coming on to the reservation.
>
> MARK POWLESS
> *Chairman, National Indian*
> *Gaming Task Force*

IN OCTOBER 1982 PRESIDENT RONALD REAGAN ANNOUNCED A NEW STRATegy to "cripple organized crime in America" whose centerpiece was a bill whose enactment by Congress would strengthen various federal criminal laws. At the direction of D. Lowell Jensen, the attorneys at the U.S. Department of Justice who had been tasked with writing the bill included a section that added a new section 1166 to Title 18 of the U.S. Code. The new section 1166 granted the states authority to enforce their gambling laws on Indian reservations.

Before the White House sends a bill to Congress, the Office of Management and Budget (OMB) distributes the bill to potentially affected executive branch departments for comment. In February 1983 OMB sent the crime bill to the Department of the Interior. When he read the bill, John Fritz, the deputy assistant secretary of the interior for Indian affairs, realized the threat section 1166 posed for the nascent Indian gaming industry. So he set about trying to persuade the White House to take section 1166 out of the bill.

Fritz had an influential ally: Ronald Reagan, who a month earlier had issued a statement on Indian policy in which, unwittingly, he had implicitly endorsed gambling on Indian reservations.

In October 1980, in Sioux Falls, South Dakota, at a meeting with tribal leaders presidential candidate Reagan had promised that when he became president he would "revitalize" the "tribal government to federal government relationship" by directing the men and women who worked in his administration to conduct "government-to-government consultation" with Indian tribes.

Three months later when he assumed office, one of the first items on the new president's agenda was reducing the federal budget deficit. To that end, in February 1981, Reagan urged Congress to cut federal spending during the 1982 fiscal year by $41.4 billion. With respect to Indian programs, the president recommended a $72.9-million reduction in funding for the Bureau of Indian Affairs (BIA), a $136.9 million reduction in funding for the Indian Health Service (IHS), and termination of funding for reservation water and sanitary facilities, the Department of Housing and Urban Development's Indian housing program, the Indian desk at the Department of Energy, and the public service employment portions of the Comprehensive Employment and Training Act that were funding 10,000 government jobs on Indian reservations.

That September, the president announced that he wanted Congress to cut the budgets of the BIA and IHS and most other federal agencies (other than the Department of Defense) by another 12 percent. The White House sent those recommendations for spending cuts to Congress without consulting tribal leaders as candidate Reagan had promised it would.

IN RESPONSE TO the September announcement, on October 21, 1981 fifty chairmen of Indian tribes who were members of the National Tribal Chairmen's Association staged a protest in front of the White House. Several wore traditional regalia, and one held up a sign that read: "Some Cowboys Never Change." When he found out the protest was being planned, John McClaughry warned Martin Anderson, the director of the White House Office of Policy Development for whom McClaughry worked, that the president was going to "catch hell from the Indians on October 21, and we have no respectable answer to their complaints about the failure to consult, and not much of an answer in defense of the 12 percent cuts themselves."

According to a biographer, Ronald Reagan "was more dependent on staff than any other recent president. It was a family secret, [CIA Director] William Casey said, that all insiders understood: Reagan initiated nothing, gave no orders, decided nothing except in the sense of choosing among options presented to him by his advisors." Inside the White House, Edwin Meese, a longtime Reagan confidant from California, supervised the development of the policy options that were presented to the president. To develop those options, Meese created working groups composed principally of individuals drawn from the various executive branch departments. The working groups then developed policy options that they submitted to one of six councils composed of members of the president's cabinet. Assistant Secretary of the Interior for Indian Affairs Ken Smith, a member of the Wasco Tribe in Oregon, was chairman of the Indian policy working group.

After warning him about the protest the National Tribal Chairmen's Association was planning, McClaughry advised Martin Anderson that "the only way we can escape the trap we are facing is to design a radically new Indian policy." Anderson accepted the advice, and eleven months later, on September 20, 1982, Secretary of Health and Human Services Richard Schweiker presided at a meeting of the Cabinet Council on Human Resources at which President Reagan was given a memorandum that described the elements of an Indian policy statement that Assistant Secretary Smith's working group had developed. After listening to a cursory explanation of the statement's content, the president compliantly initialed his approval on the memorandum.

Two months later, Elizabeth Dole, the director of the White House Office of Public Liaison, recommended that the president unveil his Indian policy statement personally at a meeting with Indian leaders. Deputy Chief of Staff Michael Deaver, who controlled the president's schedule, rejected the idea because, as another member of the staff told Dole, Deaver thought bringing in a group of Indians to meet with Ronald Reagan was "a candidate for the worst schedule proposal of the week." Dole's informant also lamented that "With his term half over, the president has never been within handshaking distance of an Indian leader."

So instead of Ronald Reagan, on January 24, 1983 Assistant Secretary Smith unveiled the Indian policy statement at a White House event timed to coincide with the winter meeting of the National Congress of American Indians (NCAI).

After announcing the president's commitment to encouraging "private involvement, both Indian and non-Indian, in tribal economic development," the policy statement cryptically noted that "in some cases, tribes and the private sector have already taken innovative approaches which have overcome legislative and regulatory impediments to economic progress." "Innovative approaches" was code for bingo halls, and "legislative and regulatory impediments" was code for state laws that limit the size of jackpots and impose other restrictions on the operation of bingo games.

Half a dozen individuals participated in writing the Indian policy statement. So who was responsible for including the oblique reference to bingo halls is not known. Also, while the statement was being written, Ken Smith asked the NCAI, the National Tribal Chairmen's Association, and the American Indian National Republican Federation (a group connected to the Republican National Committee) for their "recommendations/suggestions for a national Indian policy." So did someone from one of those organizations arrange to have the working group include an implicit reference to bingo halls in the policy statement? Whoever was responsible, when John Fritz read section 1166 in the crime bill the OMB was circulating, he sent OMB director David Stockton a letter written on Secretary of the Interior James Watt's letterhead in which he protested that section 1166 was "inconsistent with the President's Indian Policy Statement" because "a number of tribes have begun to engage in bingo and similar gambling operations on their reservations for the very purposes enunciated in the President's message."

At the White House, policy disagreements between executive branch departments were resolved by the appropriate cabinet council. The disagreement between the U.S. Department of Justice and the Department of the Interior regarding section 1166 would be resolved by the Cabinet Council on Legal Policy that Attorney General William French Smith chaired and of which Secretary Watt was a member. But John Fritz derailed that process.

A time-tested way to prevent a decision from being made is to suggest that the subject of the decision needs additional study. Employing that tactic, in his letter to Stockton, Fritz informed the OMB director that the BIA was establishing "an Ad Hoc Task Force on bingo and related gambling activities undertaken by the tribes." He then argued that "premature action" taken before the task force submitted its findings would "hinder our efforts to strengthen tribal government."

At the White House, a meeting of the Cabinet Council on Legal Policy was scheduled for March 15, 1983 to resolve the disagreement regarding section 1166. But that morning, Michael Uhlmann, who worked with John McClaughry in the Office of Policy Development, sent Edwin Meese and his deputies, Edwin Harper and Craig Fuller, a note in which he asked whether—since all but one of the other disagreements regarding the crime bill had been worked out—the meeting was necessary. It was not. Because prior to the meeting, Meese, Harper, or Fuller made the decision to remove section 1166 from the crime bill in order to give Fritz's task force time to submit its findings. A handwritten notation on the memorandum Uhlmann prepared for the Cabinet Council on Legal Policy explaining the disagreement over section 1166 recorded: "no item in the bill—set up a commission."

Through astute bureaucratic maneuvering, John Fritz had prevented the president from recommending that Congress give the states authority to enforce their gambling laws on Indian reservations. But on Capitol Hill, Frank Ducheneaux was worried.

A SIOUX INDIAN from South Dakota who, after graduating from law school, had served a brief tenure as executive director of NCAI, Ducheneaux was the principal member of the staff of the House Committee on Interior and Insular Affairs who handled Indian-related bills for the committee. When he learned that the White House had taken section 1166 out of the crime bill, Ducheneaux understood that John Fritz had only won a reprieve. As Ducheneaux later explained,

> I knew that as more tribes began to [open bingo halls and other types of gambling facilities], there was going to be a backlash from the non-Indian community. From the State and local governments, from the commercial gaming interests, the casinos in Nevada and New Jersey, the horse and dog racing people, from the charities and from the morals.

When the backlash happened, the odds would go up that members of Congress who opposed gambling on Indian reservations would have the votes they needed to pass a bill that would give the states authority to enforce their gambling laws.

Four months later, Ducheneaux also became concerned about the U.S. Supreme Court.

EACH TERM, THE COURT receives thousands of requests—called petitions for a writ of certiorari—to review decisions of the courts of appeals. In 1982, Broward County sheriff Bob Butterworth filed a petition that requested the

Court to review the decision the U.S. Court of Appeals for the Fifth Circuit had issued in *Seminole Indian Tribe of Florida v. Butterworth*. And in 1983, San Diego County sheriff John Duffy filed a petition that requested the Court to review the decision the U.S. Court of Appeals for the Ninth Circuit had issued in *Barona Group of the Capitan Grande Band of Mission Indians v. Duffy*. The Court denied both petitions.

However, in 1981, President Reagan had appointed Sandra Day O'Connor, a state court judge from Arizona, to the Court. Most justices arrive at the Court having had little to no personal experience with Indians. Justice O'Connor, by contrast, had grown up on a ranch on the Arizona–New Mexico border sixty miles southeast of the San Carlos Apache Reservation. So she had a practical understanding of day-to-day life on Indian reservations that her colleagues on the Court lacked.

In July 1983, Justice O'Connor wrote the Court's decision in *Rice v. Rehner*, a case that, when the justices were debating how each would vote, Justice Lewis Powell told Justice William Brennan that "Sandra . . . feels very strongly about." In that decision, the Court decided that the state of California had authority to enforce its alcohol control laws on the Pala Reservation north of San Diego by requiring an Indian owner of a liquor store that many non-Indians patronized to obtain a state liquor license. Justice O'Connor began her decision by noting that several of the Court's more recent decisions had "established a trend . . . away from the idea of inherent tribal sovereignty as a bar to state jurisdiction and toward reliance on federal pre-emption." She then pointed out that the liquor store owner's "distribution of liquor has a significant impact beyond the limits of the Pala Reservation" and that the state of California had "an unquestionable interest in the liquor traffic that occurs within its borders." Justice O'Connor also noted that history instructed that Indian tribes had no "inherent authority" to regulate the sale of alcohol.

Since history also instructed that Indian tribes had no inherent authority to operate bingo games that catered to non-Indian players, Frank Ducheneaux considered the *Rice v. Rehner* decision a harbinger that "did not bode well for any eventual Court review of the pro-tribal rationale in the *Seminole* and *Barona* cases." To try to prevent that review, in September 1983, Duchenaux discussed the situation, first with other members of the staff of the Committee on Interior and Insular Affairs, and then with members of the staff of the Senate Select Committee on Indian Affairs. They all agreed that "legislation might be necessary, both to secure the right of tribes to engage in [gambling] for governmental revenue purposes and to set in place necessary controls."

So, with the approval of Arizona representative Morris "Mo" Udall, the chairman of the Committee on Interior and Insular Affairs, Ducheneaux, his deputy, an Indian named Alex Tallchief Skibine, and Michael Jackson, who worked for the Republican members of the Committee, wrote a bill. According to Skibine, "[O]ur idea behind the bill at the time was a simple one: enact an Indian gaming bill before the issue reached the Supreme Court and establish a federal scheme that would pre-empt state regulation of Indian gaming," because "in the wake of decisions like *Rice v. Rehner* . . . some of us did not trust the Supreme Court to decide such state jurisdictional issues in favor of tribal interests."

On November 18, 1983 Representative Udall introduced the bill as H.R. 4566. H.R. 4566 prohibited gambling in "Indian country" (a term that includes Indian reservations) unless the gambling was conducted pursuant to an ordinance that had been approved by both the appropriate "Indian tribal government" and the secretary of the interior. It required the money a tribe earned to be used "solely to fund tribal government operations or programs." And it required the secretary of the interior to approve management agreements and conduct audits.

ON JUNE 19, 1984, THE Committee on Interior and Insular Affairs held a hearing on H.R. 4566 that Representative Udall attended but New Mexico representative Bill Richardson chaired. Representing the Department of the Interior, John Fritz was the first witness. Fritz began by informing the committee that eighty Indian tribes were operating, or would soon open, a bingo hall; and that as many as twenty-five of those halls had gross revenue of $100,000 to $1 million a month.

Although few, if any, of the halls had controls adequate to prevent bingo games from being rigged and money from being skimmed, Fritz told the committee that the Department of the Interior recommended that "action on this legislation be deferred" because each tribe should be able to decide for itself whether the tribe wanted the secretary of the interior to

approve its gaming ordinances. Fritz concluded by lecturing that the Department of the Interior "recognizes tribal sovereignty and promotes the
removal of obstacles to self-government, a goal endorsed by this administration as reflected in the government-to-government policy enunciated in
January 1983."

The next witness, Deputy Assistant Attorney General Mark Richard,
told the committee that the U.S. Department of Justice had a different view.
Richard said his department opposed H.R. 4566 because assigning the secretary of the interior the task of regulating gambling on Indian reservations
"simply does not provide for the degree of supervision and auditing to safe-
guard against skimming, [money] laundering, kickbacks, manipulation,
and other criminal activity."

But then Richard obfuscated.

When Representative Richardson asked, "Do you see Mafia infiltration
in Operation X and State Y?" Richard answered, "I would really prefer not
going into it in a public setting, just in terms of what our intelligence is."
Richard's next exchange was with New Mexico representative Manuel Lujan:

LUJAN: Do you have any indication that there is any organized crime
activity in any of the bingo operations, any inroads by organized
crime?

RICHARD: To my knowledge, we have not prosecuted any organized
crime elements for activities on Indian reservations.

LUJAN: You haven't prosecuted, but have some been brought to your
attention?

RICHARD: Mr. Congressman, we know from the activities of organized crime elements in this country that it is a natural for them, this
kind of operation.

LUJAN: So we've got to be very careful, basically?

RICHARD: Yes, extremely so.

Then Richard volunteered that

I want to make sure my remarks regarding organized crime are not
misconstrued. I am not suggesting that we have evidence of *massive*

infiltration of organized crime elements in this area. That is not what I am suggesting at all. I am suggesting that our experience in the field of organized crime, and just in criminal law enforcement in general, suggests that unless we address these issues we will be leaving ourselves vulnerable to infiltration along these lines and that we should approach this in a preventative mode before it is too late and where we have a massive crime problem to deal with. That was the point I was trying to make. (emphasis added)

At the time Richard gratuitously offered that assurance, attorneys in the Criminal Division of the U.S. Department of Justice had known for more than four years that Seminole Management Associates was controlled by associates of Meyer Lansky and the LaRocca Mafia family in Pittsburgh. They knew individuals who had felony convictions and organized crime connections were involved in the management of the Little Six Bingo Palace and had been involved with the failed attempt to open a blackjack casino on the Lummi Reservation in Washington state. And, as will be discussed, they knew a Mafia associate named Rocco Zangari had been involved in the management of a gambling facility on the Cabazon Reservation in southern California.

If (to placate the BIA?) Mark Richard downplayed the extent to which the U.S. Department of Justice knew that individuals who had organized crime connections were involved in the management of Indian bingo halls, the Indian witnesses were just as misleading.

In March 1983, John Fritz appointed thirteen BIA employees and tribal leaders of his acquaintance to serve on his ad hoc task force, which he assigned a BIA employee named Hazel Elbert to chair. However, in August when Elbert and the other members of the task force met in Minneapolis, the representatives of the sixty tribes who attended the meeting took the task force over. They reorganized the membership, changed the name to the National Indian Gaming Task Force, demoted Elbert and the other BIA employee-members to "non-voting technical advisors," and elected Bill Houle, a member of the Fond du Lac Band of Lake Superior Chippewas in Minnesota, to replace Elbert as chairman. When Houle decided he could not serve, he was replaced as chairman by Mark Powless, an Oneida Indian from Wisconsin.

When Powless and the other members of the National Indian Gaming Task Force read H.R. 4566, they lambasted the bill, calling it "anti-Indian" and "paternalistic," because it restricted the ability of tribes that were operating bingo halls to continue to operate them however they wished. So they decided to write their own bill.

Their bill authorized an Indian tribe to offer all forms of gambling at any location within its jurisdiction, unless a particular form was "prohibited within Indian country by federal law or within the state by state public policy." No approval by the secretary of the interior was required unless a tribe's constitution required the secretary to approve the tribe's ordinances. While the bill authorized the secretary to approve management agreements, existing agreements were grandfathered. If a tribe managed its own bingo hall, it could continue to do so with no oversight. In addition, the last section of the bill provided: "No part of this legislation shall apply to tribes who [sic] expressly do not desire to be included." In other words, if Congress passed the bill, any tribe that wished to do so could ignore it.

On January 31, 1984, Mark Powless and Ronald Gutierrez, a member of the Spokane Tribe in Washington state, presented the task force's bill to Representative Udall, Frank Ducheneaux, and Alex Skibine at a meeting in Washington, D.C. After the meeting, Ducheneaux complained to Udall that the task force John Fritz had created had

> been taken over by a leadership which is strictly opposed to any real effort to bring about even a minimum of Federal regulation of Indian gambling activity. Mark Powless of the Wisconsin Oneida Tribe and Ron Gutierrez of the Spokane Tribe have the idea that the Committee can take no action in this matter unless the task force, led by them, consent to it. After you left the . . . meeting, we had somewhat of a confrontation with them on proposed amendments to the bill. They felt we, on your behalf, should make commitments to various amendments they wanted. While we did indicate that some of them might be acceptable, we did not make any commitment on them. It was, in part, because of the attitude of Powless and Gutierrez that we recommended to you that the hearings [on H.R. 4566 that Ducheneaux had scheduled for April 26 and May 5] be cancelled.

Then in March, when the National Indian Gaming Task Force met in Minneapolis, Powless and Gutierrez had a change of heart. After the meeting, Alex Skibine reported to Udall that the task force members had "decided that they were, after all, not opposed to legislation but wanted to push their own legislation, therefore, they want you to go on with the hearings."

The hearing on H.R. 4566 the committee held on June 19, 1984 then was scheduled.

AT THE HEARING, after John Fritz and Mark Richard testified, Mark Powless presented the task force's bill. Then Joseph Bowen, the attorney representing the Puyallup Tribe in Washington state who had accompanied Powless to the witness table, vouched that "there isn't an example of organized crime now on the 80 reservations that have gaming." Then Suzan Harjo, the executive director of NCAI, told the committee that, while there had been "rumors of criminal elements and unsavory characters," all she had seen in Indian bingo halls was "seniors playing multiple bingo cards."

Since the Department of the Interior and the U.S. Department of Justice opposed H.R. 4566, and since neither Mark Powless nor any of the other Indian witnesses said they supported it, when the hearing concluded, Mo Udall announced that he did not support H.R. 4566 either. Rather, the bill was just something he had "throw[n] on the table so we would have something concrete and specific to discuss." The Committee on Interior and Insular Affairs took no further action on H.R. 4566, and when the Ninety-Eighth Congress adjourned, the bill died.

Frank Ducheneaux thought Powless and the other members of the National Indian Gaming Task Force had squandered an opportunity that would not come their way again. As he years later would reminisce: "The legislation in the 98th Congress was the last opportunity for enactment of a simple, minimally intrusive, preemption bill before the storm of anti-Indian backlash broke in the 99th Congress."

7: NINETY-NINTH CONGRESS: HOUSE OF REPRESENTATIVES

> For most of you this bill is not important and
> will not affect your state.
>
> Nevada representative BARBARA VUCANOVICH

IN JANUARY 1985, THE NINETY-NINTH CONGRESS CONVENED. TWO MONTHS later, Rep. Morris "Mo" Udall, the chairman of the Committee on Interior and Insular Affairs, introduced H.R. 1920, a bill whose text was based on, but was not identical to, the text of H.R. 4566. Most of the changes were cosmetic. Frank Ducheneaux changed the name of the bill from "Indian Gambling Control Act" to "Indian Gaming Control Act" and substituted the more innocuous sounding word "gaming" for "gambling" throughout the text—a change the National Indian Gaming Task Force had made in its bill. In the congressional findings section, Ducheneaux removed a finding he had included in H.R. 4566, which had acknowledged that "some Indian tribes have expressed concern about their ability to continue to regulate or operate gambling activities free from the influence of organized crime." In June of that year, the Committee on Interior and Insular Affairs held the first of the three hearings it would hold on H.R. 1920. By then the "anti-Indian backlash" Ducheneaux predicted had begun.

At the hearing the committee had held on H.R. 4566 in June 1984, gambling on Indian reservations had been a parochial matter. Of the nine witnesses, Deputy Assistant Attorney General Mark Richard was the only non-Indian. But by June 1985, bingo halls and other gambling facilities were operating on Indian reservations in twenty states. And the success of the bingo halls on the Barona, Sycuan, and four other reservations in southern California demonstrated that gambling facilities on Indian reservations in the Golden State had the potential to draw customers away from casinos in Las Vegas. As a consequence, according to Mo Udall, prior to the hearing "we had a list of up to 75 or 100 people who wanted to testify."

Of that number, Frank Ducheneaux invited nineteen. The witnesses included the attorney general of Arizona, a deputy attorney general from California, representatives of the horse and dog racing industries, and a member of the Nevada Gaming Control Board. They all opposed H.R. 1920.

To add to the calliope of objection, because three of the six bingo halls in southern California were located on Indian reservations in San Diego County, Democratic representative Jim Bates who represented the southern half of the county, asked Udall to hold a hearing in San Diego. The hearing, which the committee held in September, provided John Duffy, the sheriff of San Diego County, an opportunity to rail about the situation the U.S. Court of Appeals for the Ninth Circuit had created when it ruled against him in the *Barona Group of the Capitan Grande Band of Mission Indians v. Duffy* lawsuit. When he finished reading his testimony, Sheriff Duffy had the following exchange with Rep. Richard Lehman, who in Udall's absence chaired the hearing.

LEHMAN: Do you have any evidence of organized crime in Indian gaming?

DUFFY: Yes, we do.

LEHMAN: I take it you have shared that with the proper authorities?

DUFFY: That is correct. The State attorneys general office, the Los Angeles County sheriff's office, this office has that evidence.

LEHMAN: You think that it is a serious problem we ought to be concerned about?

DUFFY: I most certainly do. It has been shared also with Federal agencies.

LEHMAN: How about skimming and the improper conduct as far as management is concerned?

DUFFY: As a matter of fact, we have had allegations on the Barona reservation.

The hearing ended the committee's investigation, such as it had been, of gambling on Indian reservations without the FBI having been invited to testify.

No witness had appeared to tell the committee what the Reagan administration's position was on Indian gaming. Four months earlier, the *Washington Post* had reported that officials from the Bureau of Indian Affairs would be meeting with their counterparts at the U.S. Department of Justice to try to end their "squabbling" over what the administration's position should be, and, if that meeting failed to produce an agreement, "Attorney General Edwin Meese III intends to attempt to resolve it with Interior Secretary Donald Hodel."*

After that attempt to reach unanimity failed, an agreement between the two executive branch departments finally was reached in November. The Committee on Interior and Insular Affairs then held a hearing to find out what the agreement was.

At the hearing, Deputy Assistant Attorney General Victoria Toensing told the committee that "if the Justice Department had its druthers it would not have any gambling whatsoever." But in 1984, when Mark Richard told the committee the U.S. Department of Justice opposed H.R. 4566 because the Department of the Interior did not have the ability to regulate gambling on Indian reservations, there were eighty bingo halls. Since there now were 104 halls and more soon would be opening, Toensing announced that the Justice Department had reluctantly concluded that bingo halls on Indian reservations were here to stay. However, rather than the Department of the Interior regulating, the U.S. Department of Justice and the Department of the Interior now were in agreement that Congress should create a commission to do the regulating.

The other Reagan administration witness was Marian Horn, the acting solicitor (chief legal officer) of the Department of the Interior. She explained that, in exchange for the U.S. Department of Justice dropping its opposition to bingo halls, the Department of the Interior had acceded to the Justice Department's insistence that all other forms of gambling—other than "social and ceremonial gaming" that Indians played among themselves—should be regulated, or prohibited, as the case might be, by the states in which Indian reservations were located because "the potential law enforcement problems are so great as to outweigh the economic benefits to the tribes."

• • •

---

*In February 1985, Meese replaced William French Smith as attorney general, and Donald Hodel, who had been serving as secretary of energy, replaced William Clark who in November 1983 had replaced James Watt as secretary of the interior.

IN THE U.S. HOUSE of Representatives, the process pursuant to which a bill moves from introduction to passage is called the "regular order." When a bill is introduced, the speaker refers the bill to usually one, but sometimes more than one, committee. Most bills then die in committee, unless the committee's chairman decides to hold, first a hearing, and then a committee meeting called a "mark-up," at which the bill is discussed and usually amended. At the conclusion of the mark-up, committee members vote on whether to send the bill to the floor of the House. On December 4, 1985, Mo Udall called the Committee on Interior and Insular Affairs to order to mark up H.R. 1920.

The committee had forty-one members, twenty-five Democrats and sixteen Republicans. Of that number, only six members—Udall, New Mexico representatives Bill Richardson and Manuel Lujan, Arizona representative John McCain, Minnesota representative Bruce Vento, and Nevada representative Barbara Vucanovich—attended the two hearings the committee had held in Washington, D.C. Six other members attended one of hearings, although several for only a minute or two. Rep. Richard Lehman, who chaired the hearing in San Diego, and the two other members who attended that hearing did not attend either of the hearings in Washington, D.C.

Prior to testifying at a hearing, a witness submits a written statement. But most members of the committee do not read most of the statements. Instead, their staffs read the statements.

Staff members also attend the hearings that the members for whom they work do not attend. The staff member then writes a memorandum for his or her member that summarizes the bill and the testimony that was presented at the hearing. The memorandum also identifies the issues on which the member may be required to vote if the chairman decides the bill will be marked up.

All House members rely on their staffs because they do not have time during their workdays to educate themselves about every bill that has been referred to the two or more committees on which they serve or to attend hearings regarding bills in which they are not interested. The lack of member participation in the committee process enhances the influence of all chairmen of all committees, and, during the 1980s when partisan rancor was not as divisive as it is today, particularly a chairman as popular with both Democratic and Republican members as Mo Udall.

A LANKY SIX-FOOT-FIVE attorney from Tucson whose dry wit and penchant for droll storytelling were legendary during the thirty years he served in the House, the sixty-three-year-old Udall was a member of one of Arizona's pioneer families. In 1880, David King Udall, the family patriarch, emigrated from Utah by covered wagon with a group of Mormon settlers to St. Johns, a frontier hamlet in the Arizona Territory. David King Udall's son, Levi Udall, who from 1947 to his death in 1960 was a justice of the Arizona Supreme Court, raised his three sons in St. Johns.

In 1954 Mo Udall's older brother, Stewart Udall, was elected to the U.S. House of Representatives, where he served until 1960, when President-elect John F. Kennedy appointed Stewart secretary of the interior. In 1961, Mo Udall won his brother's House seat in a special election, and when he arrived on Capitol Hill he inherited his brother's seat on the Committee on Interior and Insular Affairs of which in 1977 he became chairman.

Because St. Johns is surrounded by the Navajo, Zuni, and Fort Apache reservations, Mo Udall grew up around Indians. And his congressional district contained several Indian reservations and communities, including, as previously discussed, Old Pascua and Pascua Pueblo. As a consequence and as his biographers would celebrate, during the fourteen years he served as chairman of the Committee on Interior and Insular Affairs, Udall "play[ed] the major House role in improving the lives of Indians in the United States." According to Frank Ducheneaux, Udall "had a lot of sympathy for Indian problems" and "bills to strike at the heart of Indian treaty and other rights never saw the light of day during Mo's chairmanship."

As a consequence of his concern about the lack of employment and economic development opportunities and the attendant social problems—alcohol and drug abuse, child sexual abuse, teen suicide, domestic violence—that were endemic on Indian reservations, no matter what law enforcement officials like Victoria Toensing thought about gambling on the reservations, according to Ducheneaux, Udall "felt if the states could do it, the tribes should have the same right." Udall also was sympathetic to the opposition the Indian witnesses who testified at the hearings on H.R. 1920 expressed to the idea of Congress giving the states authority to enforce their gambling laws on the reservations.

After the hearing at which Victoria Toensing and Marian Horn testified, Frank Ducheneaux wrote a new bill for Udall to offer during the mark-up as a substitute for the original text of H.R. 1920. The bill differed from H.R. 1920 in four principal respects.

First, as the Department of the Interior had recommended in the written statement Marian Horn submitted, the definition of "gaming" divided gambling into three classes:

> CLASS I: "social games [played] solely for prizes of minimal value" and "traditional forms of Indian gaming engaged in by individuals as a part of or in connection with tribal ceremonies or celebrations";
> CLASS II: bingo and "pull-tabs, punch boards, and other games similar to bingo"; and
> CLASS III: all other forms of gambling.

Second, whereas Class I forms of gambling would be "within the exclusive jurisdiction of the Indian tribes," Class II and III forms of gambling would be regulated by the tribe on whose reservation the gambling was conducted and by a National Indian Gaming Commission, whose seven members would be appointed by the secretary of the interior.

Third, neither bingo nor any Class III form of gambling could be conducted by an Indian tribe if bingo or that Class III form of gambling was "prohibited by the State within which such tribe is located as a matter of State public policy and criminal law." And fourth, if a particular Class III form of gambling was not prohibited by the public policy and criminal law of the state, the commission would regulate that Class III form of gambling pursuant to regulations whose content would be "identical to that provided for the same or similar activity by the State within which such gaming activity is to be conducted."

WHILE HIS PREROGATIVES as chairman and his personal popularity gave Mo Udall considerable influence over committee decision-making, at the mark-up of H.R. 1920 Udall could not impose his new bill on the other members of the committee by fiat. And insofar as support for the bill was concerned, the committee was divided into three factions.

The first and largest faction was composed of members of both political parties who had little or no interest in gambling on Indian reservations. Of the forty-one members of the committee, more than half did not attend the mark-up. The second faction, whose bipartisan membership included New Mexico Democratic representative Bill Richardson and Alaska representative Don Young, the ranking Republican member of the committee, supported Udall. The third faction, whose membership also was bipartisan, ranged from Montana Republican representative Ron Marlenee, who opposed all forms of gambling on Indian reservations, to California Democratic representative Tony Coelho, who was adamant that, if Congress was going to allow them, all Class III forms of gambling on Indian reservations should be regulated by the states.

For members of the committee who opposed the new Udall bill, the first line of defense was delay. When the mark-up began, Representative Marlenee moved to table consideration of H.R. 1920 because "we are about to take an action that has a nationwide impact, and I think that it is time that we slow down the process a little bit, look at what we are doing, evaluate this thing." His motion lost by a vote of 9 to 10.

Then New Mexico representative Bill Richardson offered the text of the new Udall bill as a substitute for the original text of H.R. 1920. Minor amendments were offered, most of which were agreed to, after which Udall adjourned the mark-up.

On December 11 when the mark-up reconvened, the major topic of contention was an amendment Representative Coelho offered to require all Class III forms of gambling on Indian reservations to be "controlled and regulated by the states." Unlike Ron Marlenee, a backbench Republican, Tony Coelho was an influential member of the chairman's party and, for Mo Udall, a formidable adversary.

AFTER GRADUATING IN 1964 from Loyola University in Los Angeles, where he had been president of the student body, Coelho joined the staff of Rep. B.F. Sisk. Sisk represented the congressional district in California's central valley, where Coelho had been raised. When Sisk retired, in 1978 Coelho was elected to Sisk's seat.

During his first two years as a member of the U.S. House of Representatives, Coelho established a reputation inside the Democratic caucus as a fast-rising new political star. When he was reelected in 1980, the members of the caucus elected the sophomore legislator chairman of the Democratic

Congressional Campaign Committee. The position's principal responsibility is raising the money Democratic candidates need to win elections.

Insofar as Indian gaming was concerned, Coelho said his paramount concern was that Indian tribes in California would build horse tracks on their reservations that would compete against Del Mar, Santa Anita, and the other tracks that were part of the state's $2 billion thoroughbred racing industry. He also was concerned that, at reservation tracks, trainers and jockeys would be licensed by the tribes, and the treatment of the horses and pari-mutuel betting would be regulated by the National Indian Gaming Commission, rather than by the California legislature and the California Horse Racing Board.

There were no horse tracks in Tony Coelho's congressional district. So why did he care whether Indian tribes built tracks that would compete against Del Mar and Santa Anita? According to Don Hellman, the member of his staff who handled H.R. 1920, the answer was money. "I'm not saying his views were all about money," Hellman would recall when he was asked about Coelho's motivation. "But as chairman of the Democratic Congressional Campaign Committee, Tony was reaching out to people who had money, and they in turn were talking to him about issues that were of concern to them. Particularly the horse people."

Prior to the December 11 mark-up, Udall and Bill Richardson tried to persuade Coelho not to offer his amendment to subject all Class III forms of gambling to state regulation. But Coelho would not be dissuaded. So when the mark-up began and Coelho offered his amendment, Udall offered an amendment to the Coelho amendment that made several cosmetic changes to the new Udall bill, but maintained the National Indian Gaming Commission as the entity that would regulate all Class III forms of gambling, including horse racing. After a morning of discussion and debate on the Udall amendment to the Coelho amendment, the chairman adjourned the mark-up for the lunch hour.

COMMITTEE MEMBERS WHO did not attend the mark-up could influence the outcome of the votes on the Udall amendment to the Coelho amendment, and then on the Coelho amendment, by giving a written "proxy" to a member who did attend. Frank Ducheneaux solicited proxies for the chairman. But the afternoon before the mark-up, he reported to

Udall that "We are having some problems in our proxy campaign because of the personal contacts by Coelho."

Tony Coelho not only collected his own proxies, he collected enough to win. But when the mark-up reconvened, Coelho announced that "The chairman and I have discussed his substitute, and I am going to vote no. But I am not going to use my proxies or the votes that we have to defeat it at this point" because "the chairman and I will continue to have discussions between now and the time that the bill comes to the floor and see if there can be some accommodations."

Why did Tony Coelho decide to lose a vote he could have won? One element of his calculation may have been that he had more to gain by losing than by winning.

A YEAR EARLIER, Massachusetts representative Thomas "Tip" O'Neill, the speaker of the House, had announced that he would retire at the end of 1986. That meant that in January 1987, when the One Hundredth Congress convened, Texas representative Jim Wright, the majority leader, would move up to speaker, and Washington representative Tom Foley, the whip (as the third-ranking position in the House leadership is called), would move up to majority leader. Foley's promotion meant that inside the Democratic caucus the election to replace Foley as whip would be wide open.

In May 1985, the *New York Times* reported that five members of the caucus were campaigning for the job, but that "Mr. Coelho, the chairman of the Democratic Congressional Campaign Committee that distributes money for members' campaigns, is seen as the front runner." In December 1986 Coelho won the whip election, defeating New York representative Charles Rangel by a vote of 167 to 78. The lopsided vote gives the appearance that Coelho's victory was preordained. But in December 1985, his election as whip was no sure thing. Because it was not, it was not in Coelho's interest to embarrass a chairman as popular with other members of the Democratic caucus as Mo Udall was if the embarrassment could be avoided by allowing the chairman to save face by keeping control of his own bill in his own committee.

• • •

AFTER THE MEMBERS of the Committee on Interior and Insular Affairs voted to substitute the text of the new Udall bill for the original text of H.R. 1920 and then send the bill to the House floor, as part of the "regular order" H.R. 1920 could not be considered on the floor until the Committee filed a report explaining the bill. In a consequential respect, the report Frank Ducheneaux wrote was purposely disingenuous.

Two years earlier when Mark Richard testified on H.R. 4566, he told the committee that the U.S. Department of Justice had no evidence of "*massive* infiltration of organized crime elements" (emphasis added) into bingo halls on Indian reservations. When she testified on H.R. 1920, Victoria Toensing continued that obfuscation by telling the committee that the Justice Department did not believe "Indian gambling operations are presently 'mobbed-up.'"

Toensing's testimony allowed Ducheneaux to continue the speak-no-evil soft-pedaling of the organized crime issue he began when he removed from H.R. 1920 the congressional finding in H.R. 4566 that had acknowledged that "some Indian tribes have expressed concern about their ability to continue to regulate or operate gambling activities free from the influence of organized crime."

Making no mention of San Diego County Sheriff John Duffy's testimony, the report Ducheneaux wrote informed the 398 members of the U.S. House of Representatives who were not members of the Committee on Interior and Insular Affairs:

> On the issue of organized crime, the Committee has not found any *conclusive* evidence that . . . infiltration [of bingo halls on Indian reservations] has occurred. The Justice Department, in its testimony on the bill stated that, while it did not claim that Indian gambling operations were presently "mobbed up", there was still a potential for such infiltration by organized crime. (emphasis added)

THE MEMBERS OF the Committee on Interior and Insular Affairs voted to send H.R. 1920 to the floor on December 11, 1985. But Frank Ducheneaux did not file the committee's report on the bill until March 10, 1986. The reason for the delay was to give Mo Udall time to negotiate with Tony Coelho.

On February 12, 1986, Ducheneaux gave Udall a memorandum titled: "'Last Mile' Compromise Offer of Mr. Coelho." Attached to it was an amendment to H.R. 1920 Ducheneaux had written to try to address Coelho's insistence that the states regulate all Class III forms of gambling on Indian reservations. The amendment authorized the National Indian Gaming Commission to contract with a state "to carry out the Commission's routine, preventative monitoring function;" a concession that Ducheneaux informed Udall "stops just this side of State jurisdiction and will probably be very much opposed by the tribe's [sic] who are already dissatisfied with your original compromise."

If Udall gave Ducheneaux's amendment to Tony Coelho, Coelho rejected it because by then he wanted Congress to impose a moratorium on all Class III forms of gambling. While Ducheneaux told Udall that a moratorium was "totally unacceptable to the Indian tribes," it was not totally unacceptable to Udall. So his negotiations with Coelho continued, and a bargain was struck.

The amendment to H.R. 1920 on which Udall and Coelho agreed imposed a four-year moratorium on all Class III forms of gambling on Indian reservations while the comptroller general* studied the subject. The comptroller general then would submit a report to Congress that contained recommendations regarding four questions, the first of which was "whether the tribes, the states, or the United States is the best regulator of Class III gaming on Indian lands."

AS PART OF the regular order, after the report on a bill is filed, the chairman of the committee that reported the bill asks the Rules Committee to write a "rule" that sets out the terms for debate on the bill, including what amendments may be offered. The rule is then considered on the floor of the House. If a majority of the members vote to approve the rule, the bill is brought to the floor and debated pursuant to the rule's terms.

Because that part of the regular order is procedurally unwieldy and time-consuming, a bill can also reach the floor if the speaker recognizes

---

*The comptroller general is the director of the Government Accountability Office (GAO), a nonpartisan watchdog agency. Congress frequently directs the GAO to conduct policy analysis and to submit recommendations regarding legislation.

the bill's manager for the purpose of making a motion to have the House suspend the regular order rules and pass the bill. A motion to suspend the rules is debated for no more than forty minutes and must pass by a two-thirds vote. During the debate, no amendments may be offered. But before he offers his motion, the bill's manager can amend the bill however he wishes.

Motions to suspend the rules may be offered only on Mondays, Tuesdays, and Wednesdays. Because most motions to suspend the rules pass on unrecorded voice votes, House members do not need to be on the floor or to actually cast a vote. For that reason, the speaker's office routinely asks committee chairmen to identify bills that have passed their committees and are noncontroversial enough for the House to pass "on suspension" on Mondays when, because many members are still traveling back to Washington, D.C., after having spent the weekend in their districts, the House has little business to conduct.

ON FRIDAY, APRIL 18, 1986, Rep. Tom Foley, the Democratic whip, informed the members that on Monday, April 21, Mo Udall would move the House to suspend its rules and pass H.R. 1920, and that the text of H.R. 1920 that would be the subject of the motion would include "a compromise amendment which would strike Class III provisions from the bill and add language providing that Class III gaming on Indian lands will be illegal during a four-year period beginning on the date of enactment."

On Monday, Udall made the motion. During the brief pro forma "debate" that followed, in addition to Udall, eight members, five of whom were members of the Committee on Interior and Insular Affairs, spoke. Six supported H.R. 1920, most enthusiastically, Republican representative Barbara Vucanovich, who represented Nevada, reluctantly. Texas representative Henry Gonzalez, a member of the Committee on Banking, Finance, and Urban Affairs who was on the floor only because he was waiting to make his own motion to suspend the rules, then asked Representative Vucanovich a question about H.R. 1920 because, while he cheerfully admitted he knew nothing about the bill, his wife had recently visited a bingo hall in Oklahoma and "they have been giving some mighty big prizes away in the bingo games in the Oklahoma Indian reservations."

California representative Norman Shumway, who was not a member of the Committee on Interior and Insular Affairs, was the only member to speak in opposition to H.R. 1920. Shumway explained that, after constituents in his congressional district expressed concern "about the construction and operation of a high-stakes bingo parlor on a small Indian rancheria in northern California," he had investigated the situation. What he discovered was that the problems his constituents had brought to his attention were "but the tip of the iceberg," because "nationwide there have been numerous efforts, some successful, by organized crime to gain a foothold in the potential lucrative Indian gaming business."

When Representative Shumway finished explaining to the nearly empty chamber why he thought that, insofar as the regulation of gambling on Indian reservations was concerned, "the Federal government would be wise to defer to the experience and the judgment of the States in which our native Americans live," Rep. Douglas Bosco, a sophomore member who, because he lacked the seniority to avoid the assignment, was presiding in the speaker's chair, called for the question. By an unrecorded voice vote, the 435 members of the House (with no more than thirty members present on the floor) then "voted" to suspend the rules and pass H.R. 1920 with only Mo Udall and Tony Coelho and a handful of other members from the Committee on Interior and Insular Affairs having any idea what was in the bill the U.S. House of Representatives passed.

Frank Ducheneaux now was halfway to achieving his and Alex Skibine's objective of having Congress "establish a federal scheme that would pre-empt state regulation of Indian gaming" before Sandra Day O'Connor and the other justices of the U.S. Supreme Court who had issued the Court's decision in *Rice v. Rehner* granted a petition for a writ of certiorari that would require the Court to decide whether states had authority to enforce their gambling laws on Indian reservations. But as Ducheneaux and Skibine would be reminded when H.R. 1920 reached the Senate, a senator has considerably more influence over the Senate's consideration of bills of which the senator disapproves than the next to none at all the House rules had given to Norman Shumway.

8: NINETY-NINTH CONGRESS: SENATE

> My entire career on the Indian Affairs Com-
> mittee was one of being defensive and putting
> holds on bills that had passed the Committee.
>
> SEN. SLADE GORTON

A FTER THE U.S. HOUSE OF REPRESENTATIVES PASSED H.R. 1920, THE BILL
was sent to the Senate, where it was referred to the Select Committee
on Indian Affairs.

In 1789 when Congress began operating under the U.S. Constitution,
because what should be done about the thousands of Native Americans
who occupied the land on the nation's western and northern borders was a
major policy concern, the Senate created a Committee on Indian Affairs. By
1890, that major concern had become a minor one; by then the U.S. Army
had moved thousands of Indians who lived east of the Mississippi River to
locations west of the river, and west of the river, most Indians had been confined on reservations. Nevertheless, the Committee on Indian Affairs continued to exist until 1946, when the Senate abolished the committee and
transferred its jurisdiction to the Committee on Public Lands, which, to exercise that jurisdiction, created a Subcommittee on Indian Affairs.

Twenty-five years later, in 1972, James Abourezk was elected to the
Senate from South Dakota. An attorney raised in Wood, a small town near
the Rosebud Sioux Reservation, according to Abourezk, "I was, in my
younger days, an anti-Indian racist, like everyone else in Wood," until "I
had an epiphany when I got to college." By 1973 when he arrived in the
Senate and was appointed to the Committee on Interior and Insular Affairs
(as the Committee on Public Lands had been renamed), Abourezk considered himself a stalwart advocate for Native American rights.

For that reason, Abourezk asked Washington senator Henry "Scoop"
Jackson, the chairman of the Committee on Interior and Insular Affairs,
to appoint him chairman of the committee's Subcommittee on Indian Affairs.
Jackson did so and assigned Forrest Gerard, a member of the committee

staff who had been raised on the Blackfeet Reservation in Montana, to staff the subcommittee.

Abourezk disliked that arrangement because "although I was the sub-committee's chairman, Gerard took his orders from Scoop." Abourezk also had a low opinion of Gerard, who he privately demeaned as an "apple" (an Indian red on the outside but white on the inside) and later publicly disparaged as a "perfect part-Indian bureaucrat." So, according to Abourezk, he "mercilessly bugged" Jackson to assign additional members of the staff of the Committee on Interior and Insular Affairs to the Sub-committee on Indian Affairs. To put an end to his pestering, Bill Van Ness, the committee's chief counsel, suggested to Abourezk that if he wanted more staff, rather than continuing to irritate the chairman, he should per-suade Congress to establish a commission to study Indian policy for which additional staff could be hired on a temporary basis.

Abourezk took the suggestion to heart and introduced a resolution whose passage by Congress in 1975 created an eleven-member American Indian Policy Review Commission (AIPRC), chaired by Abourezk and vice-chaired by Washington representative Lloyd Meeds, the chairman of the Subcommittee on Indian Affairs of the House Committee on Interior and Insular Affairs. The resolution directed the AIPRC to submit a report to Congress that would contain recommendations for legislation that would improve the lives of Native Americans.

When Congress appropriated the first installment of what became more than $2.5 million to fund the AIPRC, Abourzek hired a staff of more than one hundred persons that included twenty-nine attorneys and other professionals, plus forty individuals who were appointed to eleven task forces. Most were young, a majority were of Native American descent, and all were votaries of "inherent tribal sovereignty," the legal doctrine Felix Cohen invented in 1934. In May 1977 the AIPRC submitted a 563-page report to Congress that was so fraught with misstatements of law and his-tory that Representative Meeds disowned its content, dismissing it as "one-sided advocacy" that "cannot be relied upon as a statement of existing law nor as a statement of what future policy should be."

• • •

By happenstance, in January 1977 at the beginning of the Ninety-Fifth Congress, as the members of the AIPRC staff were finishing writing their report the Senate decided to reorganize its committee structure. The reorganization plan divided jurisdiction over Indian-related bills between the Committee on Energy and Natural Resources (as the Committee on Interior and Insular Affairs would be renamed) and the Committee on Human Resources.

When the Committee on Rules and Administration began reviewing the reorganization plan, Abourezk asked Nevada senator Howard Cannon, the chairman of the committee, to recommend to the Senate that, rather than dividing the jurisdiction, the Senate should create a Select Committee on Indian Affairs. The select committee's principal responsibility would be to consider bills whose enactment would implement the recommendations in the AIPRC's report. Cannon agreed to do so, but with the caveat that the select committee complete its work within two years, at which time it would "cease to exist at the conclusion of the 95th Congress."

When, with that understanding, the Senate created the select committee, Abourezk, who became chairman, began hiring members of the AIPRC's staff to staff the select committee. Ernie Stevens, an Oneida Indian who had been staff director of the AIPRC, became staff director of the select committee. Alan Parker, a Chippewa-Cree who had been a member of one of the AIPRC task forces, became the select committee's chief counsel.

In 1978, Abourezk, whose blunt-talking sharp-elbowed style was ill-suited to the decorum of the Senate, decided not to run for reelection. Before retiring, he tried to persuade the Senate to make the select committee permanent. He was not successful, but he was able to extend its life for two years. Two years later, the Senate extended the select committee's life again. Then in 1984, North Dakota Republican senator Mark Andrews, who had become chairman the preceding year, negotiated an agreement that made the select committee permanent. As a consequence, in 1986 when H.R. 1920 was referred to the Select Committee on Indian Affairs, the select committee's twenty-member staff was ensconced in a suite of offices on the eighth floor of the Hart Senate Office Building.

• • •

THE SENATE HAS the same amount of legislative work the U.S. House of Representatives has, but it must accomplish it with fewer than a quarter of the members—100 senators versus 435 House members. As a consequence, as a member of the select committee explained to the *New York Times*, senators "are assigned to so many committees that we can't become experts on much of anything."

So while Senator Andrews, the chairman of the select committee, would decide whether the committee would hold a hearing on H.R. 1920 and, if a hearing was held, whether the bill would be marked up, inside the select committee, the legislative process was even more staff-driven than it had been inside the House Committee on Interior and Insular Affairs. The first hearing the select committee held on the subject of gambling on Indian reservations illustrates how that reality played out in practice.

ON JUNE 26, 1985, WHEN Senator Andrews gaveled the hearing to order, Andrews and four of the eight other members of the committee were sitting on the dais. When the first witness finished testifying, two of the four departed. Then when the first panel of witnesses finished testifying, another senator departed. That left Andrews and Arizona senator Dennis DeConcini, who had introduced the bill that was the subject of the hearing, as the only senators still present. Andrews then gave the gavel to Pete Taylor, the staff director of the select committee, and departed. Senator DeConcini listened to one more witness and then he departed. The thirty-five witnesses remaining in the hearing room, most of whom were Indian representatives from tribes that operated bingo halls, were left to present their testimony only to Pete Taylor.

A year later, on June 17, 1986, the select committee held the only hearing it would hold on H.R. 1920, and member attendance was even worse.

When Senator Andrews gaveled the hearing to order, Senator DeConcini was the only other member present. After listening to two colleagues testify and then to witnesses from the Department of the Interior and the U.S. Department of Justice, Andrews handed the gavel to Deconcini and left the room. When he returned, he and DeConcini listened to several more witnesses. Then Andrews announced:

I think Senator DeConcini has had to leave. Senator Melcher has not been able to come. Senator Goldwater has not been able to come. I have a conference with the House that I am late for. . . . I think that what I will do is have our chief of staff conduct the hearing so we could just keep going right through the noon hour.

Andrews then handed the gavel to Pete Taylor, who proceeded to conduct the hearing by himself in order to provide the twenty-seven witnesses who remained an opportunity to make their oral presentations. As a consequence, no senator heard San Diego County Sheriff John Duffy testify. Duffy told Taylor:

On the reservations in California [on which bingo halls are being operated], virtually all of them, the Indians are exploited and they're cheated by unscrupulous profiteering companies with established connections to organized crime. In some cases organized crime is directly involved in the bingo operation itself, and many of them are involved in drug trafficking.

That led to the following exchange:

SHERIFF DUFFY: The obvious connections which we've established through investigation by my criminal intelligence unit, the Los Angeles Sheriff's Office Intelligence Unit, the State [of California] department of justice and with other agencies throughout the United States are the definite interconnections between most of these management companies and established criminals. The principals in those management companies are, in some instances, convicted felons. In other cases they are connected, not only to convicted felons but to established organized crime families, as well. Let me name some: The Genovese family, the Buffalino family, the Lucchese family. All of those could be linked to Barona bingo.

PETE TAYLOR: And you are also saying that they're linked to many other management companies?

SHERIFF DUFFY: That's correct. The Pan American Management Co., for example, is one with connecting companies [i.e., the New England Entertainment Company] with organized crime connections and criminal involvement in that company.

Not only did no member of the select committee listen to Sheriff Duffy testify, it is unlikely that any member read the written statement he submitted prior to the hearing in which, in an obvious reference to Rocco Passanante, he related that "an associate of a Los Angeles organized crime family was generally believed to be a hidden owner in the management company [that operated Barona Bonus Bingo]." (Steward Siegel, who two months earlier had pled guilty to rigging bingo games at Barona Bonus Bingo, undoubtedly was the source for Duffy's information.) After the hearing, Duffy had a meeting at the select committee at which he reiterated "the concerns of law enforcement." But rather than with Senator Andrews, he met with Pete Taylor. After the hearing at which Taylor presided, Senator Andrews directed Taylor to write a new bill for Andrews to offer as the chairman's substitute for the text of H.R. 1920 when the members of the select committee met to mark-up the bill.

ALTHOUGH HE WAS not an Indian, the forty-nine-year-old Taylor was a longtime Indian rights activist. Born, raised, and educated in Kansas, Taylor attended the George Washington University Law School in Washington, D.C., and was admitted to the District of Columbia bar in 1964. He then practiced law with a private firm until 1971, when he went to work at the Department of the Interior, directing a task force on Indian rights. In 1975, James Abourezk hired Taylor as one of the AIPRC's special counsels. Two years later when he staffed the Select Committee on Indian Affairs, Abourezk hired Taylor as special counsel. In 1981, when the Republican Party took control of the Senate and Maine Republican senator William Cohen became chairman of the select committee, he promoted Taylor to general counsel, the position in which he served until 1985 when Mark Andrews, who succeeded Cohen as chairman, promoted Taylor to staff director.

Although Taylor based the bill he wrote on H.R. 1920, his bill differed from H.R. 1920 in important particulars, two of which merit mention. First, like H.R. 1920, Taylor's bill divided gambling into three categories: Class I, Class II, and Class III. H.R. 1920 defined "Class II gaming" as bingo, pull-tabs, punch boards, "and other games similar to bingo." By 1986, 108 gambling facilities were operating on Indian reservations. Most of those facilities were bingo halls; however, fifteen tribes were offering card games, including blackjack and poker. One of those was the Spirit Lake Tribe in North Dakota, the state Senator Andrews represented. So Andrews directed Taylor to include "card games" in his definition of Class II gaming.

Second, Taylor's bill eliminated the moratorium on Class III forms of gambling on Indian reservations on which Morris Udall and Tony Coelho had agreed. In its place, the bill provided that if a particular Class III form of gambling was "otherwise legal within the State where [a tribe's 'Indian lands'] are located" the tribe could operate that Class III form of gambling if "the Indian tribe requests the Secretary of the Interior to consent to a transfer of specific jurisdiction over such gaming enterprise to the State within which such gaming enterprise is located."

On September 15, 1986 when Andrews and four other members of the select committee met to mark-up H.R. 1920, Andrews explained that he would

> like to have the tribes be able to go along with their bingo and pull-tab and small-stakes card games with a minimum amount of interference, and let them run them out on their own reservations. I think for Class III, the dogs and the ponies and everything else, it ought to either be prohibited or it ought to be subject to State law.

The procedure Pete Taylor invented to enable a tribe to request that the secretary of the interior transfer jurisdiction over Class III forms of gambling to the state in which the tribe's reservation was located was Taylor's attempt to write a bill whose content conformed to the chairman's view about state regulation without offending the ideological sensibilities of Indian leaders for whom state regulation was an anathematic intrusion on inherent tribal sovereignty. As Taylor explained the situation as he saw it in a memorandum he sent Andrews before the mark-up:

> The Committee [i.e., Taylor] draft . . . prohibits any Class III game unless the tribe and the state have agreed on a transfer of jurisdiction to the state . . . [This procedure] avoids the perceived stigma of subjecting tribes to state jurisdiction against their wishes and avoids penetration of the Federal shield of tribal rights provided by Federal preemption of the field of regulation of Indian affairs. *These are important considerations to the Indian tribes.* (emphasis in original)

When Pete Taylor finished writing his bill and tried to schedule a meeting of the select committee for August 13 to mark up H.R. 1920, the members' reaction was disinterest. "I'm not about to serve as chairman of a committee that is not functioning because staff can't get the members to show up," Mark Andrews complained to a reporter. The Associated Press reported the chairman's exasperation:

> Andrews said he had fought previous efforts to abolish the Indian Affairs panel but would change his mind if he is unable to get a quorum for a meeting after Congress returns from a three-week summer recess Sept. 8. Abolishing the committee would save taxpayers $350,000 a year in staff costs, Andrews said, adding that the work could be transferred to other committees.

When Congress returned from its recess, Pete Taylor tried again. This time, he was successful in scheduling a meeting for September 15 that five of the nine members of the select committee attended to mark up five bills. When the discussion reached H.R. 1920, Washington Republican senator Slade Gorton was the only member of the select committee, including Mark Andrews (who was not an attorney), who fully understood the content and legal consequences of the bill Pete Taylor had written.

A TALL, GAUNT man whose emotionally restrained countenance personifies High Episcopalian rectitude, Thomas Slade Gorton III is a member of an old New England family. In 1883, Gorton's great-grandfather founded Slade Gorton & Company, which brokered the cod and mackerel caught on the Grand Banks by the fishing fleet based in Gloucester, Massachusetts. Gorton's grandfather lost the family business to the bank in 1923, after which Gorton's father moved to Chicago, where the future senator was born in 1928.

In 1953, after graduating from Dartmouth College and the Columbia Law School, Gorton moved to Seattle. A small town in a young state, the Queen City was a place in which an ambitious young Republican could have a political career that might someday lead to the Senate, the career goal on which Gorton had settled in high school. He joined the Young Republican organization in Seattle's King County, where he became a leader of a group of moderate young conservatives. In 1958, Gorton was elected to the Washington House of Representatives where he served until 1968, when he was elected attorney general.

Fastidious, razor-smart, and always well-prepared, Gorton is a talented appellate litigator who argued fourteen cases before the U.S. Supreme Court during the years he served as attorney general. But he was an odd politician—easy to respect but difficult to like. As *Seattle Times* political columnist Richard Larsen noted, "Slade Gorton is not a guy you go out and drink beer with. He is stern, politically tough, humorless."

By 1980—when he defeated Warren Magnuson, Washington's revered, but doddering, senior senator, to win Magnuson's seat in the Senate—no one disliked Slade Gorton more than the leaders of Washington's Indian tribes.

In 1854 AND 1855, Isaac Stevens, the superintendent of Indian affairs for the territory of Washington, negotiated the Treaty of Medicine Creek and the other treaties in which Indians who lived around Puget Sound agreed to move onto reservations. Each treaty included a clause that guaranteed to the members of each tribe "the right of taking fish . . . in common with all citizens of the territory." Throughout the 1960s Bob Satiacum, who in 1966 would open the first smoke shop on the Puyallup Reservation, and other Indian activists repeatedly confronted the state of Washington regarding its regulation of Indian commercial fishermen in a manner that Satiacum and the other activists asserted violated their treaty rights.

In 1970 the U.S. Department of Justice sided with the activists and filed suit against the state of Washington in the U.S. District Court in Seattle. In 1974 District Judge George Bolt issued a decision in which he announced that in each of the treaties he negotiated Isaac Stevens intended the phrase "in common with all citizens of the territory" to give members of the tribes whose headmen had signed their marks on the treaties the right to catch one-half of all of the salmon and steelhead that spawned in rivers that emptied into Puget Sound.

Attorney General Gorton thought Judge Bolt was wrong. He thought Stevens included the phrase "in common with all citizens of the territory" in the treaties simply to assure Indian fishermen that they would have the same fishing rights as non-Indian fishermen. And even if Judge Bolt's decision regarding Stevens's intent was correct, Gorton thought the treaties were "anachronisms" that were "100 years old and out of date."

So, on behalf of the state of Washington, Gorton appealed Judge Bolt's decision, first to the U.S. Court of Appeals for the Ninth Circuit, where he lost, and then to the U.S. Supreme Court, where he lost again when the Court refused to review the decision of the court of appeals. However, in 1978 in *Oliphant v. Suquamish Indian Tribe*, one of the appeals he argued in the U.S. Supreme Court, Gorton persuaded the Court that within the boundaries of their reservations Indian tribes have no criminal jurisdiction over non-Indians.

Gorton also was attorney general when Robert Pirtle, the Seattle attorney who represented tribes whose members had opened smoke shops, filed *Confederated Tribes of the Colville Indian Reservation v. State of Washington*, the lawsuit in which Pirtle hoped to establish that the state of Washington had no authority inside the boundaries of Indian reservations to require smoke shops to collect the state's cigarette tax from their non-Indian customers. In 1978 Pirtle won in the district court. Gorton appealed the decision to the U.S. Supreme Court, personally argued the appeal, and in 1980 won when the Court decided that "the State may validly require the tribal smoke shops to affix tax stamps purchased from the State to individual packages of cigarettes prior to the time of sale to nonmembers of the Tribe" because "principles of federal Indian law, whether stated in terms of preemption, tribal self-government, or otherwise, [do not] authorize Indian tribes thus to market an exemption from state taxation to persons who would normally do their business elsewhere."[25]

Rather than responding to the legal arguments and policy concerns on which his objections to inherent tribal sovereignty were based, throughout the state of Washington, Indian leaders demonized Groton by dismissing him as a racist.

IN NOVEMBER 1985 WHEN she and Marian Horn appeared before the Committee on Interior and Insular Affairs to explain the agreement regarding gambling on Indian reservations the Department of the Interior and the U.S. Department of Justice had negotiated, Victoria Toensing told the committee that "very soon we will offer specific legislation for you." But the Reagan administration did not send Congress a bill until May 1986.

When the administration's bill, which Nevada senators Paul Laxalt and Chic Hecht introduced in the Senate as S. 2557, was referred to the Select Committee on Indian Affairs, Mark Andrews ignored it. But Slade Gorton instructed Deborah Storey, the member of his staff who monitored the activities of the select committee, to write a bill based on the text of S. 2557 for Gorton to introduce during the mark-up of H.R. 1920 as a substitute for the bill Pete Taylor had written for Senator Andrews.

Like S. 2557, the Gorton bill established an American Indian Bingo Commission. In addition to approving management contracts and issuing licenses to tribes that wanted to operate bingo halls, the commission would decide the hours and conditions of play in the halls; the cost of admission; and "the value of the cash or other property that may be, or that shall be required to be, awarded as prizes for bingo," as well as make all of the other major decisions that the management of a bingo hall involved. With respect to all forms of gambling other than bingo, the bill extended "all State laws pertaining to the licensing, regulation, or prohibition of gambling" to "all persons (including Indians and Indian tribes) in Indian country in the same manner and to the same extent as such laws apply elsewhere in the State."

At the meeting the select committee held on September 15 to mark up H.R. 1920, no votes were taken because Arizona senator Barry Goldwater asked for additional time to consider Pete Taylor's bill. So a second meeting was scheduled for September 17. At that meeting, in addition to Mark Andrews and Slade Gorton, six of the seven other members of the select committee were present: Arizona senators Barry Goldwater and Dennis DeConcini, Alaska senator Frank Murkowski, Hawaii senator Daniel Inouye, Montana senator John Melcher, and North Dakota senator Quentin Burdick.

When the discussion turned to how Pete Taylor's bill regulated Class III forms of gambling, Mark Andrews argued that the only difference between authorizing the states to regulate Class III forms of gambling on Indian reservations as Slade Gorton's bill did and the procedure Pete Taylor had invented—which authorized a tribe to request the secretary of the interior to transfer jurisdiction to the state in which the tribe's reservation was located—was that Taylor's approach honored "the old tribal customs" by "deal[ing] with the sensitivities of the tribal councils as independent agents." Gorton responded that Andrews had lost sight "of who it is that is being regulated," because "in both Class II and Class III, we are dealing with forms of gambling in which the overwhelming bulk of the players are not members of the tribe." They are "citizens of the state, which is deprived—in the case of Class II—of any opportunity to regulate." And while it was true that Taylor's bill authorized the states to regulate Class III forms of gambling, the states had "a somewhat shakier right under the Andrews proposal than under mine."

During the desultory back-and-forth discussion that followed Senator DeConcini admitted that he had not read Gorton's bill, and Senator Melcher complained that he did not understand the minutia in Pete Taylor's bill, which he described as "35 pages or 50 pages of stuff" that had been thought up upstairs "in that staff room" in the select committee's suite of offices in the Hart Senate Office Building.

When discussion ended Andrews called for a vote on whether Slade Gorton's bill should be substituted for Pete Taylor's bill, Senators Gorton, Murkowski, Melcher, and Inouye voted yes, and Senators Andrews, Goldwater, and Burdick voted no. When all the votes were counted, however, Slade Gorton lost four votes to five because Andrews voted proxies he had obtained from Dennis DeConcini—who by the time the vote was called had left the mark-up—and South Dakota senator James Abdnor. A majority of the members of the select committee then voted to substitute the text of Pete Taylor's bill for the text of the version of H.R. 1920 that had passed the U.S. House of Representatives. The senators then voted to send H.R. 1920 to the Senate.

Nine days later, Pete Taylor filed the report the Senate rules required in which the select committee explained its version of H.R. 1920.

AS SHE HAD when she testified before the Committee on Interior and Insular Affairs, when Assistant Attorney General Victoria Toensing testified before the select committee and Senator Andrews asked, "What evidence do you have that organized crime has gotten involved in tribal gaming operations," Toensing answered, "Mr. Chairman, I have been testifying for over one year now that we do not see organized crime in Indian gaming at this stage." That answer allowed Pete Taylor to inform the Senate in the select committee's report on H.R. 1920 that "According to the Criminal Division of the Department of Justice, Indian gaming operations currently regulated by tribal governments, with limited federal supervision are not now infiltrated by Organized Crime." The report pointedly did not mention that San Diego County Sheriff John Duffy had told the select committee that, insofar as bingo halls on Indian reservations in southern California were concerned, what Victoria Toensing had told the committee was wrong.

DURING THE THREE weeks that remained before the Ninety-Ninth Congress adjourned, Kansas senator Bob Dole, the Republican majority leader, did not call up H.R. 1920 for debate because any senator may, for any reason, prevent a bill from being brought to the floor by placing a "hold" on the bill. The identity of a senator who places a hold supposedly is secret. But two days after Pete Taylor filed the select committee's report on H.R. 1920, the *Press-Enterprise* in Riverside, California, reported that Slade Gorton, Hawaii senator Daniel Inouye, and Nevada senators Paul Laxalt and Chic Hecht had placed holds on H.R. 1920 because, as Gorton explained to the *Press-Enterprise*, the bill was "dangerously deceptive legislation" that "merely ratifies the status quo and leaves the tribes free to do about what they already are doing."

Over the next two weeks, Pete Taylor wrote a new bill that incorporated a package of amendments to the select committee's version of H.R. 1920 that Mark Andrews hoped would persuade Gorton, Inouye, Laxalt, and Hecht to lift their holds. To try to placate the Nevada senators, the bill amended the definition of Class II gaming to designate card games as a Class III form of gambling that would be subject to state regulation if the games were played on an Indian reservation located in "a state that has a legalized commercial gaming industry and comprehensively regulates such commercial gaming including casino gaming such as roulette and slot machines." But even if that concession had been enough to satisfy Laxalt and Hecht, as a member of his staff told the press, Senator Gorton "is not willing at this point to talk compromise."

In a last-ditch effort to persuade Dole to ignore the holds, Mark Andrews and seven other senators sent Dole and West Virginia senator Robert Byrd, the Democratic minority leader, a letter in which they urged Dole to bring up "H.R. 1920, with amendments by Chairman Andrews" for "immediate consideration by the Senate" because "a significant amount of effort has been undertaken to resolve the issues after mark-up" and "the amendments that are now proposed should adequately resolve all reasonable concerns with this legislation." Dole, however, refused to bring H.R. 1920 to the floor until and unless the holds were lifted. They were not lifted, and on October 18 when the Senate adjourned, H.R. 1920 died.

Slade Gorton, Daniel Inouye, and the Nevada senators each had his own reasons for killing what they thought was a bad bill. But a major reason they placed holds on H.R. 1920 was that, at the time they did so, the conventional wisdom was that there soon might be no reason that Congress needed to pass any bill. Because four months earlier, the U.S. Supreme Court had done what, in 1983, Frank Ducheneaux had feared it might.

9: CABAZON AND MORONGO: NINETY-NINTH CONGRESS

We have ourselves a little gold mine.

JOHN PAUL NICHOLS
Manager, Cabazon Indian Casino

IN SOUTHERN CALIFORNIA, SAN GORGONIO PASS SEPARATES THE BASIN IN which Los Angeles is located from the Coachella Valley on the western end of the desert that runs from the pass east 140 miles to the Colorado River. In 1876 President Ulysses S. Grant withdrew 2,400 (later reduced to 1,400) acres of sun-scorched desert on the eastern end of the Coachella Valley as a reservation for Cahuilla Indians who gathered mesquite beans in the surrounding vicinity.

The reservation, which the Bureau of Indian Affairs (BIA) named Cabazon, was a poor location for Indians to settle at because, as Francisco Estudillo, the local BIA agent, reported in 1894, it had "practically no water." Almost a century later, the situation was the same. Of the twenty-two children and adults the BIA had enrolled to the Cabazon Reservation in 1970, only six lived there.

One of the six was Joe Benitez, a Chemehuevi (rather than a Cahuilla) Indian whose parents had moved onto the Cabazon Reservation in the 1930s. According to Benitez, when he was a boy, the reservation was nothing but "sage brush and rabbits." Until the 1950s, there was no electricity and no running water.

In 1963, the less than one dozen adults enrolled to the Cabazon Reservation elected Benitez chairman of the Cabazon council, the entity with which the BIA dealt with respect to matters affecting the reservation. When he became chairman, the only money the Cabazon council had was a few hundred dollars it received occasionally from the BIA. But as it did for the Seminoles in Florida, Lyndon Johnson's war on poverty began making money available from federal agencies other than the BIA. Some of that new federal money was used to create Riverside–San Bernardino County Indian Health, Inc., a nonprofit corporation that operated medical and dental clinics for low-income Indians in the Coachella Valley, and for which in 1976 Joe Benitez was working as a project manager. As part of his job, that year Benitez attended a training program and met John Philip Nichols.

A PORTLY MAN with a white beard, the fifty-one-year-old Nichols was a self-described "radical" union organizer who, after graduating from the University of Wisconsin with a degree in social work, had worked for the Teamsters Union. But he made no mention of the fact that he had been arrested in Milwaukee in 1959 for mishandling Teamster funds, and in 1964 had been arrested in Washington, D.C., on a fugitive warrant.

It apparently was after his second arrest that Nichols expatriated with his wife, Joann, and five children to South America, where he worked for an evangelical organization that promoted local economic development projects. Nichols said that, after he returned to the United States, in 1972 he earned a doctoral degree in religious education from the Philathon Theological Seminary. Although there is no evidence other than his say-so that he did, like Hunter S. Thompson, Nichols began calling himself "Doctor" Nichols.

In the mid-1970s, Nichols moved to Sarasota, Florida, to work for Pro Plan International, a consulting firm that trained employees of organizations like Riverside–San Bernardino County Indian Health, Inc., about grant writing and government contracting. The world being a small place, in Sarasota Nichols met Osley Saunooke. According to Saunooke, "My kids went to school with his kids. I ran for the Florida House of Representatives when Joann ran for the Sarasota County Charter Review Board. I lost. She won."

Having been impressed during the training program he attended with Nichols's enthusiasm and acumen, in March 1978 Joe Benitez arranged for the Cabazon council to contract with Nichols to write an economic development plan for the reservation and provide "secretarial, bookkeeping and administrative services." Nichols and his wife then moved to Indio.

Through his work with Pro Plan International, Nichols knew that section 8(a) of the Small Business Act gives businesses in which minority groups are the majority owners a preference for contracting with the federal government. For the Cabazon Band of Mission Indians, as the BIA called the Indians who had been enrolled to the Cabazon Reservation, Nichols's first section 8(a) business was the Shaman Corporation. While the band would be the majority owner, the minority owner would be P.N. Associates, a corporation whose shareholders were Nichols and his children and Al Pearlman, an acquaintance of Nichols's who owned a pharmaceutical drug distribution business. The Shaman Corporation would purchase pharmaceutical drugs in bulk that, after they were repackaged at a facility Pearlman would build on the reservation, would be resold to the federal government.

Nothing came of that plan. But a second business Al Pearlman financed initially made money.

IN 1876, THE Cabazon Reservation was an isolated patch of desert. By 1978, however, Interstate 10, the freeway that runs from Los Angeles through San Gregorio Pass and then east to Arizona, touched the southern boundary of the reservation. So the reservation was easily accessible.

According to Osley Saunooke, "When John moved to California, because I was the guy who was doing all the stuff with the Seminoles, we kept in contact. He would call me all the time, sharing ideas back and forth."

Undoubtedly through Saunooke, Nichols learned that B.J. and Ray Turnipseed and Marcellus Osceola were selling untaxed cigarettes on the Seminole Reservation in Hollywood. In January 1979, Nichols flew to Florida and toured Osceola's Trading Post. While there, he asked his twenty-five-year-old son, John Paul Nichols, who was working in Miami, to move to Indio and manage the smoke shop on the Cabazon Reservation his father had decided to open. John Paul agreed to do so because, as he later explained, "I had seen what the Seminoles had been doing with cigarettes."

The Cabazon smoke shop, which P.N. Associates managed, opened in May 1979. According to John Paul Nichols, "Forty days later, we were selling $100,000 worth of cigarettes a week out of a 24-by-60 trailer."

In December 1979, P.N. Associates opened a liquor store on the reservation that sold tax-free alcohol purchased from a distributor in Oklahoma

City. According to John Paul Nichols, "We were going through a semi load of liquor out of this building [which had been built to replace the trailer] a week. It was just amazing!"

P.N. Associates also began selling tax-free cigarettes through a mail order business that John Paul Nichols advertised in publications such as the *New York Post*. He also persuaded *The National Enquirer* to publish a story about the business.

Then, the mail order business, and soon thereafter the smoke shop, imploded.

A FEDERAL LAW called the Jenkins Act imposes criminal penalties on any person who mails cigarettes into a state without providing the state's tax administrator the name and address of each customer so that the administrator can collect the state's cigarette tax. When the U.S. Department of Justice informed the Cabazon Band that for the purposes of the Jenkins Act the band was a "person," the mail order business instantaneously was no longer economically viable.

Then, in June 1980, in its decision in *State of Washington v. Confederated Tribes of the Colville Indian Reservation*, the U.S. Supreme Court ruled that states could require smoke shops to collect the states' cigarette tax from the shops' non-Indian customers. Shortly thereafter, John Paul Nichols informed the Cabazon council that, as a consequence of the *Confederated Tribes* decision, the Board of Equalization, the state agency that collected California's cigarette tax, had "adopted the position that retail sales of cigarettes [on the Cabazon Reservation] are to be phased out."

Soon after the smoke shop and liquor store (which had proven to be a high-volume, but low profit margin, business) closed, John Philip Nichols decided to open another new business.

CALIFORNIA LAW AUTHORIZED municipalities to license poker rooms. In September 1978, the city council of Coachella, the town next door to Indio, passed an ordinance that authorized the council to license two poker rooms. Six months later, Coachella voters repealed the ordinance when they passed a referendum that had been placed on the municipal election ballot by local residents who opposed gambling. But the publicity the referendum generated gave John Philip Nichols the idea of remodeling the building in which the smoke shop and liquor store had been housed into a poker room.

Before Coachella voters repealed the city's licensing ordinance, the local newspaper had reported that an unsuccessful applicant for one of the licenses had been a partnership whose owners were "Leo Durocher, the former major league baseball player and manager who now lives in Palm Springs, Rocco Zangari of Palm Springs, and Dr. Henry Baron, a Sharon, Pennsylvania, resident who also owns a home in the resort city." As John Paul Nichols subsequently told the story:

> Dad and I and [Joe Benitez's half-brother] Art Welmas were sitting around one day and said, "If [the Coachella city council] can do it, why can't we?" It wasn't exactly a rocket scientist's idea. We had the newspaper [article], and the whole intent was to replicate what they were doing. Out of that, Dad or Art wrote a letter to the L.A. Dodgers—we didn't even know where Leo Durocher lived—and we got a phone call a few days later, and Leo said, "I want to bring this guy Rocco down. Let's get together." That's how the whole thing started. . . . Leo was our initial contact. None of us had any experience in the poker-card-room-casino business. . . . We thought Leo Durocher, a huge baseball name, a legend, Hall of Famer, would be a great host. And we thought Rocco, if he's associated with Leo Durocher, was okay.

Rocco Zangari introduced the Nicholses to Tommy Marson, who loaned $50,000 that P.N. Associates used to remodel the building that had housed the smoke shop and liquor store. According to John Paul Nichols, "[We] put drywall up, bought tables, bought chips, bought aprons for the chip girls, bought cards, built a cage, put restrooms in, and we were in the cardroom business."

On the evening of Wednesday, October 15, 1980, Rocco Zangari, who P.N. Associates hired to manage the business, opened the Cabazon Indian Casino, which began hosting poker games twenty-four hours a day, seven days a week. Three nights later, the Indio Police Department raided the casino and issued citations for illegal gambling to ninety-eight patrons and arrested four others.

Chief of Police Sam Cross ordered the raid because, in 1970, the city of Indio, which prohibited gambling, had annexed the portion of the Cabazon Reservation on which the building that housed the poker room was located. By the night of the raid, Cross also had run a background check on John Philip Nichols and had decided he was a con man and a grifter. After conducting its own investigation, the *Los Angeles Times* agreed with Cross when it reported:

> Nichols had been involved with Indian tribes in the past as a grant seeker with a company known as Pro Plan International. One former client, the Gila River Indians in Arizona, sent a letter to dozens of tribes in the West warning that they had been duped by him. An investigation by the U.S. Indian Health Service charged that Nichols' company had been involved in the collapse of health programs at four Indian centers and that Nichols' company kept most of the grant money it helped obtain. Charles Bunch, head of the health service in California, said Nichols had been barred from contract work for the health service and that he had called for an FBI investigation of Nichols' company.

Sam Cross also knew Rocco Zangari. The forty-seven-year-old Zangari was a member of the crew Jimmy Caci, a capo in the Los Angeles Mafia family who lived in Palm Springs, supervised. In 1983, the *Miami Herald* would report that the California Department of Justice had identified Zangari as "a onetime mob enforcer and former associate of the Stefano Magaddino crime family of Buffalo, New York."

In 1987 Zangari and Caci would be named with Peter Milano, the boss of the Los Angeles family, in an eighteen-count racketeering indictment . They all pled guilty. In 1998, Zangari and Caci would be indicted in Las Vegas with Carmen Milano, the underboss of the Los Angeles family, Zangari for having sold counterfeit travelers checks to an undercover FBI agent. He again pled guilty.

In addition to Rocco Zangari, Tommy Marson was on the premises when the Indio Police Department raided the Cabazon Indian Casino and was issued a citation.

• • •

A CORPULENT SEVENTY-year-old Polish immigrant whose real name was Thomas Marsonak Dolowski, Marson was an associate of the Gambino and Genovese Mafia families. His arrest record went back to 1928 and included a conviction in 1950 in Detroit for counterfeiting, for which he served five years in the federal penitentiary at Leavenworth, Kansas. After his release, Marson became a salesman for Vulcan Industries, a company that arranged for homeowners to obtain fraudulent loans to finance remodeling projects.

In the 1960s, Marson moved, first to Queens and then to Scarsdale, New York, where he became president of the Vulcan Basement and Waterproofing Company. By the mid-1970s Marson was a millionaire, although his FBI file does not detail precisely how he became one.

At that point, Marson moved to Rancho Mirage, an affluent resort community in the Coachella Valley next door to Palm Springs, where he lived with his wife, who was almost forty years his junior, and their daughters in a home on the sixteenth fairway of the Tamarisk Country Club, around the corner from the compound in which Frank Sinatra lived and with whom Marson was acquainted.

In 1978 Marson was indicted for stock and bankruptcy fraud for having participated with members of the Gambino and Genovese families in a conspiracy to skim the Westchester Premier Theater in Tarrytown, New York, at which Sinatra and other A-List entertainers performed until the skim forced the corporation that owned the theater into bankruptcy. Marson pled guilty and spent another year in prison.

WHEN HE RETIRED from the Senate, James Abourezk joined a law firm in Washington, D.C. When John Philip Nichols went to Florida to tour Osceola's Trading Post, he stopped in Washington, D.C., on his way back to California and hired Abourezk to represent the Cabazon Band.

In May 1980 in Fort Lauderdale, District Judge Norman Roettger had issued the decision in *Seminole Tribe of Florida v. Butterworth* in which he announced that Broward County Sheriff Bob Butterworth had no jurisdiction on the Seminole Reservation in Hollywood to require the Seminole Tribe to comply with Florida's bingo law. By October when the Indio Police Department raided the Cabazon Indian Casino, the West Publishing Company had published Judge Roettger's decision in its advance sheets to which most law firms subscribed.

Several days after the raid, Glenn Feldman, an attorney who worked for Abourezk's law firm, tried to replicate the *Seminole Tribe of Florida v. Butterworth* lawsuit by filing *Cabazon Band of Mission Indians v. City of Indio* in the U.S. District Court in Los Angeles. The lawsuit was assigned to Judge Laughlin Waters, who knew nothing about federal Indian law. As a consequence, at the first hearing, when Glenn Feldman presented the legal arguments regarding inherent tribal sovereignty that Judge Roettger had found persuasive, according to Feldman, "Judge Waters thought I was completely out of my mind and denied my motion [for a temporary restraining order]." Two weeks later, however, Waters had a change of heart and ordered the Indio Police Department not to interfere with the operation of the Cabazon Indian Casino until he decided the merits of Feldman's lawsuit.

On May 4, 1981, Judge Waters issued his decision on the merits, and Feldman lost. Waters ruled that the city of Indio had lawfully annexed the portion of the Cabazon Reservation on which the building that housed the Cabazon Indian Casino was located, and he rejected the arguments regarding inherent tribal sovereignty that Judge Roettger had accepted.

Feldman then asked Judge Waters for a stay, which Feldman described as "a bizarre legal device where we asked the judge who had just ruled against us and said we were not entitled to have the card club remain open, to give us a ruling which allowed it to remain open while that decision was appealed." To his surprise, Waters issued the stay, because by then Feldman had persuaded him that, if he ordered the Cabazon Indian Casino to close its doors, seventy employees would lose their jobs, the Cabazon Band's share of the profit would not be available to pay the premiums on a health insurance policy the Cabazon council had purchased for members of the band, and the band would not be able to pay back the money it had borrowed to remodel the building in which the poker room was located and then operate the business. Art Welmas told the press that debt now totaled $250,000.

The problem with Judge Waters's concern that the Cabazon Band needed the money the poker room was earning was that the Cabazon Indian Casino had been losing money. But why was a business that seemingly should have been profitable unprofitable? By the time Judge Waters issued his decision, a member of the Cabazon Band had discovered that the reason was that John Philip Nichols and Rocco Zangari had been skimming.

ALMOST SIX FEET tall and weighing 250 pounds, Fred Alvarez, who was thirty-two-years-old, had shoulder-length black hair and tattoos, and wore a Fu Manchu mustache, was a physically imposing figure.

The BIA had enrolled Alvarez's father, Leroy, to the Cabazon Reservation, even though he lived in Susanville, a logging town in the northeastern corner of California more than 500 miles north of the Coachella Valley. And because Leroy was enrolled, the BIA enrolled his son.

Ray Couso, who grew up with Fred Alvarez in Susanville, remembers his boyhood friend as "easygoing," except when he was competing in sports at which he excelled. A high school football star and wrestling champion who attended Utah State University on a football scholarship, in 1971 Alvarez signed a contract with the Calgary Stampeders to play in the Canadian Football League. According to a press account, he was cut from the team "after suffering a badly sprained ankle and knee problems." But according to John Philip Nichols's biographer, Alvarez said the Stampeders let him go after he was caught selling drugs.

Nichols's biographer also said Alvarez, who rode a Harley, was a Hells Angel. He was not. But in 2008, a friend who said he smoked marijuana and snorted cocaine with Alvarez said they both had ridden with the Mescaleros motorcycle gang.

After he was cut by the Stampeders, Alvarez worked construction in Truckee, the resort town in the Sierra Nevadas on the north end of Lake Tahoe to which his parents had moved from Susanville. He also worked weekends as a bouncer at a bar, which is where in 1978 he met a waitress named Lynn Lamm, who by late that year was pregnant.

By then, the BIA had subdivided 466 of the Cabazon Reservation's 1,400 acres into forty-acre parcels called allotments that the BIA gave to enrolled members of the Cabazon Band. Fred Alvarez received an allotment, and, because he thought "things were starting to happen down there," he convinced Lamm to move with him to Thousand Palms, a community on Interstate 10 west of the reservation. After their son was born,

Lamm ended her relationship with Alvarez and returned north, although they remained in cordial communication.

When Lamm left, Alvarez moved to Hawaii to work a construction job. He then returned to the Coachella Valley and rented a small house with no air conditioning in a run-down neighborhood in Rancho Mirage. In October 1980, when the Cabazon Indian Casino opened, P.N. Associates hired Alvarez as the poker room's chief of security. It was on the job that Alvarez discovered the Cabazon Indian Casino was being skimmed.

TWO YEARS EARLIER, Joe Benitez, the chairman of the Cabazon council, had been instrumental in persuading the council to hire Nichols. He soon regretted having done so. But when Benitez attempted to have the council rid the reservation of Nichols, in November 1978 Nichols orchestrated an election in which, by a vote of 6 to 1, the adult members of the Cabazon Band elected Benitez's half-brother, Art Welmas, to replace Benitez as chairman. The members of the Welmas-led council then accused Benitez of financial misconduct and passed a resolution that called for him to be sanctioned for "failure to carry out his chairmanship responsibilities" To defend himself against the charges, Benitez hired Stephen Rios, an attorney whose law office was in San Juan Capistrano, a beach town south of Los Angeles.

At the meeting at which Joe Benitez was ousted as chairman of the Cabazon council, Alvarez sided with Nichols and Welmas. But by the time he realized Nichols was skimming, he had realigned himself with Benitez. Early in June 1981, Joe Benitez, Fred Alvarez, and a member of the Cabazon Band named William Callaway met with Stephen Rios. According to Benitez, at that meeting Alvarez told Rios that money was being skimmed and "the Mafia was connected with some of the people that were working inside the casino." When Alvarez said he wanted to file a lawsuit against the individuals involved in the skim, Rios told him, "You have no proof. I would need evidence."

Several weeks later, Benitez phoned Rios to report that Alvarez had the evidence. What it was is not known, but according to Lynn Lamm, with whom he remained in touch, Alvarez told her he had discovered that a double set of books was being kept at the poker room. Before he rang off, Benitez made an appointment for Benitez, Alvarez, and Callaway to meet with Rios on July 1.

That morning, Joe Benitez and William Callaway arrived at Fred Alvarez's house in Rancho Mirage at 6:00 a.m. to pick up Alvarez for the drive to meet Rios in San Juan Capistrano. In the backyard, they discovered Alvarez and two friends, Patty Castro and Ralph Boger, sprawled on the patio. Each had been shot to death with a single gunshot to the head. There was no evidence of a struggle, Alvarez's and Bolger's wallets were untouched, and the neighbors had not heard gunshots, which suggests that the .38-caliber handgun the shooter used might have been equipped with a silencer.

The gunman who murdered Fred Alvarez, Patty Castro, and Ralph Boger has never been publicly identified, and the crimes remain unsolved. Who ordered the killings and why?

THE INDIO *DAILY NEWS* reported that, beginning three weeks before he was murdered, Alvarez met five times with the paper's editor and one of its reporters to urge them to investigate the "mismanagement of tribal monies." During those meetings, he twice told the editor that, because he "knew too much . . . they're going to kill me."

The investigation into who "they" were quickly went cold and stayed cold until 1984, when a twenty-seven-year-old U.S. Army veteran named Jimmy Hughes, who was working for P.N. Associates at the Cabazon Indian Casino when the Alvarez murders were committed, told his story. *Spy* magazine reported that the story Hughes told was that

> after the murders, Nichols and two of his sons, John Paul and Mark, counted out $5,000 in front of him and told him to deliver the money to two men in Idyllwild, a nearby town. The money, Hughes said, was the balance owed for the murder of Alvarez.
>
> After Hughes spoke to the police, he was interviewed by the FBI and offered a spot in the witness-protection program, which he refused. Instead, he went on the run, hiding out until a deal could be arranged with the Riverside County district attorney, who gave Hughes immunity.

That account differs from the story the *Los Angeles Times* reported, which was that Hughes said, "[H]e had been instructed in [John Philip] Nichols' presence to take $25,000 to the mountain community of Idyllwild in the summer of 1981 and to give the money to a man there as partial payment for the Alvarez killings."

Whatever its particulars, Hughes told his story to a Riverside County grand jury. But no indictments were issued. Hughes, who had become a Born Again Christian, then moved to Central America, where he founded Jimmy Hughes Ministries, which operates a drug rehabilitation clinic, a school, and children's home in Honduras.

In 2008, when Hughes returned to the United States to attend an evangelical event in Fresno, California, Ralph Boger's daughter, Rachel Begley, and Fred Alvarez and Lynn Lamm's son, Mikel Alvarez, confronted him. During the conversation, which Begley surreptitiously videotaped, Hughes told Begley and Alvarez "your parents got killed in a Mafia hit." Hughes also claims to have been "a professional hit man for the Mafia" who had a "$30,000 a month cocaine habit," and that until he became Born Again he consumed a "gallon of liquor" a day. Such assertions, which reek of fabulism, may explain why, after listening to Hughes testify, the Riverside County grand jury did not issue any indictments.

Four months after the Alvarez murders, John Philip Nichols and Rocco Zangari had a falling out. In November 1981, Nichols fired Zangari, and John Paul Nichols began managing the poker room. A month later, the Cabazon Indian Casino filed for bankruptcy to discharge debts totaling $567,577.*

Throughout the bankruptcy, the poker room stayed open.

IN DECEMBER 1982, A three-judge panel of the U.S. Court of Appeals for the Ninth Circuit issued a decision in which it announced that Judge Waters had been wrong that the city of Indio had lawfully annexed the land within the boundaries of the Cabazon Reservation on which the

---

*Judge Waters assumed the Cabazon Band owned the Cabazon Indian Casino. The poker room was actually owned by a partnership that, in addition to Art Welmas and other members of the Cabazon Band, included John Paul Nichols. According to the bankruptcy court, in its business dealings, the Cabazon Indian Casino "regard[ed] itself as an entity independent from the Cabazon Band of Mission Indians."

Cabazon Indian Casino was located. Because the annexation was invalid, Sam Cross and his officers had had no authority to conduct their raid. The decision was a victory for Glenn Feldman, but two months later the Cabazon Indian Casino was raided again; this time by the Riverside County Sheriff's Department, whose deputies issued citations to thirty-one customers and employees for violating the county's ordinance that prohibited gambling.

In response to the raid, Feldman filed a lawsuit against Riverside County in the U.S. District Court in Los Angeles, where the lawsuit again was assigned to Judge Waters. In the lawsuit Feldman had filed against the city of Indio, Waters had rejected his arguments regarding inherent tribal sovereignty. But this time, Feldman seemingly had a slam-dunk case. The week after the three-judge panel issued its decision in *Cabazon Band of Mission Indians v. City of Indio*, a different three-judge panel of the U.S. Court of Appeals for the Ninth Circuit had issued its decision in *Barona Group of the Capitan Grande Band of Mission Indians v. Duffy*, the lawsuit Harry Hertzberg had filed. That panel had accepted Judge Roettger's reasoning regarding inherent tribal sovereignty in the decision he had issued in the *Seminole Tribe of Florida v. Butterworth* lawsuit.

Armed with that "very strong precedent," Feldman persuaded Judge Waters to issue a temporary restraining order that required the Riverside County Sheriff's Department to allow the Cabazon Indian Casino to stay open. In May 1983, Waters replaced the temporary restraining order with a preliminary injunction. And, in October, he consolidated Feldman's lawsuit with a lawsuit an Indian who lived on the Morongo Reservation forty-three miles west of the Cabazon Reservation had filed.

In 1876 and 1877, presidents Ulysses S. Grant and Rutherford B. Hayes withdrew 46,640 acres of federal land in San Gorgonio Pass as a reservation for a group of Cahuilla and Serrano Indians who had settled near a creek on the north side of the pass. By 1915, the reservation had been reduced to 32,000 acres and named Morongo in honor of John Morongo, a Serrano Indian who in 1892 the BIA had appointed to head the detachment of Indian police that maintained order on the reservation.

In 1919, the BIA subdivided 1,489 of the reservation's 32,000 acres into five- and six-acre allotments. By 1927 sixty-two families were growing apricots, almonds, peaches, prunes, grapes, and hay on their allotments. Many raised cattle. And the men worked for wages on the surrounding ranches and fruit farms.

Fifty years later, employment opportunities on the Morongo Reservation were not that different from what they had been in 1927, except that the reservation now bordered Interstate 10, the freeway from Los Angeles that runs past the Cabazon Reservation. To take advantage of the automobile traffic, by 1980 a smoke shop had opened on the Morongo Reservation. In November of that year, the building in which the smoke shop was housed was destroyed in a fire that had been intentionally set. At the time of the fire, the manager of the smoke shop was a thirty-seven-year-old Indian named Clive "Sonny" Miller, who owned one of the allotments.*

Two years later when Steve Whilden began traveling from reservation to reservation negotiating management agreements for the construction of bingo halls, he met Sonny Miller. By then, Whilden also had met Michael Frechette and Allen Arbogast. According to Frechette, "Steve said, 'You guys go out to Palm Springs.' So we went out and met Sonny and signed an agreement to do the bingo and a casino." Also according to Frechette, during one of the meetings he had with Miller, he brought along a "fat guy" who bragged he was a friend of Frank Sinatra's.

The management agreement Frechette signed with Sonny Miller on behalf of the New England Entertainment Company (NEEC) required NEEC to make an up-front $50,000 payment. But not only did Frechette and Arbogast not have $50,000, Frechette was trying to raise the million dollars NEEC needed to build the bingo hall on the Shakopee Mdewakanton Sioux Community's reservation at Prior Lake, Minnesota.

It was at that point that Whilden introduced Frechette to Walter Justus, a real estate developer from Indianapolis who had a home in Fort Lauderdale. The arrangement Frechette worked out with Justus was that Justus would finance construction of the bingo hall at Prior Lake. In return, Frechette and Aborgast would let Justus take over the management agreement Frechette had signed with Sonny Miller to build and manage a bingo

---

*Miller was best known locally for fighting pit bulls. In 1990, when Riverside County Sheriff's Department deputies raided Miller's house on the Morongo Reservation, they discovered the garage had been outfitted to stage dog fights, found thirty-seven dogs, and arrested Miller for possession of narcotics.

hall on Miller's allotment. But instead of financing construction of the bingo hall at Prior Lake, Justus negotiated his own agreement with Miller and, according to Frechette, as a consequence of Justus's duplicity, "We lost the Morongo contract."

Walter Justus then constructed a 1,400-seat bingo hall on Sonny Miller's allotment, which he hired David Ingenito, who had been working at the bingo hall Skip Weisman was managing for Seminole Management Associates on the Seminole Reservation in Hollywood, Florida, to manage. When he came west, Ingenito brought along his brother, Robert. There also may have been someone else who had worked at the bingo hall on the Seminole Reservation in Hollywood involved in opening the bingo hall on Sonny Miller's allotment.

AT THE TIME the hall was under construction, Myles Anderberg was remodeling the community center on the Barona Reservation into a bingo hall. According to Anderberg,

> Joe Welch, the chairman of the Barona Tribal Council, came to me and said he had had a telephone call from a guy named Sonny Miller at the Morongo Tribe up in Riverside, and Sonny wanted a pow-wow with Joe because he understood Barona was about to open a bingo hall, and they were going to get screwed by the white folks. So Miller wanted to tip Joe off on how to handle them.

When Welch, his wife Myrtle, and a Barona Indian named Shirley Curo drove up to the Morongo Reservation to meet with Miller, Anderberg went along disguised as a Barona Indian who Welch introduced to Miller as "Mike." To reduce the chances Miller would notice he was not an Indian, Anderberg mumbled he was hungover and feigned nodding off. Here is his recollection of what happened next:

> I was astounded at how unsavory Sonny Miller was. He said he had been involved in a number of scams. He boasted about having been in jail. It was strictly Indian-to-Indian talk. "Here's what you should do because these white sons-of-bitches are going to screw you." He urged Joe Welch to get as much cash up front as possible. I was sur-

prised at how vitriolic Sonny Miller was about non-Indians. During interruptions that happened when other people would come and go, I would mumble questions to Joe, Myrtle, or Shirley that they should ask Miller. The answers Sonny Miller came up with were pretty hateful. He hated non-Indians.

After three-quarters of an hour, Sonny brought the white guy into the meeting who he said was going to manage his bingo hall. The guy said he had been involved with charity bingo all his life. He was in his mid-forties. A very sleazy character. He boasted about knowing how to scam bingo games. How to cheat at them. How to skim. He bragged about having spent time in jail. And he hated Catholics. He said that the Catholic churches had dominated bingo and that they all were a bunch of pious bloodsuckers.

Indian Mike just kept snoring over in the corner. This guy went through all he was going to do. How you can skim money and weight the wheel of fortune that you spin around. If you put the weight on a certain number, and you control who's got the ticket for that number, it'll come up. But you've got to change it. Don't keep the same number all the time. All the things Jeff Cooper [the expert on bingo Anderberg had hired to help him set up the bingo hall on the Barona Reservation] had told me about the way you cheat in bingo.

WHEN RIVERSIDE COUNTY Sheriff Bernard Clark found out Sonny Miller was planning to open a bingo hall that would offer games played in violation of California's bingo law, he had his deputies tell Miller that, when the hall opened, it would be raided, and he would be arrested. In response, Miller and Walter Justus hired an attorney who, on February 17, 1983, filed a lawsuit against Riverside County in the U.S. District Court in Los Angeles. The lawsuit was assigned to Judge Waters.

THE SAME WEEK Waters granted Glenn Feldman's motion for a temporary restraining order against Riverside County, he denied a motion for a temporary restraining order that Miller and Justus's attorney had filed. His reason was that, unlike the Cabazon Indian Casino, which Waters thought was owned by the Cabazon Band, Indian Village Bingo, as Miller and Justus had named their bingo hall, was a private business of "no general benefit" to the Morongo Band. After Waters refused to issue a restraining order, the only way Walter Justus could prevent Sheriff Clark's deputies from raiding Indian Village Bingo was to lease the hall to the Morongo Band of Mission Indians and then negotiate an agreement that would allow the Ingenito brothers to operate the hall for a percentage of the profit as Justus's management fee.

Walter Justus and the Morongo council negotiated an agreement, which the members of the Morongo Band approved by a vote of 150 to 149. A week later, Indian Village Bingo opened and, as the bingo halls on the Seminole and Barona Reservations had been, was an immediate success.

The grand opening attracted eight hundred customers. Open seven nights a week, players paid a $45 admission to play twenty-six bingo games for jackpots that collectively paid out $20,000. In December, a single jackpot paid $48,000. After visiting Indian Village Bingo, a newspaper reporter reported that

> Since the parlor opened on April 30, an average of a thousand players a night have come from as far away as Los Angeles, San Diego and Calexico [a town on the Mexican border east of San Diego] for the chance to win bingo jackpots that routinely exceed $1,000 and have gone as high as $81,000.

> For those players who have a hard time keeping up with the relentless pace—a new number is called every 15 seconds—seven giant computerized boards display all the numbers called during the game in progress. For deaf players, 11 television screens flash the last number called. For blind players, electronic Braille bingo boards are on the way. . . . For the faint-hearted and light-headed, there are wheelchairs, oxygen tanks and first-aid kits.

Indian Village Bingo made so much money so quickly that within eight months of opening night, Walter Justus had recouped his entire $1.7 million investment. From that point forward, Justus's profits would be exorbitant because, while the management agreement he negotiated gave the Morongo Band 51 percent of the profit, it also provided that after the band received $500,000 during a calendar year, its share would be reduced to 5 percent. And before the profit was calculated, Sonny Miller would be paid a management fee, plus $876,000 a year for leasing the land on his allotment on which the bingo hall had been built.

When Walter Justus refused to renegotiate those lopsided terms, the Morongo council voted to terminate its management agreement with Justus, close Indian Village Bingo, and find an investor who would finance the construction of a bingo hall for the Morongo Band at a location closer to Interstate 10 than Sonny Miller's allotment. In response, Justus announced that he had a binding contract and intended to "continue operating on the same routine basis as [Indian Village Bingo] has been operating." But on the day before the day in February 1984 that the council had announced it would close Indian Village Bingo, Sonny Miller preemptively locked the bingo hall's doors and barricaded the parking lot.* Several months later, the Morongo council found an investor, a Korean businessman from Los Angeles named Dong Choi.

HARRY HERTZBERG HAD wanted the management agreement for the new bingo hall on the Morongo Reservation. Then Dong Choi invited Rocco Passanante to a meeting at the Beverly Wilshire Hotel.

When he arrived, Passanante found a "huge Japanese guy with tattoos" standing in front of the door to Choi's suite. Inside the suite was another Japanese bodyguard of similar bulk. According to Passanante, Choi asked him to the meeting to tell him to tell Hertzberg to stay away from Morongo because if he disregarded the advice, "We're going to kill him."

Passanante passed along the message and Hertzberg had no further contact with the Morongo Band. In May 1984, Dong Choi signed a management agreement in which the CBA Development Company, the management company Choi created, agreed to build a new bingo hall on the Morongo Reservation in exchange for the right to manage the hall for five years.

---

*After closing Indian Village Bingo, Miller found a new partner to replace Walter Justus, a professional bingo hall manager named Frank Rose. The Morongo Band filed a lawsuit to prevent Rose from reopening Miller's hall. During the trial that resulted in a court order prohibiting Rose from reopening the hall it was revealed that during the nine months Indian Village Bingo had operated, Rocco Zangari and Tommy Marson had "hung out" at the hall.

As Indian Village Bingo had been, the hall the CBA Development Company opened in October 1984 was an immediate success. One evening in February 1985, 2,300 players paid admission to try to win $1,000 jackpots. Three months later, that attendance record was broken when half an hour after the doors opened 2,700 players had jammed into the hall and another 400 were turned away.

WHILE THE CONFLICT regarding the competing bingo halls on the Morongo Reservation was being sorted out, the lawsuits Glenn Feldman and Sonny Miller had filed against Riverside County, which Judge Waters had consolidated, were proceeding with the Morongo Band having replaced Miller as the plaintiff in the second lawsuit.

As Glenn Feldman had predicted, in December 1984 when Judge Waters issued his decision on the merits of the consolidated lawsuits, he ruled that the decision the three-judge panel of the U.S. Court of Appeals for the Ninth Circuit had issued in the *Barona Group of the Capitan Grande Band of Mission Indians v. Duffy* lawsuit was the controlling precedent. He then issued an injunction that prohibited the Riverside County Sheriff's Department from interfering with the operation of the Cabazon Indian Casino— and the 500-seat bingo hall the Cabazon Band by then had opened across the parking lot from the poker room—and the bingo hall the CBA Development Company was managing on the Morongo Reservation.

Riverside County appealed Waters' decision. In April 1986, a three-judge panel of the U.S. Court of Appeals for the Ninth Circuit issued a decision in which the panel agreed with Judge Waters that it was "bound by the precedent established in *Barona* which is factually and legally indistinguishable from the case at bar." To get to that result, the panel had to explain away *Rice v. Rehner*, the decision the U.S. Supreme Court had issued six months after the *Barona* decision was issued. In *Rice v. Rehner*, the Court had decided that the state of California could enforce its alcohol control laws on the Pala reservation, in part because history instructed that Indian tribes had no inherent authority to regulate the sale of alcohol.

The members of the three-judge panel that decided Riverside County's appeal avoided deciding whether the Cabazon and Morongo Bands had inherent authority to operate bingo halls and a poker room whose customers were non-Indians by misconstruing the *Rice v. Rehner* decision. According to the panel:

> The focus in determining whether a tribal tradition exists should . . . be on whether the tribe is engaged in a traditional governmental function, not whether it historically engaged in a particular activity. [By operating their bingo halls and the Cabazon Band its poker room, the Cabazon and Morongo Bands] are engaged in the traditional governmental function of raising revenue. They are exercising their inherent sovereign governmental authority.

Riverside County immediately asked the U.S. Supreme Court to review the panel's decision.

In 1982, when Broward County Sheriff Bob Butterworth asked the U.S. Supreme Court to review the decision of the three-judge panel of the U.S. Court of Appeals for the Fifth Circuit in the *Seminole Tribe of Florida v. Butterworth* lawsuit, Sheriff Butterworth had done so on his own. And in 1983, when San Diego County Sheriff John Duffy asked the Court to review the decision of the three-judge panel of the U.S. Court of Appeals for the Ninth Circuit in the *Barona Group of the Capitan Grande Band of Mission Indians v. Duffy* lawsuit, Sheriff Duffy also had done so on his own. By 1986, however, the situation had changed. Indian tribes now were operating bingo halls and card rooms on 108 reservations in twenty states that were collectively grossing more than $100 million annually.

So unlike Sheriffs Butterworth and Duffy, Riverside County did not file its request with the U.S. Supreme Court on its own. Rudolph Corona, the deputy attorney general at the California Department of Justice responsible for dealing with the Indian gambling issue, thought the *Barona Group* decision had been wrongly decided. And even if it had been correctly decided, he thought the decision had been superseded by the U.S. Supreme Court's decision in *Rice v. Rehner*. So Corona asked Judge Waters to allow the state of California to join Riverside County as a defendant in the consolidated *Cabazon and Morongo Bands* lawsuit.

When Judge Waters granted the request, Corona arranged for Deputy Attorney General Roderick Walston to take over the case. Having represented the state of California before the U.S. Supreme Court in five previous cases, according to Walston, "I was brought in because I had a lot of Supreme Court experience."

Because, according to Walston, he "had a lot of contacts in the offices of the various attorneys general in other states," when the three-judge panel of the U.S. Court of Appeals for the Ninth Circuit issued the decision in which it affirmed Judge Water's decision, Walston began calling his contacts. As a consequence, when he filed the state of California and Riverside County's request with the U.S. Supreme Court asking the Court to review the panel's decision, attorneys general from twenty other states filed briefs as *amici curiae* (friends of the court) in which they urged the U.S. Supreme Court to grant the request.

On June 6, 1986, the Court did so. Why? According to Glenn Feldman, "Amicus briefs make some difference. But my feeling is that the time just became ripe. In 1982 and 1983, gambling on Indian reservations seemed like a local issue. By 1986 it had become a national issue."

Two WEEKS AFTER the U.S. Supreme Court agreed to review the three-judge panel's decision in *California v. Cabazon and Morongo Bands of Mission Indians*, the Select Committee on Indian Affairs held the only hearing it would hold on H.R. 1920. As has been discussed, the hearing was conducted principally by Pete Taylor, the staff director.

When he testified at the hearing, Glenn Feldman, who would represent the Cabazon and Morongo Bands before the U.S. Supreme Court, pointedly told Taylor that it would be a "serious mistake" for the select committee to "defer action on the pending legislation while the Supreme Court acts," because doing so "would represent a disservice to the tribes that are engaged in gaming." What he left unsaid—but what Taylor and everyone else in the hearing room understood—was that the "disservice" delay risked was the likelihood that the Court would rule that the state of California (and by inference all other states) had authority to enforce its (and their) gambling laws on Indian reservations. As Feldman later described his view at the time, "I think everybody felt in their heart of hearts that the reason the Court took the case was to reverse it." And according to Frank Ducheneaux, "In the minds of a lot of Indian people . . . we *knew* the only reason the Court would take this case . . . was to overrule not only *Cabazon*, but also to overturn *Seminole v. Butterworth* and *Barona* while they were at it." (emphasis in the original)

Since an adverse decision from the U.S. Supreme Court was an outcome that Senator Mark Andrews, the chairman of the select committee, (and Pete Taylor) wanted to prevent, after the select committee reported H.R. 1920 to the Senate, Andrews proposed amending the bill in ways he hoped would persuade Slade Gorton, Daniel Inouye, and Nevada senators Paul Laxalt and Chic Hecht to remove their holds. When that failed, Andrews urged Bob Dole, the Republican majority leader, to bring H.R. 1920 to the Senate floor despite the holds.

When Dole refused to do so, the Senate adjourned, and H.R. 1920 died, the fate of gambling on Indian reservations seemingly was sealed. Both the proponents and the opponents of gambling on Indian reservations assumed that when the U.S. Supreme Court issued its decision in *California v. Cabazon and Morongo Bands of Mission Indians*, the Court would reverse the decision of the three-judge panel of the U.S. Court of Appeals for the Ninth Circuit.

But four months later, the U.S. Supreme Court would demonstrate to Slade Gorton and the other senators whose holds had killed H.R. 1920 the continued validity of the ancient Chinese curse: "May your fondest wish come true."

10: CABAZON AND MORONGO: ONE HUNDREDTH CONGRESS

> On February 25, 1987, the Supreme Court issued its ruling in *Cabazon* and, as the old expression goes, "All hell broke loose."
>
> SEN. DANIEL INOUYE, Chairman,
> Select Committee on Indian Affairs

WHEN RONALD REAGAN DEFEATED JIMMY CARTER IN THE 1980 PRESidential election, Reagan's coattails were long enough for the Republican Party to take control of the U.S. Senate. But three weeks after the Ninety-Ninth Congress adjourned, Republican candidates lost twenty of thirty-four Senate elections in the November 1986 elections, and the Democratic Party regained control. As a consequence, in January 1987 when the One Hundredth Congress convened, the senior Democratic member of each Senate committee became the committee's new chairman.

The senior Democratic member of the Select Committee on Indian Affairs was Montana senator John Melcher. But Melcher, who also was the senior Democratic member of the Select Committee on Aging, decided to become chairman of that committee. So Hawaii senator Daniel Inouye, the second most senior Democrat, became chairman of the Select Committee on Indian Affairs.

A significant number of Inouye's constituents were of indigenous Polynesian descent. But they were not "Indians," and they were not eligible for services and health care benefits that the Bureau of Indian Affairs (BIA) and the Indian Health Service provided. Having no reason to be interested in Indians, in 1979 Inouye had joined the Select Committee on Indian Affairs only as a favor to West Virginia senator Robert Byrd, the Democratic majority leader, when Byrd could not find any other senator who was willing to serve. According to Inouye,

When I became a member, I knew absolutely nothing about Indians. . . . If you had asked me, 'Name three Indian leaders,' I would have said Sitting Bull, because most people know Sitting Bull. He's from Hollywood. And maybe Geronimo—he's the bad Indian in Hollywood. And the other one is Tonto. Tonto was the best known Indian in America.

So, according to Inouye, when he became chairman of the select committee, "I had no idea where I should begin or what legislation was important, and that's when I met Patricia Zell."

Short, smart, intellectually energetic, and committed to the Native American cause as she saw it, Patricia Zell, who is of Arapaho and Navajo descent, had been a member of the staff of the American Indian Policy Review Commission (AIPRC). After graduating from Georgetown University Law School in 1982, she joined the select committee as a staff attorney; which was her position when Inouye promoted her to chief counsel.

Over the next twenty-three-years, Patricia Zell would become one of Daniel Inouye's closest confidants, and insofar as his role as chairman of the select committee was concerned, his alter ego. According to Arizona senator Dennis DeConcini, a member of the select committee for eight of the years Zell served as either chief counsel or staff director, "She was a pistol. Really good. Tough as can be. And she was smart, and she did really want to do something for Native Americans." And DeConcini and the other members of the select committee understood that her relationship with the chairman was such that when Patricia Zell spoke, "You knew that was Inouye talking."

Since he knew next to nothing about the work of the committee he now chaired, Inouye asked his new chief counsel to give him a tutorial on federal Indian policy. She began by giving Inouye three books. According to Inouye,

All three were on Indian massacres. I had no idea as to the treatment that Indians had received throughout the years. So help me. I'd been a United States senator. All I knew was what Hollywood had taught me: Indians were sinister, Indians were cruel, Indians scalped, Indians stole, and Indians got drunk. And when I read about those massacres by the U.S. government, I just couldn't believe what I was reading. . . . The more I looked, the more I got horrified. And I got angry.

As the popularity of films such as *Dances with Wolves* and books such as Dee Brown's *Bury My Heart at Wounded Knee* (which since its publication in 1970 has never been out of print) demonstrate, the story of the mistreatment to which Indians were subjected during the eighteenth and nineteenth centuries remains one of the most emotionally powerful narratives in American popular culture.

Captured by that narrative, under Patricia Zell's tutelage, Daniel Inouye quickly became as committed to the Native American cause as Zell was, and he gave the select committee's new chief counsel and the attorneys she supervised a blank check to write—and in his name try to persuade the Senate to pass—whatever bills would, in their judgment, make the world a better place for Indians. As Patricia Zell would remember years later, "He [Inouye] really got fired up from the very beginning. We [the staff of the select committee] were just like horses let out of the gate . . . for all of us who were sitting on the committee, wishing and hoping and praying that we could do more for Indian country, it was like carte blanche."

WHEN THE MEMBERS of the select committee marked up H.R. 1920 during the Ninety-Ninth Congress, Inouye had voted for the version of the bill Washington senator Slade Gorton had written, which was based on the bill the Reagan administration had belatedly sent to Capitol Hill. When, by a single vote, a majority of the members of the select committee rejected Gorton's version of the bill and then voted to report to the Senate the version Pete Taylor had written, Inouye joined with Gorton and Nevada senators Paul Laxault and Chic Hecht in putting holds on H.R. 1920 to prevent the Senate from considering it.

But now newly committed to the Native American cause, six weeks after he became chairman of the select committee, on February 19, 1987 Inouye introduced S. 555. The bill had been written principally by Virginia "Ginny" Boylan, one of the attorneys Patricia Zell supervised, and its content was based on Pete Taylor's version of H.R. 1920, which Inouye had opposed.

Patricia Zell, Ginny Boylan, and Alan Parker—another alumnus of the AIPRC staff who in 1977 James Abourezk had appointed as the select committee's first chief counsel and who, when he became chairman, Inouye hired as his staff director—initially hoped the members of the select committee would rubber-stamp S. 555 by voting to report the bill to the Senate without holding a hearing. But three months earlier, Slade Gorton had been one of the Republican senators who lost their bids for reelection.

On the select sommittee, Gorton was replaced by Dan Evans, a former Republican governor of the state of Washington who had been elected to the Senate in 1982. While Gorton and Evans were close friends, according to Gorton, he and Evans "profoundly disagreed on Indian issues" because Evans, who was not an attorney, was more willing than Gorton was to try to find a political accommodation with the ideology of inherent tribal sovereignty.

In order to give S. 555 a veneer of bipartisanship, two days before Inouye introduced it Patricia Zell, Ginny Boylan, and Alan Parker suggested to Inouye that he ask Evans, who had agreed to serve as the Republican vice chairman of the select committee, to cosponsor the bill. However, because Evans "may be reluctant to cosponsor if your plan is to take the bill directly to mark-up," they recommended "that one hearing be scheduled on an expedited basis (i.e., within two to three weeks of the bill's introduction) with the announced intentions of then moving to mark-up, again, on an expedited basis."

So when Evans agreed to cosponsor S. 555 and the bill was introduced, Inouye announced that the select committee would hold a hearing on the bill on March 12. But then six days later, the U.S. Supreme Court issued its decision in *California v. Cabazon and Morongo Bands of Mission Indians*. By a vote of 6 to 3, with Justice Sandra Day O'Connor one of the dissenters, the Court ruled in Glenn Feldman's and his clients' favor.

HERE IS WHAT the Court decided:

California is subject to Public Law No. 83-280, a law Congress passed in 1953 that grants California and a handful of other states (that eventually would include Florida) authority to enforce their criminal laws, and some of their civil laws, in "Indian country" (a legal term of art that includes Indian reservations).

Justice Byron White, who wrote the majority decision in *California v. Cabazon and Morongo Bands of Mission Indians*, accepted the interpretation of Public Law No. 83-280 that District Judge Norman Roettger and the three-judge panels of the U.S. Courts of Appeal for the Fifth and Ninth Circuits had accepted in their decisions in *Seminole Tribe of Florida v. Butterworth* and *Barona Group of the Capitan Grande Band of Mission Indians v. Duffy*. That interpretation assumed that Congress did not intend Public Law No. 83-280 to grant the named states authority to enforce their civil "regulatory" laws in Indian country. Justice White then concluded that since the California legislature had authorized charitable organizations to operate bingo games and municipalities to license more than 400 poker rooms, the state statutes that regulated the terms and conditions pursuant to which bingo and poker could be played were "regulatory," even if the statutes imposed criminal penalties for their violation. After disposing of a related legal issue, Justice White turned to the balancing test Justice O'Connor had invented in the decision she had written for the Court in *Rice v. Rehner*.

Five years earlier, in 1982 nine law professors who specialized in federal Indian law had published a book on that subject that, presumably for marketing purposes, they titled *Felix S. Cohen's Handbook of Federal Indian Law*, even though Cohen had been dead for almost thirty years. The professors all were proponents of the doctrine of inherent tribal sovereignty, which Felix Cohen had invented in 1934, and their book authoritatively asserted that

> the most basic principle of all Indian law, supported by a host of decisions, is that those powers which are lawfully vested in an Indian tribe are not, in general, delegated powers granted by express acts of Congress, but rather "inherent powers of a limited sovereignty which has never been extinguished."

The book also authoritatively asserted that "State law generally is not applicable to Indian affairs within the territory of an Indian tribe, absent the consent of Congress."

In her decision in *Rice v. Rehner*, Justice O'Connor cited *Felix S. Cohen's Handbook of Federal Indian Law* as authority for a different principle of law. But she rejected the law professors' contention—which Felix Cohen had first asserted in the original version of his *Handbook*—that a state may not enforce its laws on an Indian reservation unless Congress has authorized the state to do so. Instead, Justice O'Connor invented a balancing test in which she weighed the interest of the state of California in requiring Indians who resided on reservations to comply with the state's alcohol control laws against the Indians' interest in not being subject to those laws. In his decision in *California v. Cabazon and Morongo Bands of Mission Indians*, Justice White applied Justice O'Connor's balancing test by weighing the interests of the federal government and the Cabazon and Morongo Bands in allowing the bands to operate their bingo halls and the Cabazon Band its poker room in violation of state law against the interest of the state of California in requiring the bands to comply with state law.

How Justice White and the five justices who joined his decision evaluated the evidentiary record regarding those competing interests illustrates how judicial outcomes can be as much the product of shrewd lawyering and luck as they are of reasoned legal analysis.

WITH RESPECT TO the federal interest, Justice White began his analysis by noting that in the American Indian Policy Statement he issued in 1983 President Reagan had "reaffirmed" the importance of "encouraging tribal self-sufficiency and economic development." As discussed in a preceding chapter, Reagan had known next to nothing about the content of the statement on Indian policy the White House issued in his name. The statement also did not mention bingo halls and poker rooms or gambling in any of its other guises, and it did not say the president thought bingo halls and poker rooms were appropriate forms of economic development on Indian reservations.

Aware of those defects, two years earlier when the consolidated *Cabazon and Morongo Bands* lawsuits had been before District Judge Laughlin Waters, Glenn Feldman, who represented the Cabazon Band, arranged for Theodore Krenzke, the BIA's director of Indian services, to file an affidavit. In it, Krenzke attested that

> It is the Department [of the Interior]'s position that tribal bingo enterprises are an appropriate means by which tribes can further their economic self-sufficiency, the economic development of their reservations, and tribal self-determination. All of these are federal goals for tribes. Furthermore, it is the Department's position that the development of tribal bingo enterprises is consistent with and in furtherance of President Reagan's Indian Policy Statement of January 24, 1983.

In his decision, Justice White cited Krenzke's affidavit as evidence that "the Department of the Interior, which has the primary responsibility for carrying out the Federal Government's trust obligations to Indian tribes, has sought to implement [the President's 1983 statement on Indian policy] by promoting tribal bingo enterprises." He also cited the descriptions of the BIA's enthusiasm for gambling on Indian reservations that Frank Ducheneaux and Pete Taylor had written into the reports on H.R. 1920 that the Committee on Interior and Insular Affairs and the Select Committee on Indian Affairs had issued. Neither report mentioned that the Criminal Division of the U.S. Department of Justice strongly objected to the gambling activities the BIA was promoting. And because no one told him, Justice White also did not know how close the Reagan administration had come to telling the U.S. Supreme Court that the Criminal Division's position that gambling on Indian reservations should be subject to state law was the official position of the executive branch of the federal government.

BEFORE THE U.S. Supreme Court, the executive branch is represented by the solicitor general, an attorney in the U.S. Department of Justice appointed by the president and supervised by the attorney general. When executive branch departments have conflicting views regarding what the legal position of the executive branch should be in a particular case, the solicitor general makes his own decision regarding the legal position communicated to the Court.

Today, when the U.S. Supreme Court agrees to review a decision of a U.S. court of appeals or a state supreme court that will require the Court to decide questions of federal Indian law, if the United States is not one of the parties in the case, the Court routinely "invites" the solicitor general to inform the Court of the position of the executive branch regarding the questions at issue. But in 1986 the Court did not invite the solicitor general to tell the Court what the Reagan administration's position was in regard to the questions of federal Indian law the Court would decide when it reviewed the decision the three-judge panel of the U.S. Court of Appeals for the Ninth Circuit had issued in the consolidated *Cabazon and Morongo Bands of Mission Indians v. County of Riverside* lawsuit.

Even though the Court had not ordered him to do so, had he wanted, the solicitor general, a former Harvard Law School professor named Charles Fried, could have filed a brief that informed the justices what the Reagan administration's position was. For that reason, emissaries from the BIA and the Criminal Division actively lobbied Fried. And, most likely at Glenn Feldman's instigation, Arizona senator Dennis DeConcini sent Fried a letter in which he told the solicitor general: "If the Government should file an amicus brief, I would urge you to submit a brief which reflects the views of the Department of Interior. If this is not possible, the Government must refrain from entering into this case."

The dispute between the BIA and the Criminal Division came to a head at a meeting in Fried's office. The solicitor general told those in attendance that, if he did file a brief, it would inform the U.S. Supreme Court that, as the Criminal Division advocated, the Reagan administration believed gambling on Indian reservations should be subject to state law.

But Fried did not file a brief.

Years later, Fried said that the reason he did not was that, after additional reflection, he decided that the disagreement between the BIA and the Criminal Division was a policy dispute, rather than a legal dispute. As such, it would have been "inappropriate" for the solicitor general to have resolved a policy dispute between two executive branch departments that should have been resolved by the White House. So thanks to Charles Fried's forbearance, Glenn Feldman and his clients dodged what might have been a fatal bullet.

That fact became apparent on December 9, 1986, when the U.S. Supreme Court heard oral argument in the case.

When one of the justices asked Roderick Walston, who was representing the state of California and Riverside County, whether "the government filed a brief in this case," the best he could answer was that "[T]he federal government has not, and I think that the failure of the federal government to file a brief in this case speaks volumes concerning the ambivalence of the federal position in this case." When the questioning then turned to H.R. 1920, the bill that had died two months earlier in the Senate, Walston was able to slip in that "[T]he Justice Department opposed it, and the views of the president, I understand, were closer to those of the Justice Department than Interior." But throughout the oral argument the justices assumed that the BIA's position that Indian tribes should be able to operate bingo halls and poker rooms on their reservations in violation of state law was the Reagan administration's position.

IN THE END, Justice White's decision turned on whether the state of California's and Riverside County's interests in requiring the Cabazon and Morongo Bands to comply with the California legislature's bingo and poker room licensing laws and the county's antigambling ordinance trumped the Cabazon and Morongo Bands' interest in the bands continuing to make money by marketing an exemption from the state's and the county's gambling laws to their non-Indian customers. During the oral argument, when the justices asked Roderick Walston why they should decide that his clients' interests trumped Glenn Feldman's clients' interests, in framing his response Walston was hamstrung because, first California voters, and then Rudolph Corona, the assistant attorney general who had represented the state of California in the consolidated *Cabazon and Morongo Bands of Mission Indians v. County of Riverside* lawsuit before he recruited Roderick Walston to take over the representation, had given away Walston's two best arguments.

IN 1983 WHEN Glenn Feldman filed the *Cabazon Band of Mission Indians v. County of Riverside* lawsuit, the state of California prohibited gambling—except for pari-mutuel betting at horse tracks, poker rooms that municipalities could license by local option, and bingo games that only charitable organizations could operate. But in 1984, California voters amended the California Constitution to authorize the state to operate a lottery.

In 1985, when the first lottery was conducted, California residents bought thirty million tickets in two days. As a consequence, during the oral argument Walston was compelled to concede that "I have deliberately not tried to advance a moral argument before this Court" because "with the recent adoption of the state lottery and other types of state-authorized gambling activities, I think that the state's moral objections to gambling have diminished."

Because of the lottery, Walston could not argue that gambling on Indian reservations violated the state of California's public policy. His next best argument was that the state had an important interest in regulating gambling on Indian reservations in order to prevent non-Indians who had connections to organized crime from gaining control of the bingo halls and poker rooms. But Rudolph Corona had given that argument away.

GLENN FELDMAN HAD been the Cabazon Band's attorney when Fred Alvarez was murdered. And he had represented the Cabazon Indian Casino during the business's bankruptcy. So it is reasonable to assume that Feldman knew who Rocco Zangari and Tommy Marson were. Nevertheless, after Judge Waters consolidated the *Cabazon Band of Mission Indians v. County of Riverside* lawsuit with the *Morongo Band of Mission Indians v. County of Riverside* lawsuit, when Feldman drafted an Agreed Upon Statement of Uncontroverted Facts, which Rudolph Corona signed, Feldman included a sentence that stated: "The defendants do not allege that the Cabazon card room or the Cabazon bingo parlor are associated with organized crime." And when Barbara Karshmer, the attorney who represented the Morongo Band, drafted her own Agreed Upon Statement of Uncontroverted Facts, which Corona also signed, she included a sentence that stated: "The Defendants do not allege that the Morongo Tribal Bingo Enterprise was or is associated with organized crime." During the oral argument Rudolph Corona's failure to object to those paragraphs put Roderick Walston in an untenable position when Justice Lewis Powell asked, "Is there any evidence that organized crime has infiltrated the operations of the tribes that are before us?"

Walston answered: "Not in the record. To fully answer your question, Justice Powell, I would have to go outside the record, and I am reluctant to do that."

Powell then responded, "Maybe I had better withdraw the question then, but you argue in your brief that that is a concern of the state of California."

Walston answered, "Yes," and years later he explained:

I had prepared for Justice Powell's question. I had become aware that there was some anecdotal evidence that I could provide to the Court, but it was outside the record. So I didn't want to offer it without his authorization to do so. But when Justice Powell withdrew his question, that was the end of the organized crime issue.

But it was not quite the end. When it was his turn to argue, Glenn Feldman told the justices that the influence of organized crime in bingo halls on Indian reservations to which Walston had alluded in his brief was "hypothetical" because the state of California had "stipulated to the fact that there is no organized crime involvement on either the Cabazon or Morongo reservation." And when he was pressed, Feldman told the justices the reports on H.R. 1920 Frank Ducheneaux and Pete Taylor had written for the Committee on Interior and Insular Affairs and the Select Committee on Indian Affairs stated "with no qualifications that there is no organized crime involvement anywhere."

What the report Ducheneaux wrote actually stated was that "On the issue of organized crime, the Committee has not found any *conclusive* evidence that such infiltration has occurred." (emphasis added) Also, six months earlier, Feldman had been in the hearing room during the hearing the Select Committee on Indian Affairs held on H.R. 1920 when San Diego County Sheriff John Duffy had told Pete Taylor that "[O]n reservations in California, virtually all of them, the Indians are exploited, and they are cheated by unscrupulous profiteering companies with established connections to organized crime."

For those reasons, what Feldman told the justices was at best disingenuous, and, at worst, a falsehood intentionally told.

GIVEN THE LACK of evidence in the record and the manner in which Glenn Feldman handled the organized crime issue, it is no surprise that in his decision Justice White concluded that "[T]he State's interest in preventing the infiltration of the tribal bingo enterprises by organized crime does not justify state regulation of the tribal bingo enterprises in light of the compelling federal and tribal interests supporting them."

Patricia Zell, who watched Feldman's performance, was lavish in her praise. "I've seen a lot of Supreme Court arguments, because the Senate is right across the street from the Court," she recalled years later. "But I've never seen one like Glenn Feldman's. . . . Every time somebody threw him a strange question, he would respond to it, even if it were far afield from the subject at hand, and just regain his equilibrium."

Glenn Feldman undoubtedly did handle himself masterfully. But as David Boies, one of the most celebrated appellate advocates of his generation, has noted: "There is no substitute for preparation, and more cases are won and lost by preparation, or the lack of it, than for any other reason." And luck "plays a key part."

More than his performance during the oral argument, Glenn Feldman won because he out-lawyered opposing counsel. First by arranging for Theodore Krenzke to file an affidavit that linked the BIA's support for gambling on Indian reservations to the president's American Indian Policy Statement. And then, with Barbara Karshmer, maneuvering Rudolph Corona into signing the Agreed Upon Statements of Uncontroverted Facts in which the state of California conceded there had been no involvement on the Cabazon and Morongo reservations of individuals who had connections to organized crime.

And Feldman had been lucky. First, when California voters authorized a state lottery, and then when Charles Fried decided not to file a brief.

AS A CONSEQUENCE of the U.S. Supreme Court's decision in *California v. Cabazon and Morongo Bands of Mission Indians*, until and unless Congress subjected gambling on Indian reservations to some sort of regulation, Indian tribes whose reservations were located in California and Florida and other states subject to Public Law No. 83-280 now were free to offer all forms of gambling on their reservations—including bingo and card games, pari-mutuel betting on horse and dog races, and jai alai—that the states authorized to be played for any purpose. If a state had a law that authorized charities to host Las Vegas Night fund-raisers, during which games such as roulette and craps could be played for low stakes, tribes in that state also could offer high-stakes forms of those games. And the Court's decision implied that tribes whose reservations were located in states not subject to Public Law No. 83-280 could do the same.

At the Select Committee on Indian Affairs, the Court's decision turned the politics inside out. As was discussed in the preceding chapter, the version of H.R. 1920 the Select Committee reported to the Senate at the end of the Ninety-Ninth Congress contained a provision Pete Taylor wrote into the bill that prohibited a tribe from offering forms of gambling other than bingo and card games unless the tribe asked the secretary of the interior to transfer jurisdiction to regulate those forms to the state within which the tribe's reservation was located and the secretary did so.

According to Bill Houle, the chairman of the National Indian Gaming

Association (NIGA), the organization that by 1986 had evolved from the National Indian Gaming Task Force that Houle and the leaders of other tribes that had opened bingo halls had created in 1983, the members of the NIGA agreed to the transfer provision Pete Taylor had included in his version of H.R. 1920 with "the utmost reluctance, and only in the face of what appeared to be a probable Supreme Court defeat." After the U.S. Supreme Court's decision, however, NIGA changed its position and now opposed any bill that would "transfer any jurisdiction to the State government over Indian people, their activities, or their lands." And since Ginny Boylan had included a transfer provision in S. 555 that was similar to the transfer provision Pete Taylor had written into H.R. 1920, the NIGA now opposed Chairman Inouye's bill.

Given that reality, two days after the U.S. Supreme Court issued its decision in *California v. Cabazon and Morongo Bands of Mission Indians*, the select committee announced that the hearing on S. 555 that had been scheduled for March 12 had been canceled " to give tribes and other interested parties time to assess the impact of the decision on the pending legislation." The stage was now set for a small group of congressional staff members and lobbyists to decide largely between themselves the forms of gambling Congress would allow on Indian reservations and how and by whom those forms would be regulated.

11: IGRA

The message is as clear as it is repugnant; under our so-called Federal System, the Congress is constitutionally empowered to launch programs, the scope, impact, consequences, and workability of which are largely unknown, at least to the Congress, at the time of enactment.

DISTRICT JUDGE ROBERT KELLEHER

WHEN THE ONE HUNDREDTH CONGRESS CONVENED IN JANUARY 1987, more than one hundred tribes were operating gambling facilities on Indian reservations in twenty-four states. Most of those facilities, which in 1986 collectively had gross revenues of $255.6 million, were bingo halls, although the Cabazon Band and fourteen other tribes operated poker rooms, and several tribes offered casino games such as blackjack, craps, and roulette. And in their bingo halls, a number of tribes had installed video gaming machines whose software had been programmed to allow players to play bingo, pull-tabs, and poker.

Those facilities were profitable because they offered non-Indians the opportunity to gamble in violation of the laws of the states in which the reservations were located; which is why, as he had been since 1983, Frank Ducheneaux continued to be worried because he accepted the conventional wisdom that when the U.S. Supreme Court issued its decision in *California v. Cabazon and Morongo Bands of Mission Indians*, the Court would require Indian tribes to comply with the gambling laws of the states in which their reservations were located. That would put an end to most gambling on most reservations.

But since the conventional wisdom also assumed that the Court would not issue its decision for several more months, there still was time for Congress to pass a bill that could allow at least the bingo halls to stay open. "To salvage as much as possible for tribal sovereignty over Indian gaming before the Court rendered its expected decision in the *Cabazon* case," Ducheneaux wrote a new bill that, on February 10, 1987, Mo Udall introduced in the U.S. House of Representatives as H.R. 1079. In a statement he had printed in the *Congressional Record*, Udall told the House that H.R. 1079 was "based upon the bill, H.R. 1920, which was reported from the Interior Committee in the 99th Congress." But the two bills were far from identical.

H.R. 1920 established an eight-member National Indian Gaming Commission, one of whose members would be selected by the attorney general of the United States, another member who would "represent the interest of the States," and only three of the eight members would be "enrolled members of Federally recognized tribes." H.R. 1920 also limited the definition of Class II gaming to bingo, pull-tabs, punch boards, "and other games similar to bingo," and required the commission to adopt regulations for the conduct of Class III gaming (i.e., all forms of gambling other than Classes I and II) that were "identical to [the regulations] provided for the same or similar gaming activity by the State within which such Indian gaming activity is to be conducted."

By contrast, the commission H.R. 1079 established consisted of five members. While the Attorney General still would select one member, three of the four other members were required to be "enrolled members of federally recognized Indian tribes." No member would "represent the interest of the States." The definition of Class II gaming was expanded to include card games. And while, with respect to Class III forms of gambling, the chairman of the commission would "adopt a comprehensive regulatory scheme for each Class III game" that was "identical to [the regulations] provided for the same or similar activity by the State within which such Indian gaming activity is to be conducted," the bill directed the chairman to exclude state regulations that imposed taxes, as well as state regulations that "would unreasonably impair the ability of the tribe to conduct its operation." In addition, H.R. 1079 granted Indian tribes authority to offer pari-mutuel betting, craps and roulette, and all other forms of Class III gambling that the states in which the tribes' reservations were located permitted "for any purpose." So rather than an attempt at "salvage," H.R. 1079 was a wish list presumably assembled by Ducheneaux to position Udall for the negotiation he would have to have with California representative Tony Coelho in order to develop a substitute bill that Coelho and a majority of the other members of the Committee on Interior and Insular Affairs would be willing to support. However, before that negotiation could take place, two weeks after Udall introduced H.R. 1079, the U.S. Supreme Court issued its decision in *California v. Cabazon and Morongo Bands of Mission Indians* and the Cabazon and Morongo Bands won.

That outcome instantaneously reordered the political calculations.

Four months earlier, members of the National Indian Gaming Association (NIGA), as well as most of the other tribes that operated bingo halls, had wanted the Senate to pass the version of H.R. 1920 reported by the Select Committee on Indian Affairs because they feared the Court would put bingo halls on Indian reservations out of business. After the U.S. Supreme Court issued its decision, however, many of those leaders no longer supported the enactment of any bill. Conversely, Tony Coelho and other members of the U.S. House of Representatives who believed that, other than bingo, gambling on Indian reservations should be regulated by the states now needed Congress to pass a bill. As a senator who agreed with Coelho later explained, the alternative was "rapid and uncontrolled expansion of unregulated casino type gambling on Indian lands."

Since the U.S. Supreme Court's decision seemingly strengthened Mo Udall's negotiating position, Frank Ducheneaux (and Virginia "Ginny" Boylan and Patricia Zell, the members of the staff of the Select Committee on Indian Affairs who were handling the Indian gambling issue and with whom Ducheneaux was in regular communication) wrote a second bill, which on May 21, 1987 Udall introduced as H.R. 2507.

The section of H.R. 2507 that established the National Indian Gaming Commission eliminated the provision in H.R. 1079 that authorized the attorney general of the United States to select one of the commission's five members. At the request of Paul Alexander, one of the NIGA's lobbyists, Ducheneaux expanded the definition of Class II gaming to include "electronic or electromechanical facsimiles" of bingo cards—legalese for video gaming machines programmed to play bingo.

But if Frank Ducheneaux thought the U.S. Supreme Court's decision had given Mo Udall leverage to improve on H.R. 1079, it became clear when the Committee on Interior and Insular Affairs held a hearing on H.R. 2507 that the decision had not lessened the Reagan administration's opposition to tribes offering Class III forms of gambling. As Assistant Secretary of the Interior for Indian Affairs Ross Swimmer explained when he testified, while the administration did not object to bingo halls, "Our preference as to so-called Class III, or what we call hard-core, gaming is one of two options, either [it] not be allowed in Indian country, or that if it is allowed in Indian country, it should be regulated by the State that has the appropriate regulatory body already in place."

Tony Coelho did not bother to attend the hearing because he already had told Udall he opposed his bill. Three weeks before Udall introduced H.R. 2507, Coelho had sent the chairman a five-page letter in which he put Udall on notice that he continued to have a "fundamental disagreement" with Udall regarding "the proper form of regulation that should be imposed on Indian tribes who wish to venture into complicated, high-stakes [gambling] enterprises."

The previous December, Coelho had been elected whip, the third-ranking position in the leadership of the U.S. House of Representatives. So in the One Hundredth Congress, Coelho was an even more influential member of the House than he had been during the Ninety-Ninth Congress. He also had two formidable allies.

The first was California representative George Miller, the second most senior Democrat on the Committee on Interior and Insular Affairs. Unlike Coelho, Miller did attend the hearing the committee held on H.R. 2507. But only long enough to announce that he was "deeply concerned with the bill of our chairman" because allowing Indian tribes in California to build horse tracks on their reservations that would compete against the existing tracks would damage the state's thoroughbred racing industry. He also told Udall that his other concerns about H.R. 2507 had been "outlined in a letter to the chairman from Congressman Coelho."

Tony Coelho's other ally was Claude Pepper, the eighty-six-year-old chairman of the Rules Committee. Pepper's congressional district in Florida included a portion of the city of Miami in which the Flagler Dog Track was located. But according to Thomas Spulak, the staff director of the Rules Committee at the time, "Pepper was not motivated by the Flagler situation. His interest was more related to the horse racing industry, which had a big presence in the greater Miami area."

When the hearing on H.R. 2507 concluded, Frank Ducheneaux would spend the next six months trying to negotiate mutually acceptable changes to the bill with the member of Tony Coelho's staff who handled the Indian gambling issue for Coelho. When the negotiations failed to produce an agreement, Ducheneaux wrote what he described as a "compromise" proposal. In January 1988 when the U.S. House of Representatives began the second session of the One Hundredth Congress, Mo Udall distributed Ducheneaux's proposal to the members of the Committee on Interior and Insular Affairs. The compromise allowed Indian tribes to license Class III gambling on their reservations but allowed the states in which the reservations were located to regulate the activity pursuant to state law, unless a particular tribe and a particular state agreed to a different arrangement.

Coelho rejected the compromise. He also decided that he was tired of dealing with Udall through Ducheneaux. So he invited Udall to meet with him and Claude Pepper in Pepper's office at the Rules Committee. According to Ducheneaux, who accompanied Udall to the meeting, when it began, "Coelho started personally attacking me."

To encourage the Ninety-Ninth Congress to pass a bill that would allow bingo halls to stay open if, as was expected, the U.S. Supreme Court ruled against the Cabazon and Morongo Bands, the NIGA had passed a resolution in which the organization announced that its member tribes did not oppose state regulation of Class III forms of gambling. During his meeting with Udall, Coelho "raised the issue of NIGA's 'protect only bingo' resolution," Ducheneaux recalled years later. He also demanded to know "how in the hell" Ducheneaux could continue to oppose H.R. 964, a bill Coelho and Pepper had introduced to do what the NIGA had said it supported. "I looked at Mo, and I'm sure he would have turned Coelho with a joke or something if he had been in his top form, but he just didn't say anything.* Finally, Coelho's attacks against me became so bad that Chairman Pepper took him on."

A veteran legislator, Udall knew that if he persuaded a majority of the members of the Committee on Interior and Insular Affairs to report H.R. 2507 to the House without adopting any crippling amendments (which, given Tony Coelho's and George Miller's opposition, was no sure thing), under the "regular order" procedure the bill would be sent to the

---

*In 1977, Udall had been diagnosed with Parkinson's disease. By early 1988, his physical condition had deteriorated to the point that he was having difficulty dressing himself.

Rules Committee. At the Rules Committee a rule would be written that would list the amendments that could be offered when the bill was debated on the House floor.

When his meeting with Tony Coelho and Claude Pepper deteriorated into rancor and ended with no agreement, Udall realized that, when H.R. 2507 arrived at the Rules Committee, Pepper would have the committee write a rule that would authorize Tony Coelho to offer an amendment that would either prohibit all Class III forms of gambling on Indian reservations or require Class III forms to be regulated by the states. And, as had been the situation during the Ninety-Ninth Congress, on the floor, Coelho might have the votes he needed to pass it.

So Udall decided to circumvent the Rules Committee. He told Ducheneaux, "We won't have a mark-up. We won't report a bill out." Instead, he told Ducheneaux to tell Patricia Zell that if she and Daniel Inouye could arrange for the Senate to pass a bill that was "minimally acceptable to the Indians," when it arrived in the House, Udall would have the bill "held at the [speaker's] desk and passed under suspension of the rules." But "if the Senate passes a bill which is not minimally acceptable to the tribes, I'll have that bill referred to the [C]ommittee [on Interior and Insular Affairs], and I'll kill it." According to Ducheneaux, that is what happened. "I let Pat Zell and the Senate staff know where we stood—what our problems were, what the prospects were, and what we could do."

TWO WEEKS AFTER Mo Udall introduced H.R. 2507, Arizona republican senator John McCain introduced the same bill in the Senate as S. 1303. In 1982, McCain, the politically ambitious son of an admiral who was the son of an admiral, had used his celebrity as a prisoner of war in Vietnam and his wife's father's money to win election in Arizona to a seat in the U.S. House of Representatives. He did so intending to serve two terms and then run for the Senate when Arizona senator Barry Goldwater retired.

According to McCain, when he was elected to the House he knew nothing about "public land management, water rights, mining and timber concerns, and Native American issues" that he needed to educate himself about if his plan "to succeed the legendary Goldwater were ever to amount to anything more than laughable arrogance." To obtain that education, McCain arranged to be appointed to the Committee on Interior and Insular Affairs, which had jurisdiction over bills that involved those subject matters.

When McCain joined the committee, Mo Udall asked the freshman Republican from his home state to serve on an informal Subcommittee on Native American Affairs. The subcommittee consisted of two members: Mo Udall and John McCain. And according to McCain, over the next four years, "Mo and I held hearings on all manner of issues related to Indians, just the two of us." So it is no surprise that McCain, who, as planned, in the 1986 election won Barry Goldwater's seat in the Senate, would introduce Udall's bill.

ON JUNE 18, 1987, the Select Committee on Indian Affairs held a hearing on S. 1303 and S. 555, the bill Ginny Boylan had written for Daniel Inouye. During the morning session, four members of the select committee attended the hearing for a moment or two. John McCain, who had joined the select committee following his election to the Senate, briefly attended during the afternoon session. With the exception of those cursory appearances, however, Daniel Inouye presided on the dais alone. In addition to the members' disinterest, the hearing demonstrated that the decision in *California v. Cabazon and Morongo Bands of Mission Indians* that the U.S. Supreme Court had issued four months earlier had done nothing to lessen disagreement regarding how Class III forms of gambling on Indian reservations should be regulated.

Assistant Secretary of the Interior for Indian Affairs Ross Swimmer told Inouye that the Reagan administration wanted Congress to subject all forms of gambling on Indian reservations other than bingo to state regulation. Roger Jourdain, the chairman of the Red Lake Band of Chippewa Indians in Minnesota, told Inouye that because "the U.S. Supreme Court held that Indian tribes have inherent sovereignty to operate and regulate tribal bingo and card games outside the scope of State and county regulatory laws," the Red Lake Band opposed S. 1303 and S. 555, as well as "any other legislation that would impose upon Indian tribes Federal standards and regulations covering the conduct of gaming activities on Indian reservations." Nevada senator Chic Hecht also objected to S. 1303. His complaint was that the bill "put substantially all regulatory control in the hands of the Indian tribes themselves."

As he had the previous year, San Diego County Sheriff John Duffy warned about the presence of organized crime in the operation of Indian bingo halls. And Bill Houle, the chairman of the NIGA, announced that the NIGA opposed S. 555 and any other bill that transferred jurisdiction over "Indian people, their activities, or their lands" to the states.

The views of the members of the select committee were just as discordant. Montana Democratic senator John Melcher appeared at the beginning of the hearing long enough to announce that he wanted Congress to pass a bill that permitted "tribes on the reservations to do as they please," but only "up to the limits that have been imposed by the individual States." Then John McCain vociferously defended S. 1303.

So it went. And the consequence of the discord was a stalemate that lasted for months.

To try to break it, Patricia Zell and Joe Mentor, the select committee's minority staff director who worked for Washington senator Dan Evans, began hosting a series of meetings. During the meetings, Zell and Mentor, Ginny Boylan, Frank Ducheneaux and his counterpart on the Republican staff of the Committee on Interior and Insular Affairs, and members of the staffs of interested members of the House and Senate negotiated between themselves a bill that a majority of the members of the select committee could support, that the Nevada senators would not prevent from being brought to the floor, and that Tony Coelho and Claude Pepper would allow the House to pass. According to Ducheneaux, "At various times, representatives of the federal and state governments participated in the negotiations." Paul Alexander and the other lobbyists who represented the NIGA and affected tribes did not "directly participate," but they "made their views known through the several participating parties." What the staff members who participated in the meetings Patricia Zell and Joe Mentor hosted did not have authority to do on their own was decide whether the bill whose content they were negotiating would allow Class III forms of gambling on Indian reservations, and, if it did, how those forms would be regulated.

On February 26, 1988, Ginny Boylan had sent Daniel Inouye a memorandum in which she reported that Mo Udall and Frank Ducheneaux had recently met with Tony Coelho and Claude Pepper. She also reported that, after that meeting, the House and Senate staffs had discussed the idea of the select committee moving a bill whose content would be based on the compromise proposal Ducheneaux had written for Udall. The memorandum ended by observing that "whether we want to get in front of this issue will hinge on whether we can persuade Senator Reid to proceed on the Udall compromise." "Senator Reid" was Nevada Democratic senator Harry Reid.

BORN IN 1939 AND raised in Searchlight, a desiccated mining camp in the desert south of Las Vegas that had thirteen whorehouses and no churches, Harry Reid graduated from high school in Henderson, forty-five miles north of Searchlight. He then worked his way through Utah State University and law school at George Washington University.

In high school, Reid had a teacher named Mike O'Callaghan, a larger-than-life personality who became the boy from Searchlight's mentor. In 1970, O'Callaghan, who had left teaching for a career in government service, was the Nevada Democratic Party's candidate for governor. Reid, then thirty years old and practicing law in Las Vegas, was his running mate. Both men were elected, and Reid became the youngest lieutenant governor in Nevada history.

In 1974 when Alan Bible, Nevada's long-serving senior senator, retired, Reid ran for Bible's seat. He narrowly lost the election to former Nevada Republican governor Paul Laxalt. Eight years later, Reid was elected to the U.S. House of Representatives in the same election John McCain was elected to the House in Arizona. Four years after that, when Paul Laxalt retired, Reid won his seat in the Senate.

IN JANUARY 1987, WHEN Harry Reid arrived in the Senate, more than 80 percent of Nevada's one million residents lived in Clark and Washoe Counties in which Las Vegas and Reno are located, and Las Vegas was one of the fastest growing cities in the United States. As it had since 1931, gambling was fueling the boom. Statewide, more than 270 casinos employed almost 150,000 people and indirectly generated several tens of thousands of additional jobs. Almost half the tax revenue the state of Nevada received came from the casinos.

Most of the people who gambled in Nevada casinos were nonresidents, many from California. The Nevada gambling industry had not been hurt by the handful of casinos that opened in 1978 along the boardwalk in Atlantic City. But what if Indian tribes in California opened casinos?

Would gamblers from California continue to travel to Nevada if they could lose their money closer to home?

As has been described, in September 1986 when Nevada senators Paul Laxalt and Chic Hecht put holds on H.R. 1920 to prevent the bill from being brought to the Senate floor, Mark Andrews, the chairman of the select committee, tried to persuade them to lift their holds by amending H.R. 1920 to address what the Nevada senators said were their concerns. But the holds remained.

In June 1987, Karl Funke, a lobbyist for the United South and Eastern Tribes who had been involved in Andrews's negotiations with Laxalt and Hecht, explained that the negotiations failed because "the State of Nevada was opposed to gambling anywhere in the United States, and particularly they were concerned about card games in California." Funke also said that during the negotiations, "the administrative assistant for Senator Laxalt" admitted "that Nevada was most concerned with competition, regardless of whether it was bingo games, card games or anything else." A month later, Chic Hecht confirmed Funke's description of Laxalt and Hecht's agenda when he bragged in *Gaming & Wagering Business* magazine that "I was able to block efforts to get an Indian gaming bill during the final hours of the last Congress. A couple of people from Florida wanted it, but I said, no, that it would wreck our industry."

The Nevada senators refused to lift their holds because the conventional wisdom was that, when it issued its decision in *California v. Cabazon and Morongo Bands of Mission Indians*, the U.S. Supreme Court would require Indian tribes to comply with the gambling laws of the states in which their reservations were located. So Laxalt and Hecht had no reason to allow the Senate to pass a bill whose enactment by Congress would have legalized what the Court soon would authorize the states to prohibit.

But when Harry Reid replaced Laxalt in the Senate and a month later the U.S. Supreme Court ruled that Indian tribes could offer bingo, poker, and many other forms of gambling without regulation by either the federal government or the states, the problem Reid faced was how to persuade Daniel Inouye to have the Select Committee on Indian Affairs send a bill to the Senate whose content would mitigate the damage that unregulated gambling on Indian reservations had the potential to inflict on the Nevada gambling industry.

To explore whether a solution of some sort might be worked out, two weeks before the Select Committee held its hearing on S. 1303 and S. 555, Harry Reid and Tony Coelho (who insofar as the horse racing industry in California was concerned had the same problem Reid had) met with Inouye. Afterward, Reid informed the chairman of the select committee that "Tony and I came away from the meeting with a good understanding of your position."

Unfortunately for Reid and Coelho, what Inouye, who by then had spent five months being tutored by Patricia Zell, likely told them was that allowing the states to regulate Class III forms of gambling on Indian reservations would violate the doctrine of inherent tribal sovereignty that Zell and all leaders of all Indian tribes considered sacrosanct.

Five months later, in October 1987, Reid decided to try to circumvent the select committee. Since he was a member of the subcommittee of the Appropriations Committee which wrote the bills that appropriated money to the Department of the Interior, Reid's plan was to insert into that year's Department of the Interior appropriations bill a provision whose enactment would grant the states temporary authority to regulate Class III forms of gambling on Indian reservations. Daniel Inouye, who was a member of the Appropriations Committee, but not the subcommittee, found out what Reid was planning and had the select committee pass a resolution in which its members opposed "any efforts to address the issue of gaming by Indian tribes through amendment to spending measures," which the resolution lambasted as "inappropriate, premature and an infringement of the Committee legislative process."

In response, Reid sent Inouye a letter in which he bluntly lectured,

> Given the chaotic situation that already exists in some areas of Indian gaming and which will most certainly become more extensive in the future without legislation, I don't think that it would be acceptable to postpone action indefinitely. We would simply be opening the door to the kind of infiltration by organized crime figures and other undesirable influences that regulatory legislation is meant to avoid.

INDEPENDENT OF HIS interest in protecting the Nevada gambling industry, Harry Reid's concern that unregulated casino gambling on Indian reservations would "open the door" to "infiltration by organized crime figures" was not disingenuous. After he lost the 1974 Senate election to Paul Laxalt and then in 1975 lost again when he impetuously ran for mayor of Las Vegas, in 1977 Nevada governor Mike O'Callaghan had appointed Reid chairman of the Nevada Gaming Commission. According to Reid, before his appointment, "I was completely naive about the inner workings of Las Vegas casinos." What he quickly learned was the extent to which—if the casinos and the people who ran them were not subjected to close and constant investigation and regulation—individuals who had organized crime connections would skim the counting rooms and control casino operations.

During Reid's four years as chairman, the Nevada Gaming Commission added Tony "the Ant" Spilotto, who represented the Chicago Outfit in Las Vegas (and who would be played by Joe Pesci in the 1995 film *Casino*) to the Black Book—the list of individuals who have been banned from setting foot in Nevada casinos. Reid also was offered bribes, had his life threatened, frequently had police protection, and one afternoon his wife discovered that the gas tank of her car had been wired to explode. By the end of his tenure as chairman, Reid carried a concealed weapon.

Given that experience, Harry Reid was not sympathetic to Inouye's view that it was more important for Congress not to compromise the doctrine of inherent tribal sovereignty than it was for Congress to grant the states authority to ensure that, if it was allowed at all, Class III forms of gambling on Indian reservations would be closely regulated. By placing a hold Reid could prevent the Senate from considering any bill the select committee reported of which he disapproved, but he did not have the ability to force Daniel Inouye, John McCain, and the other members of the select committee to report a bill to the Senate that he considered acceptable.

Hence the impasse between Inouye and Reid that Reid finally figured out how to end.

IN THE DESERT south of Searchlight, the Colorado River marks the border that divides the states of Nevada, Arizona, and California. In 1964, Don Laughlin, who having recently sold a bar in Las Vegas had money to invest, flew over the area and saw the future. In 1966 he bought six acres of desert on the Nevada side of the river on which a boarded-up motel was located.

He reopened the motel as the Riverside Resort with twelve slot machines and two gaming tables. Two other casinos soon opened, and by 1968 Laughlin's prescience had created a town, which the U.S. Postal Service named in honor of its founder. In addition to the Riverside Resort, which by then had expanded to include a gaming floor that contained more than 1,000 video gaming machines and two fourteen-story hotel towers, by 1986 Laughlin, Nevada, had five other casinos, 1,661 hotel rooms, and was annually attracting 1.5 million visitors.

Ten miles south of Laughlin, on the Arizona side of the Colorado River, in 1859 the U.S. Army had established an outpost called Fort Mojave. In 1890 the army transferred the fort and the surrounding 14,000-acre military reserve to the Bureau of Indian Affairs, which opened a boarding school in the buildings. In 1910 and 1911 President William Howard Taft designated the reserve, as well as 28,000 additional acres of federal land on both sides of the Colorado River, as the Fort Mojave Reservation. Because the highway from Los Angeles to Laughlin runs past the reservation, on the Nevada side of the Colorado River, the Fort Mojave Reservation was an ideal location for a casino.

Unlike many other Indian leaders, Nora Garcia, who in 1981 had been elected chairwoman of the tribal council that represented the Mojave Indians who lived on the reservation and in the nearby town of Needles, was a pragmatist more than ideologue. So she did not object to the state of Nevada regulating gambling in the casino the Fort Mojave Tribe was planning to open because, as she explained in 1986 when she testified before the Select Committee on Indian Affairs, "[S]tates are in a better position to regulate Class III gambling within their respective borders than is the United States."

In October 1987, Garcia signed an "intergovernmental agreement" in which the Fort Mojave Tribe transferred its civil and criminal jurisdiction to regulate gambling on the Fort Mojave Reservation to the Nevada Gaming Commission and the Nevada Gaming Control Board. A month later, in a speech he delivered in Atlantic City at the annual World Gaming Congress & Expo, Michael Rumbolz, the chairman of the Nevada Gaming Control Board, touted the agreement as a "significant step forward," because the "cooperative atmosphere" the Fort Mojave Tribe and the state of Nevada had developed "is the key to resolving the regulatory questions facing Congress, federal agencies, States, and Native Americans."

Harry Reid agreed and, as he later recalled, "I suggested to Chairman Inouye that we use the concept of tribal-state compacts to determine the regulatory structure of Class III gaming."

ON MAY 13, 1988, Inouye gaveled a meeting of the Select Committee on Indian Affairs to order. The purpose of the meeting was to report to the Senate a substitute for the original text of S. 555. The substitute was a new bill whose content reflected the outcome of the negotiations between staff members that Patricia Zell and Joe Mentor had hosted. Inouye explained that the bill had been written

> principally by two ladies of the staff, two very bright attorneys. The one who spent many sleepless nights, I'm certain, and long hours for the past several weeks is Virginia Boylan, who is sitting before us. . . . Working with her was the chief counsel of the committee, Patricia Zell.

After a cursory explanation of the bill by Inouye, and after Ginny Boylan answered several questions, the members voted to report to the Senate—without any amendments—not only a bill that, until the meeting, the members (other than possibly Inouye) likely had not read , but a section of the bill that did not exist.

Prior to the meeting, June Tracy, the member of the staff of the select committee who worked for Arizona senator Dennis DeConcini, had reported to DeConcini that "It is anyone's guess what Inouye will do on Class 3. His staff does not know what he is honestly comfortable with as an option. He may not have been completely candid with them on what he prefers."

In settling on what he preferred, Inouye had the same problem Harry Reid had, except in reverse. Because he knew that, by putting on a hold, Reid could prevent the Senate from considering any bill the select committee reported of which he disapproved. So to obtain Reid's support, at the May 13 meeting Inouye announced that he had directed Ginny Boylan and Patricia Zell to write, and then add into their bill, a section that would au-

*Anna Nicole Smith promotes
the Seminole Hard Rock Hotel &
Casino in Hollywood, Florida.*
PHOTO: ZUMA PRESS, INC./ALAMY

Seminole Hard Rock Hotel & Casino in Hollywood, Florida.
PHOTO: ROSA IRENE BETANCOURT 8/ALAMY

Felix S. Cohen.

Photo: Yale Collection of
Western Americana, Beinecke Rare
Book and Manuscript Library

Stogie Shop, Colville Indian Reservation.

Photo: Barry George

Howard Tommie.

PHOTO: HOWARD TOMMIE

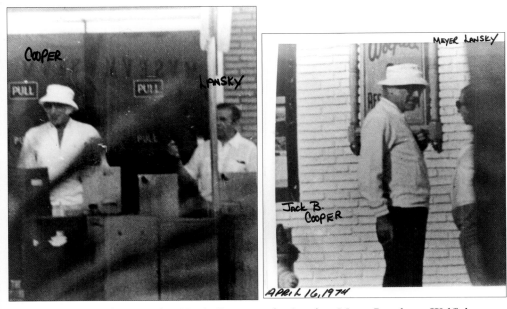

FBI surveillance photographs of Jack Cooper and crime boss Meyer Lansky at Wolfie's Restaurant in Miami Beach, Florida.

PHOTO: NATIONAL ARCHIVES AND RECORDS ADMINISTRATION

Seminole bingo hall in Hollywood, Florida, June 24, 1980.

PHOTO: RAY FISHER

Nightclub comedian Allan Drake.

PHOTO: WANDA AND CARY DRAKE

Steward Siegel and Sammy Davis Jr. at harness track in Northfield, Ohio. PHOTO: *HOOFBEATS MAGAZINE*

Steve Whilden.

PHOTO: MARK ZERBEL/*STAR TRIBUNE*

Victoria Toensing, deputy assistant attorney general, and Frank Ryan, deputy assistant secretary of the Interior for Indian Affairs, testify on S. 902 and H.R. 1920 before the Select Committee on Indian Affairs, June 17, 1986. Senator Mark Andrews, chairman of the select committee, presides. To Andrews's right is Pete Taylor, staff director. To Andrews's left is Senator Dennis DeConcini. <small>PHOTO: U.S. SENATE HISTORICAL OFFICE</small>

Frank Sinatra and Tommy Marson at the Westchester Premier Theater, September 26, 1976. Shown from left to right are Gregory De Palma, a capo in the Gambino Mafia family; Sinatra, Marson, Carlo Gambino, the boss of the Gambino Mafia family; and Jimmy "The Weasel" Fratianno, the acting boss of the Mafia family in Los Angeles. <small>PHOTO: ASSOCIATED PRESS</small>

Fred Alvarez.

PHOTO: DUGAN AGUILAR

U.S. Marshals remove video gaming machines from the bingo hall on the Tohono O'odham Reservation, May 12, 1992. PHOTO: DAVID SANDERS/ARIZONA DAILY STAR

John "Roddy" Sunchild, chairman of the Chippewa Cree Tribe in Montana, addresses President Bill Clinton, Hillary Clinton, Vice President Al Gore, and Tipper Gore at the president's meeting with Indian leaders at the White House, April 29, 1994. Gaiashkibos, the president of the National Congress of American Indians, sits on the president's left. PHOTO: WILLIAM J. CLINTON PRESIDENTIAL LIBRARY

Mary Ann Martin at the grand opening of the Augustine Casino, July 18, 2002.

PHOTO: *DESERT SUN*

Fond-du-Luth Casino in Duluth, Minnesota.

PHOTO: DONALD CRAIG MITCHELL

thorize an Indian tribe and the state in which the tribe's reservation was located to negotiate a "compact" that would set out the terms for regulation of Class III forms of gambling. Inouye explained that he had done so

> as the result of a suggestion made by our colleague, Senator Reid of Nevada. He pointed out to us that the State of Nevada has entered into a compact with the Fort Mojave Indian Tribe and suggested that this concept would keep intact the sovereignty of the Indians and the sovereignty of the State.

How the compact process would work was so little understood that when Ginny Boylan asked for permission to make technical changes to the text of the bill without having to bring the changes back to the members for a vote, Inouye quipped, "You will be given time to not only to make technical amendments, but also to come up with a compact concept," after which the stenographer transcribing the meeting recorded: "Laughter."

During the discussion that preceded the vote, Dan Evans, the vice chairman of the committee, told Boylan that he wanted her to write a compact provision that would put "pressure on the side of the state to move ahead on a compact" because

> I would be quite unhappy if we adopted a provision that would require a compact as the only method to get into class III gaming, only to find that the state just sits on it and through inaction or obstruction would keep even the best of the Indian tribes from entering into those games.

Prior to the meeting Boylan and Patricia Zell had expressed the same concern to Inouye in a memorandum in which they recommended that, if he decided "to go forward with a compact provision," the provision should be written to authorize a tribe that failed to negotiate an agreement with the state in which the tribe's reservation was located to file a lawsuit in the U.S. District Court. If the court found that the state had been "remiss for any reason in failing to reach an agreement," the provision should direct the secretary of the interior to impose a compact on the state.

After the members of the select committee reported S. 555, Boylan and Zell converted the compact concept into a bill text that required a state to negotiate in "good faith" and authorized a tribe that believed the state in which the tribe's reservation was located had not been negotiating in good faith to file a lawsuit in which the state, rather than the tribe, would bear the burden of proving the state's good faith. If the court determined the state had not been negotiating in good faith, it would appoint a mediator. If the state refused to accept the terms in the compact the mediator recommended, the mediator would notify the secretary of the interior, who then would implement the terms in the mediator's compact.

IN AUGUST, THE select committee filed the report on S. 555 that the Senate's rules required. In September, Daniel Inouye and Dan Evans worked out a time agreement with Robert Byrd and Bob Dole, the Senate majority and minority leaders, to bring S. 555 to the floor for two hours of debate and then a vote. The agreement provided that during the debate a package of amendments Ginny Boylan and Patricia Zell had assembled were the only amendments that could be offered.

Three months earlier, William Foster, the chairman of the NIGA, had informed Inouye that the NIGA "must oppose S. 555 as reported" because the bill "does not adequately protect Indian rights, but rather resolves practically all open legal issues, against Indians, and reduces rights recognized in *Cabazon*." Before he walked through the revolving door and into private practice, Paul Alexander, had served with Patricia Zell on the staff of the American Indian Policy Review Commission, and he had supervised Zell and Ginny Boylan when he had been staff director of the select committee before Pete Taylor was promoted to the position. So even though his client opposed the bill, Alexander spent the summer lobbying his friends and former colleagues to amend S. 555 in ways the NIGA considered advantageous. That effort resulted in Boylan and Zell including several of the changes Alexander wanted in their amendment package.

On September 15, 1988, Daniel Inouye went to the Senate floor and moved that the Senate take up S. 555. Two weeks earlier the NIGA had sent a letter to every Senate office in which the association described its member tribes' objections to S. 555 and asked the senators to oppose the bill's passage. And several days before Inouye made his motion, members of the NIGA held a press conference at which they again voiced their objections.

But the only response the letter and press conference generated was apathy.

When S. 555 was brought to the floor, of one hundred senators, only six—Daniel Inouye, Dan Evans, John McCain, Chic Hecht, North Dakota senator Quentin Burdick, and New Mexico senator Pete Dominici—walked over from their offices to participate in the discussion that preceded the unrecorded voice vote. No senators from California, Minnesota, Michigan, Wisconsin, New York, Connecticut, Oklahoma, or Florida—the principal states in which, over the next twenty years, tribes would transform bingo halls that in 1988 were earning millions of dollars annually into casinos that would earn tens of billions—participated.

Rather than the two hours the time agreement authorized, the discussion that preceded the vote lasted, start to finish, only thirty-six minutes. Daniel Inouye began by assuring the nearly empty chamber that "in 15 years of gaming activity on Indian reservations, there has never been one clearly proven case of organized criminal activity." While the files of the FBI contradict that assertion, the senator was just reading from a script Ginny Boylan and Patricia Zell had written. When he finished his explanation of the bill, Inouye asked for "unanimous consent that colloquies entered into with Senators Pell, Chaffee, Domenici, Reid, and the vice chairman of the Committee, Senator Evans, be made part of the record."

A colloquy is a script a senator's staff writes in which the senator asks the manager of a bill questions about the bill that the manager answers. The rules for publication in the *Congressional Record* require "all unspoken prepared statements submitted for printing" to be printed with a black dot called a "bullet," whose presence on the page informs the reader that a statement was not spoken on the floor and was not considered by the senators before they voted.

Inouye's motion required the Government Printing Office to print the colloquies about S. 555 without bullets. As a consequence, unless he or she watches the video of the discussion that preceded the vote on S. 555 that C-Span recorded, there is no way for anyone who reads the *Congressional Record* to know that the colloquies were not spoken on the floor, and that Senators Pell, Chaffee, and Reid had not been on the floor at all.

After passing the Senate, S. 555 was sent to the U.S. House of Representatives. The inclusion of the compact provision in the bill had assuaged Tony Coelho's and Claude Pepper's concerns about Class III gambling regulation, so they now supported the bill. Nevada representatives Barbara Vucanovich and James Bilbray; Alaska representative Don Young; the ranking Republican member of the Committee on Interior and Insular Affairs; and twenty-eight of the thirty-six other members of the committee, both Democrats and Republicans, also supported the bill. That bipartisan support allowed Mo Udall to arrange with the speaker's office to add S. 555 to the list of bills that could be passed by suspending the House rules.

On Monday, September 26, 1988, with Frank Ducheneaux sitting at his side on the mostly deserted House floor, Mo Udall moved "to suspend the rules and pass the Senate bill (S. 555) to regulate gaming on Indian lands." In a halting voice debilitated by Parkinson's disease, Udall then read parts of a speech explaining the bill that Ducheneaux had written. Nevada representative Barbara Vucanovich also read a speech, after which Tony Coelho vouched that S. 555 was a "fair and reasonable approach" to resolving a "difficult issue."

But then the Kabuki theater was disrupted.

First, by Michigan representative Paul Henry. In Michigan, the five tribes that operated bingo halls also had been offering blackjack. S. 555 designated blackjack as a Class III form of gambling that a tribe could not offer unless the state in which the tribe's reservation was located allowed blackjack to be played and the tribe negotiated a compact. Henry was outraged that the definition of Class II gaming in S. 555 had been written to grandfather blackjack games that tribes in Michigan were "actually operating . . . on or before May 1, 1988," even though blackjack was illegal in Michigan. Henry also complained that he was being required to vote on a bill "which at this point is not yet even printed" and has "not been made available to the Members."

Then Minnesota representative William Frenzel, whose congressional district included the reservation at Prior Lake on which the Shakopee Mdewakanton Sioux Community operated the Little Six Bingo Palace, voiced the opposite complaint. He was upset that S. 555 excluded "electronic or electromechanical facsimiles" and "slot machines of any kind" from the Class II gaming definition, even though "in my own district there is a very small tribal unit which uses . . . television games" that generate "an important part of its revenue."

For Mo Udall, Representatives Henry's and Frenzel's objections, as well as the objections two other members from Minnesota voiced regarding the designation of video gaming machines as Class III forms of gambling, were inconsequential annoyances. However, when the presiding officer called for a voice vote on Udall's motion to suspend the rules and pass S. 555, and then, as a matter of routine, announced that "in the opinion of the chair" the bill had been passed by the required two-thirds vote, Representative Frenzel demanded the "yeas and nays" to force the more than four hundred members who were not on the floor to cast a roll call vote.

The next day when the roll was called the House passed S. 555 by a vote of 323 to 84. There is no way to know how many of the 199 Democrats and 124 Republicans who voted in the affirmative read the bill before they did so, or how many of those who did read the bill understood all of the legal consequences buried in its text. But when the Office of Management and Budget (OMB) distributed S. 555 to executive branch departments for comment, Assistant Secretary of the Interior for Indian Affairs Ross Swimmer and attorneys in the Criminal Division at the U.S. Department of Justice concluded that Congress had presented the president with a Hobson's choice.

A memorandum OMB director James Miller sent to the White House summarize their views. Miller reported that the Department of the Interior had three concerns about S. 555, the most important of which was that the compact provision did not "fully protect State interests and consequently may not further the Administration's Federalism goals." Nevertheless, because signing the bill would "settle a controversial issue" by establishing "a reasonable procedure to protect the interests of the tribes, the State governments, and the gaming public," the Department of the Interior did not object to the president doing so.

The memorandum also informed the White House that the U.S. Department of Justice objected to S. 555 because the National Indian Gaming Commission, which the bill created, "is not vested with powers comparable to those given to gaming authorities in Atlantic City and Nevada" and "does not have the power to do what is necessary to protect the games from criminal influence." But that said,

> Justice notes that, during the 99th Congress, the Administration had offered its own gambling bill which would have banned all high-stakes games except bingo, and would have subjected bingo operations to reg-

ulation by a strong Federal commission. This bill attracted almost no congressional support. Justice concludes that a bill more sensitive to law enforcement concerns is unlikely, and a veto of S. 555 would either result in a weaker bill or lead to several more years of congressional wrangling, during which time more games would come into existence that future legislators would feel obligated to grandfather. For these reasons, Justice advises that it has no objection to approval of S. 555.

After communicating those unenthusiastic nonobjections, Miller advised the White House that, because S. 555 "represents the best that can be expected of the affected parties and Congress," the president should sign the bill.

With no fanfare and no signing ceremony, on October 17, 1988 Ronald Reagan did so.

If Mo Udall (and Frank Ducheneaux) and Daniel Inouye (and Patricia Zell and Ginny Boylan) thought the enactment of the Indian Gaming Regulatory Act, as the law was named, would end the controversy that had swirled since 1979 when Seminole Management Associates opened the nation's first Indian bingo hall on the Seminole Reservation in Hollywood, Florida, and if Harry Reid thought requiring tribes to negotiate compacts with the states in which their reservations were located before they could offer Class III forms of gambling would protect the Nevada gambling industry from unwanted competition, they soon would be educated to the contrary.

12: ARIZONA MACHINES

When we put 50 slot machines in, I always
consider them 50 more mousetraps. You have
to do something to catch a mouse. It's our duty
to extract as much money from the customers
as we can.

BOB STUPAK
Las Vegas Casino Owner

Any tribe that doesn't want slot machines is
foolish.

HERBERT WHITISH
Chairman, Shoalwater Bay Tribe

I N H.R. 4566, THE BILL FRANK DUCHENEAUX WROTE IN 1983 TO REGULATE
gambling on Indian reservations, the secretary of the interior did the regulating. When the Committee on Interior and Insular Affairs held a hearing on H.R. 4566, John Fritz, the deputy assistant secretary of the interior
for Indian affairs, complained that saddling the secretary with that responsibility would impede the efforts of the Bureau of Indian Affairs (BIA) to
encourage tribal "self-determination." In response to that criticism, New
Mexico representative Bill Richardson suggested that maybe Congress
should create a regulatory commission, after which Arizona representative
Morris "Mo" Udall, the chairman of the committee, mused that an even
better idea would be "to get a retired Federal judge or a tough guy like the
football and baseball leagues have as a commissioner."

In l985, when Ducheneaux wrote his second bill, H.R. 1920, the bill
continued to require the secretary of the interior to approve tribal gaming
ordinances and management agreements, and conduct audits. However, in
1985 Representative Richardson introduced a bill to establish a thirteen-
member National Indian Gaming Commission (NIGC), six of whose seven
voting members would be retired judges and law enforcement officials.
That was the high-water mark insofar as Congress's creation of an independent and impartial regulatory commission was concerned.

The bill Virginia "Ginny" Boylan and Patricia Zell wrote in 1988, which the Select Committee on Indian Affairs reported as S. 555, created a five-member NIGC: a chairman appointed by the president and four members appointed by the secretary of the interior. The bill also required three of the five members to be enrolled members of Indian tribes.

When S. 555 reached the Senate floor, the Senate accepted a package of amendments Boylan and Zell had assembled, which, with no explanation of their content, Daniel Inouye, the manager of the bill, described as mostly "technical in nature." At the request of the National Indian Gaming Association (NIGA), one amendment reduced the commission from five members to three, two of whom were required to be enrolled members of Indian tribes. When President Ronald Reagan signed S. 555 into law as the Indian Gaming Regulatory Act (IGRA), that became the composition of the NIGC.

IN THE IGRA, the chairman of the NIGC was empowered to approve tribal gambling ordinances and management agreements, issue closure orders for "substantial" violations of the IGRA, and levy fines. The most important duty of the three commissioners acting collectively was to adopt "regulations and guidelines" for the NIGC's regulation of Class II forms of gambling. All Class III forms of gambling would be regulated pursuant to terms contained in compacts tribes would negotiate with the states in which their reservations were located.

While that regulatory system was facially reasonable, the IGRA provided that, until the commissioners adopted all the regulations the NIGC needed to have in place in order to begin its work, the secretary of the interior would continue to regulate gambling on Indian reservations pursuant to whatever legal authority he had to do so prior to the enactment of the IGRA.

"Secretary of the Interior" meant "BIA."

Years later, North Dakota senator Byron Dorgan, who from 2007 to 2011 was chairman of the Select Committee on Indian Affairs, would lament that trying to deal with the BIA was like "walking through wet cement." Given that reality, requiring the BIA to regulate Class II forms of gambling until the NIGC began functioning meant that bingo halls and card rooms on Indian reservations would be unregulated throughout the interregnum.

• • •

THREE WEEKS AFTER Ronald Reagan signed S. 555 into law, George H.W. Bush was elected president. In February 1989, the Senate confirmed Manuel Lujan, a recently retired Republican member of the U.S. House of Representatives from New Mexico, as the new president's new secretary of the interior. But it did not confirm Eddie Brown, a former social worker and middle-ranking BIA bureaucrat who President Bush nominated to be assistant secretary of the interior for Indian affairs, until almost July.

Lujan, Brown, and the White House then had to settle on a candidate for the president to nominate as chairman of the NIGC, and the FBI had to conduct a background check. As a consequence, President Bush did not nominate Tony Hope, the adopted son of comedian and film star Bob Hope, to be chairman until April 1990, and the Senate did not confirm Hope's nomination until May.

A graduate of the Harvard Law School and a former partner in the Touche Ross accounting firm, Tony Hope knew nothing about Indians or the gambling industry. But he had an important qualification: he could be an impartial regulator, because he was not a member of an Indian tribe and he had no personal relationships with senior members of the BIA bureaucracy, or with the leaders of the tribes whose bingo halls and card rooms the NIGC would regulate.

The same could not be said of the other commissioners. In November 1990, Secretary Lujan appointed Joel Frank, an enrolled member of the Seminole Tribe of Florida who had been working as the tribe's executive administrator, as the NIGC's second commissioner. The IGRA prohibited the appointment of anyone who had a "financial interest" in a "gaming activity," Frank's interest in the profitability of the Seminole Tribe's bingo halls in Hollywood and Tampa, Florida, should have been disqualifying. Even more disqualifying, until his appointment, Frank had been vice chairman of the National Indian Gaming Association (NIGA). But rather than evidence of a conflict of interest, the press release the Department of the Interior issued when his appointment was announced celebrated Frank's "experience as Vice Chairman of the National Indian Gaming Association" as "an especially important asset in helping build a framework for successful operation of the Commission."

In March 1991 Lujan appointed Jana McKeag, an enrolled member of the Cherokee Nation in Oklahoma, as the third commissioner. A former member of the staff of the American Indian Policy Review Commission, from 1979 to 1990 McKeag had worked for the BIA in Washington, D.C., before becoming director of Native American programs at the Department of Agriculture.

A year later, in February 1992, the Select Committee on Indian Affairs held its first oversight hearing on the IGRA. What the members discovered was that, during the more than three years that had passed since President Reagan signed the IGRA into law, the NIGC had adopted only one of the three sets of regulations it needed to adopt. In addition, the BIA had assigned no full-time employees to monitor the bingo halls and card rooms that were operating on more than 150 reservations to ensure that only bingo and other Class II forms of gambling were being offered, that management companies had no organized crime connections, and that the companies' employees had not been skimming.

Asked to explain that dereliction, Assistant Secretary of the Interior for Indian Affairs Eddie Brown told the senators that the bureaucracy he supervised simply could not have foreseen "there would be such a tremendous expansion of Indian gaming as has occurred, as well as the introduction of high-technology through the use of video machines" (about which more will be said).

Three weeks before the hearing, Chris Petti, who represented the Chicago Outfit in San Diego; Donald Angelini, who supervised the Outfit's gambling operations; and seven other individuals connected to the Outfit had been indicted for conspiring to take control of the bingo hall and poker room on the Rincon Reservation north of San Diego. With those indictments fresh in mind, when Deputy Assistant Attorney General Paul Maloney finished reading his testimony at the oversight hearing, Sen. John McCain asked him whether the Criminal Division of the U.S. Department of Justice had "any evidence of infiltration of organized crime into any of the Indian gaming operations." When Maloney demurred, McCain tried again. After pointing out that there had been "widespread media reports and allegations," he asked Maloney to "describe the situation from your view." When Maloney again demurred, McCain tried one last time. "I don't like to beat a dead horse here," he lectured,

> but the fact is that we're going to have witnesses from the tribes who will appear after you who will say that there is no evidence whatsoever, that they are getting a bum rap, and that the media is exploiting this issue, and it is harming their ability to conduct legitimate gaming operations on Indian reservations. I have seen many media reports which

at least on the face of them would indicate that there's a very, very serious problem out there. Mr. Maloney, I think that it is appropriate for you to testify before this committee frankly, and with candor, as to what you think the extent of the problem is. The American people who will [be] patronizing these games deserve to know, and certainly the Indian tribes deserve to have a straightforward answer so that they can be more vigilant. I would suggest that even the Indian Gaming Commission deserves a fairly definitive answer. Can you provide that?

When Maloney again refused to respond, McCain gave up and moved on.

Because there were few prosecutions, the extent to which individuals with organized crime connections were involved in the management and operation of gambling facilities on Indian reservations during Indian gaming's formative years will never be known. But without identifying tribes or mentioning the word "Mafia," ten months after the oversight hearing, the inspector general of the Department of the Interior concluded:

> Approximately 260 gambling operations that generate revenues of $2 billion a year have been established on Indian lands with minimal or no effective oversight from Federal or state governments. As a result, substantial amounts of gaming revenues that should have been realized by the tribes are instead being siphoned off by enterprises hired to manage and equip the gaming operations. During our limited review, we identified situations where gaming revenues of over $12 million may have been improperly diverted from tribes to operators and suppliers, principally because of theft and mismanagement by contracted operators of gaming establishments.

If Deputy Assistant Attorney General Maloney was less than forthcoming regarding the extent to which the Criminal Division of the U.S. Department of Justice and the FBI knew individuals with organized crime connections were involved in the management of bingo halls and card rooms on Indian reservations, what the oversight hearing did reveal was the extent to which, by 1992, the tribes and their management companies were transforming their bingo halls into what they are today: casinos whose gaming floors are stuffed to bursting with blinking and beeping video slot machines.

• • •

IN 1899 IN SAN Francisco, Charles Fey, a German immigrant, built a mechanical device that had three rotating reels on which liberty bells, horseshoes, and playing card suits were depicted. A player dropped a coin into a slot, pulled a handle, and the reels spun. When the spinning stopped, if the reels displayed the right combination of symbols, the player won. If they displayed the wrong combination, the player lost his coin.

The Liberty Bell, as Fey named his invention, and its competitors so quickly became so ubiquitous throughout California that in 1911 the legislature outlawed "slot machines," as the devices were called. Other states followed suit. In 1978 when the first casinos opened along the boardwalk in Atlantic City, Nevada was the only state other than New Jersey in which slot machines could be operated lawfully for gambling purposes. But for more than sixty years, they had been operated unlawfully.

During the Roaring Twenties, slot machines—which because to lose his money a player had to pull a lever had been nicknamed "one-armed bandits"—were installed in thousands of speakeasies that served bootleg liquor during Prohibition. In 1931 there were 25,000 machines in New York City. In 1946 there were 8,000 machines in Minnesota, principally in resort areas. In 1957 when police raided a casino in Galveston, the "wide open" Texas beach town on the island of the same name, they confiscated 2,000 machines. In the early 1960s in Hot Springs, Arkansas, another "wide open" resort town, the town's casinos had "dozens of slot machines."

Into the 1970s, the clocklike mechanism inside spinning reel slot machines was not that different from the mechanism inside the Liberty Bell. Then, in 1975 an engineer named James Saxton patented a device in which a random number generator (RNG) decides the outcomes.

Every millisecond, the RNG generates a number that ranges from zero to several billion. When a player pulls a handle or pushes a button, the pull or push assigns the most recent number to the game being played. A microprocessor checks a microchip to determine the reel-stopping positions that correspond to that number, spins reels that exist only on a video screen, and stops the reels at those positions. The outcome of the game is determined when the RNG selects the number, rather than when the reels displayed on the video screen stop spinning. The RNG-based technology is versatile in that the software in a machine can be programmed to display on the video screen whatever game the programmer wishes.

For a new generation of gamblers that came of age watching television, video gaming machines—with their blinking lights and beeping sound effects—were more fun to play than table games like roulette and craps. As a consequence, casino managers in Nevada and Atlantic City began removing tables to make room on their gaming floors for more machines. However, a federal law called the Johnson Act prohibited managers of bingo halls on Indian reservations from doing the same.

IN 1950, ATTORNEY General James McGrath hosted a conference on organized crime at the U.S. Department of Justice in Washington, D.C., after which he sent Congress two bills that the participants at the conference had recommended. One of the bills, which was enacted into law in 1951, became known as the Johnson Act after Colorado senator Edwin Johnson, the chairman of the Committee on Interstate and Foreign Commerce, who had introduced the bill in the Senate.

The Johnson Act prohibits the possession of "slot machines" and other "gambling devices" in states in which their possession is illegal and at all locations within the territorial jurisdiction of the United States, including "Indian country," a term of art that includes Indian reservations. Violating the Johnson Act is a felony, and a gambling device found in Indian country is forfeited. In 1973, for example, when the FBI discovered that slot machines had been installed in a bar on the Blackfeet Reservation in Montana, the bar was raided and the machines seized.

In 1962, Congress amended the Johnson Act to expand the definition of the term "gambling device." Although in 1962 James Saxton had not yet invented the video gaming machine, the definition includes within its purview machines that contain RNGs and microprocessors, as well server-based machines that, while they look like video gaming machines, are computer terminals whose video screens display outcomes that have been generated by an RNG in a server to which the machines have been connected.

For the managers of the more than 150 bingo halls that by the mid-1980s had opened on Indian reservations, the solution to the Johnson Act's prohibition of gambling devices in Indian country was to ignore the act on the theory that the BIA did not care and the local U.S. attorneys would not send the FBI onto the reservations to confiscate the machines and arrest the managers. They also pretended that the Johnson Act only prohibited slot machines, rather than also "gambling devices," and that video gaming machines were not slot machines. According to D. Robert "Bob" Sertell, one of the nation's foremost experts on video gaming machines, "The Indians were permitted bingo. So they called a lot of their machines 'bingo machines.' But they were no more bingo machines than I'm an astronaut."

Consistent with Sertell's recollection, two months after the Select Committee on Indian Affairs held its oversight hearing, in April 1992 the Fort Lauderdale *Sun-Sentinel* reported:

> More than 90 electronic gaming machines line the back of the Seminole Bingo Hall on State Road 7 and Stirling Road. . . . Almost all were in use on Wednesday night. As soon as one gambler left, another sat down. Players feed quarters into the machines and touch boxes on the screen. Various symbols appear—globes, Ferris wheels, even bingo numbers. When the right combinations come up, the machine spits out a piece of paper, redeemable for winnings from 25 cents to $15,000. Indian tribes argue that the games are nothing more than state-of-the-art bingo.

Because a conviction for violating the Johnson Act would result in the revocation of their licenses to sell video gaming machines to casinos in Nevada and Atlantic City, the mainstream manufacturers would not put their machines into Indian bingo halls. However, according to Bob Sertell, companies that manufactured machines for the "gray market" that existed in states where the machines were illegal were "quite big in Indian country," and "all of their machines were either slot machines with random number generators in the belly masquerading as something else, or they were server-based slot machines masquerading as bingo or pull-tabs or something."

For example, in 1987, Greyhound Electronics. a gray market manufacturer in New Jersey, sold thirty machines whose software had been programmed to enable a player to play poker to the White Earth Nation, which had opened a bingo hall on the nation's reservation in Minnesota. The company was owned by Carmen Ricci, an associate of "Little Nicky". Scarfo, the head of the Mafia in Philadelphia. In 1990, Ricci and Scarfo were indicted for putting Ricci's machines into taverns and other locations throughout Philadelphia. In 1991, SMS Manufacturing, a New Jersey gray market manufacturer that had been started with financing from a member of the Scarfo family, provided the machines that were installed in the bingo halls at Pascua Pueblo and on the Tohono O'odam Reservation in Arizona.

In 1982 Mariana Shulstead was the Department of the Interior attorney who advised Norman Crooks when Crooks and Steve Whilden negotiated the management agreement that resulted in the Little Six Enterprises joint venture constructing, and then managing, the Little Six Bingo Palace on the Shakopee Mdewakanton Sioux Community's reservation at Prior Lake, Minnesota. According to Shulstead, the year after the bingo hall opened, Little Six Enterprises built an addition that ran the length of the hall in which "machines that were supposedly bingo-like games" were installed. And on every other reservation in Minnesota, North and South Dakota, and Nebraska, "Wherever there were bingo halls, they also had machines."

The Nevada Gaming Control Board and the New Jersey Division of Gaming Enforcement require video gaming machine manufacturers to submit a prototype of each model of their machines for testing to ensure that the RNGs, microprocessors, and software have not been rigged to pay out less than the amount the laws in Nevada and New Jersey require or to allow winning combinations to be manipulated.

The gray market machines in bingo halls on Indian reservations were subjected to no such testing. And because they were gray market, they were of low quality. According to Bob Sertell, many of the machines in casinos on Indian reservations in southern California had doors that did not lock, contained RNGs that did not generate numbers randomly, and "if you slammed them on the side of the cabinet in a particular place in a particular pattern, the machine would pay off twenty dollars."

The machines also were easy to rig. As Sertell, who the NIGC hired as a consultant, explained to the NIGC, some of the machines had been programmed "to never deliver a winning outcome when the player has bet the maximum amount," while others were programmed to give an "undercount." "A $5.00 bill, inserted into a machine which charges a nickel per play, might only register 80 credits." And the amount of money a machine paid out could be changed using a remote control transmitter.

Gray market machines also could be rigged to cheat the tribe that owned the bingo hall. As Sertell explained in 1999:

In some instances, casinos have discovered that [gray market] machines which have never received prototype approval from a gaming laboratory contain illegal subroutines within their software that contain recognition algorithms that allows a player to adjust the amount of credits bet in a coded sequence which the machine will "recognize." Upon recognition, the machine will either deliver an unusually high frequency of winning outcomes, or an inflated "overpayment" of credits on each winning occasion.

How much cheating went on? The evidence is anecdotal. But here is what the *St. Petersburg Times* reported about the machines Seminole Management Associates (SMA) and Pan American & Associates (PA&A) installed in the bingo halls they managed on the Seminole reservations in Hollywood and Immokalee, Florida.*

Dominick Sgarlata walked into the Seminole casino in Hollywood, Fla., one night in April 1995 and won $200,021. The next day, he won again—$2,500 in the morning, $4,300 several hours later. In fact, Dominick Sgarlata beat the video slot machines in the Hollywood casino 22 times in 1995. His total take: $532,727. The *St. Petersburg Times* has tried to find Sgarlata. . . . But no such luck.

In just six months, one woman playing video slot machines at the Immokalee casino won 57 jackpots worth a total $475,000. . . . When officers of the Seminole police force gave federal officials evidence of suspicious payouts in the casinos, the tribe's leaders acted promptly. They fired the officers.

WHEN FRANK DUCHENEAUX wrote H.R. 4566 in 1983, there were few, if any, video gaming machines in bingo halls on Indian reservations. As a consequence, the bill prohibited a tribe from offering a "gambling activity" that

---

*In 1978, Steve Whilden discovered that five acres the county owned in Immokalee, a farm town in southwestern Florida, had a covenant in its deed that required the land to be used to provide housing for Seminole Indians. So he persuaded the county to deed the land to the Seminole Tribe so that Indians "residing on said lands may be eligible for a broader range of Federal grants and services." The tribe then deeded the land to the secretary of the interior. The secretary's acceptance of the deed transformed the five acres into an Indian reservation. Since Immokalee is a convenient drive from Naples and Fort Myers, James Billie, the chairman of the Seminole Tribe, and James Clare, the PA&A partner who managed the tribe's bingo hall in Tampa, signed a management agreement in 1994 pursuant to which PA&A finished the construction of, and then managed, a bingo hall on the five acres in Immokalee.

was "prohibited within Indian country by Federal law," which was legalese for "prohibited by the Johnson Act." In 1986 when Mo Udall and North Dakota senator Mark Andrews accepted the Reagan administration's suggestion that Congress divide gambling that would be permitted on Indian reservations into three classes, the definition of Class II gaming in the versions of H.R. 1920 the U.S. House of Representatives passed and the Select Committee on Indian Affairs reported during the Ninety-Ninth Congress did not include video gaming machines in the definition.

But by 1987 video gaming machines had become commonplace in bingo halls on Indian reservations. In recognition of that fact, when Ginny Boylan and Patricia Zell wrote the bill Daniel Inouye, the new chairman of the Select Committee on Indian Affairs, introduced at the beginning of the One Hundredth Congress as S. 555, they included a provision that waived the Johnson Act for Class III forms of gambling that were lawful in the state in which a tribe's reservation was located. But to confuse the legal situation, they included a sentence in their definition of Class II gaming that read: "Class II gaming may include electronic or electromechanical facsimiles of [bingo or lotto], where devices of such types are otherwise legal under State law."

After the U.S. Supreme Court issued its decision in *California v. Cabazon and Morongo Bands of Mission Indians*, when Boylan and Zell and Frank Ducheneaux wrote the bill Mo Udall and John McCain introduced as H.R. 2507 and S. 1303, the bill made no mention of the Johnson Act. But it changed the definition of Class II gaming in S. 555 by eliminating the requirement that "electronic and electromechanical facsimiles" of bingo and lotto (and now also poker, blackjack, and all other "card games") be "otherwise legal under State law." The consequence was that video gaming machines whose software had been programmed to play bingo, poker, blackjack, and other card games were permissible Class II forms of gambling, even if possession of the machines was prohibited by the Johnson Act and by the laws of the state in which a bingo hall was located.

If Ginny Boylan, Patricia Zell, and Frank Ducheneaux had quietly done what they could to have Congress legalize video gaming machines, all of the members of the Select Committee on Indian Affairs, including Daniel Inouye, for whom Boylan and Zell worked, opposed the idea. So in the bill Boylan and Zell wrote that on May 13, 1988 the select committee reported to the Senate as a substitute for the original text of S. 555, a sentence was added into the Class II gaming definition that stated: "The term 'class II gaming' does not include . . . electronic or electromechanical facsimiles of any game of chance or slot machines of any kind." And during the May 13 meeting, Inouye assured the other members that the bill "exclude[s] from class II slot machines that some call 'bingo slots' which, in the minds of most of us here, are slots, pure and simple."

The leaders of the tribes that were members of the NIGA understood the legal consequence. In June in a letter that, in addition to its other officers, Vice Chairman Joel Frank signed, the NIGA informed Inouye that the organization opposed S. 555 because

> It is our view that S. 555 does not adequately protect Indian rights, but rather resolves practically all open legal issues against Indians, and reduces rights recognized in Cabazon. An example of an open legal issue is which, if any, video devices are prohibited slot machines within the meaning of [the Johnson Act].

In August, Paul Alexander knew that when Congress returned to Washington, D.C., from its summer recess Inouye intended to bring S. 555 to the Senate floor. The NIGA lobbyist sent his client a list of amendments to the bill that the NIGA should consider instructing him to lobby the Senate to accept. One amendment authorized bingo halls on Indian reservations to continue to operate "electronic or electromechanical facsimiles of any game of chance that were actually operated by an Indian tribe before the date of enactment of this Act." Another modified the Class II gaming definition to state: "The term 'class II gaming' includes electronic or electromechanical facsimiles of any class II game." Since neither amendment was included in the version of S. 555 that passed the Senate, when President Reagan signed the bill into law as the IGRA, every manager of every bingo hall on every reservation was on notice that the video gaming machines that had been installed in the halls were being operated in violation of both the IGRA and the Johnson Act.

There was, however, one way machines could continue to be operated. The IGRA provided that, if video gaming machines were lawful in the state in which a tribe's reservation was located, and if the tribe and the state negotiated a compact that authorized machines, the Johnson Act was waived. That is what happened in Minnesota.

In 1984 the Minnesota legislature had legalized the gray market by authorizing establishments that had liquor licenses to license their machines. Although the law disingenuously prohibited the machines from being used for gambling purposes, the state was not in a position to object to the fact that the eleven Indian tribes in Minnesota that operated bingo halls had the same gray market machines in their halls. As a consequence, the compacts Minnesota governor Rudy Perpich signed with the tribes between 1988 and 1991 authorized video gaming machines, but required the tribes to phase out their gray market machines and buy or lease new machines from a licensed manufacturer. The compacts also required the tribes to submit prototypes of the new machines for testing and required the machines to pay out at least 80 percent of the money players paid in.

While the compacts gave video gaming machines in bingo halls on Indian reservations in Minnesota a veneer of regulation, the state had no ability to know whether a tribe was complying with the terms of its compact. By 1992, there were 7,200 machines in thirteen halls. While the compacts allowed the Division of Gaming Enforcement of the Minnesota Department of Public Safety to make unannounced inspections, because it had only five enforcement agents, the Division could annually spot-check no more than 3 percent of the machines.

Minnesota was unique because the possession of video gaming machines was legal. On Indian reservations in states in which the machines were illegal, bingo hall managers continued to ignore the Johnson Act. And when challenged, the tribes' attorneys claimed that video gaming machines were "technologic aids" that assisted players to play bingo and poker and which the Class II gaming definition in the IGRA allowed, rather than "electronic or electromechanical facsimiles" of bingo and poker, which the definition prohibited. And the BIA continued not to care and the local U.S. attorneys continued not to send the FBI into the halls to enforce the Johnson Act and confiscate the machines.

That was the situation Tony Hope faced in May 1990 when he became chairman of the NIGC and began meeting with the leaders of tribes that were operating bingo halls about the content of the regulations the NIGC would write to clarify the confusion the same tribal leaders and their attorneys had created regarding the difference between "technologic aids" and "electronic or electromechanical facsimiles."

Since he was a graduate of the Harvard Law School, Hope was as qualified as Michael Cox, the NIGC's general counsel, was to discern the meaning of the term "electronic or electromechanical facsimiles" that the "class II gaming" definition in the IGRA excluded from the definition. So he agreed with Cox that the term included within its purview video gaming machines whose software had been programmed to play bingo, as well as all other types of machines that were "gambling devices" as the Johnson Act defined that term.

Seven months after Secretary of the Interior Manuel Lujan appointed Jana McKeag as the third NIGC commissioner, in November 1991 the NIGC published proposed regulations in the *Federal Register*. Two of the regulations announced the conclusion regarding the meaning of the term "electronic or electromechanical facsimiles" to which Hope and Cox had reasoned.

In response, the NIGC received 1,700 written comments. It also held hearings in St. Paul, Phoenix, Seattle, Oklahoma City, and Washington, D.C., at which the leaders of tribes that were operating video gaming machines in their bingo halls argued that, no matter what the Class II gaming definition said, the NIGC had an obligation to allow tribes that were making money to keep making it. But as Michael Cox explained when the hearings concluded, "Some tribes think our job is to promote Indian gaming, while we think our duty is to primarily regulate the [Indian Gaming Regulatory A]ct the way Congress intended." In April 1992, the NIGC published its proposed regulations in the *Federal Register* as a final rule. The publication finally motivated a U.S. attorney to take action.

A NUMBER OF STATES had Las Vegas Night laws that allowed churches and nonprofit organizations to host fund-raising events at which casino games like blackjack and roulette and slot machines could be played for small stakes. As has been described, after the U.S. Supreme Court issued its decision in *California v. Cabazon and Morongo Bands of Mission Indians*, Frank Ducheneaux, Ginny Boylan, and Patricia Zell wrote a new bill that Mo Udall and John McCain introduced as H.R. 2507 and S. 1303. Section 10 of the bill granted an Indian tribe the right to offer both Class II and Class III forms of gambling on its reservation "where such Indian gaming is located within a State that permits such gaming for any purpose by any person, organization or entity and such gaming is not otherwise specifically prohibited on Indian lands by Federal law [i. e., by the Johnson Act]."

To clarify the meaning of that language, when the Select Committee on Indian Affairs held a hearing on S. 1303—and on S. 555, the bill Daniel Inouye had introduced before the U.S. Supreme Court issued the *Cabazon and Morongo Bands* decision—Victoria Toensing, the assistant attorney general who represented the U.S. Department of Justice, and Inouye, who chaired the hearing, had the following exchange:

> TOENSING: Very few States really allow casino gambling, but there are many more States that for one or two nights a year and for certain charitable purposes allow the local churches to have Las Vegas evening[s], and therefore allow for a brief period and for limited amounts, the crap games and the roulette wheels and card playings that are in the casino gambling. We [i.e., the U.S. Department of Justice] would hope—we expect that your intent is that because there is this limited permission for certain evenings with very strict rules and only for charitable purposes, that would not mean that the whole area of casino gambling is then allowed on Indian reservations under that civil regulatory analysis. So we ask that we could look at that again and make sure that really is strengthened and made clear in the bill.
>
> INOUYE: I can assure you that is my intent as author of the measure.
>
> TOENSING: I assumed that it was, but our lawyers looked at it and thought that it might be unclear in the legislation, so we would like to work with you on that.

Despite the chairman's assurance, when they wrote the bill that Inouye and the other members of the select committee voted to send to the Senate as a substitute for the original text of S. 555, Ginny Boylan and Patricia Zell did not change the text to conform to what Inouye had told Victoria Toensing was his intent. Instead, the bill President Reagan signed into law as the IGRA directed that "class III gaming activities" were lawful on an Indian reservation if the reservation was "located in a State that permits such gaming for any purpose by any person, organization, or entity." In Arizona, that provision was consequential, because state law allowed the possession of video gaming machines as long as the machines were not used for the purpose of gambling. And another state law allowed video gaming machines to be played at Las Vegas Night fund-raising events.

Another section of the IGRA allowed a tribe that had video gaming machines in its bingo hall to continue to operate the machines for one year, but only if the machines were "legally operated on Indian lands on or before May 1, 1988," and within thirty days from the date of the enactment of the IGRA the tribe requested the state in which its reservation was located to negotiate a compact. Because prior to May 1, 1988 the Johnson Act prohibited all video gaming machines on all reservations, that provision had no legal consequence. But it gave tribes semi-straight-faced political cover to keep operating their machines while they tried to negotiate compacts.

In Arizona, the tribes that wanted compacts argued to Gov. Rose Mofford that, since state law authorized the possession of video gaming machines for the purpose of recreational play and for gambling purposes at Las Vegas Night fund-raising events, the IGRA required the state to agree to allow the tribes to operate the same machines. However, Mofford rejected that interpretation of the IGRA. And in March 1991 when he succeeded Mofford, Arizona Governor Fife Symington announced that he had the same legal position. Nevertheless, even though they did not have compacts, all of the tribes in Arizona that had video gaming machines in their bingo halls prior to Congress's passage of the IGRA continued to operate them.

In FEBRUARY 1990 President George H.W. Bush appointed Assistant U.S. Attorney Linda Akers as U.S. attorney for the district of Arizona. A no-nonsense prosecutor, before joining the U.S. Attorney's Office, Akers had been the head of the Organized Crime and Racketeering Division of the Office of the Arizona Attorney General.

Inside the U.S. Department of Justice an advisory committee composed of U.S. attorneys from around the nation advises the attorney general regarding legal matters of common concern. U.S. Attorney Akers became a member of the advisory committee's subcommittee on Indian affairs. According to Akers, the subcommittee met "regularly to discuss the problems as they exist and to share solutions that have occurred on one reservation or another." One of the problems was what to do about video gaming machines that were being operated in violation of the IGRA and the Johnson Act.

Five days after the NIGC published its proposed regulations that made clear that video gaming machines were a Class III—rather than a Class II— form of gambling, Akers decided to begin enforcing the law. In a letter dated November 6, 1991, she notified the leaders of every tribe in Arizona that was operating machines in its bingo hall that, while her predecessor had "elected to forego prosecutions of gambling activity on the reservations until after the passage of the Indian Gaming Regulatory Act and the staffing of the National Indian Gaming Commission," beginning January 1, 1992, she would "take appropriate action against gaming activity conducted in violation of the IGRA," including any Class III form of gambling, "which is not conducted under a tribal-state compact (regardless of the current status of negotiations)."

The tribal leaders responded by sending a letter to Governor Syming-ton in which they argued that "the time has come for the State and the tribes to sit down, on a government-to-government basis, and begin th[e] process" of negotiating compacts that would authorize the tribes to keep their machines. But Symington remained adamant that—because Arizona law prohibited video gaming machines from being used for gambling pur-poses except at Las Vegas Night fund-raising events—he would not agree to compacts that allowed tribes to operate machines.

That was the situation when—with Tony Hope and Jana McKeag voting yes and Joel Frank voting no—the NIGC voted to publish its pro-posed regulations in the *Federal Register* as a final rule. The regulations went into effect on May 7, 1992.

At U.S. Attorney Akers' direction, at 6:00 a.m. on May 12, trucks towing moving van trailers drove into the parking lots of bingo halls on five reservations in Arizona. They were accompanied by FBI agents and U.S. marshals who began loading into the trailers what by the end of the morning would be 750 video gaming machines. The operation went smoothly at four of the five halls, but not at the Ba'Ja Bingo Center on the Fort McDowell Reservation east of Scottsdale.

IN 1984, THE FORT McDowell Mohave-Apache Indian Community signed a management agreement with Mid-America Trust, Inc. (MATI), a management company based in Kansas City, for MATI to construct, and then manage, a 1,600-seat bingo hall in which MATI installed several hun-dred gray market video gaming machines.

MATI's first manager was a Kansas City resident named Bernie

Black, who, according to Clinton Patta, the president of the Fort McDowell Mohave-Apache Indian Community, "[W]as in the hall all the time running things. We never had any contact with him. We asked who he was. We asked for a background check on him. That's when he stopped coming around." The reason Black stopped coming around was that a background check would have revealed that he was a felon who in 1966 had pled guilty to managing an illegal casino in Leavenworth, Kansas.

In 1990 the Fort McDowell Mohave-Apache Indian Community bought MATI out of its management agreement. "There were a number of people who suspected that money was being skimmed," Gilbert Jones, the tribe's vice president, would recall as to why. "There were things that reaffirmed that belief. But there was never anything that we could prove."

During the year prior to the morning the FBI and the U.S. marshals raided the Ba'Ja Bingo Center, the bingo hall grossed $30 million, 80 to 85 percent of which had been generated by the 358 video gaming machines the FBI agents and U.S. marshals loaded into eight trailers in the center's parking lot.

It was when the trailers had been loaded that members of the Fort McDowell Mohave-Apache Indian Community blockaded the parking lot exits with a water truck, two dump trucks, and a front-end loader. An FBI agent armed with an M-16 rifle was on the roof of the bingo hall. According to Richard La Fountain, the special agent in charge of the BIA police, "The potential for violence was very high." And according to an FBI agent who was in the parking lot: "We could have busted out of there. But people would have been arrested. Cars would have been wrecked." So the FBI supervisor at the scene made the decision to stand down.

When Governor Symington was informed of the situation, he agreed to meet with Clinton Patta at the public library in the town down the road from the reservation. At the meeting, Symington and Patta negotiated a ten-day "cooling off period," pursuant to which an exit was cleared to allow the trucks to leave the parking lot as tribal members jeered and several threw soft drink cans at the departing vehicles. But the trailers stayed because, as Symington told the press, "It's just not worth having bloodshed over an issue like this."

Ten days later, with the trailers still barricaded in the parking lot, Symington announced that he now was willing to negotiate compacts that would authorize each tribe in Arizona to operate one casino that could contain no more than 250 video gaming machines.

Having pushed the situation as far as it could without provoking an armed confrontation with the FBI, after twice extending the cooling-off period, in June the tribal council allowed the trailers to be driven out of the parking lot. The video gaming machines in the trailers then were stored in the warehouse in which the other machines the FBI agents and U.S. marshals had confiscated were being stored. The council then decided to accept the governor's offer and in July signed a compact that allowed the tribe to operate 250 machines.

While the Fort McDowell Mohave-Apache Indian Community had used the threat of violence to intimidate the governor into agreeing to allow the tribe to operate legally most of the video gaming machines it had been operating illegally, three other tribes attempted to achieve an even better result through a less confrontational means.

ONE OF THE other bingo halls the FBI agents and U.S. marshals raided was located on the Yavapai-Prescott Reservation north of Phoenix. The month after President Reagan signed S. 555 into law as the IGRA, the Yavapai-Prescott Tribe began negotiating a compact with Governor Mofford. But the negotiations broke down when Mofford refused to discuss including video gaming machines in the compact. When he succeeded Mofford as governor, Fife Symington adopted the same position. In response to what its leaders considered Symington's intransigence, seven months before its bingo hall was raided, the Yavapai-Prescott Tribe filed a lawsuit against the state in which it alleged that the governor had refused to negotiate in good faith.

After the White Mountain Apache and Pascua Yaqui Tribes, and Tohono O'odam Nation joined the lawsuit , in December 1992, District Judge Paul Rosenblatt appointed Frank X. Gordon, a retired justice of the Arizona Supreme Court, as a mediator and ordered the tribes and the governor to each submit proposed compacts to Gordon.* In the compact he

---

*Rosenblatt appointed Gordon as a mediator without first deciding that Governor Symington had negotiated in bad faith and without deciding whether the IGRA imposed a legal duty on the governor to negotiate compacts that would allow the tribes to operate video gaming machines. For those reasons, Patricia Zell confidentially advised Daniel Inouye that Rosenblatt's action violated the IGRA.

submitted, Symington offered to allow each tribe to operate 250 video gaming machines. In the compacts they submitted, the White Mountain Apache and Pascua Yaqui Tribes requested Gordon to allow each tribe to operate 1,800 machines, and the Tohono O'odam Nation requested Gordon to allow it to operate 2,600 machines.*

In February 1993, Gordon selected the tribes' compacts and rejected the governor's because

> Charity "Las Vegas Nights" or "Casino Nights" are permitted in Arizona, without regulation. In such events non-profit organizations can raise funds for charitable purposes by providing full-scale casino-type gambling to its patrons, including blackjack, poker, dice, roulette, and slot machines.
>
> . . .
>
> It seems cruel to allow non-Indian charities in Arizona to use casino gambling to raise substantial sums of money for such purposes as: providing scholarships for educational needs, raising money for medical services and supplies for the sick, the elderly and the disabled, and yet to deny the Indian tribes of Arizona that same opportunity for the very same purpose.

When he read Gordon's decision, Governor Symington asked Arizona senator John McCain whether the result Gordon had announced regarding Las Vegas Nights was the result Congress had intended the IGRA to require. McCain responded that the

> Arizona legislature has explicitly decided to permit and regulate casino-style gaming activities by authorizing "casino nights." As long as this law is in effect, tribes can properly insist on the inclusion of casino-style gaming in any compact. On the other hand, if the state legislature acts to criminally prohibit casino-style gaming, then such activity is illegal for everyone, including tribes. This was clearly the intent of Congress under the Act.

Acting on McCain's implicit suggestion, Symington called the Arizona legislature into session to repeal the Las Vegas Night law. Over the

---

*The previous July, the Yavapai-Prescott Tribe accepted Governor Symington's offer and signed a compact that authorized the tribe to operate 250 video gaming machines.

previous five years, the Cactus-Pine Girl Scout Council, Planned Parenthood, the Arthritis Foundation, and dozens of other nonprofit organizations had hosted more than seven hundred Las Vegas Night events at which they collectively raised several million dollars. So the vote in the legislature to end a source of funding on which those organizations depended was close. However, first the Senate, and then the House, voted for repeal. When Symington signed the repeal bill into law, he announced he was doing so because "I will not, and I cannot, idle in my office while this state, without the consent of its people, is transformed into a haven for full-scale casino gambling and all of the social consequences it brings."

Then he flew to Washington, D.C.

A month earlier, in February 1993, Symington had been in the national capital to attend the winter meeting of the National Governors' Association (NGA). By then, in addition to the lawsuit the Yavapai-Prescott Tribe had filed in Arizona, Indian tribes had filed lawsuits in more than a dozen other states. Like the Yavapai-Prescott Tribe's lawsuit, in those suits the tribes alleged that the governors of the states in which their reservations were located had been negotiating compacts in "bad faith" because they refused to allow the tribes to offer forms of gambling that the states' Las Vegas Night laws allowed or to allow all forms of Class III gambling because the state operated a lottery.

In response to the lawsuits, the governors passed a resolution that urged Congress to amend the IGRA to eliminate the language that authorized a tribe to offer every form of Class III gambling the state in which the tribe's reservation was located permitted "for any purpose by any person, organization, or entity." Symington returned to Washington, D.C., in March to join Colorado governor Roy Romer, the chairman of the NGA, and three other governors for a meeting at the Department of the Interior to discuss the NGA resolution with Bruce Babbitt, the new secretary of the interior.

A SCION OF A prominent ranching and mercantile family in northern Arizona, Babbitt had been both attorney general and governor of Arizona. In 1987 when his governorship ended, Babbitt joined a large international law firm that had an office in Phoenix and began campaigning for the 1988 Democratic presidential nomination. After losing, first the Iowa caucuses, and then the New Hampshire primary election, Babbitt reinvented himself as a leader of the national environmental movement by becoming president of the League of Conservation Voters. In November 1992 when Bill Clinton won the presidency, the league and other environmental organizations that had supported candidate Clinton persuaded President-elect Clinton to appoint Babbitt secretary of the interior.

Having been raised in Flagstaff, which is east of the Hualapai and Havasupai reservations and west of the Navajo reservation, Babbitt grew up around Indians. He had been governor in 1983 when the Pan American Management Company opened the first bingo hall on an Indian reservation in Arizona at Pascua Pueblo. And when he practiced law in Phoenix, the Yavapai-Prescott Tribe had been a client. So Babbitt knew about Indians, and he knew that tribes in Arizona were operating hundreds of video gaming machines in their bingo halls.

During his confirmation hearing Babbitt had not been asked about gambling on Indian reservations. However, four days after he was confirmed, the new secretary of the interior appeared before the Select Committee on Indian Affairs to discuss his views on Indian policy.

When the discussion turned to gambling, Babbitt told Daniel Inouye and John McCain, who had replaced Dan Evans as vice chairman of the committee, that "properly worked out" gambling presented "an extraordinary opportunity to start economic engines in a lot of reservation areas" where other types of economic development "might be very, very slow in coming." But he acknowledged that many governors were "up in arms" that tribes in their states were attempting to use the IGRA to compel the governors to agree to compacts that would authorize the tribes to operate video gaming machines and offer other Class III forms of gambling that state law did not permit other than for the limited purpose of Las Vegas Night fund-raising events.

When it was his turn to question the witness, John McCain began by blaming the Las Vegas Night situation on the U.S. Supreme Court because "the aspect of the Supreme Court decision [in *California v. Cabazon and Morongo Bands of Mission Indians*] that a lot of people didn't anticipate" was "that if there is charitable gaming, such as a 'Las Vegas Night' allowed in the State, it is translated into the right of an Indian tribe to set up a gambling casino."

When McCain then asked him what his view of the situation was Babbitt did not correct the senator's self-serving misassertion that the Court had created the Las Vegas Night problem. Instead, he deftly shaded his answer by responding: "The courts are now painting in some results that [Congress] may or may not have contemplated. I was not a party to it, and I don't know." Six weeks later, when he met with Romer and Symington to discuss the NGA resolution, Babbitt told them he understood the governors' concerns and would ask Congress to amend the IGRA to clarify what forms of gambling a tribe could offer, as well as what "good faith" meant.

The next day, Babbitt met with Charles Keechi, the chairman of the NIGA, and a dozen other tribal leaders. After the meeting Keechi told the press that, after having discussed the situation with Babbitt, he was confident "we have a friend in the secretary of the interior" who "feels the American Indian should have the upper hand whenever possible." However, Michael Anderson, a former member of the staff of the Select Committee on Indian Affairs who attended the meeting, more realistically described the message Babbitt delivered as follows: "Secretary Babbitt was very candid on what the political landscape is. Obviously, the governors are putting a lot of pressure on him."

And they were. Several weeks later, when he attended the spring meeting of the Western Governors' Association, Babbitt was overheard saying that he wished he had never heard of Indian gaming, which he complained was "an 800-pound gorilla falling through the transom."

To calm the situation in Arizona, Babbitt used his good offices to broker a deal. As Fife Symington's press secretary subsequently explained: "The governor made numerous trips to Washington. Babbitt came out here to Arizona. There were many, many phone calls. There was almost constant daily phone contact with him."

In June, a bargain was struck and Symington signed compacts with eight tribes that, as Babbitt suggested, allowed each to operate between 475 and 1,400 video gaming machines depending on the size of the tribe. No casino could have more than 500 machines. So if a tribe had enough members to be entitled to more than 500 machines, it would have to open a second casino located at least a mile and a half from the tribe's first casino. Symington capitulated because, as his press secretary explained, the governor was told that, "If we don't sign these compromise compacts, the mediated compacts will be signed by Babbitt."

If Symington had held firm and Babbitt then had implemented the three compacts Frank X. Gordon had selected, the governor could have litigated the question of whether—after the Arizona legislature repealed the state's Las

Vegas Night law—the terms in the compacts were consistent with the re-
quirements of the IGRA. But a lawsuit would have dragged on for years. And
since, in response to the Fort McDowell Mohave-Apache Indian Community's threat of violence, Symington had agreed to compacts that allowed
every tribe to operate 250 machines, he was poorly positioned politically to
object to compacts that differed only in the number of machines.

Symington's acceptance of the compacts Bruce Babbitt brokered accel-
erated the conversion of bingo halls on Indian reservations in Arizona that in
1993 contained hundreds of machines into the twenty-six casinos tribes operate in Arizona today, whose gaming floors collectively contain more than
14,000 machines.

At the Fort McDowell Reservation, in front of the Radisson Fort Mc-
Dowell Resort & Casino, a complex that contains a five-story hotel and
convention center, a golf course, a 1,700-seat bingo hall, and more than
800 video gaming machines, a ten-foot-tall sculpture of an Indian beating
on a gourd drum commands a patch of grass. In front of the sculpture is a
marble pedestal at the top of which is a plaque that reads: "Remembering
May 12, 1992." On each side of the walkway that leads to the sculpture
two other plaques are mounted on poles. One reads: "It was on May 12,
1992, that federal agents and marshals raided Fort McDowell Gaming
Center to confiscate slot machines that had been installed at this facility.
May 12th has become a historical marker for the Fort McDowell Indian
Tribe; a day when words were backed by action; a day when a community
stood together as one, claiming the right to exist as a sovereign nation."

13: CALIFORNIA MACHINES

> The tribes and their members have shown
> themselves to be law abiding citizens and
> their compliance is anticipated.
>
> JANET RENO
> *Attorney General of the United States*

AS EARLY AS 1984, COMPANIES THAT MANUFACTURED VIDEO GAMING machines for the gray market began marketing their machines to managers of bingo halls on Indian reservations in California. In October of that year, Mark Nichols, who managed the hall on the Cabazon Reservation east of Palm Springs, told *Gambling & Wagering Business* magazine that he had been approached, but the Cabazon council had rejected the idea "because federal law prohibits gaming machinery on Indian lands." However, the $100 to $400 a day a video gaming machine could earn eventually persuaded Nichols and the other managers to ignore the fact that the possession of a "gambling device" on an Indian reservation in violation of the Johnson Act was a felony.

As described in chapter four, in March 1986, a grand jury in San Diego indicted Steward Siegel, the former manager of the bingo hall on the Barona Reservation, for using shills to rig bingo games. After Siegel pled guilty, the Barona Group of the Capitan Grande Band of Mission Indians terminated its management agreement with American Management & Amusement, Inc., the company for whom Siegel had worked.

The bingo hall on the Barona Reservation was reopened by a new management company. In 1989, it was being operated by Gary Triano, the Arizona real estate developer who was one of the owners of Bingo Enterprises, Inc., the company that constructed, and, in 1983, had begun managing, the bingo hall on the Papago Reservation south of Tucson.

When Triano assumed control of the hall at Barona, John Turner, his attorney in San Diego, read the definitions of Class II gaming and Class III gaming in the Indian Gaming Regulatory Act (IGRA). He concluded that video gaming machines were a Class III form of gambling that the IGRA prohibited Triano from installing in the Barona Group's bingo hall until and unless the group negotiated a compact with the state of California that authorized Triano to do so. Triano rejected that advice and spent $150,000 to purchase thirty gray market machines programmed to play bingo.

Still concerned the machines were illegal, Turner sent letters to the U.S. attorney in San Diego and to San Diego County Sheriff John Duffy that, according to Turner, said: "We have brought these machines in, and we would like you guys to tell us whether you have a problem." The U.S. attorney did not respond, and someone from Sheriff Duffy's office informed Turner that he did not think the sheriff had any objection.

Triano put the machines out on the floor, and for the next several months they earned considerable money. Then, according to Turner, on April 27, 1989, "I was lying in bed about nine-thirty at night, and I get a call from Frank Buscemi [who was managing the hall for Triano] and he says, 'I'm locked in the counting room. The sheriff has invaded us. They are banging at the door. What should I do?'" When Turner told Buscemi to open the door, Sheriff Duffy's deputies confiscated both the money in the counting room and the machines.

THREE YEARS EARLIER, in May 1986 the Reagan administration sent Congress a bill whose content reflected the agreement regarding how gambling on Indian reservations should be regulated that officials at the Bureau of Indian Affairs (BIA) and the Criminal Division of the U.S. Department of Justice had negotiated between themselves. The attorneys who wrote the bill knew that the U.S. Courts of Appeals for the Fifth and Ninth Circuits had ruled that Congress did not intend Public Law No. 83-280 to delegate Florida and California (and by inference other states) authority to enforce their gambling laws on Indian reservations if those laws regulated, rather than prohibited, a particular form of gambling. To reverse those rulings, the bill writers included a provision in their bill that added a new section 1166 to Title 18 of the U.S. Code. Subsection (a) of the new section 1166 stated that all state gambling laws would apply in "Indian country," a legal term of art that includes reservations. Subsection (d) stated that prosecutions for violations of those state laws should be undertaken by the states.

When Pete Taylor, the staff director of the Select Committee on Indian Affairs, began writing a new bill for North Dakota senator Mark Andrews, the chairman of the select committee, to offer as a substitute for the text of H.R. 1920 (the bill that had passed the U.S. House of Representatives), he decided to include the new section 1166 in his bill. But he made a consequential change. The text of subsection (a) in Taylor's bill was identical to the text of subsection (a) in the Reagan administration's bill. But Taylor rewrote subsection (d) to *prohibit* states from prosecuting violations of their gambling laws. Instead, prosecutions were to be undertaken by the local U.S. attorneys, "unless a tribe has consented to State criminal prosecution on the tribe's lands."

On September 17, 1986 when the members of the select committee voted to substitute the text of Taylor's bill for the version of H.R. 1920 that had passed the U.S. House of Representatives, no member asked Taylor to explain what the legal consequences would be if Congress passed his bill. H.R. 1920 died when the Ninety-Ninth Congress adjourned.

When the One Hundredth Congress convened in January 1987, Virginia "Ginny" Boylan and Patricia Zell, his chief counsel, wrote a new bill that Hawaii senator Daniel Inouye, the new chairman of the select committee, introduced as S. 555. When Boylan and Zell decided to include section 1166 in their bill, they rewrote the text of the subsection (d) Pete Taylor had written to state: "The United States shall have *exclusive jurisdiction* over criminal prosecutions of violations of State gambling laws . . . unless an Indian tribe . . . has consented to the transfer to the State of criminal jurisdiction with respect to gambling on the Indian tribe's lands." (emphasis added) With inconsequential amendment, that is the text of section 1166(d) that was included in the version of S. 555 Ronald Reagan signed into law as the IGRA.

How many senators and members of the U.S. House of Representatives knew S. 555 contained section 1166? And how many of the few who may have known understood the legal consequences Ginny Boylan and Patricia Zell had written their version of subsection (d) in order to achieve; which was to expand the *Seminole Tribe of Florida v. Butterworth* and *Barona Group of the Capitan Grande Band of Mission Indians v. Duffy* decisions and nullify the possible application of the U.S. Supreme Court's decision in *Rice v. Rehner* by prohibiting states from enforcing their gambling laws on Indian reservations—even if those laws completely prohibited, rather than merely regulated, a particular form of gambling?

Section 330b of the California Penal Code was one of those laws. The section prohibited the possession of a "slot machine or device," which section 330b defined as any "mechanical, electromechanical, or electronic contrivance, component, or machine used remotely or directly in connection with gaming or any game which affects the result of a wager by determining win or loss." Because section 1166(d) prohibited Sheriff Duffy from enforcing section 330b, a month after his deputies raided the bingo hall on the Barona Reservation, Gary Triano and the Barona Group filed a lawsuit against Duffy in the U.S. District Court in San Diego. The case was assigned to Judith Keep, the district judge who in 1982 had ruled against Harry Hertzberg in the lawsuit Hertzberg had filed against Duffy.

At the hearing, Judge Keep held on John Turner's request that she order the sheriff to return Triano's video bingo machines, Turner argued that, since section 1166(d) prohibited the state from prosecuting Triano, Duffy's deputies had no authority to seize the machines. But according to Turner,

> Judge Keep was just death on gambling. She hated it. When I finished making my pitch, the county attorney had a law enforcement officer wheel one of the machines into the courtroom, and they proceeded to put money in it and spin the reels. After watching them spin, Judge Keep said, "Mr. Turner, if it walks like a duck and it quacks like a duck, it's a duck."

Insofar as Judge Keep was concerned, a video gaming machine that had "bingo slapped across it rather than bars, cherries and stars" was a slot machine, and "slots are illegal in California."

As a consequence, Sheriff Duffy kept Triano's machines, and soon thereafter Triano's management company filed for bankruptcy. But that was not the end of machines at Barona.

THE IGRA REQUIRED the BIA to review management agreements until the National Indian Gaming Commission (NIGC) began functioning and the chairman of the NIGC took over that responsibility. As part of the review process, the IGRA required the BIA to disapprove an agreement if an individual who would be involved in the management of a bingo hall or card room had a criminal record, a questionable reputation, or suspect associations that would "pose a threat to the public interest or to the effective regulation and control of gaming" or "enhance the dangers of unsuitable, unfair, or illegal practices, methods, and activities in the conduct of gaming." In derilection of that duty, in October 1990, the BIA official who supervised Indian reservations in southern California approved a management agreement that authorized National Gaming, Inc., a management company owned by a Las Vegas resident named Emmett Munley, to reopen the bingo hall on the Barona Reservation.

In 1960 when Munley managed the casino in the Riverside Hotel in Reno, a patron who lost $12,000 at the craps table sued Munley because the shift boss, who was Munley's uncle, had given him loaded dice to play with. In 1981, Munley applied for a license to manage a casino in Laughlin. But he withdrew the application when it became apparent the Nevada Gaming Control Board was going to deny it because its members suspected that Munley was a strawman for the Partnership, as the Mafia in Detroit is called. In 1983 when Munley applied for a license to manage another casino, the board denied the application "with prejudice because of some admitted and implied associations that Mr. Munley has had with persons of questionable and unsavory reputation."

Munley then moved on to Indian bingo. Between 1984 and 1988, he was an owner of management companies that opened bingo halls on Indian reservations in New York, Oklahoma, Wisconsin, Florida, and Washington state. In New York, he was accused of skimming, which he denied. In Wisconsin and Washington state, when the Forest County Potawatomi Community and the Puyallup Tribal Councils found out that the Nevada Gaming Control Board had refused to license Munley to manage casinos, they terminated their dealings with him.

Nevertheless, the BIA official who supervised Indian reservations in southern California approved the management agreement Munley signed with the Barona Group. In December 1990, when National Gaming, Inc., reopened the bingo hall on the Barona Reservation, players who drove up Wildcat Canyon Road to play bingo discovered that Munley had installed sixty video gaming machines.

Four months after Munley reopened the bingo hall on the Barona Reservation, the manager of the bingo hall on the Morongo Reservation installed fifty-four machines in his hall. Over succeeding months, more than four hundred more machines were installed in bingo halls on seven other reservations in southern California, including Cabazon and Sycuan.

The month before Munley reopened the bingo hall on the Barona Reservation, California voters elected Dan Lungren, a former Republican member of the U.S. House of Representatives, attorney general. On Capitol Hill, Representative Lungren had made his right-of-conservative reputation by being "tough on crime." So it is no surprise that Attorney General Lungren was outraged when he discovered that video gaming machines were being operated in bingo halls on Indian reservations in California. "I don't care if you're an Indian or not Indian," Lungren railed, "You don't have a right to ignore the law."

On October 6, 1991, the *Los Angeles Times* began publishing a series of articles about gambling on Indian reservations. Two days after the first article appeared, Lungren sent "All District Attorneys, City Prosecutors, Sheriffs, and Chiefs of Police" a memorandum in which he expressed concern about "the recent proliferation of gambling machines found on California Indian reservations." He urged the recipients "to undertake appropriate action against unlawful gambling activity on Indian lands within your jurisdiction, including seizure of illegal gambling devices and prosecution of those responsible."

In response, George Forman, the attorney who represented the Morongo and Sycuan Bands, as well as two other tribes whose managers had installed video gaming and pull-tab machines in their bingo halls, sent Lungren a letter, which he copied to the sheriffs and district attorneys in the counties in which his client tribes' reservations were located. Forman put the attorney general on notice that section 1166(d) of Title 18 of the U.S. Code prohibited the state from enforcing section 330b of the California Penal Code on Indian reservations. The letter concluded by lecturing that the course of action Lungren had urged the sheriffs to pursue "could expose local law enforcement agencies and personnel to liability for unlawful arrest, seizure of property and possibly violation of rights protected under the Constitution and/or laws of the United States."

Jim Roache, who had succeeded John Duffy as sheriff of San Diego County, disregarded Forman's warning and sent his deputies into the bingo halls on the Barona and Sycuan Reservations. They also raided the Viejas Casino & Turf Club, a bingo hall and off-track betting parlor that had recently opened on the Viejas Reservation east of the Sycuan Reservation. Sheriff Roache's deputies confiscated more than 280 video gaming and pull-tab machines.

After the raid, San Diego County District Attorney Edwin Miller filed criminal prosecutions against the managers of the three halls, one of whom was Emmett Munley. In response, George Forman, who represented the Sycuan Band, and Art Bunce, the attorney who represented the Barona and Viejas Groups of the Capitan Grande Band of Mission Indians, filed lawsuits against District Attorney Miller and Sheriff Roache in the U.S. District Court in San Diego.

The cases were assigned to Judge Marilyn Huff, who issued first a temporary restraining order and then a preliminary injunction that prohibited Miller from "continuing with criminal prosecutions" and prohibited Roache from "destroying or removing any of the seized property without prior court approval." In February 1992, Judge Huff made her preliminary injunction permanent in a decision in which she held, correctly, that as a consequence of section 1166(d) of Title 18 of the U.S. Code "the defendants were without authority to execute the October 1991 warrants or to criminally prosecute [the managers of the halls]."

EACH OF THE fifty states has been divided into one or more federal judicial districts in which a U.S. attorney appointed by the president and supervised by the attorney general represents the United States. California has been divided into four districts.

While section 1166(d) of Title 18 of the U.S. Code prevented Sheriff Roache and other state law enforcement officials from enforcing section 330b of the California Penal Code on Indian reservations, section 1166(d) explicitly authorized the U.S. attorneys in California to do so. They also had authority to enforce the Johnson Act.

In October 1988 when Ronald Reagan signed S. 555 into law as the IGRA, Nevada senator Harry Reid assumed that Indian tribes would have to remove the video gaming machines they had installed in their bingo halls unless and until each tribe negotiated a compact with the state in which the tribe's reservation was located that allowed machines. But as early as March 1989 Reid discovered that "in states where such devices are clearly illegal" tribes were continuing to operate machines. When two more years passed and the local U.S. attorneys still had made no effort to enforce the Johnson Act, in June 1991 Reid and Nevada senator Richard Bryan (who in 1988 had defeated Chic Hecht) complained to Attorney General Richard Thornburgh.

The complaints were to no avail. Throughout the presidency of George H.W. Bush, the raids on the five bingo halls Linda Akers, the U.S. attorney for the district of Arizona, ordered were one of few enforcement actions a U.S. attorney initiated.*

In 1993 when Bill Clinton became president, his attorney general proved to be as unenthusiastic as Thornburgh had been about enforcing the Johnson Act, and her disinclination appears to have reflected the attitude of the president for whom she worked.

WHILE HE WAS born in Hope, a small town in southwest Arkansas, Bill Clinton was raised in Hot Springs, Arkansas, which he would describe as "a town with the largest illegal gambling operation in America when I was a kid." So the future president knew about gambling. However, since the federal government had removed the Quapaw, Caddo, Osage, and Cherokee Indians from Arkansas more than a century before he was born, the only thing Clinton knew about Indians when he was growing up was what he read about them in books. As he would recall of his reading list during his grade school years:

> I was most fascinated by books about Native Americans and read children's biographies of Geronimo, the great Apache; Crazy Horse, the Lakota Sioux who killed Custer and routed his troops at Little Big Horn; Chief Joseph of the Nez Pearce, who made peace with his

---

*In February 1991, the FBI raided the bingo hall on the Robinson Rancheria, a small reservation north of San Francisco, and confiscated fifty video gaming machines. The raid was an anomaly, however, as it was conducted because the former chairman of the rancheria, who had been removed from office in an intratribal coup, had lobbied the BIA and the FBI to confiscate the machines.

In June 1992, the U.S. attorney for the eastern district of Wisconsin ordered the Forest County Potawatomi Community to turn off the two hundred video gaming machines the community had installed in the bingo hall it had opened on a tract of land it had purchased in an industrial area in the city of Milwaukee. (With the city's approval, the community had arranged for the secretary of the interior to transform the tract into an Indian reservation.) The community complied with the order and turned off the machines until it negotiated a compact with the state of Wisconsin that authorized the machines to be turned back on.

powerful statement, "From where the sun now stands, I will fight no more forever"; and the great Seminole chief Osceola, who developed a written alphabet for his people. I never lost my interest in Native Americans or my feeling that they had been terribly mistreated.

Because there were no Indian tribes in Arkansas, between 1983 and 1992 when he was governor, Bill Clinton had no involvement with Indian gaming. However, during those years, he attended meetings of the National Governors' Association (NGA), at which other governors expressed their concerns about gambling that was being conducted on reservations in their states. And in 1987 when the U.S. Supreme Court issued its decision in *California v. Cabazon and Morongo Bands of Mission Indians*, Bill Clinton was chairman of the NGA.

Two weeks after Governor Clinton became President Clinton, on February 1 and 2, 1993, the NGA held its winter meeting in Washington, D.C. At the conclusion of the meeting, the governors adopted a resolution that urged Congress to amend the IGRA to make clear that a state was not required to negotiate a compact with an Indian tribe that would authorize the tribe to offer Class III forms of gambling that the state prohibited other residents from offering.

The president, who gave a speech at the meeting, had departed by the time the governors discussed the resolution. But he was told about it. Because three months later when he attended a town hall meeting in San Diego and was asked whether he would be willing to meet with leaders of Indian tribes that were operating video gaming machines in their bingo halls that the governor was demanding that they stop operating, the president said he knew that a number of governors were "nervous" because "they think that they'll have to turn their states into Nevada."

During the 1992 presidential election, the Clinton campaign had courted leaders of Indian tribes in states that had significant numbers of Native American voters. That effort paid its benefit when voter registration and get-out-the vote drives those leaders helped to organize helped candidate Clinton win Montana, New Mexico, Colorado, Oregon, and Washington, and come within striking distance of winning in Arizona and South Dakota. To maintain that political support, which candidate Clinton would need again during the 1996 election, in 1994 President Clinton hosted a meeting on the south lawn of the White House at which a dozen of the more than three hundred leaders of Indian tribes who attended were afforded an opportunity to educate the president and members of his cabinet about the economic and attendant social problems that were rampant on their reservations.

In his autobiography Bill Clinton recalled that "Some [of the tribal leaders who attended the meeting] were so wealthy from Indian gaming that they flew to Washington in their own planes." And when the speeches by tribal leaders ended and the president delivered his prepared remarks, he signaled that he knew those leaders had become wealthy because—on reservations in California, New Mexico, Florida, and other states in which state law prohibited video gaming machines—the tribes the leaders represented were earning millions of dollars annually by operating hundreds, and in several cases as many as a thousand, machines in violation of the Johnson Act.

But rather than telling those tribal leaders to comply with the Johnson Act before they were arrested for not doing so, the president told his audience: "My goal is this: I want the tribes to continue to benefit from gaming, and I want current disputes over the 1988 gaming regulatory act to be worked out."

How should those disputes be worked out? The president didn't say. But a month earlier, his attorney general had told the U.S. attorneys who had Indian reservations in their districts that they were not to send the FBI onto the reservations as U.S. Attorney Akers had done. And they were not to file Johnson Act prosecutions.

WHEN HE ASSUMED office, Bill Clinton wanted to be the first president to appoint a woman as attorney general. But his effort to do so deteriorated into fiasco when his first two nominees, Zoe Baird, a corporate attorney, and Kimba Wood, a federal judge, withdrew when it was revealed they both had employed undocumented immigrants as nannies. So in February 1993, the president nominated Janet Reno.

A graduate of Harvard Law School, Reno had the proper paper credentials. And for fourteen years she had been the chief prosecutor in Miami-Dade County, Florida. But for the new president, her most politically useful qualification was that Reno was a fifty-four-year-old spinster who had no nannygate problem.

According to her biographer, in 1978 when Florida governor Reuben Askew appointed Reno to replace the chief prosecutor in Miami-Dade County, who had resigned in the middle of his term, her "eye was on the calendar" because, to keep the job, she had to win a special election. Prior to the election, one of the ways Reno kept her name in the *Miami Herald* was by ordering the Miami police department to raid the professionally managed "charitable" bingo halls that were operating in Miami because, as Reno told the *Herald*, "organized crime is behind the operation of the major halls." During the new prosecutor's first three months in office, four halls were raided and twenty-three managers and employees were arrested.

The bingo halls Seminole Management Associates and Pan American & Associates managed for the Seminole Tribe were located outside her jurisdiction. So during her years as a prosecutor, Reno had no involvement with them. As a consequence, during her confirmation hearings to be attorney general, when South Dakota senator Larry Pressler asked Reno, "What is your view of Indian gaming?" she forthrightly responded, "I don't have the expertise at this point to really give you an informed judgment on it."

As DESCRIBED IN the previous chapter, in April 1992 the NIGC published regulations to guide the implementation of the IGRA. One regulation made clear that the Class III gaming definition in the IGRA included within its purview "slot machines as defined in [the Johnson Act] and electronic or electromechanical facsimiles of any game of chance." Another regulation defined "electronic or electromechanical facsimile" to mean any video gaming machine that was a "gambling device" for the purposes of the Johnson Act.

When the regulations were issued, in the U.S. District Court for the District of Columbia, Glenn Feldman, who represented the Cabazon Band, and attorneys who represented six other tribes, filed *Cabazon Band of Mission Indians v. National Indian Gaming Commission*, a lawsuit in which the tribes challenged the validity of the regulations. In June 1993, District Judge Royce Lamberth ruled that the tribes' objections to the regulations were "meritless." And in January 1994 a three-judge panel of the U.S. Court of Appeals for the District of Columbia Circuit affirmed Judge Lamberth.

Two months later, on March 25, 1994, Attorney General Reno sent U.S. attorneys who had Indian reservations in their districts a memorandum in which, for the first time, she addressed "the truly sensitive issue of what should be done about illegal gaming conducted by tribal authorities." The memorandum directed each U.S. attorney to "review the status of gaming that may be operating in your district." It then instructed: "If you find any illegal gaming, the *peaceful* termination of those illegal operations should be *negotiated* with the Tribes within a brief but reasonable time." (emphases added) Attorney General Reno concluded her memorandum on the upbeat by assuring the U.S. attorneys she was confident their negotiations would be successful because "The tribes and their members have shown themselves to be law-abiding citizens and their compliance is anticipated." However, that is not how the situation played out in California.

IN 1990, PETE WILSON, the former mayor of San Diego who had recently finished serving one term in the U.S. Senate, was elected governor of California in the same election in which Dan Lungren was elected attorney general. Wilson had a personal dislike for gambling that he had acquired during law school when he had a job parking cars at a horse track. According to Wilson:

> One afternoon a guy pulled up in a terrible old heap and got out. I started to get in to drive this jalopy away. I looked in the back seat and there was no back seat. But on the floor boards were two little boys. I lost it. I went after this guy and grabbed him and spun him around and said, "You sonofabitch. You get in that car and drive out of here. If you think you're going to go in and play the ponies and leave these two little kids unattended in that jalopy, then you're crazy. You got two choices. You get in and drive away or else I'm going to call the cops."

Father and sons drove away. But the experience informed Wilson's view that gambling was a predaceous recreation. "I don't care what the hell rich people do. They've got money to waste," the governor would lecture. "But too many of the wrong people gamble."

But no matter what Pete Wilson thought of gambling, the IGRA authorized Indian tribes in California to negotiate compacts for the conduct of Class III forms of gambling. It also required the state to negotiate in "good faith" regarding any Class III form of gambling the state "permits . . . for any purpose by any person, organization, or entity."

Because the state allowed pari-mutuel betting at horse tracks, in 1990 the Cabazon and Sycuan Bands and the Viejas Group of the Capitan Grande Band of Mission Indians asked California governor George Deukmejian to negotiate compacts whose approval would authorize the bands and the group to operate off-track betting parlors. California Attorney General John Van de Camp directed Deputy Attorney General Cathy Christian, who had been doing legal work for the California Horse Racing Board, to represent the state in those negotiations, which had a successful outcome when Deukmejian signed the compacts.

In 1992, the Cabazon and Sycuan Bands, the Viejas Group, and fourteen other tribes requested the state to negotiate compacts whose approval would allow the tribes to continue operating the video gaming machines they had installed in their bingo halls. Since she had negotiated the first three compacts, Attorney General Lungren directed Cathy Christian to meet with George Forman, Glenn Feldman, and the other attorneys who represented the tribes that wanted compacts. This time the negotiations ended shortly after they began when Christian said she had no authority to negotiate compacts that would allow tribes to operate video gaming machines that section 330b of the California Penal Code prohibited.

As discussed in chapter ten, in 1984 California voters had passed an initiative that amended the California Constitution to authorize the California State Lottery Commission to operate a lottery. In 1992 the Lottery Commission began installing computer terminals and video screens in more than 5,000 retail businesses throughout California that allowed players to play Keno. To play, a player fills in up to ten numbers on a playslip and inserts the slip into a computer terminal. Out of a field of eighty numbers, a random number generator then selects twenty numbers that are displayed on the video screens. If the numbers on the playslip are among the numbers displayed on the video screens, the player wins. If they are not, the player loses. The random number generator selects twenty new numbers once every five minutes.

When Cathy Christian told the attorneys who represented the tribes that wanted compacts that she had no authority to negotiate regarding video gaming machines, the attorneys argued that the Lottery Commission's computer terminals, random number generator, and video screens were no different than the video gaming machines their clients were operating. When Christian disagreed, the attorneys proposed that they file a "test case" in order to have the federal courts decide whether, for the purposes of the IGRA, there was any difference between video gaming machines and the Lottery Commission's Keno game.

When Attorney General Lungren agreed to that approach, Christian and the attorneys negotiated a stipulation in which the state and the tribes agreed to have the U.S. District Court for the Eastern District of California settle their dispute. The stipulation also provided that the state and the tribes would have the right to file an appeal.

Two lawsuits were filed, which were consolidated under the caption: *Rumsey Indian Rancheria of Wintun Indians v. California Governor Pete Wilson.* On July 20, 1993, District Judge Garland Burrell issued a decision in *Rumsey* in which he sided with the tribes. Pete Wilson appealed, and on November 15, 1994, a three-judge panel of the U.S. Court of Appeals for the Ninth Circuit reversed Judge Burrell in a decision in which the panel concluded that Congress did not intend the IGRA to

> require a state to negotiate over one form of a gaming activity simply because it has legalized another, albeit similar form of gaming. Instead the statute says only that, if a state allows a gaming activity "for any purpose by any person, organization, or entity," then it also must allow Indian tribes to engage in that same activity. In other words, a state need only allow Indian tribes to operate games that others can operate, but need not give tribes what others cannot have.

While a victory for Pete Wilson, the panel muddied the analytical waters at the end of its decision. The lawsuit was sent back to Judge Burrell to decide "whether California permits the operation of slot machines in the form of the state lottery or otherwise."

OTHER THAN AT the Robinson Rancheria in northern California in 1991, since 1988 when Congress enacted the IGRA, the U.S. attorneys in California had taken no action to enforce section 330b of the California Penal Code or the Johnson Act on Indian reservations. However, in March

1994, Attorney General Reno instructed them to begin negotiating the "peaceful termination" of illegal gambling Indian tribes were conducting on reservations in their districts.

In June, when the U.S. attorneys met in San Francisco to discuss how to begin doing so, Alan Bersin, the U.S. attorney for the southern district, proposed that no action be taken until the U.S. Court of Appeals for the Ninth Circuit, and, if necessary the U.S. Supreme Court, decided the appeal Pete Wilson had filed in the *Rumsey* test case. In exchange for that forbearance, no new machines would be allowed during the interregnum.

According to Bersin, the other U.S. attorneys "were not enthusiastic" about the moratorium on filing enforcement actions he had proposed. Nevertheless, he decided to impose a moratorium in his district, which included San Diego County in which the Barona and Viejas Groups of the Capitan Grande Band and the Sycuan Band of Diegueno Mission Indians were collectively operating 2,230 machines, 1,000 each at Barona and Viejas, and 230 at Sycuan. Bersin rationalized his decision to continue not enforcing the Johnson Act by explaining that, "To the same extent one would not shut down the business of a defense contractor pending final adjudication," it would not be fair "in this context" to confiscate the groups' and the band's machines. While his assertion that the two situations were analogous was a stretch, Bersin meant what he said about no new machines.

IN AUGUST 1994, COLUMBIA Group, Inc. (CGI), a corporate shell an Arizona resident named Paul Helton had incorporated in Nevada, signed a management agreement with the Rincon Band of Luiseño Mission Indians to remodel, and then manage, the bingo hall on the band's reservation in San Diego County. As part of the remodeling, CGI installed 230 video poker machines. In April 1995 when the hall opened, Bersin filed suit against CGI in the U.S. District Court in San Diego. District Judge Marilyn Huff, who four years earlier had prevented San Diego County Sheriff Jim Roache from enforcing section 330b of the California Penal Code on the Barona, Sycuan, and Viejas Reservations, issued an injunction that required CGI, first to turn off, and then remove the machines.

The NIGC had approved CGI's management agreement. But in 1994 when it did so, Tony Hope and the other commissioners had no more ability to investigate Paul Helton and CGI than the BIA official who supervised Indian reservations in southern California had to investigate Emmett Munley and National Gaming, Inc. As a consequence, until confidential informants told the FBI, the NIGC did not know that, rather than the doctors and attorneys Helton said were his investors, CGI's owners were Pasquale Ferruccio, Henry Zottola, Dominic Strollo, and John "Duffy" Conley. Ferruccio was a member of the LaRocca Mafia family in Pittsburgh, and Zottola, Strollo, and Conley were associates.

In 1997, grand juries in San Diego and Pittsburgh indicted Helton, Ferruccio, Zottola, Strollo, Conley, and twelve other participants in the conspiracy to take control of the bingo hall at Rincon. They all pled guilty.

IN NOVEMBER 1994, PETE Wilson was reelected governor. A week after the election, the three-judge panel of the U.S. Court of Appeals for the Ninth Circuit issued the decision in which it reversed Judge Burrell in the *Rumsey* test case. But two months after Wilson began his second term, the legal situation regarding video gaming machines, which the panel's decision had clarified, again became muddled.

In 1993, the California Horsemen's Benevolent & Protective Association, a trade group that represented trainers whose horses raced at tracks whose revenue from pari-mutuel betting had been reduced when the California State Lottery Commission began offering Keno, had filed *Western Telecon, Inc. v. California State Lottery*, a lawsuit in which the association asserted that the computer terminals the Lottery Commission had installed in retail businesses throughout California were "slot machines" that section 330b of the California Penal Code prohibited. In March 1995, the California Court of Appeal agreed that the terminals were "slot machines." But the court then concluded that in 1984 when California voters passed the initiative that enacted the California State Lottery Act, they intended the act to supercede section 330b.

The Court of Appeal's decision meant that, as the plaintiff tribes had argued in the *Rumsey* test case, California law—i.e., the Lottery Act—permitted the Lottery Commission to operate computer terminals that, since they were connected to a random number generator, were tantamount to the video gaming machines the tribes were operating. As a consequence, when it reported the *Western Telecon* decision, the *Los Angeles Times* theorized that the decision "steps up the pressure on Gov. Pete Wilson to negotiate agreements with California tribes that would significantly expand the range of gaming activities they may offer."

The California Supreme Court agreed to review the *Western Telecon* decision, and in June 1996 the justices of that court reversed the Court of Appeal. But they did so on the ground that the Lottery Commission's Keno game was a banked game that the California Constitution prohibited, rather than a lottery that the Lottery Act allowed. After so holding, the justices pointedly announced that "We therefore need not decide whether CSL [California State Lottery] Keno also involves the use of slot machines" or whether the Lottery Act granted an exemption that allowed the Lottery Commission to "conduct any authorized games whether or not the game is prohibited by Penal Code section 330."

The day after the California Supreme Court issued its decision in *Western Telecon*, the *San Francisco Examiner* reported that Attorney General Lungren had said, "[T]here can now be no doubt the video gambling machines now operated on Indian reservations are illegal." While the justices had said no such thing, when the *Rumsey* test case and *Western Telecon* decisions were considered in tandem, they for the most part settled in Pete Wilson's favor the question of whether the IGRA required Wilson to negotiate compacts that would allow tribes to operate video gaming machines that section 330b of the California Penal Code prohibited.

AT THE BEGINNING of his second term, Pete Wilson appointed a Los Angeles attorney named Dan Kolkey as his legal advisor. After the California Supreme Court issued its decision in *Western Telecom*, Kolkey informed the tribes that wanted compacts that Governor Wilson had authorized him to resume the negotiations that had been suspended when the *Rumsey* test case was filed. But the governor had a precondition: Kolkey could not negotiate with a tribe that was operating video gaming machines in violation of section 330b of the California Penal Code until the tribe turned off its machines.

The governor was adamant about that precondition for two reasons. The first was that, during the four years it had taken to litigate the *Rumsey* test case and then *Western Telecon*, a number of tribes had increased the number of machines they were operating in violation of the spirit (although not the letter) of the stipulation their attorneys had negotiated with Cathy Christian.

For example, in January 1994, the Barona Group of the Capitan Grande Band of Mission Indians, which had been operating almost 400 video gaming machines, opened what it advertised as the "largest tented casino in the world." The structure had cost $3.5 million to construct using the same material the U.S. Army had used to construct helicopter hangars in Kuwait and Iraq during the Desert Storm war. Inside the tent, Inland Casino Corporation, the Barona Group's new management company, installed six hundred additional machines. And five months later when Alan Bersin met with the leaders of the Viejas Group of the Capitan Grande Band to announce his moratorium, according to George Forman "[T]he first thing that happened was the guy from Viejas went out into the hall— this was before cell phones—and he was on the phone ordering more machines before the stand-still kicked in."

The other reason the governor was adamant about his precondition was that if a tribe could operate its machines while its attorney negotiated with Dan Kolkey, the tribe would have no reason to ever stop negotiating.

From Pete Wilson's perspective, his precondition was reasonable because, as he described his view of the situation, "The financial benefit Indian tribes may derive from casino-style gaming does not excuse their knowing and deliberate violation of the law." But if a video gaming machine earned, on average, $200 a day, a tribe like the Barona Group, which had a thousand machines, was earning $200,000 *a day*. So none of the thirty-four tribes in California that were collectively operating 12,000 machines would agree to turn them off.

The impasse between Pete Wilson and the tribes was finally broken by a subterfuge in which all parties were complicit.

On the evening of August 31, 1996, Pete Wilson, Dan Kolkey, and Dave Sterling, Attorney General Lungren's principal deputy, were in the hallway of the capitol building in Sacramento on the last night of that year's session of the California legislature. Because the legislature was considering a gambling control bill that might affect their clients, George Forman and several of the other attorneys who represented tribes that wanted compacts also were there.

At some point during the evening, one of the attorneys suggested to Sterling that if the governor would not allow Dan Kolkey to negotiate compacts with tribes that refused to turn off their video gaming machines, Kolkey should negotiate with a tribe that did not have any machines in order to develop a model compact that could serve as a template for other compacts. When Sterling mentioned the idea to Wilson, according to Dan Kolkey, "The governor asked me what I thought, and I said I thought it was the right way to go."

THE TRIBE DAN Kolkey would negotiate with was the Pala Band of Luiseño Mission Indians.

In 1810, the padres at the Franciscan mission on the San Luis Rey River on the coast of California in what today is northern San Diego County built a granary in the Pala Valley twenty-four-miles up the river, and then in 1816 at that location they opened San Antonio de Pala Asistencia, a small auxiliary mission, around which a number of Luiseño Indians settled. In 1875, President Ulysses S. Grant withdrew 160 acres of federal land in the Pala Valley whose boundaries encircled the village that had grown up around San Antonio de Pala Asistencia. In 1903, the BIA purchased 3,438 adjacent acres from private landowners onto which Charles Lummis, the local Indian agent, relocated 144 Cupeno and Kumeyaay Indians the U.S. Supreme Court had ordered to move off land on which they had been living east of the Pala Valley.

In 1927, a public health nurse named Florence Ames visited the Pala Reservation. She found thirty-five Luiseño, Cupeño, and Kumeyaay Indian families living in one-room houses that were "in a state of disrepair," and whose out-houses were "in need of attention," because there had been five cases of typhoid that the physician who treated the sick attributed "to flies due to the insanitary conditions of outdoor privies and their close proximity to the homes." Ames also recorded that "many people enrolled on this reservation do not live here" because "insufficient employment in surrounding territory, combined with lack of sufficient income from land, has caused them to leave."

In 1996, the conditions on the Pala Reservation, which by then had been expanded to 12,000 acres, were not that different from what they had been when Florence Ames visited. The housing was substandard. The economy was based on subsistence agriculture, wage work on the surrounding farms and ranches, and a quarry the Pala Band leased to a company that used the materials it excavated to manufacture concrete and asphalt. And unlike the Rincon Band, whose reservation farther up the San Luis Rey River was only a few miles distant, the Pala Band had not been able to find an investor willing to finance construction of a bingo hall.

A Sacramento attorney named Howard Dickstein represented the Pala Band. Dickstein also represented the Table Mountain Rancheria, whose members lived on a small reservation in the Sierra Nevada foothills. In 1991, the Table Mountain Rancheria had installed video pull-tab machines in its bingo hall. However, even though Dickstein owed the Table Mountain Rancheria the same legal duty to protect its ability to continue to operate its machines that George Forman and the other attorneys who represented tribes that were operating machines had, Forman and the other attorneys were not about to let Dickstein negotiate with Dan Kolkey on his own.

In October 1996 when Kolkey and Dickstein held their first meeting, George Forman, Glenn Feldman, Art Bunce, and Jerry Levine—who collectively represented most of the tribes in California that had refused to turn off their video gaming machines—were in the room participating as Dickstein's "co-counsels." "I didn't want to breach the governor's condition that we don't negotiate with gaming tribes," Kolkey would recall of that wink-wink arrangement. "But we found a clever way to allow those tribes' attorneys, not only to be in the room, but to be full participants in the negotiations."

While Forman and the other attorneys ostensibly were members of the Pala Band's legal team, they took their direction from their real clients. According to Forman,

> There was a protocol that the tribes we represented had laid down. Before a particular subject got talked about during a negotiating session, it would come to the tribal group to reach consensus on what the position was going to be. Then after a negotiating session, there would be a debriefing at which the members of the tribal group would be apprised of what had been talked about, what had been agreed to in principle, and what had not been agreed to.

With that arrangement in place, Dan Kolkey and Howard Dickstein and his co-counsels began meeting and progress was made, until the negotiations imploded in acrimony.

• • •

DICKSTEIN'S CO-COUNSELS AND their clients had agreed that the subjects discussed during the negotiations would remain confidential in order, as Robert Smith, the chairman of the Pala Band, later explained, to prevent "leaks to the media" that might "force one or both sides to harden their positions."

That agreement held for eleven months, until September 1997 when a draft of a section of the compact was circulated whose content revealed that, at Dan Kolkey's insistence, Howard Dickstein had agreed to limit the number of video gaming machines a tribe could operate. When he read the draft, Richard Milanovich, the chairman of the Agua Caliente Band of Cahuilla Indians, which two years earlier had opened a casino in Palm Springs that had 1,065 machines, was outraged.

Milanovich had been instrumental in organizing the Tribal Alliance of Sovereign Indian Nations, a trade organization of sorts whose membership was composed of eleven tribes in southern California. When Milanovich and the other leaders of the tribes that were members of the alliance found out Howard Dickstein had agreed to limit the number of machines their tribes could operate, they protested in a letter to Pete Wilson. When someone gave a copy to the *San Diego Union-Tribune*, which on September 11, published an article in which the letter was mentioned, according to George Forman, "Dan Kolkey went nuts. Howard Dickstein went nuts."

On September 16, Richard Milanovich informed Robert Smith, the chairman of the Pala Band, that because "the continued participation of Mr. [Art] Bunce [the Agua Caliente Band's attorney] on behalf of the Pala Band's compact could be misconstrued as an endorsement of the terms of the Pala Band's compact by the Agua Caliente Band," Bunce would no longer be participating in the negotiations.

On September 18, Howard Dickstein demanded that his co-counsels not disclose to the leaders of the tribes they represented what was discussed during negotiating sessions "without the agreement of the State and the Pala Band." In response, on September 29 George Forman informed Dan Kolkey that, like Art Bunce, he no longer would attend Kolkey's meetings with Dickstein.

By then, the U.S. attorneys in California were losing patience.

• • •

SEVERAL DAYS AFTER Dan Kolkey and Howard Dickstein and his co-counsels began meeting, the panel of the U.S. Court of Appeals for the Ninth Circuit that decided Pete Wilson's appeal in the *Rumsey* test case denied the plaintiff tribes' request that the panel reconsider its decision. At that point, the moratorium on filing enforcement actions that Alan Bersin had imposed in the southern district—and which the other U.S. attorneys had eventually decided to observe in their districts—expired. But Bersin and the other U.S. attorneys decided to keep the moratorium in place as long as Kolkey and Dickstein made progress in their negotiations.

However, when after five months the negotiations had not produced a compact, on March 17, 1997 the *Los Angeles Times* reported that

> By the end of this month, federal prosecutors have warned, the tribes must have a plan to stop the illegal gaming now conducted on the 12,000 electronic machines stacked row on row through 34 tribal casinos throughout California. If not, the tribes face prosecution or civil action later this spring,

which the *Times* explained meant May 1.

According to George Forman, two months after Alan Bersin announced his moratorium in the southern district, Nora Manella, the U.S. attorney for the central district, which contained nine reservations in Santa Barbara, Riverside, and San Bernardino Counties, "[C]alled everybody in, all the tribes, both those that were operating machines and those that weren't, and said no expansion, no new openings." In defiance of that edict, in 1995 the Twenty-Nine Palms, Agua Caliente, and Pechanga Bands opened casinos in Riverside County in which by 1997 they were collectively operating more than 2,000 video gaming machines.

When those machines were turned on, Manella took no action. But two years later when the tribes in her district made it clear they had no intention of developing a plan, by March 31 or any other date, for turning off their machines, in the U.S. District Court in Los Angeles, Manella filed *United States v. Santa Ynez Band of Chumash Mission Indians*, an enforcement action in which she requested District Judge John Spencer Letts to order the tribes in the central district to turn off their machines.

When May 1 came and went and none of the tribes in their districts had turned off their machines, instead of following Manella's lead, the other U.S. attorneys again relented and announced that they would not file enforcement actions until Dan Kolkey and Howard Dickstein concluded their negotiations. Manella, however, tired of excuse and delay, asked Judge Letts to issue a preliminary injunction requiring the tribes that were defendants in *United States v. Santa Ynez Band of Chumash Mission Indians* to turn off their machines.

When Manella filed her enforcement action, George Forman, who represented one of the defendant tribes, the Morongo Band, arranged for the chairpersons of all of the defendant tribes to accept service of their summonses at the federal courthouse in Los Angeles. "Then we bused in hundreds of people," Forman would recall years later with a grin, "and we had a rally on the steps." The *Los Angeles Times* reported the event on its front page:

> In a downtown Los Angeles rally punctuated by drumbeats, chants, and a traditional burning of sage, 3,000 Native Americans and gaming industry workers vowed Monday to fight a proposed government shutdown of tribal casino slot machines and other types of gambling. Calling the slots the main moneymaker in a business that has begun to defeat grinding poverty on the reservations, the leaders of several California tribes said a federal civil lawsuit seeking to unplug the machines is the latest example of oppression against American Indians. The tribes refused to sign an agreement with the federal government to give up the slots.
>
> "We feel an injustice is being done to us, and we're here to fight for what we deserve," said a tribal coalition spokeswoman, Lynn LeRoy, to the cheers of the crowd. "We're not going back to the way it was." The protesters, most of them casino workers who are not Native Americans, rooted loudly for the nine leaders as they climbed the steps of the federal courthouse on Main Street to receive copies of the lawsuits. Bearing placards with slogans such as "Support our right to support ourselves" and "Indian gaming means getting well, not welfare," the crowd later walked to the south lawn of City Hall for a picnic.

Unimpressed with the political theater, when asked to comment on the rally, U.S. Attorney Manella, responded, "The fact that an illegal activity is profitable is not a defense. If it were, cocaine traffickers would have a perfect defense."

But Judge Letts's was the opinion that mattered, not Manella's. Six weeks later, when he held a hearing on Manella's motion for a preliminary injunction, the publicity the rally on the courthouse steps generated accomplished its purpose. Minutes after gaveling the hearing open, Letts gaveled it closed and ordered the attorneys into his chambers. When they came out, the tribes' attorneys announced that Letts had denied Manella's motion. The following November, Letts issued a written decision in which he explained his reasoning:

> There is evidence that the United States has known for years that Class III gaming is being conducted by the Indians and has allowed the gaming to continue and grow without ever attempting to shut it down. Moreover, in the other districts in California, the United States Attorneys have stated that they will stay enforcement against the Indians pending the finalization of a model tribal-state compact. If the public interest in shutting down Class III gaming were so great, one would expect all of the districts to be behaving the same way and bringing enforcement actions.

When Judge Letts denied her motion, Manella announced that, like the other U.S. attorneys, she would take no further action until Dan Kolkey and Howard Dickstein concluded their negotiations, which four months later they did.

ON MARCH 6, 1998, PETE Wilson announced that he had signed "a ground-breaking compact with the Pala Band to allow legal gaming on tribal lands" that "can serve as a model and a starting point for negotiations with other tribes." When the leaders of those other tribes read the 119-page compact, they were apoplectic.

During the negotiations, Dan Kolkey had five objectives, all of which he achieved: he wanted tribes to only operate video gaming machines that allowed players to play a game that was a form of lottery that the California State Lottery Act authorized; he wanted to provide employees of tribal gambling facilities the workplace protections that the state's workers' compensation law, the federal Occupational Safety & Health Act, and similar statutes conferred; he wanted to protect patrons of tribal gambling facilities by, among other safeguards, requiring the tribes to purchase liability insurance; he wanted every tribe in California to benefit from gambling; and because in 1984 the initiative in which California voters enacted the California State Lottery Act had also amended the California Constitution to prohibit "casinos of the type currently operating in Nevada and New Jersey," Kolkey wanted to prevent tribes from operating gambling facilities that were tantamount to Nevada and New Jersey casinos, even though the amendment that established the prohibition did not identify the characteristics that made a gambling facility a "Nevada or New Jersey type casino."

To achieve the last objective, the compact prohibited the Pala Band from conducting Class III forms of gambling in a hotel, offering card games "in the same room in which any non-card Class III Gaming is conducted," serving players complimentary alcoholic beverages, and extending players credit.

From the other tribes' perspective, that was bad enough. But even worse, the compact allowed the Pala Band to operate only 199 "lottery devices" as the compact called the video gaming machines the Sierra Design Group, a video gaming machine manufacturer Howard Dickstein had hired, was designing.

The compact also contained provisions that applied to every tribe: like the Pala Band, every tribe could operate 199 lottery devices. If a tribe did not want to open its own gambling facility, it could license its right to operate its 199 devices to another tribe for annual compensation not to exceed $5,000 per device. But no tribe could purchase more than 776 licenses, which meant no tribe could operate more than 975 devices. And statewide, all tribes were limited to a total of 19,900 machines.

The Barona and Viejas Groups of the Capitan Grande Band and the Agua Caliente and San Manuel Bands each were operating 1,000 or more machines that played faster, and as a consequence made more money, than the devices the Sierra Design Group was designing. So why would they sign the Pala compact?

The reason is that David Ogden, the official at the U.S. Department of Justice in Washington, D.C., who Janet Reno finally had belatedly assigned to bring order to the situation in California, had flown to Sacramento and worked out a new enforcement policy with Dan Kolkey.

At the press conference at which he announced the Pala compact, Pete Wilson revealed that "Earlier this morning, the state reached agreement with the United States Department of Justice on a new policy." Each tribe would have sixty days to either sign the Pala compact and begin abiding by its provisions or turn off its video gaming machines and begin negotiating with Dan Kolkey regarding the terms of a different compact. Then the governor delivered an ultimatum: "For those tribes that fail to elect one of those two alternatives and who deliberately choose not to put a halt to their illegal gaming, in 60 days U.S. attorneys will take immediate enforcement actions against them." Presented with that Hobson's choice, the Table Mountain Rancheria and four other tribes signed the Pala compact.

The other tribes pulled out all the stops.

First, the California Nations Indian Gaming Association (which tribes operating bingo halls and card rooms in California created when Congress enacted the IGRA) decided to ask President Clinton to issue an executive order that would maintain the status quo while a mediator tried to work something out with the governor. When nothing came of that, the Pechanga and San Manuel Bands filed a lawsuit in the U.S. District Court in Washington, D.C., to try to prevent Secretary of the Interior Bruce Babbitt from approving the Pala compact; which they lost. In the U.S. District Courts in San Francisco and Los Angeles, tribes filed lawsuits to try and obtain orders that would prohibit the U.S. attorneys from filing enforcement actions; which they lost.

On May 13 when the sixty-day deadline expired, the U.S. attorneys could have sent the FBI onto the reservations to confiscate the machines. Instead, on May 14 in the U.S. District Courts in San Francisco, Sacramento, and San Diego the U.S. attorneys filed enforcement actions (U.S. Attorney Manella having filed her action a year earlier).

Three weeks later, the California Nations Indian Gaming Association flew more than one hundred tribal members to Washington, D.C., to lobby Bruce Babbitt to disapprove the Pala compact, lobby California senator Barbara Boxer and other members of Congress to amend the IGRA in their favor, and try to persuade Attorney General Janet Reno to disavow the new enforcement policy David Ogden had worked out with Dan Kolkey.

To find someone to organize the lobbying effort, according to George Forman, "we first interviewed Bob Dole [the former Republican leader of the Senate who was practicing law in Washington, D.C., after having lost the 1996 presidential election to Bill Clinton]. But we ended up with Lanny

Davis, because it was felt that a Democratic lobbying firm would have better juice with the Clinton administration."

From December 1996 to February 1998, Davis, who had been a Friend of Hillary's at Yale Law School, had been special counsel to the president. The job required Davis "to deal with the press on behalf of the president and the White House on a variety of 'scandal' stories, primarily the ones dealing with the allegations of Democratic campaign-finance abuses." Because of the relationships he developed when he was special counsel, Davis had "juice" at the White House.

But while senior members of the White House staff routinely tell the attorney general what policies the president wants the U.S. Department of Justice to implement, no member of any White House staff would direct an attorney general to order a U.S. attorney to dismiss an enforcement action that already was underway. And that would have been the situation even if relations between the Clinton White House and the U.S. Department of Justice had not been as arm's length as they had become because of the scandal regarding the president's relationship with a former White House intern named Monica Lewinsky.

So Lanny Davis's juice at the White House was of no value. Having no personal relationship with her, Davis also had no "juice" with the attorney general; when the California Nations Indian Gaming Association asked for a meeting with Reno, her staff denied the request.

The association then organized a march down Pennsylvania Avenue from Capitol Hill to the main building of the U.S. Department of Justice in which Reno had her office. According to Carole Goldberg, a UCLA law professor and prominent Indian rights advocate, when the marchers were "less than half a block away, the doors to the Department of Justice finally opened."

Five days later, Reno met for an hour with six tribal leaders, while the more than one hundred Indians who had participated in the march sat in the audience. Whether the U.S. attorneys were correct that the tribes that refused to sign the Pala compact were violating section 330b of the California Penal Code and the Johnson Act by refusing to turn off their video gaming machines was a question of law. But rather than a legal argument, what the attorney general sat through were speeches that tried to appeal to her emotion.

Maria Figueroa, a non-Indian whose husband had been killed in a gang fight, said her job as a video gaming machine technician at the casino on the San Manuel Reservation had allowed her to buy her seven-year-old son eyeglasses. "If they take the machines out of the casino," Figueroa told Reno in a speech punctuated by sobs, she and thousands of other employees "will be the ones affected." Then tribal leaders told Reno that, before they installed video gaming machines in the bingo halls on their reservations, the members of their tribes had lived without electricity and indoor plumbing, and 90 percent had been unemployed. "This is not a fight about machines or gaming," Mary Ann Martin Andreas, the chairwoman of the Morongo Band, argued, "but about our rights to make choices as a people."

When the speechmaking ended, Reno expressed her empathy, but she refused to order the U.S. attorneys to stand down. That outcome was no surprise to David Ogden because, "What they were complaining about was her policy. It wasn't something I and other people cooked up on our own without her buy-in."

If the meeting with the attorney general had been a waste of time, by the time they flew home to California, the leaders of a small group of tribes already were well along in implementing a truly audacious scheme.

THE CALIFORNIA CONSTITUTION contains an initiative provision that authorizes laws to be enacted by a vote of the people. If Pete Wilson had no authority to sign compacts that would authorize tribes to operate video gaming machines that section 330b of the California Penal Code prohibited, what if California voters passed a law that allowed tribes, and tribes only, to operate machines?

According to George Forman, the idea of sponsoring an initiative was first discussed in March 1997 when he and Mary Ann Martin Andreas and other tribal leaders organized the rally on the steps of the federal courthouse in Los Angeles. To assess the feasibility of an initiative, that December, the Morongo and San Manuel Bands hired Winner/Wagner & Mandabach, a Los Angeles consulting firm. Polling the firm conducted revealed that "a significant majority of voters were not opposed to gambling *per se*, and supported Indian tribes having casinos on their own land."

Three months later, when Pete Wilson and Robert Smith, the chairman of the Pala Band, signed the Pala compact, Richard Milanovich, the chairman of Agua Caliente Band, hosted a meeting of leaders of the tribes whose reservations were in Riverside, Santa Barbara, and San Bernardino Counties. That meeting led to a larger meeting in Sacramento at which the decision was made to sponsor an initiative.

George Forman; Jerry Levine, the attorney who represented the San Manuel Band; and Glenn Feldman then wrote a bill they titled the "Tribal Government Gaming and Economic Self-Sufficiency Act." The act directed the governor of California to sign a compact within thirty days after a tribe requested him to do so. It also set out the terms that would be included in the compact, which included allowing a tribe to operate as many "gaming devices" as it wished. California voters' passage of the initiative would enact Forman, Levine, and Feldman's bill.

To qualify the initiative for the November general election ballot, the tribes needed to submit petitions to the California Secretary of State that had been signed by 467,000 registered voters. And they had only three weeks to collect the signatures. To get them, the Agua Caliente, Morongo, and Cabazon Bands mailed a solicitation to 55,000 households in Riverside County requesting the recipients to sign the petition attached to the solicitation and mail it back. Other tribes did the same. And Winner/Wagner & Mandabach produced television commercials that featured Mark Macarro, the thirty-five-year-old chairman of the Pechanga Band who, after several professional actors were auditioned for the role, had been selected to be the public face of the initiative campaign.

Raised in Colton, a blue-collar railroad town three miles south of San Bernardino, where he played the trombone in his high school marching band, Macarro had graduated from the University of California at Santa Barbara. So his upbringing was hardly representative of the hardscrabble lives that thousands of uneducated descendants of California's indigenous peoples were leading, mired in poverty on reservations where there were few opportunities for employment. But so what? As the *Los Angeles Times* described Macarro's qualifications to be a television pitchman:

> By most everyone's assessment, Macarro was a natural for the job. He's handsome, articulate, charming, warm, passionate—and, yes, part Indian. Who better to look square into the camera—TelePrompter

notwithstanding—and present the message that Indians need support?

The commercials in which Mark Macarro appeared were broadcast in the major television markets. And the tribes flooded the state with signature-gatherers who stood in front of supermarkets and shopping malls. That full-court press allowed the tribes to collect more than a million signatures, twice the number they needed to qualify their initiative, which would be numbered Proposition 5, for the November general election ballot.

Obtaining that many signatures that quickly was an extraordinary achievement. But more than Mark Macarro's charisma, what made it possible was the $11.3 million the tribes spent to hire Winner/Wagner & Mandabach, send out the direct mail solicitations, produce and broadcast the television commercials, and pay the signature-gatherers.

Where did they get $11.3 million?

It was money the San Manuel, Morongo, Cabazon, Sycuan, and Agua Caliente Bands; the Barona and Viejas Groups of the Capitan Grande Band; and the other tribes that financed the signature-gathering had in the bank because of the years they had spent operating unlawfully the video gaming machines that passage of Proposition 5 would legalize. As the *Los Angeles Times*, without a hint of irony, reported: "By their own accounting, the 41 California tribes that operated casinos in 1997 made about $632 million in net profit—at a time when Gov. Pete Wilson and federal authorities said the casinos were operating illegal slot machines."

If $11.3 million was an astronomical amount of money to have spent to collect signatures, between April and November, Californians for Indian Self-Reliance, the organization the tribes created to manage the initiative campaign, spent another $51.6 million to pay consultants, produce and broadcast television and radio commercials, publish newspaper advertisements, and inundate mailboxes with direct mail. That was more money than had ever before been spent in an initiative campaign.

Ostensibly, eighty-five of the 104 tribes in California were members of Californians for Indian Self-Reliance. But most were members in name only. The involvement of the Tule River Indian Tribe, which operated 150 video gaming machines in a small casino on its reservation in the foothills northeast of Bakersfield, was typical. According to UCLA law professor Carole Goldberg,

Late one night in the early months of 1998, tribal leaders at Tule

River got a phone call from their counterparts at the San Manuel Band of Mission Indians in San Bernardino County. . . . San Manuel's leaders knew that Tule River was unable to help out with money, but what they wanted was Tule River's public endorsement.

The San Manuel Band, whose 800-acre reservation on a hillside close-by the Interstate 10 freeway is an hour's drive east of Los Angeles, did not need the Tule River Indian Tribe's money because it was operating a thousand machines. If each machine earned $200 a day, the Band was earning $73 million a year. So the Band had no difficulty writing Californians for Indian Self-Reliance checks that totaled $27.7 million.

But if Californians for Indian Self-Reliance was a front for the fewer than one dozen tribes that were operating thousands of video gaming machines on reservations located within a convenient automobile drive from metropolitan locations at which tens of thousands of non-Indian customers resided, the campaign Winner/Wagner & Mandabach developed focused on the plight of Indians who were not members of those tribes.

In addition to the television commercials in which Mark Macarro appeared, another commercial featured Francine Kupscha, a member of the Los Coyotes Band whose reservation in San Diego County was too remote to make a bingo hall economically feasible. In her commercial, after describing how she had grown up in a shack lit with kerosene lamps, Kupscha told voters that, if Proposition 5 passed, she finally would be able to get electricity and maybe even a refrigerator.

Californians for Indian Self-Reliance featured Karen Kupscha in its commercials because her message resonated. As one political consultant explained to the *Los Angeles Times*, "When you go into focus groups, people tell you that the Indians have been screwed for hundreds of years and deserve a break. Their ads tap into this overwhelming sense of sympathy. That's smart."

Proposition 5 had an organized opposition. By 1998 bingo halls, card rooms, and video gaming machine casinos on Indian reservations in California had 15,000 employees, 90 percent of whom were non-Indians.

In the Pala compact, the Pala Band agreed to allow its employees to "bargain collectively through representatives of their own choosing." In other words, to form unions.

By contrast, the Tribal Government Gaming and Economic Self-

Sufficiency Act said nothing about collective bargaining. For that reason, the Hotel Employees and Restaurant Employees International Union, known by its acronym as HERE and whose local union in Nevada represented workers in the casinos on the Las Vegas Strip, and the California Labor Federation AFL-CIO, which represented 2,000 local unions in California, opposed Proposition 5.

Proposition 5 also was opposed by Mirage Resorts, Circus Circus Enterprises, and the other owners of the major casinos in Las Vegas that depended on gamblers from California for 30 percent of their business. Collectively, ten of those owners spent $25.4 million to broadcast television commercials whose message was that if Proposition 5 passed, Indian tribes would open Las Vegas–style casinos (like the ones they owned) throughout California in communities that wanted nothing to do with gambling.

While in the years ahead that argument would prove prescient, on Election Day, November 3, 1998, 62.38 percent of California voters approved Proposition 5. The "no" vote carried in only eight of California's thirty-four counties, all rural and sparsely populated. In San Diego, Riverside, and San Bernardino Counties, in which the reservations of most of the tribes that had funded Californians for Indian Self-Reliance were located, Proposition 5 passed by a 2-to-1 margin. And it did the same in Los Angeles County.

For Mary Ann Martin Andreas, the chairwoman of the Morongo Band; Richard Milanovich, the chairman of the Agua Caliente Band; and the other leaders of the handful of tribes that had financed Californians for Indian Self-Reliance, the passage of Proposition 5 was a victory of historic import.

But there was a rub.

THE CALIFORNIA CONSTITUTION prohibited "casinos of the type currently operating in Nevada and New Jersey" without saying what characteristics made a casino a Nevada and New Jersey–type casino. Because the California Constitution can be amended by initiative, a provision could have been included in Proposition 5 whose passage would have amended the constitution to exempt casinos on Indian reservations from the prohibition against Nevada and New Jersey–type casinos. But to amend the California Constitution by initiative would have required the tribes to collect 780,000 signatures. And no one thought they could collect that many signatures in three weeks.

So when George Forman, Jerry Levine, and Glenn Feldman wrote the Tribal Government Gaming and Economic Self-Sufficiency Act, they included a provision that stated: "The people of the state . . . find that casinos of the type currently operating in Nevada and New Jersey are materially different from the tribal gaming facilities authorized under this chapter."

While a clever try, the California Supreme Court (not the voters who passed Proposition 5) was the only entity that could decide what the California Constitution meant. So, three weeks after the November election, HERE petitioned the Court to declare that Proposition 5 was invalid because it authorized Indian tribes to operate "casinos of the type currently operating in Nevada and New Jersey."

Two weeks after HERE filed its petition, the Court issued an order in which it prohibited Pete Wilson from implementing Proposition 5 until the Court ruled. Eight months later, on August 23, 1999, the Court issued a decision in which it agreed with HERE that, with the exception of one relatively inconsequential provision, Proposition 5 was invalid.

But by then the tribes were on the cusp of not having to care.

IN 1994 WHEN PETE Wilson and Dan Lungren ran for second terms as governor and attorney general, tribes that were operating video gaming machines contributed $1 million to the California Democratic Party and another $800,000 to Lungren's Democratic opponent. But Wilson and Lungren both were reelected.

Four years later, when Lungren was the Republican Party's candidate in the November 1998 election to succeed Wilson as governor, the tribes tried again. They gave Lungren's Democratic opponent, Gray Davis, the lieutenant governor of California, $902,000.

What was Davis's position on Proposition 5?

In August at a debate with Dan Lungren in San Diego, Davis said he had no position. But four months earlier, in a letter to the California Nations Indian Gaming Association, Davis told the association what its members wanted to hear. He excoriated the Pala compact, because it had "not given even the slightest deference to the sovereign independence of the California tribes."

That expression of solidarity persuaded the Cabazon Band not only to give Davis, who in the run-up to the June primary election was being heavily outspent by his two multi-millionaire opponents, $100,000, but on four occasions the band chartered airplanes that Davis used to travel to campaign events. And several other tribes collectively gave Davis an additional $95,500.

After Davis won the primary election, during the general election the money kept coming. And when Davis was elected, the Cabazon, San Manuel, and Agua Caliente Bands each contributed $100,000, and the Sycuan Band and four other tribes collectively contributed another $145,000 to the committee that organized Governor Davis's inauguration.

What did the leaders who wrote the checks think their tribes' money was buying?

According to George Forman, two months after the inauguration, in March 1999 at a meeting in Los Angeles to which he invited representatives of all of California's 104 tribes, Davis suggested that "as a hedge against a bad result in the California Supreme Court [which had not yet issued a decision in the lawsuit HERE had filed to invalidate Proposition 5]," the tribes should negotiate a new model compact that would replace the Pala compact. When the tribes' representatives agreed to do so, Davis appointed a retired judge named William Norris as his negotiator.

By then the tribes that wanted compacts had divided themselves into three groups. The largest was a coalition of sixty-three tribes that had a steering committee chaired by Mary Ann Martin Andreas, the chairwoman of the Morongo Band, and whose other members included Mark Macarro. Apparently on the theory that he had influence with the governor, the steering committee hired Mickey Kantor—a Los Angeles attorney who had been secretary of commerce during the Clinton administration—as the committee's lead negotiator.

On May 13 when the members of the steering committee met with Judge Norris their expectation was that the negotiations would proceed pro forma. But it soon became apparent that Norris had no authority to agree to all of the compact terms in the Tribal Government Gaming and Economic Self-Sufficiency Act.

Throughout his political career, Gray Davis had depended on support from organized labor. And prior to the Democratic primary election, he had taken more money from labor—$656,000—than he had from the

Cabazon Band and the other tribes. So Davis would not allow Norris to agree to a compact that would prohibit employees of bingo halls, card rooms, and video gaming machine casinos on Indian reservations from organizing unions. Norris also had no authority to agree to allow a tribe to operate an unlimited number of video gaming machines.

Then, on August 23, the California Supreme Court invalidated Proposition 5. Davis's response, on the same day the court issued its decision, was to invite Mark Macarro and two dozen other tribal leaders to meet with him in Sacramento for what turned out to be a two-hour meeting. John Burton, the president of the California Senate, and Antonio Villaraigosa, the speaker of the California Assembly, also attended. The message Davis delivered was that if the tribes would agree to a compact whose terms were acceptable to Davis, Burton and Villaraigosa would arrange for the California legislature to put an initiative on the March 2000 primary election ballot whose passage would exempt casinos on Indian reservations from the provision in the California Constitution that prohibited "casinos of the type currently operating in Nevada and New Jersey."

After dangling that carrot, Davis reminded that the U.S. attorneys still had their stick. A year earlier, when the May 13, 1998, deadline passed, and the nine tribes in Santa Barbara, Riverside, and San Bernardino Counties that were defendants in *United States v. Santa Ynez Band of Chumash Mission Indians* refused to sign the Pala compact or turn off their video gaming machines, U.S. Attorney Manella brought the tribes' intransigence to Judge Letts's attention. In July, Letts reluctantly concluded that, while the situation had been confused "largely by the Indian tribes . . . . Gaming cannot be done without a compact." He then told the tribes' attorneys that their clients had until September 15 to sign compacts. If by that date a tribe had not done so, he would issue an order that would require the tribe to turn off its machines.

When the September 15 deadline came and went, even Richard Milanovich, the chairman of the Agua Caliente Band, thought Letts's patience with the tribes' flaunting of the law had finally run out. But at the next hearing, Letts said he was concerned about throwing the 4,000 employees who worked in the tribes' casinos out of work. So instead of signing the injunction he had promised in July that he would sign, Letts directed Nora Manella and the tribes' attorneys to file briefs that set out their views on how Letts should write the injunction so that "people don't suffer more than they have to."

In November when Judge Letts finally issued his injunction, rather than complying with it, the tribes appealed Letts's action to the U.S. Court of Appeals for the Ninth Circuit. Several days later, that court issued an order in which it stayed enforcement of the injunction until the appeal was decided.

The passage of Proposition 5 that same month mooted the injunction and the appeal. But now that the California Supreme Court had invalidated Proposition 5, who could say what the U.S. Court of Appeals for the Ninth Circuit would decide. And the enforcement actions the other U.S. attorneys had filed were pending.

During the meeting in Sacramento, Davis told the representatives of the tribes who attended that he had asked Attorney General Reno to direct Nora Manella and the other the U.S. attorneys not to press their enforcement actions because "I don't want you to fear bringing down the house of cards." What was left unsaid, but which everyone in the room undoubtedly understood, was that, if there was no agreement on a new compact, the U.S. attorneys were positioned to proceed.

Anticipating that HERE might win its lawsuit, several weeks earlier Richard Milanovich, the chairman of the Agua Caliente Band, persuaded the band's governing council to approve spending $20 million to collect the 670,816 signatures needed to put an initiative to amend the California Constitution on the March 2000 primary election ballot. And by the date of the meeting with Davis, the band's signature-gatherers had collected 500,000 signatures. Nevertheless, the representatives of the tribes who attended the meeting decided that the sensible course was to negotiate.

Three days after the meeting, Judge Norris distributed a thirty-seven-page proposal for a model compact. The proposal allowed casino employees to organize unions, allowed tribes that were operating video gaming machines to collectively install five thousand more machines, limited new casinos to 350 machines, and divided 25 percent of the tribes' gross profit between the state to fund its regulation of gambling on Indian reservations, tribes like the Los Coyotes Band that did not have a casino, and programs to combat gambling addiction.

In response, the tribes rented a conference room at the convention center in Sacramento across the street from the capitol in which more than three hundred tribal representatives and their attorneys discussed, and then rejected, Norris's proposal. That began back-and-forth bargaining that continued into the following week. On Friday, September 10, 1999, the last day the California legislature was in session, hands finally were shaken.

The new model compact gave every tribe the right to operate two casinos and up to 2,000 video gaming machines. Every tribe that had 250 or more employees was required to adopt a Model Tribal Labor Relations Ordinance that created a procedure for employees who wished to do so to organize unions. And revenue would be shared with tribes that did not have casinos and with the state to reimburse the state for its regulatory costs.

As Gray Davis, John Burton, and Antonio Villaraigosa had promised they would arrange, before the California legislature adjourned, the members voted to put an initiative—which would be known as Proposition 1A—on the ballot for the March 2000 primary election. California voters' passage of the amendment would amend the California Constitution by authorizing the governor to sign the new compacts.

The Morongo and San Manuel Bands and the other tribes that had funded Californians for Indian Self-Reliance then spent another $20 million to fund a new campaign. Television commercials featuring Mark Macarro were broadcast and again accomplished their objective when Proposition 1A passed with 64.5 percent of the vote.

TWO YEARS LATER, Gray Davis, who by then was deeply unpopular, was elected to a second term as governor in a mudslinging campaign he won only because his Republican opponent was even more unpopular than he was. Ten months after his inauguration, in October 2003, Davis became the first governor in California history to be recalled after 1.36 million voters signed a petition to put the recall to a vote. Davis was replaced by Arnold Schwarzenegger, the action-movie star whose Colonel Klink accent and "Hasta la vista, baby" swagger had made him an international celebrity.

At the beginning of the recall election, Davis and two of the men who wanted to replace him, Democratic lieutenant governor Cruz Bustamante and a Republican state senator Tom McClintock, met in Sacramento with members of the California Nations Indian Gaming Association. Bustamante won the pandering contest and the prize that went with it—$5.15 million in campaign contributions—by promising that, if he replaced Davis, he would amend the compacts the tribes had signed with Davis to remove the 2,000 video gaming machines per tribe limitation.

Arnold Schwarzenegger, by contrast, refused to accept campaign contributions from members of the California Nations Indian Gaming Association. He also broadcast a television commercial that opened with a picture of a video gaming machine and Arnold reminding voters that Indian casinos "make billions, yet they pay no taxes and virtually nothing to the state." The commercial concluded with the candidate vowing that it was time for the tribes "to pay their fair share."

Even if the commercial had been just a campaign tactic, in November when he took office Governor Schwarzenegger needed money from any and everywhere he could find it because the national economic recession and years of profligate spending by the California legislature had created a $15 billion budget deficit.

In January, in his first State of the State address, Schwarzenegger announced that, just as he respected "the sovereignty of our Native American tribes," he expected the tribes to "respect the economic situation that California faces." Because he was sure they would, he announced he was appointing a "negotiator who will work with the gaming tribes so that California receives its fair share of gaming revenues."

The negotiator he appointed was Dan Kolkey. During the new round of negotiations Kolkey conducted, the only thing he had to trade for a share of the tribes' video gaming machine revenue was the governor's willingness to allow the tribes to earn that revenue and more by raising, and in some compacts completely eliminating, the 2,000 machine limit on the number of video gaming machines a tribe could operate.

As a result, in 2014, sixty-two groups in California the BIA says are Indian tribes operated casinos whose gaming floors contained 67,725 slot, poker, blackjack, and other Class III video gaming machines. The tribes also operated thousands of additional machines programmed to play bingo and pull tabs.* In 2014, those machines and other forms of gambling in casinos on Indian reservations in California earned $7.3 billion.

In 1988 when S. 555 passed the Senate without a recorded vote, Cal-

---

*In 2002, the NIGC amended the regulations it adopted when Tony Hope was chairman and reclassified video gaming machines whose software had been programmed to play bingo and pull-tabs as Class II forms of gambling a tribe may offer without a compact.

ifornia senator Pete Wilson voiced no objection. And when the U.S. House of Representatives suspended its rules and passed S. 555, thirty-three of the forty-five members who represented congressional districts in California voted for the bill, one of whom was Rep. Dan Lungren. Two years later when they were elected governor and attorney general, Wilson and Lungren would spend the next eight years trying—and in the end failing—to force Indian tribes in California that were operating video gaming machines unlawfully to comply with the IGRA.

Wilson and Lungren's failure is a textbook example of why on Capitol Hill the devil is at all times in the details buried in the texts of seemingly minor bills that most members of Congress have neither the time nor the interest to read. Because when they wrote S. 555, the bill Congress would enact as the Indian Gaming Regulatory Act, if Ginny Boylan and Patricia Zell had not included a new section 1166 to Title 18 of the U.S. Code in the bill, and if they then had not written subsection (d) of section 1166 to prohibit states from enforcing on Indian reservations within their borders, not only their laws that regulated, but also their laws that completely prohibited gambling, during Pete Wilson's and Dan Lungren's tenures as governor and attorney general the story of Indian gaming in California would have turned out very differently than it did.

14: FAKE TRIBES

Hey, everybody wants to be a Mashantucket.

JOSEPH CARTER
Member, Mashantucket Pequot Tribe

I N 1941, FELIX COHEN, THE DEPARTMENT OF THE INTERIOR ATTORNEY WHO invented the doctrine of inherent tribal sovereignty, cautioned that "The term 'tribe' is commonly used in two senses, an ethnological sense and a political sense" and "It is important to distinguish between these two meanings of the term." The distinction is important, because only a group whose members are a tribe in a "political sense" may operate a casino, bingo hall, or other gambling facility pursuant to the Indian Gaming Regulatory Act (IGRA). To be an IGRA "Indian tribe," a group must meet two criteria: the members of the group must be eligible to receive programs and services from the Bureau of Indian Affairs (BIA), and the group must be "recognized as possessing powers of self-government."

In the arcane world of federal Indian law, a group that "possesses powers of self-government" is called a "federally recognized tribe." In 1979, when Seminole Management Associates opened the nation's first Indian bingo hall, there were 277 groups in the coterminous states the BIA said were federally recognized tribes. In 2015, there were 340.

How did those sixty-three new federally recognized tribes each become one? And for that matter, how did each of the original 277? Every federally recognized tribe has its own story, and telling those stories would fill volumes, rather than just a book. But since the 1970s, all federally recognized tribes have acquired that legal status through one of two means: the disinterested inattention of Congress and unilateral (and unlawful) administrative action by the assistant secretary of the interior for Indian affairs, the political appointee who supervises the BIA inside the Department of the Interior.

• • •

THE U.S. SUPREME COURT has defined an ethnological tribe as "a body of Indians of the same or a similar race, united in a community under one leadership or government and inhabiting a particular though sometimes ill-defined territory." In 1783, when the Revolutionary War ended, ethnological tribes whose members occupied land west and north of the thirteen original states had the military capability to resist the efforts of white settlers to intrude into their territories. The nonmilitary means the new federal government chose to try to end that resistance was to negotiate a treaty with each ethnological tribe. When the headmen of an ethnological tribe signed a treaty, the signing had the legal consequence of transforming the ethnological tribe into a federally recognized tribe.

By 1871, however, the U.S. Army had relocated thousands of Native Americans who had occupied land east of the Mississippi River to locations west of the river. And west of the river, while Custer's defeat at the Battle of the Little Big Horn was still five years away, the depredations that members of ethnological tribes continued to inflict on white settlers had become more of an annoyance than a military threat. So members of the U.S. House of Representatives included a provision in an appropriations bill that prohibited the president from negotiating, and the Senate from ratifying, any more treaties.

When treaty-making ended, the only way members of an ethnological tribe could become a federally recognized tribe was to acquire that status in a bill passed by Congress and signed by the president. However, that fact was of no consequence, because by 1880 the objective of Congress's Indian policy had shifted from clearing the public domain of Native Americans to assimilating those who survived the clearing into American society. For that reason, for the next almost one hundred years Congress created no new federally recognized tribes. Then, in 1972, with no understanding of the precedent doing so would establish, Congress reversed course.

IN 1872, WHEN President Ulysses S. Grant established the San Carlos Apache Reservation in what is today southeastern Arizona, the U.S. Army confined members of the Chiricahua and other Apache bands whose men had been raiding white settlements and ranches on the reservation at bayonet point. A number of Apaches, the most famous being Geronimo, escaped and had to be recaptured. But by 1889 the Apaches living on the San Carlos Reservation no longer posed a threat. So that year, several families quietly moved away and built an encampment near Payson, a small ranching and mining town west of the reservation.

By 1967, sixty-four descendants of those families were living on the outskirts of Payson, squatting on land in the Tonto National Forest. After inspecting their encampment, the BIA area director in Phoenix reported:

> The buildings are constructed of scrap lumber from the nearby mill where ten of the family heads are employed seasonally. There is no electricity and water must be hauled from town. The privies do not meet minimum standards and are considered a menace to the health of the camp as well as Payson itself.

The BIA area director had conducted his inspection at the request of Doris Sturgis, the manager of the Payson Chamber of Commerce, who had begun a letter-writing campaign to convince the members of Arizona's congressional delegation to relocate the members of what by then was known as the Payson Band from the land on which they were squatting to a permanent location in the forest at which proper houses and a water and sewer system could be constructed.

At Sturgis's urging, in 1968 Rep. Sam Steiger, whose congressional district included Payson, introduced a bill in the U.S. House of Representatives to authorize the Payson Band to select eighty-five acres of land in the Tonto National Forest as a village site. The title to the land would be "held by the United States in trust as an Indian reservation." The bill also "recognized" the band "as a tribe of Indians within the purview of the [Indian Reorganization Act of 1934]."

In 1971, when they reported the bill to the U.S. House of Representatives, the members of the Committee on Interior and Insular Affairs rewrote the text to remove the band's recognition as a tribe. As Rep. Wayne Aspinall, the chairman of the committee, explained: "The Payson Band is a part of the San Carlos Tribe," and the Department of the Interior had told the committee, "[W]e do not now recognize this group and believe that we should not now recognize them. If this group wishes to avail itself of Indian services, they need only remove themselves to the San Carlos Indian Reservation."

However, because Arizona senator Paul Fannin and other members of the Senate Committee on Interior and Insular Affairs apparently wanted members of the Payson Band to be able to receive health and other services without having to travel to the San Carlos Reservation, the version of the bill Richard Nixon signed into law in 1972 recognized the Payson Community of Yavapai-Apache Indians as a "tribe of Indians."

When, with no debate or recorded votes, first the U.S. House of Representatives, and then the Senate, passed Sam Steiger's bill, the only consequences were that eighty-five acres of land were removed from the Tonto National Forest and members of the Payson Community became eligible to receive services and programs from the BIA and the Indian Health Service without having to travel to the San Carlos Reservation. But sixteen years later, Congress enacted the IGRA. As a consequence, today on its reservation on the outskirts of Payson, the Tonto Apache Tribe (as the Payson Community now calls itself) operates the Mazatzal Hotel & Casino, whose gaming floor, in addition to blackjack and poker tables, contains more than 400 video gaming machines.

If the Tonto Apache Tribe is a federally recognized tribe because Congress, with few members knowing they had done so, conferred that legal status on sixty-four individuals who had been squatting in a national forest in abject poverty, there is no question that the members of the Tonto Apache Tribe are descendants of Apache Indians who lived in Arizona during the nineteenth century. The same cannot be said for another federally recognized tribe Congress created.

THE INDIAN NONINTERCOURSE Act, which Congress enacted in 1790, prohibited the sale by any tribe of Indians of land its members occupied, unless the sale had been approved by the federal government. Four years later, the Commonwealth of Massachusetts entered into a treaty with the Passamaquoddy Indians, an ethnological tribe whose members occupied a large portion what today is the state of Maine.* In the treaty, the tribe's members relinquished their land occupancy rights and agreed to relocate onto two reservations.

---

*In 1820, residents of Maine voted to secede from the Commonwealth of Massachusetts, and Congress admitted the state of Maine into the Union.

In 1969 a twenty-five-year-old graduate of the George Washington University Law School named Tom Tureen took a job as a staff attorney with Pine Tree Legal Assistance, a federally funded antipoverty law firm, at the firm's office in Calais, Maine, a small town near the Passamaquoddy Reservations. When Tureen arrived, the tribal council was involved in a dispute regarding the ownership of land within the boundaries of one of the reservations. When Tureen investigated the dispute, he realized the federal government had never approved the 1794 treaty with the Commonwealth of Massachusetts.

In 1972 Tureen and a team of lawyers he assembled filed a lawsuit in the U.S. District Court in Maine against the secretary of the interior in which the Passamaquoddy Tribe requested District Judge Edward Gignoux to order the secretary to file a lawsuit against the state of Maine to enable the tribe to obtain monetary compensation for the value of the land its members had lost in violation of the Indian Nonintercourse Act.

In response to the lawsuit, the attorneys at the U.S. Department of Justice argued that in 1790 Congress intended the word "tribe " in the Indian Nonintercourse Act to mean "tribe" in its political sense, rather than "tribe" in its ethnological sense. And because the Senate had not ratified a treaty, and Congress had not enacted a statute that recognized the Passamaquoddy ethnological tribe, the Passamaquoddy ethnological tribe was not a "tribe" of Indians for the purposes of the Indian Nonintercourse Act.

In 1975 Judge Gignoux rejected that argument and held that in 1790 Congress intended the term "tribe" in the Indian Nonintercourse Act to include ethnological tribes that had not been recognized. His decision set into motion events in Maine and Washington, D.C., that in 1980 resulted in Congress enacting the Maine Indian Claims Settlement Act. The act extinguished the land occupancy rights of the members of the Passamaquoddy Tribe, as well as two other ethnological, but unrecognized, tribes in Maine. As compensation, the act authorized the tribes to receive $81.5 million, much of which the tribes used to buy land from the timber companies that were Maine's largest private landowners.

When Tom Tureen thought up his theory regarding the present-day consequence of a failure to comply with the Indian Nonintercourse Act, a Passamaquoddy Indian of his acquaintance named John Stevens was dating an anthropologist named Susan MacCulloch whose area of interest was unrecognized ethnological tribes. MacCulloch suggested to Tureen that there might be other unrecognized ethnological tribes whose history regarding their members' land occupancy rights was similar to that of the Passamaquoddy Tribe's. To find out, Tureen arranged for Stevens and MacCulloch to drive around New England to look for descendants of members of unrecognized ethnological tribes for Tureen to sign up as clients.

IN THE SEVENTEENTH century, Pequot Indians lived in villages along several of the major rivers in what today is the state of Connecticut. In 1637, English settlers, aided by Mohegan and Narragansett Indians, launched a war of annihilation against the Pequots. More than 700 Pequots were killed, and most of those who had not been were enslaved by the Mohegans and Narragansetts.

A few Pequots escaped capture, and by 1649 they had grouped themselves into two bands, one under the leadership of a headman named Robin Cassacinamon. In response to a petition from Cassacinamon's band for a permanent home, in 1667 the General Court of the Connecticut Colony designated a 2,000-acre tract of land in southeastern Connecticut at a location the Indians called "Mushantuxet" as a reservation for the band.

In 1761, when the Connecticut General Assembly reduced the reservation to 989 acres, 176 Indians lived on the reservation. By 1852, only twenty did, and in 1856 the state of Connecticut sold 800 of the 989 acres at public auction.

In 1910, only six adults lived on the reservation. In 1935, only three adults did, one of whom was a forty-year-old woman named Elizabeth George. In May 1973, when John Stevens drove down from Maine to investigate whether anyone lived on the Mashantucket Reservation, Elizabeth George, now seventy-eight, was the only resident.

According to Jeff Benedict, an author and attorney who investigated her genealogy, while Elizabeth George had been born on the Mashantucket Reservation in 1895, her father was an African American who when he was seventy years old had listed himself as a Narragansett Indian on a state enumeration record, and her mother was a blue-eyed Caucasian. They had lived on the reservation because, according to Benedict, "Largely neglected by state overseers, the [several Indian] reservations [in Connecticut] attracted squatters and paupers alike."

When John Stevens got out of his car in front of Elizabeth George's ramshackle house, rather than George, he met Skip Hayward and his wife Aline. Hayward, who was twenty-five years old, lived in Mystic, a resort town on the seacoast where he managed a restaurant. When Stevens explained that he was trying to find members of the Pequot Tribe and Hayward said he was Elizabeth George's grandson and "a member of the tribe," Stevens—who, being an Indian, knew one when he saw one—was incredulous. Nevertheless, he explained to Hayward how Tom Tureen had been assisting the Passamaquoddys, and he invited Hayward to visit the Passamaquoddy Reservations to "see how our tribal administration is set up."

What happened next is a long story Jeff Benedict tells in his book, *Without Reservation*, and which also is told in Kim Isaac Eisler's *Revenge of the Pequots* and Brett Fromson's *Hitting the Jackpot*. While those accounts differ in their details, in summary:

The month after John Stevens's chance meeting with Skip Hayward, Elizabeth George died.

In Maine, in January 1975 Judge Gignoux issued his decision in which he held that Congress intended the term "tribe of Indians" in the Indian Nonintercourse Act to include ethnological tribes that had not been recognized.

In March 1975, Skip Hayward visited the Passamaquoddy Reservations. Several weeks later, Tom Tureen met in Connecticut with Hayward, Hayward's mother and sister, and several other Hayward relatives. At the meeting, the Haywards retained Tureen to file a lawsuit on behalf of the "Western Pequot Tribe" against the present-day owners of the 800 acres the state of Connecticut had auctioned in 1856.

In August 1975, Hayward invited his mother and sisters; aunts, uncles, and cousins he had never met; and as many other relatives of Elizabeth George as he could locate to a meeting in the front yard of his grandmother's vacant house. At Hayward's urging, his relatives organized themselves as the Western Pequot Tribe, approved a tribal constitution Tureen had written, and elected Skip Hayward tribal chairman.

In May 1976 in the U.S. District Court in Connecticut, Tureen filed *Western Pequot Tribe of Indians v. Holdridge Enterprises* in which he requested the court to invalidate the landowners' title to the 800 acres because the state of Connecticut had not obtained the federal government's approval before it sold the land at auction.

When he filed the lawsuit, Tureen had no intention of litigating it to a judgment because, as he would admit years later,

These land claims are something that we made up. It was an utterly untested theory. If the [United States] Supreme Court ever tested the issue, it would say that the Nonintercourse Act did not apply to *any* of these tribes. So settlement was critically important to our strategy in all of these cases. (emphasis in original)

As it had in Maine, that is how the situation played out in Connecticut.

Tureen convinced Connecticut senators Lowell Weicker and Christopher Dodd, and all six of Connecticut's members of the U.S. House of Representatives that having Congress quiet the landowners' title to the 800 acres and pay the tribe monetary compensation was a quicker and cheaper way to resolve the dispute than spending the years it would take the landowners to fight the *Western Pequot Tribe* lawsuit in the courts. Tureen then wrote a bill that in July 1982 Senators Weicker and Dodd introduced as S. 2719.

In addition to quieting title to the 800 acres, the bill authorized the appropriation of $900,000 for the purpose of buying land from private landowners. It also designated the 189 acres that remained of the Mashantucket Reservation, as well as the land that would be purchased, as an Indian reservation whose title would be owned by the United States in trust for "the Mashantucket Pequot Tribe (also known as the Western Pequot Tribe)." And, most important, the bill provided that "Notwithstanding any other provision of law, Federal recognition is extended to the Tribe." What the text of S. 2719 did not say was that Tureen had written it to have a legal consequence of which he made no mention.

In 1978, when Tureen wrote the bill that in 1980 President Jimmy Carter signed into law as the Maine Indian Claims Settlement Act, the attorneys who represented the state of Maine had been adamant that the bill give the state jurisdiction to enforce all state laws—including state laws that regulated and prohibited gambling—on the Passamaquoddy and Penobscot Reservations. Tureen had not had a negotiating position strong enough at that time to allow him to resist that hard line.

That experience educated Tureen. He also likely was educated by the decisions District Judge Norman Roettger and the U.S. Court of Appeals for the Fifth Circuit issued in 1980 and 1981 in the *Seminole Tribe of*

Florida v. Butterworth lawsuit. So through subtle wordsmithing, Tureen included language in S. 2719 that, without explicitly saying so, avoided giving the state of Connecticut the jurisdiction to regulate gambling on the Mashantucket Reservation that the Maine Indian Claims Settlement Act had given to the state of Maine.

The attorneys in the Connecticut Attorney General's Office either did not understand what Tureen intended his wordsmithing to achieve, or they did understand and did not care. Nor did Senators Weicker and Dodd and of Connecticut's five congressmen and one woman who introduced S. 2719 in the U.S. House of Representatives as H.R. 6612.

Someone who did understand was Tim Woodcock, the staff director of the Select Committee on Indian Affairs. Woodcock telephoned Perry Pockrose, who worked for Connecticut representative Sam Gejdenson, whose congressional district included the towns that surrounded the Mashantucket Reservation, and explained the situation. Several days later, Pockrose told Woodcock, "I checked with Sam Gejdenson and the Connecticut Attorney General's Office, and we don't care if there is federal jurisdiction there." So Woodcock let the matter drop.

But Tureen still had a problem: the members of the select committee and the House Committee on Interior and Insular Affairs would not report S. 2719 and H.R. 6612 until each committee held a hearing at which the members might discover that Congress's enactment of Tureen's bill would create an Indian tribe that was one only because Skip Hayward and Tureen had created it.

To finesse the problem, Tureen wrote a witness statement for Hayward to read at the hearings, and prior to the first hearing, Hayward spent the evening with Tureen rehearsing his performance. The next morning, when Maine senator William Cohen, the chairman of the select committee and the only member who attended, gaveled the select committee's hearing on S. 2719 to order, Hayward read from his script. Then Tureen took over.

Four years earlier, the BIA had issued regulations (about which more will be said) that authorize a group that wants to be a federally recognized tribe to petition the secretary of the interior to grant that legal status. For tactical reasons, in 1979 Tureen had filed a petition in which he requested the secretary to "recognize" the Mashantucket Pequot Tribe. But he did not submit any supporting documentation.

When Hayward finished reading his testimony, Tureen told Senator Cohen that it was his understanding that the "Federal acknowledgment people" who were processing the petition he had filed "believe that [Skip Hayward and the other members of Hayward's tribe] could easily establish recognition status through [the BIA administrative] process." Since they could, it would be "far more efficient all around, inasmuch as we all know that they will be recognized, to simply do it in the legislation."

And when Cohen asked, "Has the state of Connecticut recognized the tribe?" Tureen continued to dissemble by answering: "The state of Connecticut has always recognized the tribe and recognizes the tribe today. That is one of the reasons why the recognition people at Interior felt that recognition would essentially be a fait accompli."

The following morning, the Committee on Interior and Insular Affairs held its hearing on H.R. 6612, which was chaired by Sam Gejdenson, rather than by Arizona representative Morris Udall, the chairman of the committee. Only five of the committee's forty-one other members attended, and each did so only briefly.

When Tureen and Hayward were asked whether there was a roll of tribal members, Tureen answered: "Yes. The Connecticut tribes have been recognized continuously by the state of Connecticut. Both the state and the tribe have maintained rolls consistently throughout history." And Hayward volunteered that the Mashantucket Pequot Tribe had 195 members, 42 of whom lived on the reservation.

In October, H.R. 6612 passed the U.S. House of Representatives and in December, the Senate passed its version of the bill, in both cases without recorded votes, and after only cursory explanations of the bill's purpose and content by Representative Gejdenson and Senators Weicker and Dodd, each of whom spoke in virtually empty chambers.

Because the Ninety-Seventh Congress adjourned before the House had time to vote to accept the Senate's version of H.R. 6612, when the Ninety-Eighth Congress convened in January 1983, Tureen's bill was reintroduced. It again passed both Houses in the same pro forma fashion, and was sent to the White House where the bill was vetoed.

Skip Hayward told the press it was a "mystery" why the president would veto a bill that "put to rest a lot of issues that have been pressing for centuries here on the reservation." But there was no mystery. While

Ronald Reagan signed the veto message, the odds he knew anything about the bill are close to zero. But officials at the Department of the Interior knew. And from the beginning they had been suspicious that the Mashantucket Pequot Tribe was a fraud.

When he testified at the hearings on S. 2719 and H.R. 6612, William Coldiron, the Department of the Interior's chief legal officer, had announced that the department opposed Tureen's bill, among other reasons, because the department did not have sufficient information to know whether there was a Mashantucket Pequot Tribe. When Representative Gejdenson, who was chairing the House hearing, challenged the suggestion that the tribe's existence was suspect, Coldiron explained the department's position during the following exchange:

> GEJDENSON: Even though they have lived on the same land for over 200 or 300 years, and the state has had them as a tribe through the entire period of time, you are saying that the Interior Department may still find that they will not be recognized as a tribe?
>
> COLDIRON: We would have to examine the evidence. There is a possibility that they might not be. If it is so simple, why haven't they come in in the last three years [with evidence that would document the facts about the tribe's present-day existence that Tom Tureen had alleged in the petition he filed in 1979]? I don't understand.
>
> GEJDENSON: The question is . . . as the fiduciary of Indians, why hasn't the Interior Department gone to these Indians and helped them prove that, if that is the case?
>
> COLDIRON: We don't even know that they are Indians.

Gejdenson's and Senators Weicker and Dodd's refusal to acknowledge the legitimacy of Coldiron's concerns was one of the reasons for the veto.

When he found out the bill had been vetoed, Weicker was so angry that he set about trying to round up votes in the Senate to override it.

The idea that the Senate, which the Republicans controlled, would embarrass a Republican president by overriding his veto of a minor bill seems unlikely. But Weicker apparently obtained commitments from enough senators to persuade Sen. Howard Baker, the Republican majority leader, to broker a compromise with the White House. In exchange for the Department of the Interior dropping its insistence that Skip Hayward and his relatives establish their legitimacy as a tribe, the state of Connecticut would contribute $200,000 to a trust fund the federal government would create to finance the tribe's land purchases. According to Jeff Benedict, "Under the agreement, the Pequots were assured that their genealogy would not come under review."

Hands were shaken, and in June 1983 Senator Weicker introduced a new bill whose text incorporated the agreed-upon changes. The bill passed the Senate and the U.S. House of Representatives pro forma and without recorded votes and was signed by President Reagan.

The preoccupying objective for Connecticut's senators and representatives had been to have Congress pass a bill whose details were unimportant as long as the bill's passage cleared the title to the 800 acres that Tureen's lawsuit had encumbered. Less than three weeks after President Reagan signed the Mashantucket Pequot Indian Claims Settlement Act into law, they learned that the details mattered when Joseph Francis, the lieutenant governor of the Penobscot Tribe in Maine, told a reporter that "as soon as we can start pouring the concrete slab," the Penobscots would begin constructing a 3,500-seat bingo hall on the Mashantucket Reservation.

Skip Hayward told the same reporter that Francis's announcement had been premature; which it was because the bingo hall did not open until 1986. Its first year of operation, the hall, which was managed by the Penobscots who bused in players from as far away as Massachusetts and Rhode Island, earned $20 million.

Financed with a $60 million loan from a Chinese-born billionaire who owned the only destination resort casino in Malaysia, in 1992 the Mashantucket Pequot Tribe opened the Foxwoods casino. Within a month, Foxwoods, which had a monopoly on lawful casino gambling throughout New England, was being patronized by 15,000 players a day. By 1994, the casino had 9,200 employees and was earning $400 million a year.

Today, the Foxwoods Resort & Casino looks from a distance like one of the cities in Lord of the Rings. The complex contains four hotels, two golf courses, a 3,600-seat bingo hall, a 50,000-square-foot convention center, a twenty-eight-bay gas station, and six gaming floors that contain 5,500 video gaming machines and 300 poker, blackjack, and baccarat tables.

During the 2014 fiscal year, the machines alone earned $467.9 million.

In 2010, the Mashantucket Pequot Tribe had 850 members. According to the BIA, who those individuals are is no one's business but the tribe's. But as Bruce Kirchner, who Skip Hayward recruited to join his tribe at the meeting Hayward hosted in the front yard of his grandmother's house, explained to Brett Fromson, the author of *Hitting the Jackpot*, "We are the first tribe in American history to be formed around money."

Another tribal member is Theresa Casanova, the daughter of a Puerto Rican father and African American mother. When Casanova and her mother were living on welfare in Florida, her mother announced they were moving to Connecticut because they were Indians who were related to the half-sister of a woman named Elizabeth George. According to Casanova, "I asked her what tribe. She said the Mashantucket Pequot. I could not pronounce it. . . . I never knew about that. At school, I told everyone that I was Puerto Rican." And with unrepentant candor, Casanova explained to Brett Fromson: "The only reason that a lot of people are here [on the Mashantucket Reservation] is for the money. That is the only reason my family is here. . . . I don't know if we deserved it or not. Maybe we were just lucky. But we deserved the money just as much as anyone else who the tribe said were Pequot."

What has Bruce Kirchner's and Theresa Casanova's membership in the Mashantucket Pequot Tribe been worth? Except for the Internal Revenue Service, no one who is not a member of the tribe knows for sure. But until 2009, when the national economic recession reduced the video gaming machine revenue the Foxwoods casino generates, Kirchner and Casanova had been receiving checks that totaled between $90,000 and $120,000 a year.

With Tom Tureen's help, Skip Hayward gamed an inattentive Congress into creating an Indian tribe that did not exist. But he is not the only fake Indian who has done so.

GREG SARRIS, WHO was born in 1952 and raised through junior college in Santa Rosa, the largest town in Sonoma County north of San Francisco, is the son of an unwed mother named Bunny Hartman, the sixteen-year-old daughter of a socially prominent Caucasian family that lived in Laguna Beach in southern California. Bunny died shortly after giving birth without revealing the name of Sarris's father.

In 1973, his adoptive mother told Sarris his birth mother had been named Hartman. That information began a search that ended a decade later when Sarris saw a photograph in a Laguna Beach High School yearbook of a teenager Sarris decided was his father.

While the teenager, Emilio Hilario, Jr., by then was dead, Emilio Hilario, Sr., who was Filipino, told Sarris that Emilio, Jr.'s, mother, who also was deceased, had been the daughter of a woman named Reinette Sarragossa. Sarris says Reinette Sarragossa was the daughter of Emily Stewart, whose father was a Scot and whose mother was a Coast Miwok Indian, and Tom Smith, whose mother was a Coast Miwok Indian and whose father was a Russian Creole who had a parent or grandparent who was a Pomo Indian.

His critics say Sarris is a self-promoting fabulist, because one of Reinette Sarragossa's great-granddaughters had her DNA tested, and the test revealed that *all* of her ancestors had come from Africa. Sarris could take his own DNA test. But rather than do so, Sarris, a college professor who is street-smart and verbally aggressive, accuses any and everyone who suggests that he might be a fake Indian of being "racist people."

In 1998, Sarris persuaded Rep. Lynn Woolsey, who represented Sonoma County in the U.S. House of Representatives, to introduce a bill to "restore" federal recognition to a tribe called "the Indians of the Graton Rancheria of California." In 2000 when he testified on the bill before the House Committee on Resources (as the Committee on Interior and Insular Affairs had been renamed), Sarris told the two members of the fifty-three-member committee who bothered to attend the hearing that in 1920 the BIA had purchased a 15.45-acre tract of land in the foothills west of Santa Rosa, which the BIA called the Graton Rancheria, as "a homeland for Coast Miwok and Southern Pomo peoples," and "seventy-five members moved on in 1920."

As historical fact, that was dissembling nonsense.

By the beginning of the twentieth century, many Indians in northern California labored as itinerant field workers who moved with their families from farm to farm, ranch to ranch. On each farm and ranch, the location at which the owner allowed his Indian workers to camp was called a "rancheria." In 1904, the Northern California Indian Association petitioned Congress to appropriate money to enable the BIA to purchase small tracts of land for those "landless" Indian families. In 1906 Congress began doing so, and over the next thirty years, the BIA purchased more than forty tracts, including the Graton Rancheria.

The Graton Rancheria, which is heavily timbered and riven with gullies, can be reached only by driving up a winding country road. It was unoccupied until 1937, when the BIA allowed, first an Indian named Andrew Sears, and then a handful of other Indians to move onto the land. In 1957, the BIA reported that six adults and one ten-year-old girl were living on the rancheria. At the urging of the Indians who were living on them, in 1958 Congress directed the BIA to convey the title to the land within the boundaries of forty-one rancherias, including Graton, in fee to the occupants. In 1966, the BIA conveyed the title to all 15.45 acres within the boundaries of the Graton Rancheria to the only people living there, Frank Truvido and his daughter Gloria.

In 1992, the Santa Rosa *Press Democrat* reported that a resident of San Jose, California, named Jeff Wilson, who was a descendant of a Pomo Indian family that had lived on a rancheria north of Santa Rosa, had asked the BIA to have the secretary of the interior take into trust the title to a 350-acre ranch south of Santa Rosa as a reservation for his "tribe" in order to build a golf course and a housing development in violation of the county zoning ordinances. Greg Sarris, who was teaching at UCLA and had decided he was the great-great-grandson of Coast Miwok Indians, was instrumental in organizing a meeting at a senior center near Santa Rosa that two hundred people who claimed descent from Coast Miwok Indians attended to discuss how to put a stop to Wilson's scheme. At the beginning of the meeting, Sarris was elected chairman of the group.

How many of the individuals who attended the meeting had a connection to the Graton Rancheria? If she was in the room, there would have been one: Gloria Truvido Armstrong, who in 1957 had been the ten-year-old girl living on the rancheria and who today still lives there, in a house on an acre lot that is part of the land the BIA gave to her and her father.

So how did Greg Sarris and the other individuals who attended the meeting become the "Indians of the Graton Rancheria of California"? After interviewing Sarris, *Indian Country Today* newspaper reported that five years after the meeting at the senior center:

In 1997 the tribe found out it originally had 15.4 acres near Graton
in Sonoma County that was set aside for them in the 1950s [sic] . . . .
The Miwoks approached Armstrong about using her land to restore
the Graton Rancheria. After being assured she would not lose her
home, she agreed. This is when the tribe became the Federated Indians of the Graton Rancheria [as the Indians of the Graton Rancheria
by then had been renamed].

Who would be members of the new tribe? In addition to Gloria Armstrong, Sarris's bill designated as members all individuals, and all descendants of those individuals, who lived in the vicinity of the communities of
Graton, Marshall, Bodega, Tomales, and Sebastopol and who had been
identified as Indians by the BIA or in any "public or California mission
records." When the director of the BIA Office of Tribal Services read that
section of the bill he was incredulous, because "As written it does not
require possession of the tribal blood which would show descendency from
past members of the Rancheria" or even possession of "California Indian
blood." The director concluded his criticism by pointing out that "Any
individual who lives in one of these vicinities, and has documents stating
he or she possesses Indian blood would be eligible to be placed on the
Rancheria's roll."

Neither Lynn Woolsey nor any member of the Committee on Resources
cared (or understood?) that "restoring" the Indians of the Graton Rancheria
of California would be creating a federally recognized tribe that had never
existed. And after the bill passed the House, nor did any member of the
Select Committee on Indian Affairs. With no explanation of the bill's content and no recorded votes, Congress passed the Graton Rancheria
Restoration Act in 2000. Today, Greg Sarris remains chairman of a federally recognized tribe that a recent press report estimated has 1,300 members. According to the BIA, who those individuals are is no one's business
but the tribe's.

At the Committee on Resources hearing at which he testified in support of his bill, when Greg Sarris was asked, "How many acres does the
bill set aside?" he answered, "Approximately one acre, sir." Had the congressman who asked the question bothered to read the bill, he would have
known that that answer was an intentional prevarication. Because in addition

to the acre on which Gloria Armstrong's house is located, the bill directed the secretary of the interior to "accept into trust for the benefit of the Tribe" any other "real property located in Marin or Sonoma County" that the tribe requested the secretary to accept into trust. Another provision designated that land as "part of the tribe's reservation."

Oddly, Lynn Woolsey did not care how much land in her congressional district became an Indian reservation. But she was adamant that the Indians of the Graton Rancheria of California not open a casino. So to obtain Woolsey's support, Sarris included a provision in his bill that prohibited his new tribe from opening one. Kevin Gover, the assistant secretary of the interior for Indian affairs, objected to that provision, because it would establish the precedent that Congress could compromise a tribe's inherent sovereignty to decide for itself whether it wanted a casino.

Two months after the U.S. House of Representatives passed Sarris's bill with the no-casino provision included, Stacey Leavandasky, the member of Lynn Woolsey's staff who was handling the bill, met with Loretta Tuell, the BIA employee who was handling the bill for Gover, as well as with members of the staff of California senator Barbara Boxer. After the meeting, Leavandasky reported to Woolsey that "the Senate Indian Affairs Committee will not hold hearings on the Miwok bill knowing that BIA opposes the gaming provision." She also reported that Tuell had been adamant the "the tribe cannot negotiate away its civil rights and that the role of the federal government/BIA is to be overseer and trustee with all Indians long term benefits in mind."

Two months later and without informing Woolsey, California representative George Miller, the ranking Democrat on the Committee on Resources and a close friend and political confidant of Barbara Boxer's, arranged for the House to suspend its rules and pass Sarris's bill, with the no-casino provision removed, as part of an Indian omnibus bill and without a recorded vote. Another two months later, the Senate did the same.

Greg Sarris has never said publically whether he privately lobbied, first Kevin Gover, and then Hawaii senator Daniel Inouye, the chairman of the select committee (or Patricia Zell?) to object to the no-casino provision. What is known is that on April 23, 2003, Sarris announced that the Federated Indians of Graton Rancheria had signed a management agreement with Station Casinos, a Las Vegas–based casino management company, pursuant to which Station Casinos would build and manage a casino and hotel for the tribe.

When I asked Lynn Woolsey how she felt when she heard that news, her answer was, "Greg Sarris sat in my office and he lied to me." Woolsey was so outraged that she introduced a bill to amend the Graton Rancheria Restoration Act by prohibiting land whose title the secretary of the interior took into trust pursuant to the act from being used for gambling purposes. But the bill went nowhere.

In 2010, Secretary of the Interior Ken Salazar accepted into trust for the Federated Indians of Graton Rancheria 255 acres of land in Rohnert Park, a bedroom community south of Santa Rosa and forty-three miles north of San Francisco. The land, which Station Casinos purchased for $100 million, is located down the street from Home Depot and within easy access to an exit of the Highway 101 freeway. No member of the Federated Indians of Graton Rancheria lives on the reservation. Instead, in 2013 Station Casinos opened the $800 million Graton Resort & Casino. Surrounded by a parking lot that contains spaces for 5,500 automobiles, the casino's gaming floor contains 3,000 video gaming machines and 144 tables at which patrons can play poker, baccarat, and blackjack. During the first three months of 2014, the casino generated $101 million in revenue, had adjusted earnings of $57 million, and was one of the five most profitable Indian casinos in California. Station Casinos has estimated that in 2015, the casino would earn $487 million.

The Graton Resort & Casino exists because Lynn Woolsey and the members of the Committee on Resources and the Select Committee on Indian Affairs, with no other members of Congress caring, created a federally recognized tribe that, other than in Greg Sarris's imagination, had never existed. But manipulating an inattentive Congress is not the only way individuals who are descendants—or, like Skip Hayward and Greg Sarris, who say they are descendants—of Native Americans can become a federally recognized tribe and open a casino.

DURING THE 1870S, THE president signed executive orders that withdrew federal land at nineteen locations in southern California, including Capitan Grande, Cabazon, Morongo, and Pala, at which Mission Indians (as Indians in southern California were called) had congregated. But in several cases, the executive orders misdescribed the boundaries of the withdrawals, and there were Indian families living on land that had not been withdrawn. In 1891, Congress passed the Mission Indians Act, which directed a commission to investigate the situation and then "select a reservation for each band or village of the Mission Indians," whose boundaries would include federal land that was "in the actual occupation and possession of said Indians."

After conducting their investigation, the commissioners reported that thirty-eight Cahuilla Indians whose headman was named Augustine were living in "bush and tule houses" on a section of land in the Coachella Valley several miles south of Indio, the farm town that had grown up near the supply depot the Southern Pacific Railroad had established at the location known as Indian Wells. Because the land on which the Indians were living was owned by the railroad and had "very poor water," the commissioners recommended that President Benjamin Harrison withdraw the adjoining 640-acre section of land, "to which [Augustine and the members of his band] can go if they are ever called upon to vacate the [land] they are on." President Harrison approved that recommendation, and in 1893 the Department of the Interior issued a patent that conveyed the Augustine Band a restricted title to the 640 acres.

Augustine and the members of his band eventually did move onto that land. But from the beginning, the location was uninhabitable because it had no water. In 1906 L.A. Wright, the local Indian agent, informed the commissioner of Indian affairs that the ten Indians living in the Augustine village had "asked that water be obtained for them." And prior to 1912, the BIA dug at least one well, which eventually went dry.

In 1947 a woman named Margaret Andreas reported to the BIA that she and nine other adults and one ten-year-old girl named Roberta Augustine were the members of the Augustine Band. Andreas lived in Palm Springs and it is unlikely that any of the other members of the band lived on the reservation. By 1956 there was Margaret Andreas and three other adults, plus Roberta Augustine. By 1972 there was only Roberta Augustine.

Rather than on the 640 acres that had been withdrawn for the Augustine Band, by the 1950s Roberta Augustine was living on the Morongo Reservation in the San Gorgonio Pass west of Palm Springs. She then met

Herman Martin, an African American with whom she had three children: Mary Ann, Gregory, and Herbert. Mary Ann Martin, who was born in 1964, was raised by her paternal grandmother in Monrovia, a small town in the San Gabriel Valley east of Los Angeles. The year after she graduated from high school, in 1984 she married an African American named William Vance.

In May 1987 Roberta Augustine died. A month later, the Select Committee on Indian Affairs held a hearing on S. 555, the bill President Reagan would sign into law as the IGRA. During the hearing, when Hawaii senator Daniel Inouye, the chairman of the select committee, asked Assistant Secretary of the Interior for Indian Affairs Ross Swimmer, "What is the largest tribe in the United States under your jurisdiction?" Swimmer answered,

> We have approximately 310 organizations now, possibly one or two new ones, that are recognized as tribes. The smallest tribe, until recently, was one individual on the Augustine Rancheria [sic] in California. She died. The Augustine Rancheria has no Indians on it, but is still a reservation.

Mary Ann Martin grew up believing she was African American and did not discover her mother was a Cahuilla Indian until her grandmother died around the time her mother died and an uncle told her she had relatives on the Morongo Reservation. When she visited the Morongo Reservation, Martin learned that her mother had been the last member of the Augustine Band and that the band had a reservation on which no one lived.

One of her newfound relatives worked for the BIA. She put Mary Ann Martin in touch with Robert Shull, an attorney who worked for California Indian Legal Services (CILS), a federally funded antipoverty law firm whose mission was similar to that of Pine Tree Legal Assistance, the federally-funded anti-poverty law firm at which Tom Tureen had worked in Maine. According to Shull, with his assistance, Martin and her brothers contacted the BIA to request "enrollment in the Augustine Band for themselves and Mary Ann Martin Vance's children, Victoria Martin and Amanda Vance."

The problem with that request was that the Augustine Band did not exist. However, with bureaucratic ingenuity, that impediment to enrollment was solved when, on July 29, 1988, Robert Shull and Mary Ann Martin and her brothers met at the office of the BIA Southern California Agency in Riverside with Frances Muncy, who supervised the agency's tribal operations office. At that meeting, Muncy explained that the BIA had invented what it called its "General Council Concept."

Pursuant to the General Council Concept, Mary Ann, Gregory, and Herbert Martin could notify each other that they were calling a meeting and then, at that meeting, pass a resolution which announced that they had formed a general council to govern the Augustine Band. The general council then could pass an ordinance that established a procedure for enrolling new members.

Acting on Muncy's instructions, later that day Mary Ann Martin and her brothers called a meeting during which, by a vote of 3 to 0, they passed the resolution Muncy had suggested, and by another vote of 3 to 0 passed an enrollment ordinance that allowed any person who was "1/8 or more of blood of the Band" to file an application for enrollment. When the general council's enrollment committee (whose members were Mary Ann, Gregory, and Herbert Martin) approved the application, the applicant became a member of the Augustine Band. Their use of the General Council Concept, which had no legal basis, allowed Mary Ann Martin and her brothers to enroll themselves and Martin's children in a federally recognized tribe that, had it ever been one (which it had not), had ceased to exist.

Robert Shull sent that paper shuffle to the BIA Southern California Agency. For two years nothing happened. When Timothy Sanford-Wachtell, the CILS attorney who by then had taken over the Martins' representation from Shull, asked Frances Muncy about the delay, according to Sanford-Wachtell, Muncy told him the BIA was concerned "that the only reason that the Roberta Armstrong descendants seek recognition is for the purpose of economic development of the reservation."

To allay that concern, Sanford-Wachtell told Virgil Townsend, the superintendent of the BIA Southern California Agency, that he had "spoken with Mary Ann Martin Vance, and she has assured me that Roberta Augustine's descendants are not seeking recognition for the purpose of monetary gain. They are seeking recognition because they wish to reside on the reservation and establish a government there."

That vouch accomplished its objective. On June 6, 1991, Townsend recommended to Amy Dutschke, the BIA area director in Sacramento, that "the descendants of Roberta Augustine be granted recognition as the governing body for the Augustine Reservation and as the legitimate members of the Band." Three weeks later, Dutschke approved the recommendation. While they now were members of their own federally recognized tribe, rather than moving onto the Augustine Reservation as their attorney had promised, Mary Ann Martin lived in Riverside, Gregory Martin lived in Monrovia, and Herbert Martin lived in Ontario, west of San Bernardino.

Three years later, Mary Ann Martin became the only adult member of the Augustine Band when Gregory Martin, whose street name was "Moto" and who was a member of the Bloods, the notorious Los Angeles street gang, was shot to death in Banning, the farm town next to the Morongo Reservation on the western end of San Gorgonio Pass. And then five months later, Herbert Martin, who also was a Blood, also was shot to death in Banning.

When Mary Ann Martin became the only adult member of her own federally recognized tribe, even if she had wanted to move onto the Augustine Reservation (which over the years had been reduced from 640 acres to 502 acres), she could not have done so because the land was covered with industrial-grade garbage. Here is how the Environmental Protection Agency described the situation:

> Unoccupied for more than 50 years, the reservation became a midnight dumping ground for area businesses, residents, and farmers. Over the years, tons of household trash, garbage, appliances, animal carcasses, commercial waste, car batteries, and more than 2,000 tires have accumulated on the reservation. At one point the reservation became a popular spot for car thieves to strip stolen cars, leaving the land littered with close to a dozen burned and abandoned vehicles.

Through the BIA, in 1993 Mary Ann Martin met Karen Kupcha, a consultant who provided financial and other types of technical assistance to Indian organizations in California. Kupcha became the Augustine Band's "tribal administrator" and began helping Martin apply for government grants to begin clearing away the garbage.

By 1996 enough progress had been made for a well to be drilled, a septic system installed, and an electricity line extended to the reservation. Mary Ann Martin then had a mobile home moved onto a cleared area into which she moved with her husband and three children. Three years later the Environmental Protection Agency reported:

> Preventing further illegal dumping is a priority for the Augustine. William Vance, the reservation's security officer, makes daily inspections of the reservation to identify any waste illegally dumped the previous night.
>
> . . .
>
> The Augustine plan [is] to remove all of the waste that has accumulated during the 50 years that the reservation has been vacant. By taking small steps, as the funding becomes available, they hope their land can be cleared for development. The ultimate use for the reservation is undecided, although commercial retail or light industry is being considered.

If by 1999 Mary Ann Martin had not decided on the "ultimate use" of her reservation, she soon would, since in her capacity as chairwoman of the Augustine Band, in March 2000 she signed a compact with California governor Gray Davis that authorized the band to open a casino that could offer blackjack and other card games and as many as 2,000 video gaming machines.

Five months later, the *Desert Sun* newspaper in Palm Springs reported that the Augustine Band soon would sign a management agreement with an unnamed investor for the construction on its reservation of the Eagle Flower Garden Resort and Casino, which would consist of a 200-room hotel, a golf course, and a casino whose gaming floor would contain 700 video gaming machines. When that deal fell through, in August 2001 Mary Ann Martin signed a management agreement with Paragon Augustine LLC, a subsidiary of Paragon Gaming, a Las Vegas–based casino management company.

On July 18, 2002, Martin was on hand to greet the first players at the opening of the Augustine Casino, a steel-framed building surrounded by a parking lot with spaces for 558 automobiles. The gaming floor contained 349 video gaming machines and ten blackjack and poker tables.

Today, the garbage that covered the reservation, the mobile home in which Mary Ann Martin and her family once lived, and Paragon Augustine LLC are gone. As it has since the evening the doors opened, the Augustine Casino, whose gaming floor now contains 804 video gaming machines, caters to a largely Spanish-speaking working-class local (rather than tourist) clientele. On the midweek morning I visited, more than two hundred players, many senior citizens, many smoking, several wearing "I Love Augustine" bracelets, were playing the machines.

In 1991 Mary Ann Martin, her brothers, and Mary Ann Martin's children became members of a federally recognized tribe because the BIA had invented a way for them to enroll themselves in an organization that did not exist that the BIA simply assumed had been a federally recognized tribe when it did exist without explaining how and when the Augustine Band acquired that legal status. But the General Council Concept is not the only means the BIA has invented to usurp Congress's authority to create federally recognized tribes.

AT THE INSTIGATION of South Dakota senator James Abourezk, in 1975 Congress created the American Indian Policy Review Commission (AIPRC) to study needed "revision in the formulation of policies and programs for the benefit of Indians." To conduct its study, the AIPRC created eleven task forces, one of which was Task Force Ten: Terminated and Nonfederally Recognized Tribes.

The chairwoman of Task Force Ten was Betty Jo Hunt, a member of the Lumbee Indians, a group whose 40,000 members claimed descent from Indians who in the eighteenth century had lived along the Lumber River in North Carolina. While a majority of the individuals who said they were descendants of Lumbee Indians lived in North Carolina, thousands of others lived in other states, both west and east of the Mississippi River. The Lumbees had no tribal organization, no reservation, and the year before Congress created the AIPRC the Senate had rejected a bill to designate the Lumbee Indians as a federally recognized tribe.

The second member of Task Force Ten was Robert Bojorcas, a member of the Klamath Indian Tribe in Oregon, whose status as a federally recognized tribe Congress had terminated in 1954. The third member of Task Force Ten was John Stevens, the Passamaquoddy Indian who had worked with Tom Tureen, who Stevens and the other members of Task Force Ten recruited to serve as their advisor.

At Task Force Ten's urging, in its report to Congress the AIPRC recommended that Congress "recognize all Indian tribes as eligible for the

benefits and protections of general Indian legislation and Indian policy."
To implement that recommendation, in December 1977 Senator Abourezk
introduced a bill whose enactment would establish an "investigative office"
inside the Department of the Interior to review petitions for acknowledgment of tribal existence and make recommendations as to whether a petition should be approved. The bill also delegated the secretary of the interior
authority to approve petitions he determined were meritorious and designate the groups that had filed the petitions as "federally acknowledged Indian tribes."In March and August 1978 similar bills, one of which was
H.R. 13773, were introduced in the U.S. House of Representatives. A year
earlier, the BIA had published a notice in the *Federal Register* in which it
announced that it was proposing to adopt regulations that would establish
a procedure to enable groups to petition the secretary of the interior to designate the groups as federally recognized tribes.

In August 1978, the subcommittee of the Committee on Interior and
Insular Affairs that handled Indian-related bills held a hearing on H.R.
13773. When Wyoming representative Teno Roncalio, the chairman of the
subcommittee, asked whether Congress had passed a statute that delegated
the BIA authority to adopt regulations that would allow the secretary to
begin creating new federally recognized tribes on his own, a Department
of the Interior attorney named Scott Keep answered that there were two
statutes: 25 U.S.C. 2 and 9.

Section 2, enacted in 1832, grants the commissioner of Indian affairs
authority to manage "Indian affairs" and "all matters arising out of Indian
relations." Section 9, enacted in 1834, grants the president authority to
adopt regulations necessary to implement "any act relating to Indian affairs." Neither statute delegates the secretary of the interior authority to
create new federally recognized tribes. But two weeks later, when it published its proposed regulations in final form, the BIA cited 25 U.S.C. 2 and
9 in the *Federal Register* as the statutes in which Congress had delegated
the secretary that authority.

Since 1978, the assistant secretary of the interior for Indian affairs
has used the authority to create federally recognized tribes that the BIA
gave the secretary of the interior in the regulations it issued to create eighteen new tribes in eleven different states. Nine operate casinos, five others
would like to. As of November 2014, 236 other groups in twenty-four

states, including seventy-two groups in California, have either filed a petition requesting the secretary of the interior to designate the group as a federally recognized tribe or notified the secretary that the group intends to file a petition.

Picking two groups at random, who are the members of the Coastanoan Band of Carmel Mission Indians in California and the Yamassee Native American Moors of the Creek Nation in Georgia? Where do those members live, and why do they consider themselves Indians? How many members of all 236 groups created their group with the idea in mind that if they can persuade the assistant secretary to approve their petition and designate their group as a federally recognized tribe the group will open a casino?

And in the twenty-first century, should Congress or the secretary of the interior be creating new federally recognized tribes whose members live scattered in cities and towns in multiple states, are assimilated into the economy and social life of the communities in which they reside, and whose claim to "Indianness" is that—as Greg Sarris says he does—they each had a great- or a great-great-grandparent, or two, or even three or four, who was a Native American?

Different people can have different answers to that question. But since 1978, when the BIA issued the regulations in which it gave the secretary of the interior authority to create new federally recognized tribes, and particularly since 1988, when Congress enacted the IGRA, on Capitol Hill that question has not been asked.

15: FAKE RESERVATIONS

Just like real estate, it's all location, location, location.

BARRY BRANDON
Former Chief of Staff
National Indian Gaming Commission

THE FOXWOODS RESORT & CASINO IS ONE OF THE MOST PROFITABLE casinos in the world because twenty-two million customers live within 150 miles of its gaming floors. The same can be said of the Mystic Lake Casino the Shakopee Mdewakanton Sioux Community opened in 1992 on its reservation at Prior Lake thirty miles southwest of Minneapolis, and of the two Hard Rock Hotels & Casinos the Seminole Tribe operates in Florida.

Most Indian reservations that were established in the nineteenth century are not so conveniently located. But there are two ways a federally recognized tribe can acquire a reservation at a location at which a casino can be profitable.

The first is that Congress can create a reservation. The story of how Congress directed the secretary of the interior to transform 255 acres of land down the street from Home Depot in Rohnert Park, California, into a reservation for the Federated Indians of Graton Rancheria is not an anomaly.

Here is another.

In 1926, the Bureau of Indian Affairs (BIA) purchased fifty acres of land at Lytton Springs near Healdsburg, a farm town north of Santa Rosa, California. The land, which became known as the Lytton Rancheria, was unoccupied until 1937 when the BIA allowed Bert Steele, a quarter-blood Indian, and his wife Mary, a half-blood, to live there. In 1938, the BIA allowed Mary Steele's brother, John Wesley Meyers, to move onto the land as well.

After Bert Steele died, at the request Mary Steele and John Wesley Myers, in 1961 the BIA terminated the Lytton Rancheria and conveyed the title to the fifty acres in fee to John Wesley Meyers's widow and thirty-two other heirs of Bert and Mary Steele and John Wesley Meyers.

A quarter of a century later, by which time the heirs had sold all fifty acres, in 1986 in the U.S. District Court in San Francisco an attorney named Stephen Quesenberry, who worked for California Indian Legal Services, filed *Scotts Valley Band of Pomo Indians of the Sugar Bowl Rancheria v. United States*, a lawsuit in which he sought to invalidate the BIA's termination of a number of rancherias. The lawsuit also sought to transform both the individuals to whom the BIA had conveyed title to the land within the boundaries of the rancherias and their heirs into federally recognized tribes.

In August 1987 Quesenberry added the "Lytton Indian Community of the Lytton Rancheria" and "Carol J. Steele, a dependent member from the Lytton Rancheria" to his list of plaintiffs. Carol Joyce Steele's connection to the Lytton Rancheria was that she was the ex-wife of Bert and Mary Steele's deceased son, Daniel Steele.

In 1991, District Judge Vaughn Walker approved a settlement agreement Quesenberry wrote and to which the attorney at the U.S. Department of Justice who represented the United States acquiesced. In that agreement, the BIA agreed that, henceforth, the heirs of Bert and Mary Steele and John Wesley Meyers and their descendants would be "eligible for all rights and benefits extended to other federally recognized Indian tribes and their members." In 1993, the BIA added the "Lytton Rancheria of California" to the list of "Indian Tribal Entities Within the Contiguous 48 States" that it publishes annually in the *Federal Register*.

Although the record is murky, the Lytton Band of Pomo Indians (as the members of the Lytton Rancheria of California renamed themselves) appears to have been invented in order to open a bingo hall. Sixteen months *before* Stephen Quesenberry added the Lytton Indian Community and Carol J. Steele to his list of plaintiffs, on April 1, 1986 a partnership called Lytton-Sonoma Ventures, Inc., (LSV) was organized. One of LSV's partners was Robert Ingenito, who after working at the bingo hall Seminole Management Associates managed on the Seminole Reservation in Hollywood, Florida, in 1983 had moved with his brother to California to open the bingo hall on Sonny Miller's allotment on the Morongo Reservation. On August 6, 1986, another LSV partner, William Pedraza, and George Vlassis, an attorney from Arizona who had been general counsel for the Navajo Nation, purchased three parcels of land located within the boundaries of the former Lytton Rancheria.

On October 9, 1988, LSV signed a management agreement with Carol Joyce Steele, the "spokesperson" for the "Lytton Springs Indian Band of California." LSV also wrote a business plan for a 2,500-seat bingo hall that LSV would build on the Lytton Rancheria. The business plan explained that the key to the hall's profitability was the rancheria's location, which was "more readily accessible to citizens of the San Francisco Bay Area than any Indian bingo currently operating."

Carol Joyce Steele later said that, while she had "discussions" with Pedraza, her signature on the management agreement was a forgery. Whatever the truth, LSV's business plan became moot when Sonoma County intervened in Quesenberry's lawsuit. The county did not care if Judge Walker's approval of the settlement agreement transformed the Steele and Meyers heirs and their descendants into a federally recognized tribe as long as the new tribe would agree not to open a gambling facility anywhere in the county. Stephen Quesenberry and Carol Joyce Steele accepted that condition. Which is how Sam Katz became involved.

In 1996, Margie Mejia, a great-granddaughter of Bert Steele who had replaced Carol Joyce Steele as the head of the Lytton Band of Pomo Indians, signed a management agreement with One Sky, Inc., a consulting firm Joel Frank, the Seminole Indian who had been one of the first commissioners of the National Indian Gaming Commission (NIGC), had created. One of Frank's partners knew Sam Katz, a Philadelphia-based expert in municipal finance who had become wealthy assisting municipalities and the owners of sports teams arrange financing for convention centers and stadiums. Katz agreed to help Joel Frank raise the money One Sky, Inc., would need to purchase land and build a bingo hall for the Lytton Band.

The management agreement required One Sky, Inc., whose assets were Joel Frank's ambition and not much else, to make a $500,000 up-front payment to the Lytton Band. When One Sky, Inc., failed to do so, Sam Katz recruited a group of investors from Philadelphia and signed his own management agreement with Margie Mejia. He then began looking for land outside Sonoma County to turn into an Indian reservation.

Katz found sixty acres on the highway that runs through American Canyon, a bedroom community on the southern end of the Napa Valley, the wine-growing region north of San Francisco Bay. But the sententious opposition of an evangelical minister who was president of the American

Canyon chamber of commerce, as well as of other American Canyon residents, made that location a nonstarter.

Depressed about that outcome, when he was driving back to San Francisco from American Canyon, Katz passed a sign at a freeway exit north of Berkeley that advertised the "San Pablo Casino." His curiosity piqued, Katz turned around and drove back to see what the San Pablo Casino was.

IN THE 1940S THE Second World War transformed San Pablo from the bucolic farm town on the northeastern shore of San Francisco Bay it had been into a bedroom community for thousands of blue-collar workers who moved from Oklahoma and the rural south to work in the nearby shipyards. When the shipyards closed after the war, San Pablo deteriorated into a blighted and crime-ridden urban environment whose predominate architectural characteristics are discount stores and fast-food restaurants. Having no tax base, by the early 1990s the city of San Pablo faced bankruptcy.

To ward it off, the city manager proposed that the city try to attract a poker room. When San Pablo voters approved the idea, the city bought 9.5 acres of land in downtown San Pablo on which a trailer park and a bowling alley had been located. The city then persuaded Ladbrokes, a company that owns casinos, card rooms, and horse tracks in Great Britain and the United States, to build a 70,000-square-foot building with a circular driveway that, according to Sharon Brown, a member of the city council at the time, looked like a "Moroccan whorehouse." Ladbrokes then leased the building and the adjoining parking lot to SF Casino Management, a management company that would operate the facility.

Initially, the 100-table poker room made money. But then poker rooms were required to comply with the ban on smoking in public places the California legislature had enacted, and according to Sharon Brown, business at the San Pablo Casino, as the poker room had been named, "went into the tank." That was the situation when Sam Katz drove into the poker room's parking lot.

When Katz soon thereafter bought the building and parking lot from Ladbrokes, he gave Margie Mejia two pieces of advice: "Do a deal with the unions. Do a deal with the city." Mejia did both: she agreed to honor the labor contract SF Casino Management had signed with HERE, the union that represented the poker room's employees, and she agreed to give the city of San Pablo 7.5 percent of the San Pablo Casino's gross gaming revenue. Doing both was the key to obtaining the support of George Miller, the pro-labor Democrat who represented San Pablo in the U.S. House of Representatives, and who, as Katz and Mejia's luck would have it, also was the senior Democrat on the House Committee on Resources.

Section 5 of the Indian Reorganization Act (IRA), which Congress passed in 1934, authorizes the secretary of the interior to take into trust the title to any land he wishes for members of a "recognized Indian tribe now under Federal jurisdiction." In 2009, the U.S. Supreme Court would hold that Congress intended the word "now" to mean "in 1934." But in 2000, the BIA and its attorneys assumed that section 5 authorized the secretary to take title to land into trust for the Lytton Band, which had not purportedly become a federally recognized tribe until 1991, when Judge Walker approved the settlement agreement in Stephen Quesenberry's lawsuit.

To explore whether Secretary of the Interior Bruce Babbitt could be persuaded to take into trust as a reservation for the Lytton Band a poker room and parking lot in downtown San Pablo, in July 2000 Sam Katz and Margie Mejia met with Assistant Secretary of the Interior for Indian Affairs Kevin Gover. Marie Howard, the member of his staff who handled Indian-related bills for George Miller, also attended the meeting.

After listening to Katz and Mejia make their pitch, Gover said he might be able to persuade Babbitt to take title to the land under the San Pablo Casino into trust. "But it wouldn't happen until the very last few days of this administration. And even then, I'm not sure I can do it. So my suggestion is that you get an act of Congress." According to Katz: "I'm sitting in this very warm room, not doing a lot of talking, but occasionally throwing in my two cents, and I suddenly feel faint. Did he say 'act of Congress'? We're not getting an act of Congress. That just doesn't happen."

But it did happen.

In October, George Miller and Marie Howard arranged to include in the Indian omnibus bill into which Miller (and Howard) also added the Graton Rancheria Restoration Act a paragraph that directed the secretary of the interior to take the title to the land under the San Pablo Casino and the adjoining parking lot into trust for the Lytton Band.

When the Indian omnibus bill was brought to the floor, Miller told the House that "most" of the bills that had been rolled into the omnibus bill "have passed out of the House or the Senate." And most had, except for the paragraph for the Lytton Band, which had never been introduced as a bill, about which no hearing had been held, and about which in his explanation of the omnibus bill Miller made no mention.

Congress passed the Indian omnibus bill after only a cursory explanation of the bill's content on the House and Senate floors and with no recorded votes. In October 2003, Gale Norton, Bruce Babbitt's successor as secretary of the interior, took the title to the land under the San Pablo Casino into trust.

In August 2005 the Lytton Band removed most of the poker tables and installed 500 video gaming machines whose software had been programmed to play bingo, which by that date the NIGC had reclassified as a Class II form of gambling that a tribe could offer without having to negotiate a compact. By September 2006, more poker tables had been removed to make room for another 548 machines. By 2008, the Lytton Band was paying the city of San Pablo $12 million a year as its 7.5 percent share of the gross gaming revenue, which meant that the "San Pablo Lytton Casino," as the former poker room had been rebranded, was earning $160 million annually.

In 1990, Stephen Quesenberry said the Lytton Band of Pomo Indians had 20 members. In 2005 Margie Mejia said the band had 275 members. Today, how many individuals are members of the band? Who are they, where do they live, and what is their connection to the Lytton Rancheria? And what have they done with the hundreds of millions of dollars the San Pablo Lytton Casino has earned? According to the BIA, the answers to those questions are no one's business but the band's.

THE SECOND WAY a federally recognized tribe can acquire a reservation at a location at which a casino can be profitable is the way Sam Katz and Margie Mejia originally contemplated: the secretary of the interior can take title to a tract of land into trust pursuant to section 5 of the IRA.

In 1979 and 1981, Secretary of the Interior Cecil Andrus took into trust the title to the land in Florida on which the Seminole Tribe today operates the Seminole Casino in Immokalee and the Seminole Hard Rock Hotel & Casino in Tampa. But when Secretary Andrus and Assistant Secretary of the Interior for Indian Affairs Tom Fredericks did so, the BIA did not know James Billie and Steve Whilden, the tribe's chairman and general counsel, wanted the title to the land taken into trust in order to open bingo halls.

The first time the BIA had a secretary of the interior use the authority section 5 delegates for the purpose of enabling a tribe to open a bingo hall happened in 1985 in Duluth, Minnesota, a dreary port town on the shore of Lake Superior.

IN THE EARLY 1980S, THE local economy was so in the doldrums that the Sears & Roebuck Company closed its department store in downtown Duluth. At the time, the Fond du Lac Band of Lake Superior Chippewa Indians was operating a bingo hall on the band's reservation twenty miles west of the city that Bill Houle, the chairman of the band, wanted to expand. When Houle asked John Fedo, the mayor of Duluth, to support the expansion, according to Fedo, who was looking for ways to reinvigorate Duluth's economy, "I suggested we think about ways we could bring Indian bingo into the city."

Fedo's first idea was to sink a barge that had been used to transport iron ore in front of downtown Duluth, have the BIA have the secretary of the interior take the title to the land under Lake Superior on which the barge would rest into trust as a reservation for the Fond du Lac Band, and then have the band remodel the barge into a bingo hall. When that plan proved impractical, Fedo came up with another idea: the Fond du Lac Band would purchase the department store and the land on which it was located from the Sears & Roebuck Company and then ask the BIA to have the secretary of the interior take title to the land into trust. The city of Duluth would build a parking garage next door to the department store. The band and the city then would organize the Duluth–Fond du Lac Economic Development Commission, a joint venture that would lease the department store from the band for 25 years and remodel the building into a bingo hall that would offer games that paid out jackpots larger than the state of Minnesota's bingo law allowed. The profit would be split three ways: 50 percent to the commission, 25.5 percent to the band, and 24.5 percent to the city. The problem with the scheme was that Ken Smith, the assistant secretary of the interior for Indian affairs, opposed the idea of turning land under a boarded-up department store in the middle of a decaying Rust Belt city into an Indian reservation.

Two years earlier, Fedo had attended a National League of Cities convention at which Ronald Reagan had lectured the nation's mayors that their cities needed to stop depending on federal funding. Fedo and several other mayors were so incensed that they held a press conference at which Fedo accused the president of being out of touch with the problems with which he and other mayors were dealing. Members of the domestic policy staff in the Reagan White House responded to the embarrassing press coverage by reaching out to Fedo, and, according to Fedo, "[F]rom that point forward, I had a personal relationship with the White House liaison to the mayors."

While a middle-ranking member of the domestic policy staff could not order Ken Smith to approve Fedo's plan to have the secretary of the interior turn part of a city block in downtown Duluth into an Indian reservation, three weeks after Ronald Reagan was elected to his second term as president, Ken Smith resigned, and his deputy, John Fritz, became the acting assistant secretary. Unlike Smith, Fritz, who was from Minneapolis and knew John Fedo, was supportive of Fedo's plan for the department store. So according to Fedo, "The project went from DOA to a success based on the fact that the individual in the decision-making position at the BIA was replaced." And because of Fedo's connection at the White House, "The project went from being killed by the BIA to being the number one White House priority for 'urban Indian economics.'"

In February 1985 the Fond du Lac Band bought the building and the land. In June, Fritz informed Earl Barlow, the BIA area director in Minneapolis, that the band's proposal "to renovate a property the Band already owns in fee status in downtown Duluth and open a bingo parlor on the site" had been "thoroughly reviewed and is hereby approved."

On behalf of the secretary of the interior, Barlow took the title to the land into trust, and in January 1986, Ross Swimmer, who a month earlier the Senate had confirmed to replace Ken Smith as assistant secretary of the interior for Indian affairs, published a notice in the *Federal Register* in which he designated the land as an Indian reservation. Nine months later,

Telly Savalas, the star of the television series *Kojak*, whose wife was from Duluth, was the unofficial master of ceremonies at the grand opening of the Fond-du-Luth Casino.

In 1987, video gaming machines arrived whose software had been programmed to let players play blackjack and poker. In 1994 real blackjack arrived. Then real poker. In 2003 the bingo games ended in order to make room for more machines. Today, the Fond-du-Luth Casino's two gaming floors contain more than 750 of them.

PRIOR TO HIS appointment as assistant secretary, Ross Swimmer had been principal chief of the Cherokee Nation in Oklahoma. One of the last things Swimmer did before he resigned as principal chief was veto a resolution the tribal council had passed to authorize the Cherokee Nation to open a bingo hall. And throughout his tenure as assistant secretary, Swimmer was "not a big fan of gaming."

While Swimmer cleared the way for the Fond-du-Luth Casino by designating the land under the Sears & Roebuck department store as an Indian reservation, he did so because when he arrived at the Department of the Interior the BIA area director in Minneapolis already had taken the title to the land on which the store was located into trust. But as a general proposition, Swimmer opposed establishing "satellite bingo reservations in or near urban areas" because he thought doing so would endanger the traditional reservation system, which was predicated on reservations being "tribal homelands."

In February 1986, Swimmer made his opposition official when he published a notice in the *Federal Register* in which he announced that, henceforth, "[I]t will be the policy of the Department of the Interior to decline to accept off-reservation lands in trust for the purpose of establishing bingo or other gaming enterprises." While that seemingly settled the matter, Swimmer's successor could abandon the Department of the Interior's new policy. However, six months before Swimmer's announcement, Nebraska representative Douglas Bereuter had introduced a bill to restrict the BIA's ability to have the secretary of the interior create "satellite bingo reservations."

• • •

IN NEBRASKA, BEREUTER'S congressional district included Thurston County, in which the Omaha and Winnebago Reservations are located, and Dakota County, in which South Sioux City, which is part of the Sioux City, Iowa, metropolitan area, is located. When the Omaha Tribe announced that it wanted to purchase twenty-two acres of land within the South Sioux City city limits and then ask the BIA to have the secretary of the interior take the title to the land into trust so the tribe could open a bingo hall, the South Sioux City city council objected. But it had no ability to prevent the secretary from doing so. Bereuter's bill gave the city council that ability by prohibiting the secretary of the interior from taking title to land located outside the boundaries of an Indian reservation into trust to enable a tribe to open a gambling facility, unless the tribe first obtained "the concurrence of the governor and the legislative bodies of all local government units in which the land is located."

While Bereuter was not a member of the Committee on Interior and Insular Affairs to which his bill was referred, the bill was taken seriously because Arizona representative Morris "Mo" Udall, the chairman of the committee, had the same problem Bereuter did. As Udall explained when Bereuter testified at the hearing the committee held on H.R. 1920, the bill Frank Ducheneaux had written and Udall had introduced to regulate gambling on Indian reservations, "We have in Arizona a group that wanted to set aside some of the Indian school land in downtown Phoenix and have not only bingo games, but a casino—Las Vegas–type operation."

And the chairman was not alone. When the members of the committee marked up H.R. 1920, Ohio representative John Seiberling offered an amendment whose text was based on Bereuter's bill because, as Seiberling explained, in the county in which Cleveland is located, an Indian tribe from Oklahoma "wanted to buy eight acres of land" to "set up a gambling casino, not just bingo," and "the real hooker was that the moving force behind this was some unsavory characters in Florida."

The Seiberling amendment, which the members of the Committee on Interior and Insular Affairs approved without a recorded vote, was so noncontroversial that, after the U.S. House of Representatives passed H.R. 1920, Pete Taylor, the staff director of the Select Committee on Indian Affairs, included the amendment in the version of H.R. 1920 he wrote, and which a majority of the members of the select committee voted to report to the Senate. Taylor also included the amendment in the version of H.R. 1920 that incorporated the changes to the select committee's version of the bill that Taylor and Senator Mark Andrews made to try to persuade Slade Gorton, Hawaii senator Daniel Inouye, and the two Nevada senators to lift their holds, which were preventing the Senate from considering H.R. 1920.

The Seiberling amendment prohibited an Indian tribe from operating a gambling facility on land located outside the boundaries of the tribe's reservation if the secretary of the interior had taken the title to the land into trust after H.R. 1920 was enacted. But the prohibition did not apply if the tribe obtained the "concurrence of the Governor of the State, the State legislature, and the governing bodies of the county and municipality in which such lands are located."

If the holds had been lifted, and Pete Taylor's version of H.R. 1920 had passed the Senate, and then the House, the Seiberling amendment would have been part of the Indian Gaming Regulatory Act (IGRA). But the holds stayed on, H.R. 1920 died when the Ninety-Ninth Congress adjourned, and in January 1987 when the One Hundredth Congress began the dance of legislation started over.

Daniel Inouye became the new chairman of the Select Committee on Indian Affairs. And under the influence of Patricia Zell, his new chief counsel, Inouye gave Zell and the attorneys she supervised wide latitude to write bills whose enactments would advance the Native American cause as they saw it. One of the ways Virginia "Ginny" Boylan, the staff attorney who did most of the writing, and Patricia Zell asserted their influence was by rewriting the Seiberling amendment.

In June 1987 when the select committee held a hearing on S. 555 and S. 1303—the bill Boylan, Zell, and Frank Ducheneaux wrote, and John McCain and Mo Udall introduced, after the U.S. Supreme Court issued its decision in *California v. Cabazon and Morongo Bands of Mission Indians*—no witness, including Ross Swimmer, mentioned that the Seiberling amendment had been rewritten in both bills. In May 1988 when the members of the select committee voted to report to the Senate a new version of S. 555 that Boylan and Zell had written, during his explanation of the bill, Inouye made no mention of the rewrite. No mention of the rewrite was made in the report explaining S. 555 that the select committee filed with the Senate. And no mention of the rewrite was made when S. 555 was briefly discussed on the Senate and House floors.

The version of the rewrite Ginny Boylan and Patricia Zell included in the version of S. 555 that became section 20 of the IGRA began by prohibiting a tribe from conducting Class II and III forms of gambling on land whose title the secretary of the interior had taken in trust after the date of enactment of the IGRA. But then come two site specific, and seven generic, exceptions to that rule. One of the site-specific exceptions directed the secretary of the interior to take the title to twenty-five acres of land located on the outskirts of Miami, Florida, into trust for the Miccosukee Tribe of Indians.

THE MICCOSUKEES ARE Seminole Indians who, rather than moving onto one of the three Seminole reservations, lived in camps along the Tamiami Trail, the two-lane highway that runs from Miami west across the Everglades. Although no treaty or statute had designated the Miccosukees as a federally recognized tribe, in 1962 the BIA arranged for the secretary of the interior to approve a constitution for the Miccosukee Tribe pursuant to section 16 of the IRA. Since then, no one has thought to question the Miccosukees' legal status as a federally recognized tribe.

In 1989, the Miccosukee Tribe signed a management agreement with the Tamiami Development Corporation, which invested $6.5 million to purchase the twenty-five acres, and, reorganized as Tamiami Partners, in 1990 to open a 2,000-seat bingo hall. The manager of the hall was David Ingenito, who, after working at the bingo hall Seminole Management Associates managed on the Seminole Reservation in Hollywood, Florida, in 1983 had moved with his brother, Robert Ingenito, to California to open the bingo hall on Sonny Miller's allotment on the Morongo Reservation. One of Tamiami Partners' partners was George Simon, who in 1978 Jack Cooper had installed as one of Seminole Management Associates' two general partners. And Ingenito purchased bingo cards and other paper bingo supplies from Nannicola Wholesale, a mob-connected company that supplied bingo halls in eastern Ohio and western Pennsylvania whose owner was the son-in-law of a member of the Pittsburgh Mafia.

Today on the twenty-five acres the Miccosukee Tribe operates Miccosukee Resort & Gaming, a complex that includes a nine-story hotel, 1,050-seat bingo hall, 1,200-seat entertainment arena, and a gaming floor that contains thirty-two poker tables and 1,700 video gaming machines.

OF THE SEVEN generic exceptions Ginny Boylan and Patricia Zell wrote into section 20 of the IGRA, one of the most consequential removed the requirement in the Seiberling amendment that the governor, the state legislature, and county and municipal officials all concur before a tribe could operate a gambling facility on the land located outside the boundaries of the tribe's reservation whose title the secretary of the interior took into trust after the date of enactment of the IGRA. In Boylan and Zell's rewrite, only the governor need concur after the secretary of the interior has determined that a gambling facility will be "in the best interest of the Indian tribe and its members" and will not be "detrimental to the surrounding community."

In 2008 BIA regional directors sent Carl Artman, the assistant secretary of the interior for Indian affairs, thirty applications that requested the secretary of the interior to take the title to the land described in the applications into trust for the purpose of enabling the applicant tribes to open a gambling facility at an economically advantageous urban location. One application requested the secretary take into trust the title to land located more than a thousand miles from the applicant tribe's reservation.

When he disapproved eleven of the thirty applications, Artman sent the regional directors a memorandum in which he directed that, in the future, land whose title the regional directors proposed that the secretary take into trust be located no farther from an applicant tribe's reservation than a resident of the reservation could reasonably commute to work at the tribe's gambling facility. Leaders of tribes whose land-into-trust applications could not meet that standard vilified Artman. In 2011, Larry Eco Hawk, who in 2009 President Barack Obama appointed assistant secretary of the interior for Indian affairs, withdrew the Artman memorandum.

Before Eco Hawk did so, the House Committee on Natural Resources held an oversight hearing on the Artman memorandum. One of the witnesses was Kevin Washburn, an enrolled member of the Chickasaw

Nation in Oklahoma who from 2000 to 2002 had been general counsel of the NIGC. Washburn criticized the "reasonable commuting distance" standard Carl Artman had invented because it assumed that the principal benefit a tribe derived from operating a gambling facility was jobs for tribal members in the facility. Washburn argued that assumption was "misguided" because the "stream of revenue" a gambling facility generated was more important than the jobs in the facility. The reason was that the revenue stream allowed the tribe that operated the facility to hire its members to work for the tribe back on the reservation "in a variety of areas, including healthcare, elderly services, social services, education, [and] law enforcement."

Washburn, who in 2012 President Obama would appoint to succeed Larry Eco Hawk as assistant secretary of the interior for Indian affairs, pointedly did not mention that most tribes that have been lucky enough to have—or to acquire—a reservation located in or near an urban area use their "streams of revenue" to give money away directly to their members. The $90,000 to $120,000 a year Bruce Kirchner and Theresa Casanova were paid because they are members of the Mashantucket Pequot Tribe has been described. In 2012, the 480 members of the Shakopee Mdewakanton Sioux Community each received monthly checks that totaled $1.08 million from the "stream of revenue" the Mystic Lake Casino generates.

The same can be said for the 200-member San Manuel Band of Mission Indians, which operates the San Manuel Indian Bingo & Casino on its 800-acre reservation east of Los Angeles. The casino's gaming floor contains 3,600 video gaming machines, also offers blackjack and poker, and generates a "stream of revenue" that in 2012 allowed the band to pay each member $100,000 a month. In 2012 the 400 members of the Miccosukee Tribe each received checks totaling $160,000 as their share of the "stream of revenue" Miccosukee Resort & Gaming generated that year.

If, as Kevin Washburn argued, it is permissible for the secretary of the interior to transform land in or near an urban area far distant from a tribe's reservation into a satellite reservation on which a casino that generates a "stream of revenue" can be built, why should the secretary not give *every* tribe that—for no reason other than the vagaries of history—does not have a reservation whose location is well-suited for a casino a satellite reservation so that its members can receive the same windfall that members of the Mashantucket Pequot Tribe, the Shakopee Mdewakanton Sioux Community, the San Manuel Band, the Miccosukee Tribe, and dozens of other tribes with casinos located in or near urban areas now consider their due? There is no better example of such a tribe than the Oglala Sioux Tribe, whose members live on the Pine Ridge Reservation in South Dakota.

IN 1869, THE U.S. Senate ratified the Treaty of Fort Laramie to which Sioux headmen, including Sitting Bull and the war chief Red Cloud, had signed their marks. The treaty established the Great Sioux Reservation, which included within its boundaries what today is all of South Dakota west of the Missouri River, much of eastern Wyoming, much of western Nebraska, and some of Montana and North Dakota. In the treaty, the United States promised that it would not permit whites to "pass over, settle upon, or reside" on the reservation.

That promise was kept until 1874, when the U.S. Army sent an expedition commanded by George Armstrong Custer into the Great Sioux Reservation to reconnoiter the Black Hills. When while panning for gold a member of the expedition found a modest amount of it, Custer ordered a scout to ride to Fort Laramie and report the news.

By 1875, more than 1,500 prospectors were in the Black Hills. Not only did the army not force them to leave, President Ulysses S. Grant secretly told Gen. George Crook to ignore the Treaty of Fort Laramie and allow as many prospectors as wished to do so to come into the region. A year later, Grant's perfidy led to the annihilation of Custer and the Seventh Cavalry at the Little Big Horn River, and then to the military campaigns that ended Sioux resistance to the president's repudiation of the Treaty of Fort Laramie. In 1889, Congress broke the Great Sioux Reservation into six smaller reservations, one of which is Pine Ridge.

Today, no one knows how many Oglala Sioux live on the Pine Ridge Reservation. Estimates range from 15,500 to 50,000. What is known is that most are desperately poor. The topography of the 2.2-million-acre reservation—bluffs dotted with copse of pine that begin the Badlands on the north and grassland prairie to the south—is majestic in its windswept desolation. But most of the land is unsuited for growing crops, and cattle ranching provides few jobs. As a consequence, 80 percent of Pine Ridge residents are unemployed. And most of those who have a job work for the BIA, the Indian Health Service (IHS), or another federal agency. Or they work for the tribal government, which gets most of its money from the federal government.

Housing on the reservation is deplorable. In 1999 when Bill Clinton visited, the president was taken to a shack attached to a trailer in which a woman named Geraldine Blue Bird was living with twenty-seven other people. And here is a contemporary description of the situation: "On an average, seventeen people live in a house that is built for a family of four. Up to thirty people have been reported in one home built for eight. Most houses are badly insulated and have insufficient heating. Approximately 40 percent of the households are without electricity."

In those households, boredom that life with no purpose and no prospects engenders begets depression and dysfunction. Of the 200,000 calls to which the tribal police respond each year, 80 percent are alcohol-related, and four of every five families have one member, and many families many members, who is alcoholic. Pandemic alcohol abuse begets domestic violence, incest and child abuse, teenage and adult suicide, and the truly heartbreaking statistic that one-quarter of all infants born on the Pine Ridge Reservation are born with fetal alcohol syndrome or worse. The Oglala Sioux also have an alarming rate of methamphetamine addiction, a rate of diabetes 800 percent higher than the national average, and a life expectancy lower than the life expectancy in every country in the Western Hemisphere but Haiti.

The depression and dysfunction passes down, father to son, mother to daughter. "I felt worthless, and I wanted a drink to get rid of my pain," a Pine Ridge resident named Ben explained when *New York Times* columnist Nicholas Kristof asked why he began drinking when he was twelve years old. According to Kristof, "Ben, now in his 30s, says he quit alcohol several years ago. But he is overweight and in poor health, surviving on disability payments and seeing no chance of getting a job."

To create jobs for tribal members like Ben, numerous economic development projects have been brought to the Pine Ridge Reservation. In 1993, the tribal council decided to try a casino. After negotiating a compact with the state of South Dakota, the tribe signed a management agreement with Turnkey Gaming, a management company a tribal member and the owner of a truck stop in Rapid City had created. In October 1994, Turnkey Gaming opened the Prairie Wind Casino in three double-wide trailers in which it installed four blackjack tables and seventy-five video gaming machines. By October 1995, the casino was employing 120 mostly reservation residents and had earned $1 million.

After falling out with Turnkey Gaming over the construction of a permanent building, the tribe replaced the double-wide trailers with a tent-like structure in which it installed 250 video gaming machines. By 2006, the Prairie Wind Casino had 209 employees and was annually earning $2.3 million. By then, the tribe had borrowed $20 million from the Shakopee Mdwakanton Sioux Community and begun construction of a permanent building to house the casino and, connected by a corridor, a seventy-eight-room hotel, both of which opened in 2007.

Less than a year later, the tribal council hired a consulting firm to review the casino and hotel operations because, as a council member explained, there was "a problem with the last audit." Since the audits have not been made public, only the tribal council and the NIGC know the extent to which, since 2007, the Prairie Wind Casino & Hotel has been profitable. But according to Jeffrey Whalen, a Pine Ridge resident and columnist for the *Native Sun News*, the 2008 and 2009 audits revealed that, during those years, food service at the casino lost $722,000 and $650,000, the hotel lost $209,000 and $262,000, and in 2009, the casino's liabilities exceeded its assets by $3.65 million.

To see the situation for myself, in September 2014, I drove into the Pine Ridge Reservation east to west on Highway 18, first into Pine Ridge, population 3,300, the largest town on the reservation and the headquarters for the tribal government and the BIA, and the location of the IHS hospital. In the center of town, the only supermarket on the reservation and the post office share a parking lot. Pine Ridge has no public library. But it has a Subway, Pizza Hut, and Taco John's and several gas stations to fuel the battered pickups and mud-caked automobiles in which young men who had no work but somehow enough money to fill their gas tanks were driving around town on the morning I drove through.

Fifteen miles farther west is Oglala, population 1,300, a cluster of shacks and house trailers, several boarded up, all in disrepair, and a windowless concrete bunker that is the Oglala post office. When I stopped to ask the postal clerk, a personable thirtysomething wearing a stocking cap pulled down over his long black hair, how I could find the Prairie Wind Casino, he walked me back out to the parking lot, pointed west, and told me to keep driving. When I asked what he thought of the casino, his answer was, "Our tribal government is pretty corrupt. If you're a member of the council, and you want to drive out and have dinner and spend the night you can. But not the rest of us."

Ten miles past Oglala, I saw the sign for the Prairie Wind Casino & Hotel and turned into the parking lot. On the left was the tentlike structure that had replaced the double-wide trailers, and in which bingo is played four nights a week. Across the parking lot was the hotel, a nondescript two-story building that appeared deserted, other than for the desk clerk who assured me the hotel had had a decent summer season.

The casino was a warehouse to which a log portico had been attached. Inside were four poker and seven blackjack tables and 250 video gaming machines. No alcohol, no entertainment, and nowhere to eat other than at a Subway counter and a dining room that had plywood walls. On the midweek afternoon I visited, the poker and blackjack tables were unattended, and no more than seventy or eighty people were playing the machines. Many were Indians, most middle-aged to elderly, many smoking.

When I checked tripadvisor.com, I found ten reviews. Here are two. Judy from Ralston, Nebraska, wrote: "The Hotel was very nice; beautiful lobby and nice rooms. The casino was a disappointment." And this from Eddie from Omaha: "There's a pool and an exercise room. No room service. The casino features slots, blackjack, and poker." Eddie concluded his review by suggesting that stopping at the Prairie Wind Casino & Hotel was something "someone heading to the Black Hills" might consider doing. Eddie from Omaha's suggestion explains what a warehouse full of video gaming machines and not much else, attached to two floors of rooms for rent, is doing in the middle of the grasslands prairie on the western edge of the poorest Indian reservation in America.

At the Oglala post office, when I asked the postal clerk who the casino's customers were, he said, "Mostly us." And when I asked Jeffrey Whalen, he said the same, "The majority of customers are local guys."

It was not supposed to be that way.

In 1994 when the tribal council was deciding where Turnkey Gaming should locate the double-wide trailers in which the Prairie Wind Casino would be housed, the Heartland Expressway, a freeway that would run north four hundred miles from Denver, past the Black Hills, and then on to Rapid City, was being planned. So the council had Turnkey Gaming put the trailers as close to the route of the Heartland Expressway as possible in order to market the casino to the thousands of motorists that the members of the council assumed soon would be driving by.

But more than twenty years later, while segments of freeway have been built, the Heartland Expressway remains a plan on a drawing board. And the Prairie Wind Casino sits by itself on the prairie at a location that is as close to the middle of nowhere as nowhere gets.

In 2013, the members of the tribe's Economic & Business Development Committee directed the tribe's attorneys to research the possibility of replicating the Fond-du-Luth Casino by opening a casino in Rapid City. The second largest city in South Dakota, Rapid City, which is thirty miles north of the reservation, has a population of 68,000.

Since then, nothing has come of the idea. But if someday something did come of it, given the ubiquity of the casinos that today operate on "reservations" that Congress and the secretary of the interior have created in Duluth, Minnesota; Rohnert Park and San Pablo, California; Immokalee, Tampa, and Miami, Florida; Mashantucket, Connecticut, and elsewhere, what would be the harm?

EPILOGUE

> Yes, in some cases Indians have gotten rich.
> But what's wrong with that?
>
> TIM WAPATO
> *Executive Director,*
> *National Indian Gaming Association*

WHEN THE FOXWOODS CASINO OPENED IN FEBRUARY 1992, 15,000 people a day crowded the gaming floor, seven days a week, twenty-four hours a day, jostling each other for a chance to lose money at the blackjack, roulette, craps, and poker tables. In January 1993, video gaming machines arrived. By June, Foxwoods was grossing $40 million a month and had become one of the most profitable casinos in the world.

Three casinos that were not so profitable were the Trump Plaza, Trump Castle, and Trump Taj Mahal in Atlantic City, which had filed for bankruptcy because their construction had been financed with junk bonds that the casinos' cash flow could not service. Donald Trump, the New York real estate mogul who owned the casinos, correctly considered Foxwoods a competitor that was stealing customers from throughout New England. While his motivation for trying to have Foxwoods shut down was entirely pecuniary, Trump's public grievance was that Skip Hayward and the other members of the Mashantucket Pequot Tribe that owned Foxwoods were fake Indians. As Trump, with signature bombast, complained on talk radio to disk jockey Don Imus:

> IMUS: A couple of these guys up in Connecticut look like Michael Jordan, frankly.

> TRUMP: I think if you've ever been up there, you would truly say that these are not Indians. One of them was telling me his name is Chief Running Water Sitting Bull, and I said, "That's a long name." He said, "Well, just call me Ricky Sanders." So this is one of the Indians. I'll tell you, they got duped in Washington, and it's just one of those things that we have to straighten out.

To try to put an end to Foxwoods, Trump filed a lawsuit in which his attorneys challenged the constitutionality of the Indian Gaming Regulatory Act (IGRA). Which got Trump nowhere. Then he recruited New Jersey representative Robert Torricelli to introduce a bill in the U.S. House of Representatives that on Capitol Hill was ridiculed as the "Donald Trump Protection Act." Which also got Trump nowhere.

But Donald Trump eventually wised up.

FOR EIGHTY YEARS, every state—except Nevada and New Jersey—had prohibited casinos, even though millions of people who lived in those states loved to gamble in them. As a consequence of Congress's passage of the IGRA, Indian tribes could open casinos on reservations in many of those states. But most tribes had neither the capital nor the know-how to do so.

One of the first casino management companies to understand that there was money to be made supplying that capital and know-how was Caesars World, which owned Caesars Palace on the Las Vegas Strip. In 1992, Caesars World signed a management agreement with the Agua Caliente Band of Cahuilla Indians to build, and then manage, a casino for the band in Palm Springs.

When Donald Trump heard that news, he sought out Richard Milanovich, the chairman of the Agua Caliente Band, according to Milanovich, "to talk about becoming the operator [of our casino]." When nothing came of that, three years later Trump flew to Florida and pitched James Billie, the chairman of the Seminole Tribe, on allowing Trump to build, and then manage, what today are the Seminole Hard Rock Hotels & Casinos.

Nothing came of that either. However, four years later, Trump Hotels and Casino Resorts signed a letter of intent with the fourteen-member Twenty-Nine Palms Band of Mission Indians to take over the management of the Spotlight 29 Casino east of Palm Springs, which after opening as a bingo hall and poker room had been reconfigured into a casino whose gaming floor contained 700 video gaming machines.

When the news that Trump Hotels and Casino Resorts would manage the Spotlight 29 Casino was announced, the *New York Times* reported that

> Casino companies from Nevada, New Jersey, and elsewhere are angling to get in on what could become a huge gambling market. Three

Las Vegas companies, Harrahs Entertainment, Anchor Gaming, and Station Casinos, have already announced deals to build and manage tribal casinos, each costing roughly $100 million.

Over the past sixteen years that is what happened.

Today, many tribes, many employing non-Indian executives who trained in the gaming industry, manage their own casinos. But many others have contracted with one of the major casino management companies. Station Casinos' construction and management of the Graton Resort & Casino has been described. Station Casinos also built and manages the Gun Lake Casino in Michigan for the Match-E-Be-Nash-She-Wish Band of Pottawatomi Indians. And it has contracted with the North Fork Rancheria, an ersatz tribe headquartered in the foothills north of Fresno, California, to build a casino on land the company has purchased for the North Fork Rancheria next to an exit of the freeway that runs from Sacramento south down the east side of the San Joaquin Valley to Los Angeles.

In North Carolina, California, and Arizona, Harrahs built and today manages casinos for the Eastern Band of Cherokees, the Rincon Band of Luiseño Mission Indians, and the Ak-Chin Indian Community. And in Jamul, a rural hamlet east of San Diego, Penn National Gaming, which operates twenty-six casinos and horse and dog tracks in sixteen states and Canada, is building, and will manage, a $360 million casino for the Jamul Indian Village.

Between 1995 and 2013, casinos and other gambling facilities on Indian reservations earned $348.75 billion. Billions of those dollars passed through to Lim Goh Tong and Sol Kerzner, the Chinese and South African casino magnates who financed the Foxwoods and Mohegan Sun* casinos in Connecticut,

---

*As has been described, in 1978 the BIA adopted regulations that allow a group of individuals to petition the secretary of the interior to designate the group as a federally recognized tribe. On behalf of the secretary, in 1994 Assistant Secretary of the Interior for Indian Affairs Ada Deer granted a petition that had been filed by a group that said its members were descendants of the Mohegan Indians who had lived in Connecticut. The new tribe, and the investors who paid for the attorneys who persuaded Assistant Secretary Deer to grant the petition, then teamed up with Sol Kerzner, the billionaire owner of a destination resort casino in South Africa, to persuade the secretary of the interior to take into trust as a reservation for the Mohegan Indian Tribe the title to 240 acres of land in southeastern Connecticut on which a boarded-up factory was located. Kerzner then invested $305 million to build the Mohegan Sun casino. In 1996 when it opened with 3,850 video gaming machines and 180 blackjack and poker tables, the Mohegan Sun immediately became one of the most profitable casinos in the United States.

to investors who own stock in Station Casinos and the other (publicly traded and privately held) casino management companies, and to investors who own stock in International Game Techology, Bally Manufacturing Company, and the other companies that manufactured the more than 346,000 video gaming machines that today are being played on gaming floors in casinos on Indian reservations.

Frank Ducheneaux, Pete Taylor, Patricia Zell, Virginia "Ginny" Boylan, Morris Udall, Daniel Inouye, and the other individuals who were involved in the events on Capitol Hill that culminated in 1988 in Congress's enactment of the IGRA did not support gambling on Indian reservations because they wanted to benefit the gaming industry. What they wanted was for the money and jobs bingo halls, card rooms, and casinos would bring to reservations to make life better for the human beings who live on them.

But the money and jobs have been irregularly distributed. In 2000, the Associated Press reported that

> Two-thirds of the American Indian population belong to tribes locked in poverty that still don't have Las Vegas–style casinos. And among the 130 tribes with casinos, a few near major population centers have thrived while most others make just enough to cover the bills. . . . Of the 500,000 Indians whose tribes operate casinos, only about 80,000 belong to tribes with gambling operations that generate more than $100 million a year.

The reason a few casinos earn more than $100 million a year, but most do not, is the location of the reservation on which a casino is located.

The 30,000-member Citizen Potawatomi Nation, for example, whose reservation is in Shawnee, Oklahoma, operates two casinos, one of which has more than 2,000 video gaming machines on its gaming floor and is attached to a fourteen-story hotel. Over the years, the tribe has used the money its casinos have earned to open a supermarket, a gas station, and a bank; build a health clinic, a wellness center, and a housing development for tribal members; and purchase a golf course. In those and other enterprises, the tribe has put more than two thousand people to work. But the casinos the Citizen Potawatomi Nation operates have changed the lives of its members for the good because the reservation on which the casinos are located is located only forty miles east on the Interstate 40 freeway from Oklahoma City.

By contrast, for all but a handful of members of the Oglala Sioux Tribe, the Prairie Wind Casino has made no difference in their lives. And the situation on the Pine Ridge Reservation is typical of the situation on other reservations located distant from large numbers of non-Indian customers.

Here, for example, is what in 2014 A.T. "Rusty" Stafne, the chairman of the Assiniboine and Sioux Tribes, told the Senate Committee on Indian Affairs about the Silver Wolf Casino—a nondescript and windowless building that houses eight-six video gaming machines and several rows of tables at which bingo is occasionally played—in Wolf Point, population 2,600, the largest town on the Fort Peck Reservation in northeastern Montana: "For the 13,000 members of the Assiniboine and Sioux Tribes, we have seen little economic benefits from Indian gaming over the last twenty-five years" because, while the casino annually grosses $10 million, when expenses are deducted, it earns less than $500,000 a year, which Stafne explained "represents less than $40 per member."

Given the importance of location, it is no surprise that in 2014 casinos and other gambling facilities on Indian reservations in California accounted for 25 percent of the $28.5 billion in revenue that all gambling facilities on all reservations in all states generated. And when the revenue from the two casinos the Mashantucket Pequot and Mohegan Tribes operate in Connecticut, the seven casinos the Seminole and Miccosukee Tribes operate in Florida, the Mystic Lake Casino in Minnesota, and the casinos surrounding Phoenix, south of Tucson, and elsewhere in Arizona are added in, it also is no surprise that in 2012 casinos and other gambling facilities in those five states generated 60 percent of total revenue.

Also in 2012, the casinos and the hotels, restaurants, golf courses, gas stations, and other businesses attached to them provided 679,000 jobs. The National Indian Gaming Association (NIGA) has estimated that 75 percent of those jobs are held by non-Indians. But that still leaves 170,000 jobs for Indians that did not exist before Indian gaming was invented.

But the jobs are distributed the same irregular way the revenue is.

In Connecticut, the Foxwoods and Mohegan Sun casinos each employ more than 7,000 people. And because it is located only forty-three freeway miles north of San Francisco, 2,000 people work at the Graton Resort & Casino. But only a handful of residents of the Pine Ridge Reservation have a full- or part-time job at the Prairie Wind Casino & Hotel.

The irregular distribution of revenue also affects the amount of money a tribe has available to give away to its members.

SECTION 6 OF H.R. 4566, the first bill to regulate gambling on Indian reservations, which Frank Ducheneaux wrote in 1983, required "net revenues from tribal gambling operations" to be used "solely to fund tribal government operations or programs." However, in 1985 when Ducheneaux wrote his next bill, H.R. 1920, he rewrote section 6 to allow a tribe to also spend the money it earned from gambling to "provide for the general welfare of the tribe and its members," which is legalese for "per capita payments." And that arrangement was continued in S. 555, the bill President Reagan signed into law as the IGRA.

During the years since, members of many tribes have never seen a cent, either because the tribes have too many members, their casinos earn too little money, or both. For example, even if the Prairie Wind Casino earns $10 million a year, and even if the Oglala Sioux Tribe distributes the entire $10 million to its members per capita, if the tribe has 40,000 members, each member would receive a check each month for $20.83. By contrast, the Shakopee Mdewakanton Sioux Community and the San Manuel Band of Mission Indians that each have only a few hundred members and operate casinos on reservations that are located within an easy freeway drive for tens of thousands of non-Indian customers send their members checks that total more than $1 million per member per year.

SIX OF THE ten richest Americans did nothing for their money except get lucky.

Other than their net worth, is there any difference between Alice Walton, who is the tenth richest person in America because she was lucky enough to have Sam Walton, who invented Walmart, for a father, and Cherie Crooks, who was lucky enough to have Norman Crooks, who invented the Shakopee Mdewakanton Sioux Community, for a grandfather? Or between Caroline Kennedy and Mary Ann Martin, the chairwoman of the Augustine Band?

If there is one, the difference is that Alice Walton's father and Caroline Kennedy's grandfather made their money on their own, whereas Cherie

Crooks and Mary Ann Martin are rich because, in the IGRA, Congress gave the Shakopee Mdewakanton Sioux Community and the Augustine Band a monopoly to sell non-Indians who live in Minnesota and California a commodity—the opportunity to gamble in a casino—that the Minnesota and California legislatures have prohibited everyone else who lives in Minnesota and California from selling.

But Congress passing laws that make some people rich but not others, and some people just well-off but not others, is nothing new. In 1964, Charles Reich, a professor at the Yale Law School, published "The New Property," one of the most influential law review articles of its era. In it, Reich pointed out that, in the early 1950s, "the emergence of government as a major source of wealth" had begun to transform the economy. And because that transformation was accelerating, in the future, an increasing number of Americans would depend for their economic well-being on "government largess—allocated by government on its own terms, and held by recipients subject to conditions which express 'the public interest.'"

At the hearing the Senate Committee on Indian Affairs held at which Rusty Stafne testified, one of the other witnesses was Ernie Stevens, Jr., the chairman of the NIGA. Stevens began his testimony by lecturing that "any discussion of Indian gaming must begin with tribal sovereignty." Then he celebrated casinos on Indian reservations because they were "helping to maintain, generate, and fuel an American economic recovery," even though he had just heard Rusty Stafne tell the committee that the Silver Wolf Casino was doing no such thing.

Ernie Stevens undoubtedly has never heard of, much less read, "The New Property." And he likely knows nothing of the story of how Felix Cohen invented the doctrine of inherent tribal sovereignty. If he did know, Stevens would understand that Indian gaming has nothing to do with tribal sovereignty.

It exists because Glenn Feldman out-lawyered Rudolph Corona and Roderick Walston, the attorneys who represented the state of California in the *California v. Cabazon and Morongo Bands of Mission Indians* lawsuit, and, after Feldman did so, Congress passed the IGRA, which gave Indian tribes a government-created monopoly, or in several states a semi-monopoly, to sell casino forms of gambling to non-Indians.

• • •

To FIND OUT how the story of Indian gaming has turned out where it began, I had lunch in Hollywood, Florida, in 2013 with Marcellus Osceola at his favorite southern barbecue restaurant a few blocks north of the Seminole Hard Rock Hotel & Casino. Marcellus, who at the time was a member of the Seminole Tribal Gaming Commission, told me that every adult member of the Seminole Tribe now receives $12,000 a month as his or her share of the multibillion-dollar cash flow from the Seminole Hard Rock Hotels & Casinos, the tribe's five other casinos, and its other businesses. Marcellus also lamented that when he was growing up on the Hollywood Reservation there was "no crime. Not like it is now. It was penny ante. Now it's major."

After lunch, I drove Alligator Alley, the freeway that runs from Fort Lauderdale west across the Everglades, to visit the Seminole Hard Rock Hotel & Casino in Tampa to try to solve a nagging mystery.

In the middle of the Hard Rock complex in Tampa, sandwiched between a parking garage and the hotel, is the smoke shop the Seminole Tribe opened in 1981, a small building at which a long line of automobiles was backed down the driveway, each waiting its occupant's turn to reach a drive-thru window and buy a carton of cheap cigarettes. But where was the cemetery James Billie and Steve Whilden told Tampa mayor Bob Martinez the Seminole Tribe would build in order to properly bury the bones of the Seminoles whose skeletons had been unearthed during the excavation for the municipal parking garage?

After walking around and not seeing a cemetery, I took the elevator to the roof of the parking garage. But from that commanding view, no cemetery. So I went into the casino, rode the escalator down to the gaming floor, and asked the woman behind the counter in the gift shop whether she knew if there was a cemetery on the premises. When she said she didn't know of one and then asked why I was interested and I explained that I had heard that there were Seminole skeletons buried somewhere on the casino and hotel grounds, her smile brightened and she gestured out through the gift shop's floor-to-ceiling glass windows toward the wall past the escalator.

Hanging on the wall next to a guitar that once had been owned by John Lee Hooker was a large photograph of Bill Haley, the spit-curled leader of Bill Haley and His Comets, whose recording, Rock Around the Clock, is one of the defining anthems of 1950s rock-and-roll.

"Do you see Bill Haley?" she asked. "I heard that when this building was built, they dug up some Seminole bones that they sealed up behind that wall."

"Is there a plaque or anything?" I asked.

"No," she answered. "Just a bunch of bones behind the sheet rock."

When I walked over and ran my hand along the wall below Bill Haley's photograph, it crossed my mind—with several thousand video gaming machines beeping and their lights blinking behind me—how amused, and then when he thought about it, how astounded, Steve Whilden would be to see what his and James Billie's bait-and-switch scheme so many years ago has become.

I know I am.

ACKNOWLEDGMENTS

Every book that purports to be nonfiction is the product of the contributions of many individuals other than the author who is publicly saddled with responsibility for the book's content. Of the many individuals whose contributions to the *Wampum* project were invaluable, I first would like to thank Al Gore and whoever really did invent the Internet. This book could not have been written without access to the research tools and communication technologies that, thanks to the Internet, the world now considers a commonplace.

In 1966 Congress enacted the Freedom of Information Act to require the FBI, the Bureau of Indian Affairs, and other executive branch agencies to open their records to researchers. But Congress keeps its own records closed for as long as fifty years. For that reason, I am indebted to former Senator Byron Dorgan and former Representative Nick Rahall, who during their tenures as chairmen of the Senate Committee on Indian Affairs and House Committee on Natural Resources opened for my inspection the files for the bills on Indian gaming that their committees considered during the Ninety-Eighth, Ninety-Ninth, and One Hundredth Congresses. With respect to congressional records that are open to researchers, I also am indebted to Rodney Ross who until his recent retirement was a Reference Archivist at the Center for Legislative Archives in Washington, D.C. I also would like to thank the staff of the Record/Information Dissemination Section of the Records Management Division of the FBI who over the years processed my FOIA requests to obtain the FBI files of numerous participants in the story of Indian gaming that contain a treasure-trove of information that would not otherwise have been available.

One of the most interesting parts of the *Wampum* project was learning about the history of organized crime in Pittsburgh and south Florida. For that reason, I am indebted to retired FBI special agent Roger Greenbank who was a member of the Organized Crime Drug Enforcement Task Force in Pittsburgh. Without Roger's assistance I could not have connected the dots between the LaRocca Mafia family and the Weisman brothers in Pittsburgh, and Jack Cooper and Meyer Lansky in Miami Beach.

Finally, there would be no book without Don Fehr, my agent at the Trident Media Group who was instrumental in placing *Wampum* at the Overlook Press, and without Allyson Rudolph, Vanessa Kehren, and Tracy Carns, my editors at the Overlook Press who saw the project through from start to completion. My thanks to them all.

NOTES

INTRODUCTION

page

1   *Indians are no different:* "Judge Upholds Indian Band's Right to Operate Bingo Parlors," *Press-Enterprise* (Riverside), November 6, 1984.

2   *In 1911, President:* Executive Order No. 1379, June 28, 1911.

2   *That year, the:* Nash, 70–71.

2   *A conservative estimate:* "Hard Rock's Revenue Equal to 8 Other So. Fla. Casinos Combined," *Sun Sentinel*, August 31, 2014.

3   *And the Seminole:* "National Indian Gaming Commission, Gaming Tribe Report," June 6, 2015, available at http://www.nigc.gov/Reading_Room/List _and_Location_of_Tribal_Gaming_Operations.aspx.

3   *In 1949, Mao:* "Beware of Card Sharks," *Newsweek*, August 24 and 31, 2009.

3   *In the United:* American Gaming Association, 26, 29.

3   *In 2008, when:* "Florida High Court Overturns Seminole Compact," *Indian Country Today*, July 23, 2008.

3   *Less than an hour:* "Quapaws Hit the Jackpot with $300 Million Resort Casino," *Indian Country Today*, July 23, 2008.

4   *That December, when:* "Red Hawk Casino Draws 10,000 on First Day," *Sacramento Bee*, December 18, 2008.

4   *The first reason:* "Jackpot! Man Wins More Than $450,000 at Riverton Slot Machine," *Casper Star Tribune*, December 10, 2007.

4   *In 2010, a retired:* "Lake County Gambler Hits $8.4 Million Jackpot," *Press Democrat* (Santa Rosa), December 30, 2010.

5   *According to geologist:* Lord, 73.

5   *When he assumed office:* Ibid., 33.

5   *In 1869, Nevada:* Message from the Governor, March 3, 1869, *Journal of the Assembly of the Legislature of the State of Nevada*, Fourth Session, at 282.

6   *This time, however:* Moody, 12.

6   *There the high-stakes:* Land, 38.

6   *George Wingfield, the richest:* Raymond, 194–195.

6   *And a year earlier:* Moody, 45.

6   *At 10:00 a.m.:* "'Old West' Returns in Nevada Gambling," *New York Times*, March 21, 1931.

7   *In a downtown:* "Reno, in Full Dress, Gambles All Night; 'Divorce Cure' Patrons Hailed in Resort Song," *New York Times*, March 23, 1931.

7   *Five years later:* Bonanno and Abromovitz, 120.

7   *After watching gambling:* Van Meter, 139.

7   *This time the idea:* Ibid., 230–231.

8   *Farley attempted to:* Sternlieb and Hughes, 37–38.

8   *McDermott's public rationale:* "Offtrack Betting Attracting Nationwide Interest," *New York Times*, April 17, 1971.

8   *But in 1971:* "Jersey Is Warned on Legal Casinos," *New York Times*, February 11, 1971.

8   *Nevertheless, the legislature:* Concurrent Resolution No. 128, New Jersey Assembly, April 1, 1974.

8   *In 1974, when:* Sternlieb and Hughes, 38–48.

9   *According to Jack Davis:* Van Meter, 256.

9   *The amendment's supporters:* Mahon, 15–16.

9   *During its first:* Sternlieb and Hughes, 188.

9   *Prior to the 1974:* "Hefner Promotes Jersey Gambling Plan," *New York Times*, October 27, 1974.

1: SOVEREIGNTY AND CIGARETTES

page

11   *That state laws: Handbook of Federal Indian Law,* 116–117.

11   *The law prohibited:* Florida Statutes, Chapter 67–178 (1967).

12   *By 1788, the situation:* Prucha, 39.

13   *However, when he:* Lipscomb, 10:370.

13   *Jefferson first advocated:* Wallace, 273.

13   *In 1825, President:* President James Monroe, Annual Message, January 27, 1825.

14   *To prevent such:* Richardson, 458.

14   *Congress accepted the:* 4 Statutes 411 (1830).

14   *Jackson had recommended:* Richardson, 458–59.

14   *The expulsion of:* de Tocqueville, 1: 340–41.

15   *To clear that:* House Executive Document 1, 31st Cong., 2d sess. 35–36 (1850).

15   *When thousands of:* Utley, 164.

15   *When the meeting:* Kluger, 48, 82.

15   *After reviewing the: United States v. Washington,* 384 F. Supp. 312, 356 (W.D. Wash. 1974).

16   *They did so:* Kluger, 83.

16   *In 1877, Commissioner:* House Executive Document 1, Part 5, 45th Cong., 2d sess. 397 (1877).

16   *In 1892, Commissioner:* House Executive Document 1, Part 5, 52d Cong., 2d sess. 28–31 (1892).

17   *The charge is:* Institute for Government Research, 772.

17   *When he had:* Collier, 126.

18   *But according to:* Mitchell, 293–94.

18   *To that end:* Sections 2 and 3, S. 2755, 73d Cong., 2d sess. (1934), reprinted in *To Grant Indians Living under Federal Tutelage the Freedom to Organize for Purposes of Local Self Government and Economic Enterprise: Hearings on S. 2755 and S. 3645 Before the Senate Comm. on Indian Affairs,* 73d Cong. 2 (1934).

18   *According to Indian:* Deloria and Lytle, 138.

19   *Perhaps the most:* "Powers of Indian Tribes," 55 Decisions of the Department of the Interior 19 (1934).

19   *But as Vine Deloria:* Deloria and Lytle, 159.

19   *Had Collier's original:* Ibid., 160.

20 *By 1938 Felix Cohen:* See generally Martin.

20 *That same month:* Littell, xiii.

20 *Littell initially thought:* Memorandum to the Attorney General re: Preparation of Manual on Indian Law, April 14, 1939. FSC.

20 *But he soon began:* Confidential Report of Assistant Attorney General Norman M. Littell, in Charge of Lands Division, at 8, July 1, 1939. NML.

20 *Cohen later conjectured:* Report of Work as Chief of Indian Law Survey, 1939–1940. n.d. FSC.

20 *But what Cohen:* Memorandum for Assistant Attorney General Littell re Conference on the Indian Law Survey Held in the Conference Room on the Afternoon of August 2, 1939, August 4, 1939. FSC.

20 *All of the material:* Memorandum for Assistant Attorney General Littell re Indian Law Survey. n.d. FSC.

21 *Charles Wilkinson, the:* Wilkinson, 60.

21 *Perhaps without appreciating:* Getches, Wilkinson, and Williams, 196.

22 *Miss Williamson also:* Letter from Doris Williamson to Felix S. Cohen, September 19, 1941. FSC.

22 *Less than three: United States v. Santa Fe Pacific Railway Company,* 314 U.S. 339, 349 n. 5 (1941).

22 *The treaty created:* 15 Statutes 667 (1868).

22 *The councils did:* Bailey and Bailey, 109–110.

23 *The secretary also:* Ibid., 62–63.

23 *In June 1923:* Iverson, 22.

23 *Thirty-six years later: Williams v. Lee,* 358 U.S. 217, 221–222 (1959).

23 *In a footnote:* Ibid., 220 note 4.

24 *As the BIA superintendent:* Letter from Superintendent, Colville Indian Agency, to Robert Holtz, BIA Area Director, April 9, 1964. Files: Washington Supreme Court. Washington State Archives.

24 *When the owners:* Minutes, Washington State Tax Commission, July 20, 1965. Washington State Archives.

25 *In December 1965: Makah Indian Tribe v. Tax Commission,* 434 P.2d 580 (Wash. 1967).

25 *During the interregnum:* "Operators' Trial Slated on Tuesday," *Okanogan Independent,* February 16, 1967; "State Closes Stogie Shop," *Omak Chronicle,* January 23, 1969.

25 *Tonasket then hired:* See *Tonasket v. State,* 488 P. 2d 281 (Wash. 1971).

25 *According to Pirtle:* Pirtle, 359.

25 *So while Tonasket:* Ibid., 378–379.

26 *As authority for: Confederated Tribes of the Colville Indian Reservation v. State of Washington,* 446 F. Supp. 1339, 1362 (E.D. Wash. 1978).

26 *As Washington senator:* 21 *Congressional Record* 7597 (1890).

26 *By 1950, the Indian:* See Error! Hyperlink reference not valid..

27 *In 1966 a Puyallup:* "The Rise and Fall of Bob Satiacum," *The Weekly* (Seattle), November 27–December 3, 1985.

27 *By 1974, the:* "Indian Cigarets: $3 1/2 Million Gross for Bob Satiacum," *News Tribune* (Tacoma), February 16, 1975.

2: Seminole Cigarettes

page

28 *They are just:* "Indian Cigarette Sales Send Tax Revenues Up in Smoke," *Miami Herald,* October 8, 1984.

29 *My Dad was:* Howard Tommie interview.

29 *When the Office:* Howard Tommie interview, January 14, 1988. Dr. Harry A. Kersey Jr. Faculty Papers Collection, 1966–2010. Florida Atlantic University.

29 *By contrast, according:* Jumper and West, 168.

30 *And according to:* Edmunds, 174.

30 *As a BIA employee:* West, "From Hard Times to Hard Rock," 4.

30 *Osceola had a job:* "Swearing-In Tribal Officials," *Alligator Times,* June-July 1975; "Indian Action Team," Alligator Times, October–November 1975.

30 *According to Osceola:* Marcellus Osceola interview.

31 *"I told Ray:* Ibid.

31 *The plan Skelding:* Jack Skelding interview.

31 *Almost immediately, the:* "Tobacco Store Vandalized," *Alligator Times,* May–June 1977.

32 *I bought six:* Marcellus Osceola interview.

32 *Sheriff Stack also:* "Stack May Halt Smokers' Good Deal," *Fort Lauderdale News,* July 27, 1977.

32 *During the meeting:* Jack Skelding interview.

32 *Two years later:* Cahill and Jarvis, 205–220.

32 *Stack and the:* 425 U.S. 463 (1976).

33 *But a few: Confederated Tribes of the Colville Indian Reservation v. State of Washington,* 446 F. Supp. 1339, 1362 (D.C.E.D. Wash. 1978).

33 *In November the: Vending Unlimited, Inc. v. State of Florida,* 364 So. 2d 548 (Dist. Ct. of Appeal of Fla. 1978).

33 *The Alligator Times:* "Indians, State Lock Horns on Tax," *Alligator Times,* October–November 1977.

34 *In 1978, the:* Spencer, 118–123.

34 *"We could have:* Osley Saunooke interview.

34 *Moxon had worked:* Bureau of Indian Affairs Press Release, "Duane C. Moxon Named Superintendent of Bureau of Indian Affairs Seminole Agency," Hollywood, Florida, June 1971. Author's collection.

35 *According to Saunooke:* Osley Saunooke interview.

3: Seminole Bingo

page

36 *People always say:* "U.S. Will Try Again for Indians' Bingo Records," *Fort Lauderdale News and Sun Sentinel,* August 30, 1980.

36 *"I watched the:* Kaye, 53.

36 *All I could:* Ibid.

37 *Also according to:* "1930s: We have a Bingo Here!," *Times Leader* (Wilkes-Barre, PA), June 25, 2006.

37 *The idea caught:* Kaye, 57.

37 *According to Howard:* Howard Tommie interview.

38   *A young attorney:* Barry Horenbein interview.

38   *When Horenbein told:* Ibid.

38   *Next to their:* Commercial High School, New Haven, Connecticut, Senior Class Book, 1933, at 48.

39   *He bought watermelons:* Barry Hornbein interview.

39   *He is regarded:* Memorandum entitled, "Jack B. Cooper Interstate Transportation of Gambling Devices," September 8, 1951. Jack Cooper FBI File.

39   *Less than a year:* "$3,650,000 Paid for 2 Dog Tracks," *Miami Herald*, December 5, 1953.

39   *It was Meyer:* Barry Hornbein interview.

39   *By the time:* Unless otherwise cited, biographical information regarding Meyer Lansky is taken from information in Lacey.

40   *As Bugsy Siegel:* Eisenberg, 143.

40   *According to his:* Lansky, 49.

40   *In 1969, Florida's:* "Faircloth's Law: A New Way to Nail Elusive Mobsters?" *Life*, October 24, 1969. See also "Florida Suing to Shut 19 Motels Allegedly Controlled by Mafia," *New York Times*, October 20, 1969; "Florida Acts on Resorts Said to Have Mafia Links," *New York Times*, October 21, 1969.

41   *According to Cooper:* "Helped Trujillo Embezzle $744,000," *Miami Herald*, April 6, 1962.

41   *Information was received:* Memorandum entitled, "Jack Ben Cooper," May 2, 1967. Jack Cooper FBI File.

42   *In July 1960:* Memorandum entitled, "Jack Ben Cooper," May 2, 1967. Jack Cooper FBI File.

43   *According to the:* Federal Bureau of Investigation, 115.

43   *And, in 1974:* Block.

43   *I asked for:* Barry Horenbein interview.

43   *"When I came:* Ibid.

44   *And according to Horenbein:* Ibid.

44   *According to Osceola:* Marcellus Osceola interview.

44   *But according to historian:* Kersey, *An Assumption of Sovereignty*, 126.

45   *In 2009, when:* Bertha Turnipseed interview.

45   *And in 2014:* George Simon interview.

46   *When Husick told:* Steve Paskind interview.

46   *And why did Steve:* Pennsylvania Crime Commission, 18.

46   *But according to Lansky:* Lacey, 413.

47   *Eugene Weisman operated:* Pennsylvania Crime Commission, 16.

47   *So when the final:* Steve Paskind interview.

47   *Cooper and his new:* George Simon interview.

48   *One of the witnesses: Financial or Business Interests of Officers or Employees of the Senate: Hearings Before the Senate Committee on Rules and Administration*, 88th Cong. 1577–1585 (1964) [hereinafter "Bobby Baker Hearings"].

48   *Years later when:* Bobby Baker interview.

49   *Here is what:* Bobby Baker Hearings, 1009.

49   *But in 1994:* George Simon deposition. *Bruce Todd Wheeland v. Seminole Management Associates, et al.*, U.S. District Court for the Southern District

of Florida, 93–6956 CIV, National Archives and Records Administration, Atlanta Records Center [hereinafter *"Wheeland Files"*].

49   *In exchange for:* Ibid.; Seminole Tribe of Florida–Seminole Management Associates, Ltd. Management Agreement, September 5, 1979.

50   *The president of City:* "Seminoles May Face Battle on Bingo," *Miami Herald,* December 7, 1979.

50   *But Steve Whilden:* "Seminoles Banking on Big Profits," *Fort Lauderdale News,* December 10, 1979.

50   *And in 1994:* George Simon deposition, Wheeland Files.

50   *According to Tommie:* Howard Tommie interview.

50   *In December, Florida:* Cahill and Jarvis, 224–225.

50   *Bogus subsequently transferred:* Steve Paskind interview.

50   *When we went:* Robert Butterworth interview.

51   *What got our:* Ibid.

51   *When Butterworth told:* James Billie interview.

51   *According to Shailer:* Phil Shailer interview.

35   *In May 1980:* Seminole Tribe of Florida, 491 F. Supp. 1015 (S.D. Florida 1980), affirmed 658 F.2d 310 (5th Cir. 1981).

52   *That evening a thousand:* "Seminoles Banking on Big Profits," *Fort Lauderdale News,* December 10, 1979; "Bingo! Seminoles Win First Court Test," *Miami Herald,* December 15, 1979; "Bingo! 1,000 Whoop It Up as Seminoles Open Hall," *Fort Lauderdale News and Sun Sentinel,* December 15, 1979.

52   *In October 1980:* "Seminoles Plan 'Super Bingo'—Despite 'Violation,'" *Fort Lauderdale News,* October 14, 1980.

52   *The bingo hall:* "Cigarette Ruling Could End Seminole Bingo," *Fort Lauderdale News,* June 11, 1980.

52   *After all 1,200:* "B-I-N-G-O: Just Call My Number Please and Turn Agony into Ecstasy," *Fort Lauderdale News,* February 1, 1982.

52   *SMA ran advertisements:* "Bingo Grand Opening Dec. 14," *Alligator Times,* December 1979.

52   *Eugene Kubitz, an:* James Weisman deposition, *Wheeland Files;* "Those Pesky Indians Are Causing Trouble Again—With Bingo," *Wall Street Journal,* September 9, 1980.

53   *In 1983, SMA:* "Tribe Profits Go Politicking," *Miami Herald,* May 30, 1983.

53   *When he was deposed:* George Simon deposition, *Wheeland Files.*

53   *When the Miami:* "Former Tribal Leader Has Won Big," *Miami Herald,* August 2, 1987.

53   *When he was asked:* Interview with Chief Billie, Tape One—November 1997, *St. Petersburg Times,* available at http://www.semtribe.com/SeminoleTribune/Archive/1997/transcription.shtml.

54   *Lane also reported that:* U.S. Department of the Interior, Office of Inspector General, Memorandum: Seminole Management Associates, Seminole Tribal Bingo, Hollywood, Florida, February 7, 1990.

54   *Wheeland hired an:* Bruce Todd Wheeland v. Seminole Management Associates, et al., U.S. District Court for the Southern District of Florida Nos. 93–2365 and 93–6956.

55 *Lyons also said:* "Seminoles Gain Entry in Caribbean Casino," *St. Petersburg Times,* December 20, 1997.

55 *During the deposition:* James Weisman deposition, *Wheeland Files.*

55 *And as he was:* Marc Sarnoff interview.

55 *According to Simon:* George Simon interview.

56 *In response, Billie:* Letter from James Billie, chairman, Seminole Tribe of Florida, to B.D. Ott, BIA Eastern Area Director, June 29, 1992. *Wheeland Files.*

56 *When Weisman suggested:* James Billie interview.

57 *According to the:* Supplementary Offense Report, Fairfield, Connecticut, Police Department Case No. 98–25736, December 22, 1998 [hereinafter "Fairfield Police Report"].

58 *Moriarty, who was:* Gary MacNamara interview. MacNamara is chief of the Fairfield Connecticut Police Department. In 1998 he was one of the officers who investigated the Moriarty home invasion.

58 *He also said:* Fairfield Police report.

4: BARONA BINGO

page

59 *A rat ran:* "Bingo! Indians Aren't Always the Winners," *Los Angeles Times,* October 12, 1986.

59 *Harry was a:* Myles Anderberg interview.

60 *So when Allan:* Wanda Drake interview.

60 *While the chairwoman:* Rocco Passanante interview.

61 *As the French explorer:* Laperouse, vol. 1, 448.

61 *In 1833, when:* Carrico, 40.

61 *Now free to stay:* Settles, 92.

62 *At the Barona:* Carrico, 168–170.

63 *Since the council:* "Barona Bingo Subject to Hearings, Probes, Raids," *San Diego Union,* December 15, 1985, reporting after interviewing her that Sister Romero "brought the idea of bingo to the tribe".

63 *On April 4:* Minutes, Barona Group, Capitan Grande Band of Mission Indians, General Council Meeting, April 4, 1981. RG 233, Records of the U.S. House of Representatives, Committee on Interior and Insular Affairs, Legislative Files, H.R. 1920, 99th Cong.

63 *In July 1981: Barona Group of the Capitan Grande Band of Mission Indians v. Duffy,* U.S. District Court for the Southern District of California No. 81–0710.

64 *She dismissed the:* Ibid.; Order Granting Defendant's Motion for Summary Judgment, April 21, 1982.

64 *Hertzberg appealed the: Barona Group of the Capitan Grande Band of Mission Indians v. Duffy,* 694 F.2d 1185 (9th Cir. 1982).

64 *As Anderberg later:* Myles Anderberg interview.

65 *As he would recall:* Ibid.

65 *But by 5:30:* "Tribe Hopes Bingo Will Hit Jackpot," *The Daily Californian (El Cajon),* April 16, 1983.

65 *At that point:* Myles Anderberg interview.

66 *In May, Anderberg:* "Barona Indians' Pot of Gold Is Bingo," *San Diego Union,* May 6, 1983.

66　*By September, Barona:* "Everyone Can Win at Bingo," *Los Angeles Times*, September 25, 1983.

66　*In October, Anderberg:* "San Diego County Digest," *Los Angeles Times*, October 2, 1983.

66　*By November, Barona:* "Indian Bingo Ill Feeling Lingers," *San Diego Union*, November 4, 1983; "Barona Bingo Offers $1-Million Prize," *Los Angeles Times*, August 2, 1984.

66　*And every Barona:* "Indian War Cry: Bingo!" *Time*, January 2, 1984.

66　*The success of Barona:* "Building Begun on Bingo Hall," *Los Angeles Times*, April 29, 1983.

66　*In August, Harry:* "Bingo Enriches Barona Indians . . . at Cost of a Tribal Feud," *Los Angeles Times*, August 15, 1983.

66　*That November, the:* "Indian Bingo Ill Feeling Lingers," *San Diego Union*, November 4, 1983.

67　*The anonymous investor:* See *McDonald's Restaurants of Illinois, Inc. v. Commissioner of Internal Revenue*, 688 F.2d 520 (7th Cir. 1982).

67　*When the new:* "New $2.5 million, 2,000-seat bingo hall opens on Barona Indian Reservation," *Daily Californian* (El Cajon), August 4, 1984.

67　*Which is why:* Anderberg v. American Amusement & Management, Inc., Superior Court for the County of San Diego No. 537547, Declaration of Myles Anderberg, August 14, 1986.

68　*Three months after:* "Indian Bingo Hall Raided in Probe of Game-Fixing," *Los Angeles Times*, December 13, 1986.

68　*In March 1986:* News Release, Office of the Attorney General of California, April 2, 1986.

68　*Before the indictment:* "Ex-Manager Admits Bingo Scam on Reservation," *Los Angeles Times*, April 3, 1986.

68　*When they were given:* "Jury Report Describes Bingo Scam," *San Diego Union*, April 8, 1986.

69　*They attempted to:* Organized Crime in Sports (Racing): Hearings Before the House Committee on Crime, 92d Cong. 551–565 (1972).

69　*As part of the:* Hoofbeats 16, October 1971.

69　*Siegel also arranged:* The Horseman and Fair World 43, July 14, 1971.

70　*A December 1983:* Ibid.; Memorandum (December 1, 1983).

70　*Siegel also told:* The People of the State of California v. Stewart Siegel, Superior Court for the County of San Diego No. CR 79502, Reporter's Transcript, December 8, 1986.

71　*During the ride:* Nesteroff.

71　*In 1983, the FBI:* Ibid.; Teletype (June 18, 1973). Allan Drake FBI File; Teletype (Aug. 15, 1983).

72　*One of those:* State of California Dept. of Justice, Organized Crime Control Commission, First Report, at 69 (May 1978).

72　*In 1964, Passanante:* "Hatchet Terror Reign in $250,000 Thefts Ends With Arrest of 2 Men," *Los Angeles Times*, June 12, 1964.

72　*Before he was:* "All-Points Bulletin Issued on 2 Gunman," *Desert Sun* (California), November 19, 1964.

72 *In 1982, Passanante:* "Fugitive Swindling Suspect Seized," *Los Angeles Times,* December 22, 1982.

72 *Also in 1982:* The People of the State of California v. Rocco Victor Passanante and Harold Joseph Golden, Superior Court for the County of Las Angeles No. A 379714, Information alleging violations of California Penal Code sections 487.3, 496, and 12021.

73 *According to Anderberg:* Myles Anderberg interview.

74 *But Dwyer was:* Personal communications from Robert Dwyer to author, February 21, 2014, and July 15, 2015.

75 *"In late 1985:* Wolf and Attebery, 212.

75 *He did not:* Federal Government's Relationship With American Indians: Hearings Before the Special Committee on Investigations of the Senate Select Committee on Indian Affairs, 101st Cong., Part 2, 233–250 (1989).

5: STEVEN WHILDEN AND PAN AMERICAN MANAGEMENT

page

77 *Steve Whilden is:* "Bingo Lawyer, Indians Didn't Know of Butcher Role," *Knoxville Journal and The Tennessean,* May 9, 1984.

77 *The next morning:* James Billie interview.

77 *What grabbed Whilden's:* Piper and Piper.

77 *Whilden later said:* "New Riches Grow From Old Burial Ground," *Miami Herald,* May 31, 1983.

78 *When he did:* Memorandum from Assistant Secretary—Indian Affairs—to Commissioner of Indian Affairs entitled "Waiver of 25 CFR section 120a—Trust Acquisition for Seminole Tribe of Florida," January 16, 1981.

78 *And in July:* "Indian Museum Plan Just a Smokescreen?" *Miami Herald,* October 18, 1981; "Seminoles Open Cut-Rate Cigarette Store in County," *Tampa Tribune,* July 16, 1981; "Smoke Signals: Officials Fume About Seminole Sales," *Miami Herald,* October 18, 1981.

79 *Players, many of:* "Seminoles Open Bingo Parlor to Overflow Crowds," *St. Petersburg Times,* June 2, 1982; "Seminole Bingo Opens With Shouts and Applause," *Tampa Tribune,* June 2, 1982.

79 *The hall was:* Statement Analysis, Seminole Economic Development, Inc., January 2, 1990. DOI FOIA.

79 *And according to:* Michael Whilden interview.

80 *But according to Estrada:* Alfred Estrada interview.

80 *According to Barry:* Barry Horenbein interview.

80 *But according to James:* James Billie interview.

80 *Ten months before:* "Bingo Hall Gutted by Fire; Officials Suspect Arson," *Tampa Tribune,* August 31, 1981.

81 *Benny introduced me:* Steve Paskind interview.

81 *In 2012, when:* Buddy Levy interview.

81 *But when I:* Michael Fisten interview.

81 *When he hung:* Barry Horenbein interview.

81 *In 1990, an:* U.S. Department of the Interior, Office of Inspector General, Memorandum: Seminole Management Associates, Seminole Tribal Bingo, Hollywood, Florida, February 7, 1990.

82   *Piazza also told:* "Loyalty Pays Off for Tampa Partner," *St. Petersburg Times,* December 20, 1997.

82   *Marcellus Osceloa, the:* "Lawyer Taught Seminoles to Play Political Hardball," *Miami Herald,* May 30, 1983.

83   *The Herald also:* "$14-Million Broward Condo Plan Hinged on Land Deal," *Miami Herald,* May 31, 1983; "Plan to Set Up Reservation Tried to Dodge Zoning Laws," *Miami Herald,* May 31, 1983.

83   *Whilden's job was: Pan American Management Company v. Stephen Whilden,* Superior Court for the County of San Diego No. 516838, Complaint (February 23, 1984) [hereinafter "PAMC Complaint"].

83   *He settled in:* Michael Freschette interview.

84   *Frechette, whose day:* Email Communication from Michael Frechette to Author, April 21, 2014.

84   *In July 1980:* "Bingo Is the Best Revenge," *Time,* July 7, 1980.

84   *According to Frechette:* Michael Frechette interview.

85   *When Little Crow:* Schultz, 28.

85   *In 1884, Minnesota:* 23 Statutes 87 (1884).

85   *In 1888, Congress:* 25 Statutes 228–29 (1888).

86   *In 1890 and 1891:* House Report No. 96–1409, at 5 (1980).

86   *According to historian:* Meyer (1967), 275–76.

86   *Instead, the BIA:* Meyer (1993), 384.

86   *When an assignee: Brewer v. Acting Deputy Assistant Secretary—Indian Affairs,* 10 Interior Board of Indian Appeals 110, 112 (September 30, 1982).

86   *Crooks would recall:* Crooks.

86   *So, in January:* The following description of the BIA's creation of the Mdewakanton Sioux Community is based on documents in the file of the Area Director of the BIA Midwest Region.

87   *When that legally:* Graves and Ebbot, 64.

87   *As Norman Crooks:* Crooks.

87   *First the House:* Public Law No. 96–557, 94 Statutes 3262 (1980).

87   *The Shakopee Mdewakanton:* Mariana Shulstad interview.

87   *After visiting reservations:* "Local Indians Sell Tax-Free Smokes," *Shakopee Valley News,* January 13, 1982.

87   *According to Frechette, "We:* Michael Frechette interview.

88   *According to Frechette, "We'd:* Ibid.

88   *While Steve Whilden:* Ibid.

88   *We had my:* Ibid.

89   *After paying other:* Meyer (1993), 388–89. *See also Indian Gaming Control Act: Hearing on H.R. 4566 before the House Committee on Interior and Insular Affairs,* 98th Cong., 2d sess., 221–236 (1984) (testimony of Norman Crooks).

89   *Mills was a:* See, generally, Mills and Mann.

89   *The land was:* "Florida Lawyer Proposes Bingo as Indian Solution," *Cape Cod Times,* February 10, 1983; "Man Who Helped Open High-Stakes Indian Bingo Operates in Fast Lane," *Arizona Daily Star,* September 9, 1984.

89   *Mills agreed that:* "Florida Firm Offers Indians Gaming Casino," *The Enterprise,* February 17, 1983.

89   *Thousands more were:* Hu-DeHart.

90   *However, because the:* Private Law No. 88–350, 78 Statutes 1196 (1964).

90   *The statute also:* Public Law No. 95–375, 92 Statues 712 (1978).

92   *In December 1982:* "Yaquis Hoping to Make Village Bingo Capital," *Tucson Citizen*, December 22, 1982.

90   *In January 1983:* "1,600 People Say Welcome to Yaqui Bingo," *Tucson Citizen*, January 24, 1983.

91   *Given the reservation's:* "Firm Parlayed Old Law Into New Lummi Income," *Bellingham Herald* (Washington), January 15, 1983.

91   *When the casino:* "The Gamble Is On," *Bellingham Herald*, January 8, 1983.

92   *According to Michael:* Michael Freschette interview.

92   *The meeting ended:* "State Raises Questions on Lummi Game," *Bellingham Herald*, January 14, 1983.

92   *When they picked: United States v. Lummi Indian Tribe*, U.S. District Court for the Western District of Washington No. 2:83-cv-94; "Indians Lost Casino and Its 158 Jobs," *Spokesman-Review* (Spokane), February 23, 1983.

92   *But as the:* "Ruling Stops Lummi Game," *Bellingham Herald*, February 17, 1983; "Federal Attorneys Link Criminal to Lummi Gambling Operation," *Seattle Times*, February 12, 1983.

93   *In 1883, when:* Jackson and Kenny, 28.

93   *Donald Valverde moved:* "Sycuan Indians to Open Bingo Palace Friday," *San Diego Union*, November 22, 1983.

93   *Five months later:* "Yaquis Reach Temporary Settlement with Bingo Operators," *Arizona Daily Star*, November 18, 1983; "Pasqua Yaquis Acquire a New Partner for Tribe's High-Stakes Bingo Game," *Tucson Citizen*, January 5, 1984.

93   *So, in February:* PAMC Complaint.

93   *We wanted to:* Buddy Levy interview.

94   *But each time:* FBI Minneapolis Field Office. Memorandum (September 8, 1986). Steve Whilden FBI File.

94   *According to his:* Michael Whilden interview.

94   *The trip was:* "Floridians Bid for Puyallup Bingo," *Tacoma News Tribune*, April 12, 1982.

94   *Then Joseph Bowen:* Ibid.

95   *I even brought:* "Bingo Deal Is Derailed by Rumors," *Miami Herald*, May 30, 1983.

95   *And then, according:* Ibid.

95   *In the end:* "Tucson Investors, Tribe Share Losses," *Tucson Citizen*, June 19, 1992.

96   *The council rejected:* "Bingo Killed in Council Action," *One Feather*, February 10, 1982.

96   *When the first:* "5,000 Bingo Players on Hand for Opening Day in Cherokee," *Asheville Citizen*, December 5, 1982.

96   *And four times:* "Biggest Bingo Game in World Planned Saturday in Cherokee," *Dispatch* (Lexington, North Carolina), June 30, 1983.

96   *Between December 1982:* "Indians Want New Contract for Bingo," Chief Says, *One Feather*, March 26, 1986; "Correction," *One Feather*, April 2, 1986.

96 *Of that amount:* "Cherokee Profits: Tribe Gets a Fair Shake 'Right Down the Line,'" *One Feather,* March 21, 1984.

96 *Sherman Lichty and:* "Principal Chief's Report," *One Feather,* April 16, 1986.

96 *They pled guilty:* "Bingo Owner Guilty of Skimming profits," *Asheville Citizen,* February 14, 1987; "Bingo Partner Fined for Mail Fraud," *One Feather,* April 8, 1987; "Two Sentenced for Skimming Bingo Money," *Asheville Citizen,* October 28, 1987.

96 *In addition to:* "Profits Game Attracting Tribes to Bingo Business," *Miami Herald,* May 29, 1983.

97 *With the BIA's:* "Spreading Bingo Business Brings Tribes Big Bucks," *Miami Herald,* May 29, 1983.

6: NINETY-EIGHTH CONGRESS

page

98 *There hasn't been: Indian Gambling Control Act: Hearing on H.R. 4566 Before the House Committee on Interior and Insular Affairs,* 98th Cong. 39 (1984) [hereinafter "1984 House Hearing"].

98 *In October 1982:* "Remarks Announcing Federal Initiatives Against Drug Trafficking and Organized Crime," October 14, 1982, 2 Public Papers of the Presidents: Ronald Reagan 1982, at 1313–1317 (1983).

98 *In October 1980:* "Have to Go, Reagan Says," *Sioux Falls Argus Leader,* October 15, 1980; Statement by the Honorable Ronald Reagan: The American Indian and Alaskan Native Leadership Meeting, Sioux Falls, South Dakota, October 14, 1980. RRWHF.

99 *With respect to:* Samuel R. Cook, "Ronald Reagan's Indian Policy in Retrospect: Economic Crisis and Political Irony," *Policy Studies Journal* 24:11–26 (1996), reprinted in Meyer, John, at 125–139; Hazel W. Hertzberg, "Reaganomics on the Reservation," *The New Republic,* November 22, 1982.

99 *Several wore traditional:* "Briefing," *New York Times,* October 23, 1981.

99 *When he found:* Memorandum from John McClaughry to Martin Anderson, entitled "Indian Wars," October 16, 1981. RRWHF.

99 *According to a:* Pemberton, 113.

99 *The working groups:* Anderson, Martin, 224–225.

100 *After listening to:* Minutes: Cabinet Council on Human Resources, September 20, 1982; Memorandum for the President from Richard Schweiker, Chairman, Pro Tem. Cabinet Council on Human Resources, September 17, 1982. RRWHF.

100 *Two months later:* Memorandum from Elizabeth Dole to William Sadleir, Director Presidential Appointments and Scheduling, November 24, 1982. RRWHF.

100 *Dole's informant also:* Memorandum from Morton Blackwell to Elizabeth Dole, entitled "Scheduling Proposal for President's Indian Policy Statement," November 4, 1982. RRWHF.

100 *So instead of:* American Indian Policy Statement, January 24, 1983. RRWHF; "Indian Group Praises Reagan Statement on Tribes," *New York Times,* January 29, 1983.

101 *Half a dozen:* Memorandum entitled "Background," n.d. RRWHF.

101 *Also, while the:* Memorandum from Ken Smith to Members, White House Working Group on Indian Policy, entitled "Agenda, Meeting of May 19, 1982; Development of Policy Statement," May 18, 1982, RRWHF.

101 *Whoever was responsible:* Letter from John Fritz, Deputy Assistant Secretary of the Interior for Indian Affairs, to David Stockman, Director, Office of Management and Budget, March 3, 1983. Files of the Office of the Secretary, Department of the Interior, Washington, D.C.

101 *He then argued:* Ibid.

101 *But that morning:* Note from Mike U. to Ed Meese, Ed Harper, and Craig Fuller, March 15, 1983, RRWHF.

102 *A handwritten notation:* Memorandum from Michael M. Uhlmann, to Cabinet Council on Legal Policy, entitled "Comprehensive Crime Control Act of 1983," March 15, 1983, RRWHF.

102 *As Ducheneaux later:* Ducheneaux, "Legislative History of the Indian Gaming Regulatory Act of 1988."

103 *In July 1983:* 463 U.S. 713 (1983); Letter from Justice Lewis Powell to Justice William Brennan regarding "82–401 Rice v. Rehner,", April 5, 1983. Harry A. Blackum Papers, Library of Congress, Washington, D.C.

103 *Since history also:* Ducheneaux & Taylor, 7.

104 *They all agreed:* Memorandum from Frank Ducheneaux to "MKU and McNulty," September 20, 1983. H.R. 4566 File.

104 *According to Skibine:* "The Indian Gaming Regulatory Act at 25: Successes, Shortcomings, and Dilemmas," *The Federal Lawyer*, April 2013.

104 *On June 19:* 1984 House Hearing.

106 *In March 1983:* "News Note: Constitutions Will Play Key Row (sic) to BIA Task Force on Bingo," *One Feather*, May 4, 1983.

106 *When Houle decided:* "Report on Bingo," *One Feather*, August 24, 1983; Brewer, 46–47; *Indian Gambling Control Act: Hearings on H.R. 1920 and H.R. 2404 Before the House Committee on Interior and Insular Affairs*, 99th Cong., 1st sess., 178 (1984), testimony of Mark Powless that the National Task Force on Indian Gaming was "re-established as an Indian government Task Force in Minneapolis, Minnesota, in 1983".

106 *When Powless and:* Memorandum from "Alex and Frank" to "Congressmen Udall and McNulty" entitled "H.R. 4566, Indian Gambling Bill," March 21, 1984. H.R. 4566 File.

107 *After the meeting:* Memorandum from Alex Skibine to Representative Morris Udall entitled "Indian Gambling," April 2, 1984. H.R. 4566 File.

108 *As he years:* Ducheneaux, "The Indian Gaming Regulatory Act," 122.

7: NINETY-NINTH CONGRESS: HOUSE OF REPRESENTATIVES

page

109 *For most of:* 132 *Congressional Record* 8185 (1986).

109 *In June of: Indian Gambling Control Act: Hearings on H.R. 1920 and H.R. 2404 Before the House Committee on Interior and Insular Affairs*, 99th Cong., Part I, 100 (1985) [hereinafter "H.R. 1920 Hearings, Part I"].

109 *But by June:* Bureau of Indian Affairs, Survey of Indian Bingo Activity, July 1, 1987, reprinted in *Gaming Activities on Indian Reservations and Lands: Hearing on S. 555 and S. 1303 Before the Senate Select Committee on Indian Affairs*, 100th Cong. 237–251 (1987).

109   *As a consequence:* H.R. 1920 Hearings, Part I, at 100.

110   *When he finished:* Ibid., 386.

111   *Four months earlier:* "U.S. Authorities Square Off Over Indian Bingo; Justice, Interior Departments Disagree on Tribal Autonomy in High-Stakes Gambling," *Washington Post,* May 2, 1985.

111   *The Committee on Interior: Indian Gambling Control Act: Hearing on H.R. 1920 and H.R. 2404 Before the House Committee on Interior and Insular Affairs,* 99th Cong., Part II (1985) [hereinafter "H.R. 1920 Hearings, Part II"].

112   *On December 4:* H.R. 1920 Mark-up Transcript, Wednesday, December 4, 1985. RG 233, Records of the U.S. House of Representatives, 99th Cong., Committee on Interior and Insular Affairs, H.R. 1920, Box 173.

113   *As a consequence:* Carson and Johnson, 203.

113   *According to Frank:* Ibid., 204–205.

113   *As a consequence:* Ibid., 205.

115   *On December 11:* H.R. 1920 Mark-up Transcript, Wednesday, December 11, 1985. RG 233, Records of the U.S. House of Representatives, 99th Cong., Committee on Interior and Insular Affairs, H.R. 1920, Box 173.

116   *According to Don:* Donald Hellman interview.

116   *But the afternoon:* Memorandum from Frank Ducheneaux to "MKU", entitled "Gambling Bill," December 10, 1985. RG 233, Records of the U.S. House of Representatives, 99th Cong., Committee on Interior and Insular Affairs, H.R. 1920, Box 175.

117   *A year earlier:* "O'Neill Hopes to Retire Soon, to Another Job," *New York Times,* March 1, 1984.

117   *In May 1985:* "Congress: The Race for Whip Wide Open," *New York Times,* May 31, 1985.

117   *In December 1986:* "Wright; Picked as Speaker Urges Limit on Tax Cuts for Rich," *New York Times,* December 9, 1986.

118   *When she testified:* H.R. 1920 Hearings, Part II, 47–48.

118   *Making no mention:* House Report No. 99–488, at 10 (1986).

119   *The amendment authorized:* Memorandum from Frank Ducheneaux to "MKU", entitled "'Last Mile' Compromise Offer of Mr. Coelho," February 12, 1986. RG 233, Records of the U.S. House of Representatives, 99th Cong., Committee on Interior and Insular Affairs, H.R. 1920, Box 175.

119   *While Ducheneaux told:* Ibid.; Memorandum from Frank Ducheneaux to "MKU", entitled "Class III Moratorium Compromise Proposal," March 24, 1986.

120   *On Friday, April 18:* Whip Advisory No. 60. RG 233, Records of the U.S. House of Representatives, 99th Cong., Committee on Interior and Insular Affairs, H.R. 1920, Box 175.

120   *On Monday, Udall:* 132 *Congressional Record* 8179 (1986).

120   *During the brief:* Ibid., 8182–8188.

120   *Texas representative Henry:* Ibid., 8186.

121   *Shumway explained that:* Ibid., 8187.

121   *By an unrecorded:* 132 Congressional Record 8179–8188 (1986).

8: NINETY-NINTH CONGRESS: SENATE

page

122 *My entire career:* Slade Gorton interview.

122 *Twenty-five years later:* E-mail communication from James Abourezk to author, July 24, 2012.

122 *An attorney raised:* Abourezk, 215.

123 *Abourezk disliked that:* Ibid., 205.

123 *Abourezk also had:* Senate Joint Resolution No. 93–133 (1975).

123 *The resolution directed:* Final Report, American Indian Policy Review Commission, at v–vi (1977).

123 *When Congress appropriated:* Ibid., 571–572.

123 *In May 1977:* Senate Resolution No. 95–4, at 10–11 (1977).

124 *The reorganization plan:* Senate Report No. 95–2, at 7 (1977).

124 *The select committee's:* "The Lessons of Capitol Hill Life Are not Wasted on the Young," *New York Times*, June 14, 1981.

125 *As a consequence: Gambling on Indian Reservations and Lands: Hearing on S. 902 Before the Senate Selection Committee on Indian Affairs*, 99th Cong. (1985).

125 *On June 26: Establish Federal Standards and Regulations for the Conduct of Gaming Activities Within Indian Country: Hearing on S. 902 and Related Bills Before the Senate Select Committee on Indian Affairs*, 99th Cong. (1986) [hereinafter 1986 Senate hearing].

125 *A year later:* Ibid., 87.

126 *Duffy told Taylor:* Ibid., 290.

127 *Not only did:* Ibid., 610.

127 *But rather than:* Transcript of Markup of H.R. 1920, September 15, 1986. Record Group 46, Select Committee on Indian Affairs, U.S. Senate, 99th Cong. Select Committee Records, 99th Cong.

128 *On September 15:* Ibid.; Memorandum from Peter S. Taylor, Staff Director, to Senator Mark Andrews, Chairman, and Committee Members, entitled "H.R. 1920 and proposed Gorton amendment (S. 2557)", September 17, 1986.

128 *As Taylor explained:* "Absent Senators Put Indian Panel Chief on Warpath," *Los Angeles Times*, August 14, 1986.

129 *The Associated Press:* The Slade Gorton biography contained herein is based principally on John Hughes.

129 *A tall, gaunt:* Ibid., 95.

130 *As Seattle Times: United States v. Washington*, 384 F. Supp. 312 (W.D. Wash. 1974).

130 *In 1974 District:* Ibid., 127.

130 *He thought Stevens:* Pirtle, 272.

130 *And even if:* 435 U.S. 191 (1978).

131 *However, in 1978:* 447 U.S. 134, 155, 159 (1980).

131 *In November 1985: Indian Gambling Control Act: Hearing on H.R. 1920 and H.R. 2404 Before the House Committee on Interior and Insular Affairs*, 99th Cong., Part II, at 46 (1985).

131 *But the Reagan:* Letter to the Honorable George Bush, President of the Senate, from Assistant Attorney General John Bolton and Assistant Secretary of the Interior for Indian Affairs Ross Swimmer, May 20, 1986. RRWHF.

132 *In addition to:* Amendment to be proposed by Senator Slade Gorton in the nature of a substitute to the Draft Bill of the Senate Select Committee on Indian Affairs, n.d. SG.

133 *The senators then:* Transcript of Markup of H.R. 1920 (September 17, 1986). Select Committee Records, 99th Cong.

133 *Nine days later:* Senate Report No. 99–493 (1986).

133 *As she had:* 1986 Senate hearing, at 53.

133 *That answer allowed:* Senate Report No. 99–493, at 5 (1986).

134 *But two days:* "Western Senators Holding Up Vote on Indian Gambling Regulatory Bill," *Press-Enterprise*, September 28, 1986.

134 *Over the next:* 132 *Congressional Record* 29,031 (1986), explanation by Senator Andrews of the content of his revised bill text.

134 *To try to:* Ibid.; Section 19(6)(B) of Andrews Amendment No. 3226 in the nature of a substitute for the text of H.R. 1920.

134 *But even if:* "Tribal Gaming Bill Is Likely to Stay on Hold," *Arizona Daily Star*, October 13, 1986.

134 *In a last-ditch:* Letter to the Honorable Robert Dole and Robert Byrd from Mark Andrews, Quentin Burdick, James Abdnor, Barry Goldwater, Alan Cranston, Jim Broyhill, George Mitchell, and Bill Cohen, dated October 7, 1986. DE.

9: CABAZON AND MORONGO: NINETY-NINTH CONGRESS

page

136 *We have ourselves:* "Indian War Cry: Bingo!," *Time*, January 2, 1984.

136 The reservation, which: Letter from Francisco Estudillo, United States Indian Agent, to the Commissioner of Indian Affairs, August 31, 1894, reprinted in 1894 Report of the Commissioner of Indian Affairs to the Secretary of the Interior, at 120.

136 *Of the twenty-two:* Almost a century: Heizer, 585.

136 *Until the 1950s:* "Famous Chase Was Family Affair," *Desert Sun*, April 12, 1991.

136 *When he became:* Lane, 19.

137 *But he made:* Connolly.

137 *According to Saunooke:* Osley Saunooke interview.

138 *According to Osley:* Ibid.

138 *John Paul agreed:* Lane, 47.

138 *According to John Paul Nichols; "Forty:* Ibid., 48.

138 *According to John Paul Nichols: "We:* Ibid., 50.

139 *He also persuaded:* "Indian Tribe Gets Rich Selling Tax-Free Cigarettes by Mail for 46 Cents a Pack," *National Enquirer*, November 1979.

139 *Shortly thereafter, John:* Lane, 59.

139 *In September 1978:* "Coachella Approves Gambling," *Desert Sun*, September 20, 1978.

139 *Six months later:* "Voters Repeal Gambling Law in Coachella," *Desert Sun*, March 7, 1979.

140 *Before Coachella voters:* "Casino Permit Winners to Hedge Bets," *Press-Enterprise*, January 4, 1979.

140 *As John Paul Nichols subsequently:* Lane, 61.

140 *According to John Paul Nichols, we:* Ibid., 107.

140 *Three nights later:* "Four Arrested and 98 Others Cited in Raid of Cabazon Indian Casino," *Press-Enterprise,* October 21, 1980; "Gambling Charges Slated," *Press-Enterprise,* October 23, 1980; Rossum, 11.

141 *After conducting its:* "Indians' Quest for Profit Ends in Barren Bitterness," *Los Angeles Times,* April 14, 1982.

141 *In 1983, the:* "Tribe's Vision of Empire Died in Bankruptcy Court," *Miami Herald,* May 29, 1983.

141 *In 1987 Zangari:* "Reputed Crime Boss in Southland Is Indicted," *Los Angeles Times,* May 23, 1987.

141 *They all pled:* Smith, John, 206.

141 *In 1998, Zangari:* "FBI Deals Crippling Blow to L.A. Mob," *Las Vegas Sun,* February 3, 1998.

141 *He again pled:* "Alleged Mobsters Plead Guilty," *Las Vegas Sun,* March 13, 2000.

141 *In addition to Rocco:* "Professional Runs Casino Gambling," *Press-Enterprise,* March 3, 1981.

142 *At that point:* Ibid., 301–303.

142 *In 1978 Marson:* "10 Charged with Fraud in Inquiry on Bankrupt Westchester Theater," *New York Times,* June 7, 1978.

142 *Marson pled guilty:* "Westchester Fraud Brings Prison Term," *New York Times,* July 7, 1979.

143 *As a consequence:* Glenn Feldman interview.

143 *Two weeks later:* "Indians Can Reopen Casino Closed in Raid, Judge Rules," *Los Angeles Times,* November 12, 1980.

143 *Waters ruled that:* "Indians Lose Plea for Card Parlor," *Los Angeles Times,* May 5, 1981.

143 *Feldman then asked:* Rossum, 12.

143 *Art Welmas told:* "Cabazon Band Plans to Appeal Court Ruling Closing Its Cardroom," *Press-Enterprise,* May 6, 1981.

144 *Ray Couso, who:* Ray Couso interview.

144 *According to a press:* "Murder Victim Knew His Life Was on the Line," *Daily News* (Indio, CA), July 2, 1981.

144 *But according to:* Lane, 90.

144 *But in 2008:* Undercover interview with Jimmy Hughes, "24 Hours in California, Part 3—Jimmy Hughes Final," You Tube, http://www.youtube.com /watch?v=1KgvW9LSbm4.

144 *He also worked:* Lynn Lamm Suedel interview.

144 *By then, the:* "Cabazons Hunting for Profits," *Desert Sun,* April 24, 1987, reporting that "Two-thirds of the Cabazon's 1,400 acre reservation is owned by the tribe as a whole".

144 *After their son:* Lynn Lamm Suedel interview.

145 *The members of:* Lane, 37–39.

145 *According to Benitez:* TV Channel 4 (Riverside, California) interview with Joe Benitez, "Old Video of Jimmy Hughes and Others," You Tube, http://www .youtube.com/watch?v=arfAGhNjiDw.

145 *When Alvarez said:* Stephen Rios interview.

145 *Several weeks later:* Ibid.

145 *What it was:* Lynn Lamm Suedel interview.

146 *There was no:* "3 Found Dead at Home in RM," *Daily News* (Indio), July 1, 1981; "Probe Continues in Triple Slaying; Victims Named," *Daily News* (Indio), July 2, 1981; "'Executr' Used Three Shots, Autopsy Reveals," *Daily News* (Indio), July 3, 1981.

146 *During those meetings:* "Murder Victim Knew His Life Was on Line," *Daily News* (Indio), July 2, 1971; "Arrest in 1981 Tribal Murders Revives Old Mystery," *Associated Press*, November 22, 2009.

146 *Spy Magazine reported:* Connolly.

146 *That account differs:* "Advisor to Indians Jailed in Murder-for-Hire Plot," *Los Angeles Times*, January 19, 1985.

147 *Hughes, who had:* See http://www.freetheoppressed.org/about-us-quienes -somos.html.

147 *During the conversation:* Undercover interview with Jimmy Hughes, "24 Hours in California, Part 3—Jimmy Hughes Final," You Tube, http://www.youtub .com/watch?v=1KgvW9LSbm4.

147 *Hughes also claims:* Jimmy Hughes, "A Hit Man With a New Mission," *Full Gospel Business Men's Fellowship International*, http://www.fgbmfivoice .com/stories/996hughes.htm.

147 *In November 1981:* In re Cabazon Indian Casino, 35 *Bankruptcy Reporter* 124, 125 (1983); "Manager Proposes Plush Indian Casino, Club," *Press-Enterprise*, March 20, 1988.

147 *A month later:* Cabazon Indian Casino v. IRS, 57 *Bankruptcy Reporter* 398 (1986); "Cabazon Indian Casino in Financial Straits," *Desert Sun*, December 18, 1981.

148 *Because the annexation:* 694 F.2d 634 (9th Cir. 1982).

148 *The decision was:* "Court Oks Cardroom Reopening," *Desert Sun*, February 25, 1983.

148 *Armed with that:* "Indians Want to Reopen Casino," *Desert Sun*, February 23, 1983.

148 *By 1915, the:* Tom Hughes, 118–120; Quimby, 10–11.

148 *In 1919, the:* Hoffman, 99.

149 *To take advantage:* "Smoke Sales Fall—Stores Turn to DMSO," *Los Angeles Times*, October 15, 1980.

149 *In November of:* "Morongo Reservation Fire Blamed on Arson," *Los Angeles Times*, November 12, 1980.

149 *According to Frechette*: "Man Bred Pit Bulls for Fighting, Officers Say After Raiding Home," *Los Angeles Times*, December 7, 1990.

150 *But instead of:* Michael Frechette interview.

150 *Walter Justus then:* "Morongos Set to Open Huge Bingo Parlor," *Press-Enterprise*, February 22, 1983.

150 *When he came:* Email communication from Robert Ingenito to author, March 4, 2013.

151 *The answers Sonny:* Myles Anderberg interview.

151 *His reason was:* "Bingo Parlor Won't Open as Scheduled," *Desert Sun*, February 26, 1983; "Indio Casino Will Reopen," *Los Angeles Times*, February 28, 1983; "Morongo Indians Decide to Postpone Bingo Decision," *Desert Sun*, March 7, 1983; "Bingo Parlor Fate Lies in Hands of Morongo Indian

Tribe Members," *Desert Sun*, April 14, 1983.

152 *Walter Justus and:* "Morongo Indians Back Plan for Bingo," *Desert Sun*, April 25, 1983.

152 *The grand opening:* "Opening of Morongo Bingo Parlor Attracts Big Crowds," *Desert Sun*, May 3, 1983.

152 *Open seven nights: "Bingo! Indians Hit the Jackpot," Los Angeles Times,* December 12, 1983.

152 *After visiting Indian:* "Indian Bingo: New Hot Spot in the Desert," *Boston Globe*, December 6, 1983.

152 *Indian Village Bingo:* "Lytton Station Bingo Business Plan," Lytton-Sonoma Ventures, October 1, 1988, copy in case file for *Scotts Valley Band of Pomo Indians of the Sugar Bowl Rancheria v. United States of America*, U.S. District Court for the Northern District of California No. C 86–333360. National Archives and Records Administration-Pacific Region.

152 *From that point:* "Bingo! Indians Hit the Jackpot," *Los Angeles Times*, December 12, 1983.

153 *And before the profit:* "Morongos Decide to Close Bingo Parlor Friday, Open Another," *Press-Enterprise*, February 7, 1984.

153 *But on the:* "Morongo Bingo Building Is Seized by Owner of Land," *Press-Enterprise*, February 10, 1984.

153 *According to Passanante:* Rocco Passanante interview.

153 *In May 1984:* Morongo Tribal Bingo Enterprise Management Agreement (May 17, 1984), reprinted in *Gambling on Indian Reservations and Lands: Hearing on S. 902 Before the Senate Slection Committee on Indian Affairs*, 99th Cong. 253–270 (1985).

154 *Three months later:* "Overflow Mother's Day Crowd James Bingo Parlor," *Press-Enterprise*, May 14, 1985.

154 *In April 1986:* 783 F.2d 900 (9th Cir. 1986).

155 *According to the:* Ibid., 906.

155 *By 1986, however: Establish Federal Standards and Regulations for the Conduct of Gaming Activities Within Indian Country: Hearing on S. 902 Before the Senate Select Committee on Indian Affairs*, 99th Cong. 162–163 (1986) [hereinafter "Senate hearing on S. 902"].

156 *Because, according to:* Roderick Walston interview.

156 *As a consequence:* Rossum, 23.

156 *By 1986 it:* Glenn Feldman interview.

156 *When he testified:* Senate hearing on S. 902, 93.

156 *As Feldman later:* Brewer, 53.

157 *And according to:* Ibid., 63.

10: CABAZON AND MORONGO: ONE HUNDREDTH CONGRESS
page

158 *On February 25:* Statement of Sen. Daniel K. Inouye, Chairman, Senate Committee on Indian Affairs, before the March 19, 1993, Meeting with Representatives of Indian Tribal Governments Engaged in Indian Gaming Activities. DD.

159 *So, according to:* Brewer, 69.

159 *And DeConcini and:* Dennis DeConcini interview.

159 *According to Inouye:* Brewer, 69.

160 *We [the staff:* "An Interview with Senate Committee on Indian Affairs Staff Member Patricia Zell," *Indian Country Today*, November 15, 2006.

160 *Patricia Zell, Ginny:* Letter from Daniel K. Inouye, Chairman, Select Committee on Indian Affairs, to the Honorable Dennis DeConcini, February 2, 1987. DD.

161 *While Gorton and:* Personal communication from Slade Gorton to author, February 29, 2008.

161 *However, because Evans:* Memorandum from Alan Parks, Patricia Zell, Virginia Boylan to Senator Daniel Inoye, entitled "Gaming Bill," February 17, 1987. DE.

161 *But then six:* 480 U.S. 219 (1987).

162 *The professors all:* Strickland, 231.

162 *The book also:* Ibid., 259.

163 *In it, Krenzke:* California v. Cabazon and Morongo Bands of Mission Indians, U.S. Supreme Court No. 85–1708, Joint Appendix, Declaration of Theodore Krenzke, Director of Indian Services, Bureau of Indian Affairs, United States Department of the Interior, in Support of Plaintiffs' Motion for Summary Judgment, August 28, 1984.

164 *In his decision:* 480 U.S. at 217.

165 *If this is not:* Letter from Dennis DeConcini, United States Senator, to Paul Fried, July 22, 1986. DD.

165 *The solicitor general:* Washburn, 311–312.

165 *As such, it:* Charles Fried interview.

165 *That fact became:* California v. Cabazon and Morongo Bands of Mission Indians, U.S. Supreme Court No. 85–1708, Transcript of Oral Argument, December 9, 1986, available at http://www.oyez.org/cases/1980–1989/1986/ 1986_85_1708.

166 *In 1985, when:* "In 2 Days, Coast Lottery Sells 30 Million Tickets, *New York Times*, October 7, 1985; "Some in Calif. Protest Lottery Winners," *New York Times*, December 8, 1985.

167 *And when Barbara:* Cabazon and Morongo Bands of Mission Indians v. County of Riverside and State of California, U.S. District Court for the Central District of California Nos. CV-83–1117 and CV-83–3073, Agreed Upon Statements of Uncontroverted Facts. DD.

167 *Walston answered, "Yes,":* Roderick Walston interview.

168 *What the report:* House Report No. 99-488, at 10 (1986).

168 *Also, six months: Establish Federal Standards and Regulations for the Conduct of Gaming Activities Within Indian Country: Hearing on S. 902 and Related Bills Before the Senate Select Committee on Indian Affairs*, 99th Cong. 82–97 (1986).

168 *Given the lack:* 480 U.S. at 220–222.

169 *Patricia Zell, who:* Brewer, 57–59.

169 *And luck "plays:* Boies, 15, 42.

170 *According to Bill: Gaming Activities on Indian Reservations and Lands: Hearing on S. 555 and S. 1303 Before the Senate Select Committee on Indian Affairs*, 100th Cong. 103 (1987).

170 *After the U.S.:* Ibid., 103–104.

170 *Given that reality:* Senate Select Committee on Indian Affairs, Press release, February 27, 1987. USS.

11: IGRA

page

171 **The message is:** *American Petroleum Institute v. Knecht,* 456 F. Supp. 889, 931 (D.C.C.D. Cal. 1978).

171 **Most of those:** *Gaming Activities on Indian Reservations and Lands: Hearing on S. 555 and S. 1303 Before the Senate Select Committee on Indian Affairs,* 100th Cong. 238–251 (1987) [hereinafter "1987 Senate hearing"].

171 **So there still:** *Oversight Hearing on Minimum Internal Control Standards for Indian Gaming Before the House Committee on Natural Resources,* 109th Cong. (2006), statement of Franklin Ducheneaux, available at http://natural-resources.house.gov/uploadedfiles/ducheneauxtestimony05.11.06.pdf.

172 **In a statement:** 133 *Congressional Record* 3264 (1987).

173 **As a senator:** Eadington, 17.

173 **Since the U.S.:** See Memorandum entitled, "Mtg. With Sen. Reid Re: Indian Gambling" from June Tracy to Senator DeConcini, May 27, 1987, reporting that "House and Senate Indian Committees staffs just finished developing a new bill on Indian gaming". DD.

173 **At the request:** Memorandum to Franklin Ducheneaux and Alex Skibine from Paul Alexander and Manny Fierro for the National Indian Gaming Association, April 10, 1987. DD.

173 **As Assistant Secretary:** *Indian Gaming Regulatory Act: Hearing on H.R. 964 and H.R. 2507 Before the House Committee on Interior and Insular Affairs,* 100th Cong. 193 (1987)[hereinafter "1987 House Hearing"].

174 **Three weeks before:** Letter from Representatives Tony Coelho and Claude Pepper to Representative Morris Udall, Chairman, Committee on Interior and Insular Affairs, June 5, 1987. USHR. See also 134 *Congressional Record* 15,747 (1988) (copy of letter published).

174 **He also told:** 1987 House Hearing, at 191.

174 **But according to:** Email communication from Thomas Spulak to Author, December 1, 2014.

175 **The compromise allowed:** Memorandum entitled "Proposed Compromise Amendment on Indian Gaming," from Virginia Boylan to Chairman Inouye, January 25, 1988 (content of Ducheneaux "compromise" amendment explained); Memorandum entitled "Gambling Legislation", from Virginia Boylan to Chairman Inouye, February 26, 1988, explaining that "Attached is a January 25 memo to you on the Udall proposed compromise on the gaming bill". USS.

175 **"I looked at:** Brewer, 63.

176 **According to Ducheneaux:** Brewer, 71.

176 **According to McCain:** McCain, 68.

177 **The subcommittee consisted:** Ibid., 78.

178 **Paul Alexander and:** Ducheneaux, "The Indian Gaming Regulatory Act: Background and Legislative History," 164.

179 **The memorandum ended:** Memorandum entitled "Gambling Legislation" from Virginia Boylan to Chairman Inouye, February 26, 1988. USS.

180 **Funke also said:** 1987 House Hearing, at 342. The published hearing record mislabels "Karl Funke" as "Carl Franke."

180 *A month later:* "Casino Beat," *Gaming & Wagering Business,* July 1987.

181 *Afterward, Reid informed:* Letter from Harry Reid to Daniel Inouye, June 2, 1987. USS.

181 *Daniel Inouye, who:* A copy of the resolution of the Select Committee on Indian Affairs is printed at 133 *Congressional Record* 27,451 (1987).

181 *In response, Reid:* Letter from Harry Reid to Daniel Inouye, October 29, 1987. DE.

182 *By the end:* See, generally, Reid, 236–272.

183 *In addition to:* "A Tiny Town Grows as Casinos Multiply," *New York Times,* April 28, 1988.

183 *In 1890 the:* Stewart, 233.

183 *So she did: Establish Federal Standards and Regulations for the Conduct of Gaming Activities Within Indian Counrty: Hearing on S. 902 Before the Senate Select Committee on Indian Affairs,* 99th Cong. 243 (1986).

183 *In October 1987:* Section Nos. 4, 5 and 8, Intergovermental Agreement Between the Fort Mojave Indian Tribe and the State of Nevada (October 15, 1987). Nevada State Library and Archives.

184 *Harry Reid agreed:* Eadington, 18–19.

184 *The purpose of:* Transcript of Markup of S. 555, May 13, 1988. USS.

184 *Prior to the:* Memorandum entitled "Indian Gambling—mark-up 5/13/88" from June Tracey to Sen. Dennis DeConcini, May 9, 1988. DD.

185 *During the discussion:* Ibid., 29.

185 *If the court:* Memorandum entitled "Outline of Proposed Compact Provision to S. 555" from Virginia Boylan and Patricia Zell to Chairman Inouye, May 12, 1988. USS.

186 *In August, the:* Senate Report No. 100–446 (1988).

186 *The agreement provided:* Time Limitation Agreement—S. 555, 134 *Congressional Record* 23,130 (1988).

186 *Three months earlier:* Letter from William Foster and other officers of the National Indian Gaming Association to Daniel Inouye, June 23, 1988. DE.

186 *So even though:* See Memorandum from Paul Alexander and Manny Fierro to National Indian Gaming Association, August 25, 1988. DE.

186 *Two weeks earlier:* Letter from William Foster and other officers of the National Indian Gaming Association to "Dear Senator," August 29, 1988. DE.

187 *When S. 555 was:* See 134 *Congressional Record* 24,016–24,037 (1988).

187 *As a consequence:* A video of the discussion on the floor of the United States Senate that preceded the voice vote to pass S. 555 can be viewed at: http://www.c-spanvideo.org/program/3880-1. Compare with the printed record of the discussion with the colloquies included at: 134 *Congressional Record* 24,016–24,037 (1988).

187 *On Monday, September:* See 134 *Congressional Record* 25,369–25,381 (1988).

189 *The next day:* Ibid., 25,781.

190 *After communicating those:* Memorandum for the President from James Miller, director of the Office of Management and Budget, entitled "Enrolled Bill S. 555—Indian Gaming Regulatory Act", October 11, 1988. RRWHF.

12: ARIZONA MACHINES

page

191 **When we put:** "America's Gambling Craze," *U.S. News & World Report*, March 14, 1994).

191 **Any tribe that:** "Lowry Assents to Quinault Casino," *Post-Intelligencer*, July 10, 1996.

191 **In response to:** Indian Gambling Control Act: Hearing on H.R. 4566 Before the House Committee on Interior and Insular Affairs, 98th Cong. 31–33 (1984).

191 **However, in 1985:** H.R. 3752, 99th Cong. (November 13, 1985).

192 **Years later, North:** "Ecohawk Has 'His Hands Full' With Bureau of Indian Affairs Position, Insiders Say," *Idaho Statesman*, July 20, 2009.

193 **But rather than:** "Interior Secretary Lujan Proposes Appointment of Joel Frank to National Indian Gaming Commission," U.S. Department of the Interior, October 24, 1990, available at http://www.bia.gov/cs/groups/public/documents /text/idc014441.pdf.

193 **A former member:** "Interior Secretary Lujan Names Jana McKeag to National Indian Gaming Commission," U.S. Department of the Interior, March 1, 1991, available at http://www.bia.gov/cs/groups/public/documents/ text/idc014441.pdf.

194 **A year later:** Implementation of the Indian Gaming Regulatory Act: Oversight Hearing on Status of the Activities Undertaken to Implement the Gaming Regulatory Act, 102d Cong. (1992).

194 **Asked to explain:** Ibid., 12.

194 **Three weeks before:** "Mafia Tied to Indian Gaming Takeover Bid," *Los Angeles Times*, January 11, 1992.

195 **But without identifying:** Office of Inspector General, U.S. Department of the Interior, Survey Report No. 93-I-349: *Implementation of the Indian Gaming Regulatory Act*, December 1992.

196 **In 1931 there:** Fey, 104–105; Nelli, 223.

196 **In 1946 there:** House Research Department, Minnesota State Legislature, *Gambling in Minnesota: A Short History*, March 2005, available at http://www .house .leg.state.mn.us/hrd/pubs/gambhist.pdf [hereinafter "Gambling in Minnesota"].

196 **In 1957 when:** "James P. Simpson, Lawyer, Dies at 87; Helped Clean Up Galveston in 1950s," *New York Times*, December 5, 2010.

196 **In the early:** Allbritton, 242.

196 **The outcome of:** "Luck, Be a Microchip Tonight," *New York Times*, December 17, 1998.

197 **The Johnson Act:** Public Law No. 81–906, 64 Statutes 1134 (1951) (codified at 15 U.S.C. 1171).

197 **Violating the Johnson:** See *United States v. Blackfeet Tribe of the Blackfeet Reservation*, 364 F. Supp. 192 (D. Mont. 1973); "Tribes Sovereignty Is Defined by Court," *New York Times*, October 14, 1973.

198 **According to D. Robert:** Robert Sertell interview.

198 **Consistent with Sertell's:** "New Rules Cut Games at Indian Halls," *Sun-Sentinel*, April 9, 1992.

198 **For example, in 1987:** "Gambling with the Mob?" *U.S. News & World Report*, August 15, 1993; "Three Who Conspired with Scarfo Plead Guilty to Gambling Charges," *Philadelphia Inquirer*, November 8, 1991.

198 *In 1991, SMS:* "Mob Ties to Tribal Gaming Feared," *Arizona Republic*, January 29, 1992.

199 *And on every:* Mariana Shulstad interview.

199 *As Sertell explained:* Robert Sertell, "VLT Machine Evaluation Spa Casino, Palm Springs, California", Casino Horizons Corporation, 2000.

200 *But here is:* "The Players Who Couldn't Stop Winning," *St. Petersburg Times*, December 19, 1997.

200 *In just six:* "In Seminole Gambling, a Few Are Big Winners," *St. Petersburg Times*, December 19, 1997.

202 *And during the:* Transcript of Markup of S. 555, May 13, 1988. USS.

202 *In June in:* Letter from National Indian Gaming Association to the Honorable Daniel Inouye, June 23, 1988. DE.

202 *Another modified the:* Memorandum from Paul Alexander and Manny Fierro to National Indian Gaming Association, August 25, 1988. DE.

202 *In 1984 the:* Williams, 13.

203 *The compacts also:* Minnesota Governor Arne Carlson, Attorney General Hubert H. Humphrey III, and Tribal-State Compact Negotiating Committee, "Report to the Legislature on the Status of Indian Gambling in Minnesota," September 5, 1991, available at http:www.leg.state.Mn.us/docs/pre2003/mandated /910715.pdf.

203 *While the compacts:* "Scams at Casinos: Good News and Bad," *Minneapolis Star Tribune*, December 20, 1992; "Indian Casinos Are Jackpot for Minnesota Economy," *International Gaming & Wagering Business*, August 15–September 14, 1992.

204 *Seven months after:* 56 *Federal Register* 56,278 (1991).

204 *But as Michael:* "NIGC Examines Comments Other Than Just Where Electronic Facsimile Games Fall," *International Gaming & Wagering Business*, February 15–March 14, 1992.

204 *In April 1992:* 57 *Federal Register* 12,382 (1992).

205 *To clarify the: Gaming Activities on Indian Reservations and Lands: Hearing on S. 555 and S. 1303 Before the Senate Select Committee on Indian Affairs*, 100th Cong. 92–93 (1987).

206 *In February 1990:* 136 *Congressional Record* 26,511 (1990), statement on the nomination of Linda Akers.

206 *U.S. Attorney Akers: Child Sexual Abuse in Indian Country: Hearing on Problems of Child Sexual Abuse in Indian Country Before the Senate Select Committee on Indian Affairs*, 101st Cong. 10 (1990), statement of Linda Akers.

207 *In a letter:* See, for example, Letter from Linda A. Akers, United States Attorney, District of Arizona, to David King, President, Mohave-Apache Tribal Council, November 6, 1991. DD.

207 *The tribal leaders:* Letter from Dale Phillips, Chairman, Cocopath Indian Tribe, to Arizona Governor Fife Symington, November 13, 1991. DD.

207 *MATI's first manager:* "Raided Tribe Losing," *Arizona Republic*, May 17, 1992.

208 *"There were a:* Ibid.

208 *During the year:* "Indians Plan to March," *Tucson Citizen*, May 16, 1992.

208 *And according to:* "FBI Agents Draw Criticism for Their Part in Casino Raid," *Phoenix Gazette*, May 16, 1992.

208   *But the trailers:* "U.S. Attorney Ordered Raids," *Phoenix Gazette*, May 14, 1992.

208   *Ten days later:* "Pact Would Allow, But Not Expand, Reservation Gaming," *Tucson Citizen*, May 22, 1992.

209   *The video gaming:* "Gambling Dispute Unresolved Despite So-Called Compromise," *Phoenix Gazette*, June 6, 1992.

209   *In response to: Yavapai-Prescott Indian Tribe v. State of Arizona*, U.S. District Court for the District of Arizona No. CIV 91–1696.

210   *In February 1993:* Memorandum marked "Confidential" from Patricia Zell to Sen. Daniel Inouye, February 23, 1993. DD; Mediator's Selection of Proposed Gaming Compacts, February 15, 1993. DD.

210   *McCain responded that:* Letter from Sen. John McCain to Arizona Governor Fife Symington, February 17, 1993. DD.

210   *Acting on McCain's:* Letter from Sen. John McCain to Arizona Governor Fife Symington, February 17, 1993. DD.

211   *However, first the:* "Senate Oks Gaming Ban Amid Threats," *Arizona Star*, March 3, 1993; "Gambling Ban Signing Imminent," *Tucson Citizen*, March 4, 1993; "Referendum on Casino Ban OK With Symington," *Tucson Citizen*, March 8, 1993.

211   *When Symington signed:* "Indians Protest Arizona Governor's Bill Banning All Gaming in State," *International Gaming & Wagering Business*, April 15– May 14, 1993; "Referendum on Casino Ban OK with Symington," *Tucson Citizen*, March 8, 1993.

211   *In response to:* Transcript of Proceedings, National Governors' Association 1993 Winter Meeting, February 1, 1993, available at http://www.nga.org/files /live/sites/NGA/files/pdf/1993NGAWinterMeeting.pdf.

212   *But he acknowledged: Views of the Secretary of the Department of the Interior on Matters of Indian Affairs: Hearing Before the Senate Select Committee on Indian Affairs,* 103d Cong. 81 (1993).

213   *Six weeks later:* "Babbitt Turning 'Neutral'," *Tucson Citizen*, March 9, 1993.

213   *However, Michael Anderson:* "We Have a Friend in Babbitt, Indian Leaders Say," *Tucson Citizen*, March 10, 1993.

213   *Several weeks later:* "Regulations Focus of Conference," *Desert Sun*, April 17, 1993.

213   *There was almost:* "Finally, an Indian Gaming Compromise Is Reached in Arizona," *International Gaming & Wagering Business*, July 15–August 15, 1993.

213   *Symington capitulated because:* Ibid.

13: California Machines

page

215   *The tribes and:* Memorandum from the Attorney General to United States Attorneys entitled "Enforcement of the Indian Gaming Regulatory Act," March 25, 1994 [hereinafter "Reno Memorandum"]. WCWHF.

215   *In October of that:* "The (Indian) Games People Play," *Gambling & Wagering Business*, October 1984.

215   *After Siegel pled:* "Company Plans to Resume Bingo Games at Barona," *Los Angeles Times*, May 16, 1986.

216   *When Turner told:* John Turner Interview. And see also "Bust Doesn't Move

Players," *The Californian* (El Cajon), April 28, 1989.

217 **Instead, prosecutions were:** See Section 22, H.R. 1920, 99th Cong., September 24, 1986.

217 **When Boylan and:** See Section 23, S.555, 100th Cong., February 19, 1987.

218 **The case was:** "Barona Sues Sheriff to Save Video Machines," *The Californian* (El Cajon), May 26, 1989.

218 **At the hearing:** "Bingo Devices' Return Denied," *San Diego Tribune*, August 12, 1989.

218 **But according to:** John Turner interview.

218 **Insofar as Judge:** "Bingo Devices' Return Denied," *San Diego Tribune*, August 12, 1989.

219 **In 1960 when:** Kling, 113, 141; *Berman v. Riverside Casino Corporation, H.J. Munley, Emmett Munley, William Miller, First Doe and Second Doe*, U.S. District Court for the District of Nevada (Reno) No. 61–1564, Amended Findings of Fact and Conclusions of Law (July 28, 1967); *Berman v. Riverside Casino Corporation*, 323 F.2d 977 (9th Cir. 1963); *Berman v. Riverside Casino Corporation*, 247 F. Supp. 243 (D. Nev. 1964), *aff'd* 354 F.2d 43 (9th Cir. 1965).

219 **But he withdrew:** "Inside Detroit's Mafia," *Detroit Free Press*, July 15, 1996.

219 **In 1983 when:** "Investigators Looking at Mohawk-Mob Links, *Times Union* (Albany), September 24, 1989.

219 **Munley then moved:** *Donald S. Jacobs v. Eastern Director, Bureau of Indian Affairs*, 20 Interior Board of Indian Appeals 68 (1991); Vegas Duo's Casino Deal Questioned," *Milwaukee Sentinel*, August 18, 1994; "Bingo Believers Cross Swamp for Chance at Record Jackpot," *Fort Lauderdale News/Sun-Sentinel*, March 22, 1987; "Investors Plan Takeover at Big Cypress Bingo," *Sun Sentinel*, May 12, 1988; "New Bingo Operator Clinches Deal," *Miami Herald*, July 31, 1988.

219 **In New York:** "Investigators Looking at Mohawk-Mob Links, *Times Union* (Albany), September 24, 1989.

219 **In Wisconsin and:** Vegas Duo's Casino Deal Questioned," *Milwaukee Sentinel*, August 18, 1994; "Puyallups' Vote Stops Bingo Deal," *Tacoma News Tribune*, November 3, 1988.

219 **Nevertheless, the BIA:** "Lady Luck Turns on Indians," *Los Angeles Times*, October 6, 1991.

219 **In December 1990:** "Bingo at Barona Returns, Grand Reopening Dec. 8," *The Californian* (El Cajon), December 5, 1990.

219 **Over succeeding months:** "Casinos Coming to Tribal Land Amid Lax Regulation," *Los Angeles Times*, October 9, 1991.

220 **"I don't care:** Transcript, "Playing with House Money?" *PBS News Hour*, August 8, 1996, available at http://www.pbs.org/newshour/bb/economy/august96/gamble_indians_8–8.html.

220 **On October 6:** "Lady Luck Turns on Indians," *Los Angeles Times*, October 6, 1991; "How the Mafia Targeted Tribe's Gambling Business," *Los Angeles Times*, October 7, 1991; "Tribe Hits Jackpot With Its Gambling Operation," *Los Angeles Times*, October 8, 1991; "Casinos Coming to Tribal Land Amid Lax Regulation," *Los Angeles Times*, October 9, 1991. "Indians See Battle Ahead Over Future of Gambling," *Los Angeles Times*, October 10, 1991.

220 *He urged the:* Memorandum from Dan Lungren, Attorney General of California, to All District Attorneys, City Prosecutors, Sheriffs, and Chiefs of Police, October 8, 1991. Author's Collection. See also "Indians See Battle Ahead Over Future of Gambling," *Los Angeles Times*, October 10, 1991.

220 *The letter concluded:* Letter from George Forman to the Honorable Daniel E. Lungren, Attorney General of California, October 11, 1991. Author's Collection. See also "Tribes Warn Lungren Against Crackdown on Slot Machine Gambling Indians: Their Attorneys Say Raids Would Be Illegal and Provoke Confrontations with Local Authorities," *Los Angeles Times,* October 13, 1991.

220 *Sheriff Roache's deputies:* "Authorities Raid Gaming Halls Run by Three Indian Tribes," *Los Angeles Times*, October 31, 1991.

221 *In February 1992:* Sycuan Band of Mission Indians v. Roache, 788 F. Supp. 1498 (D.C.S.D. Cal. 1992).

221 *But as early:* Eadington, 20.

221 *When two more:* "Indians See Battle Ahead Over Future of Gambling," *Los Angeles Times*, October 10, 1991.

222 *While he was:* Remarks at a Town Hall Meeting in San Diego, May 17, 1993, 1 Public Papers of the Presidents, William J. Clinton, at 680, 689 [hereinafter "Clinton Town Hall Meeting"].

222 *As he would:* Clinton, 30.

223 *Because three months:* Clinton Town Hall Meeting.

223 *During the 1992:* "Campaign Trail; A Clinton Team Maps Plans to Get Out the Indian Vote," *New York Times*, September 25, 1992.

224 *In his autobiography:* Clinton, 594.

224 *But rather than:* "Remarks to Native American and Native Alaskan Tribal Leaders," April 29, 1994, reprinted in 1 Public Papers of the Presidents, William J. Clinton, 1994, at 800, 802.

225 *Prior to the:* "Bingo Players Out of Luck; Hall Closed by Raid," *Miami Herald*, February 23, 1978.

225 *During the new:* Ibid. And see also "Police Ruin Jackpot Night for Crowd of Bingo Faithful," *Miami Herald*, March 15, 1978; "Police Raid Bingo Hall, Arrest Four," *Miami Herald*, March 16, 1978; "Bingo Hall Is Raided," *Miami Herald*, March 30, 1978.

225 *As a consequence:* Nomination of Janet Reno to Be Attorney General of the United States: Hearings Before the Senate Committee on the Judiciary, 103d Cong. 109 (1993).

225 *In June 1993:* Cabazon Band of Mission Indians v. National Indian Gaming Commission, 827 F. Supp. 26 (D.C.D.C. 1993).

225 *And in January:* Cabazon Band of Mission Indians v. National Indian Gaming Commission, 14 F.3d 633 (D.C. Cir. 1994)

226 *The memorandum directed:* Reno Memorandum.

226 *According to Wilson:* "Wilson Lays His Cards on the Table in Gaming Debate," *Los Angeles Times*, July 13, 1998.

226 *But the experience:* Ibid.

227 *California Attorney General:* Cathy Christian interview.

228 *The stipulation also:* Agreement for Submission of Class III Tribal-State Compact Dispute to United States District Court. Author's collection.

228 *Two lawsuits were: Rumsey Indian Rancheria of Wintun Indians v. Wilson,* 1993 Westlaw 360652 (E.D. California).

228 *Pete Wilson appealed: Rumsey Indian Rancheria of Wintun Indians v. Wilson,* 41 F.3d 421 (9th Cir. 1994).

228 *The lawsuit was:* Ibid., 428.

229 *In June, when:* "Showdown at Hand Over Indian Video Gaming Boom," *Los Angeles Times,* July 12, 1994.

229 *According to Bersin:* Alan Bersin interview.

229 *Bersin rationalized his:* "Showdown at Hand Over Indian Video Gaming Boom," *Los Angeles Times,* July 12, 1994.

229 *In April 1995:* "Indian Casinos in Middle of Battle Over Slots," *Los Angeles Times,* May 9, 1995; "California Tribes' Slot Machines Shut Down," *Gaming & Wagering Business,* June 1, 1995.

230 *In 1997, grand:* "17 Indicted in Indian Casino Probe," *Los Angeles Times,* April 19, 1997; *United States v. Henry Zottola, Dominic Strollo, Dennis Miller, John Conley, and Pasquale Ferruccio,* U.S. District Court for the Western District of Pennsylvania, Indictment, March 27, 1997. Author's Collection.

230 *But the court: Western Telecon, Inc. v. California State Lottery,* 39 Cal. Reptr.2d 273 (Cal. App. 1995).

230 *As a consequence:* "Ruling May Let Tribes Offer Slot Machines," *Los Angeles Times,* March 29, 1995.

231 *After so holding: Western Telecon, Inc. v. California State Lottery,* 917 P.2d 651 (Cal. 1996).

231 *The day after:* "Slots Targeted After Keno Ruling," *San Francisco Examiner,* June 25, 1996.

232 *Inside the tent:* "Native-American Casino Gets 'Pitched' in Lakeside, California," *Gaming & Wagering Business,* April 5, 1994.

232 *And five months:* George Forman interview.

232 *The other reason:* Dan Kolkey interview.

232 *From Pete Wilson's:* "Indian Gaming and the Rule of Law," *San Diego Union-Tribune,* September 30, 1997.

233 *When Sterling mentioned:* Dan Kolkey interview.

233 *In 1903, the:* Hyer, 116–135.

233 *Ames also recorded:* Ames, 18–19.

233 *The economy was:* "Pala Tribe Gamely Accepts Its Role in Gambling Battle," *Los Angeles Times,* May 13, 1998.

233 *And unlike the:* "Pala Indians OK Plan for Their Own Casno," *San Diego Union-Tribune,* September 12, 1998.

234 *"I didn't want:* Dan Kolkey interview.

234 *According to Forman:* George Forman interview.

235 *Dickstein's cocounsels and:* Testimony of Robert Smith before the National Gambling Impact Study Commission, July 29, 1998, available at http://govinfo .library.unt.edu/ngisc/meetings/jul2998/p210729.html.

235 *When someone gave:* "Tribes Split Over State Gaming Pact," *San Diego Union-Tribune,* September 11, 1997; George Forman interview.

235 *On September 16:* Letter from Richard Milanovich to Robert Smith, September 16, 1997. DK.

235 *On September 18:* Letter from Howard Dickstein to Jerry Levine, Glenn Feldman, George Forman, and Art Bunce, September 22, 1997. DK.

235 *In response, on:* Letter from George Forman to Daniel Kolkey, September 29, 1997. DK.

236 *However, when after:* "Tribes Given Deadline on Slot Machines," *Los Angeles Times,* March 17, 1997.

236 *According to George:* George Forman interview.

236 *In defiance of:* See "When 'Have-Nots' Become 'Haves,'" *Desert Sun,* September 22, 1996, reporting that in its Spa Casino that Agua Caliente Band was operating 1,065 video gaming machines, and in its Spotlight Twenty-Nine Casino, the Twenty-Nine Palms Band was operating 700 machines. And see "Casino Applies for Permit," *Rancho News* (Temecula), September 28, 1995, reporting that the Pechanga Band was installing 200 more video gaming machines in its casino.

237 *"Then we bused:* George Forman interview.

237 *The Los Angeles:* "3,000 Rally for Indian Casinos," *Los Angeles Times,* March 25, 1997.

237 *Unimpressed with the:* Ibid.

238 *When they came:* "Judge Holds Closed Meeting in U.S. Suit Against Casinos," *Los Angeles Times,* May 6, 1997.

238 *The following November: United States v. Santa Ynez Band of Chumash Mission Indians,* U.S. District Court for the Central District of California No. CV 97–1716, Opinion and Order re Motion for Preliminary Injunction (November 4, 1997), 25 Indian Law Reporter 3001, 3005 (1998).

238 *When Judge Letts:* "U.S. Attorneys Likely to Stand Pat on Gaming," *Desert Sun,* April 2, 1998.

238 *On March 6:* Office of Governor Pete Wilson, "Fact Sheet: Tribal Gaming in California: The Historic Pala Compact," March 6, 1998. Author's Collection.

239 *And statewide, all:* See Tribal-State Compact Between the State of California and the Pala Band of Mission Indians, March 6, 1998, copy available at http://www.bia.gov/cs/groups/xoig/documents/text/idc 038217.pdf.

240 *Then the governor:* Transcript of March 6, 1998, press conference announcing the Pala compact. DK.

240 *Presented with that:* "Five More Tribes Sign Compacts," *Desert Sun,* July 14, 1998.

240 *First, the California:* "Tribes Want Clinton to Block State Compact," *Desert Sun,* March 18, 1998.

240 *When nothing came:* "Tribes File Suit Over Pact," *Desert Sun,* April 24, 1998. "Judge Won't Block Gaming Pact," *Los Angeles Times,* April 25, 1998.

240 *On May 13:* "U.S. Files Seizure Papers for Tribes' Casino Games," *Los Angeles Times,* May 15, 1998.

240 *But we ended:* George Forman interview.

241 *The job required:* Davis, 39.

241 *Having no personal:* "Reno to Meet With Tribes Seeking to Defend Calif. Gaming," *Washington Post,* June 7, 1998.

241 *According to Carole:* Frank and Goldberg, 246.

242 *This is not:* "Reno Declines to Enter Gambling Dispute," *Los Angeles Times,* June 11, 1998.

242   *That outcome was:* David Ogden interview.

242   *According to George:* George Forman interview.

242   *Polling the firm:* Meyer, John, 110.

242   *Three months later:* "Indians Denounce Gambling Accord," *Los Angeles Times*, March 10, 1998.

243   *To get them:* "Tribes Mail Petition on Gaming," *Desert Sun*, March 27, 1998.

243   *Raised in Colton:* "Prop. 5 Pitchman Has Starring Role," *Los Angeles Times*, Oct. 25, 1998. And see "Mark Macarro Chairman," available at http://www .pechanga nsn.gov/page?pageId=128.

243   *As the Los Angeles Times described:* "Prop. 5 Pitchman Has Starring Role," 9, October 25, 1998.

244   *And the tribes:* "Tribes Face Deadline on Slot-Like Games," *Los Angeles Times*, April 30, 1998.

244   *But more than:* Scott and Mikesell.

244   *As the Los Angeles Times, without:* "Tribes, Casinos Roll Dice With Early Ad Blitz," *Los Angeles Times*, July 27, 1998.

244   *That was more:* Scott and Mikesell. And see also California Voter Foundation, Follow the Money: Top Ten Contributors—California Propositions, December 31, 1998 [hereinafter "Follow the Money"], available at http://www.calvoter .org/voter/elections/archive/98general/followthemoney/topten1.html.

244   *According to UCLA:* Frank and Goldberg, 249.

245   *So the Band:* Follow the Money.

245   *In her commercial:* "Indian Gaming Initiative Ads Simplify Complex Issue," *Los Angeles Times*, October 2, 1998.

245   *As one political:* Ibid.

245   *For that reason:* "Battle Lines Blurred on Gaming Initiative," *Los Angeles Times*, November 1, 1998.

246   *Collectively, ten of:* Follow the Money.

247   *Two weeks after:* "State High Court Blocks Indian Gaming Measure," *Los Angeles Times*, December 3, 1998.

247   *Eight months later:* Hotel Employees and Restaurant Employees International Union v. Davis, 981 P.2d 990 (Cal. 1999).

247   *In 1994 when:* "Indian Casinos Not Ready to Remove Slots," *Los Angeles Times*, November 17, 1994; Tom Umberg—Attorney General, 1993–1994 Campaign Contribution Disclosure Statements. California State Archives. Sacramento, California.

247   *They gave Lungren's:* Brenkert, 152–153.

247   *In August at:* "Lungren, Davis Spar on Abortion, Gun Control," *Los Angeles Times*, August 1, 1998.

247   *He excoriated the:* "Tribes Put Their Bets on Davis, Campaign Now Declines Casinos' Contributions," *Sacramento Bee*, July 27, 1998.

248   *And several other:* Ibid.

248   *And when Davis:* "Tribal Leaders Confident of Davis' Support," *Los Angeles Times*, December 25, 1998.

248   *According to George:* George Forman interview.

248   *Apparently on the:* "Mickey Kantor Appointed to Assist CA Indians on Tribal

Gaming," *PRNewswire*, May 4, 1999; "Indian Gaming, Clinton Advisor to Represent Tribes," *Las Vegas Sun*, May 6, 1999; "California Tribal Leaders to Meet With Governor's Representatives for Tribal-State Gaming Talks," *PRNewswire*, May 11, 1999; "63 Tribes, Davis Aide Will Begin Talks on Gambling," *Los Angeles Times*, May 13, 1999.

248 **And prior to:** "Tribes Donate Heavily to State Candidates," *Los Angeles Times*, May 24, 1998.

249 **John Burton, the:** "Davis Holds Summit on Indian Casino Issue," *Los Angeles Times*, August 26, 1999.

249 **In July, Letts:** "Judge Against Video Gaming," *Desert Sun*, July 21, 1998.

249 **If by that:** "Tribes Confident Machines Will Stay," *Desert Sun*, July 22, 1998. "Judge Asks U.S., Tribes for Feedback on Workers," *Los Angeles Times*, September 16, 1998.

249 **So instead of:** Ibid; "Judge Set to Crack Down on Indian Gaming," *Sacramento Bee*, September 16, 1998.

250 **During the meeting:** "Davis, Legislative Leaders Hold Gaming Summit With Indians," *Sacramento Bee*, August 26, 1999; "Davis Holds Summit on Indian Casino Issue," *Los Angeles Times*, August 26, 1999.

250 **And by the:** "Indians Launch New Try," *Sacramento Bee*, August 24, 1999.

250 **In response, the:** "Negotiations Continue on Indian Gaming," *Sacramento Bee*, September 2, 1999.

251 **And revenue would:** Simmons, 11, 33, 58.

251 **The Morongo and:** "Backers of Indian Casino Measure Double War Chest," *Los Angeles Times*, February 29, 2000.

251 **Bustamante won the:** "Bustamante and McClintock Deny Any Dealing for Donations," *Sacramento Bee*, August 29, 2003; "Tribes Have Become Players in Sacramento," *Los Angeles Times*, September 20, 2003.

252 **The commercial concluded:** "Ad Watch: Arnold Schwarzenegger," *Los Angeles Times*, September 24, 2003.

252 **Because he was:** California Governor Arnold Schwarzenegger, State of the State Address, January 6, 2004, transcript posted at http://www.govspeech.org/#2004.

14: Fake Tribes

page

254 **Hey, everybody wants:** "With Casino Profits Indian Tribes Thrive," *New York Times*, January 31, 1993.

254 **In 1941, Felix:** Cohen, 268.

254 **To be an:** Section 4(5), Public Law No. 100–497, 102 Statutes 2467, 2468 (1988).

254 **In 1979, when:** "Indian Tribal Entities That Have a Government-to-Government Relationship With the United States," 44 *Federal Register* 7231, February 6, 1979.

254 **In 2015, there:** "Indian Entities Recognized and Eligible to Receive Services From the United States Bureau of Indian Affairs," 80 *Federal Register* 1942, January 14, 2015.

256 **After inspecting their:** Report from Albert Lassiter, Acting Area Director, BIA, to Commissioner, BIA, July 19, 1967. DSH.

256 **The title to:** H.R. 18565, 90th Cong., July 15, 1968.

256 **As Rep. Wayne Aspinall:** Authorizing the Acquisition of a Village Site for the Payson Band of Yavapai-Apache Indians," 117 *Congressional Record* 41,136 (1971).

256 **Department of the Interior:** Letter from Harrison Loesch, assistant secretary of the interior, to the Hon. Wayne N. Aspinall, September 20, 1971, reprinted in House Report No. 92–635, at 3–7 (1971).

257 **However, because Arizona:** Public Law No. 92–470, 86 Statutes 783 (1972).

258 **In 1972 Tureen:** Brodeur.

258 **In 1975 Judge:** *Joint Tribal Council of the Passamaquoddy Tribe v. Morton*, 388 F. Supp. 649 (D. Me. 1975, *affirmed*, 528 F.2d 370 (1st Cir. 1975).

258 **His decision set:** Maine Indian Claims Settlement Act, Public Law No. 96–420, 94 Statutes 1785 (1980).

259 **To find out:** Benedict, 20–23.

259 **In response to:** De Forest, 262–263.

259 **In 1910, only:** Hauptman and Wherry, 135–136.

259 **They had lived:** Benedict, 148–149.

260 **Nevertheless, he explained:** Ibid., 35–36.

261 **When he filed the lawsuit:** Ibid., 102.

262 **Several days later:** Ibid.

263 **And when Cohen:** *Chitimacha and Mashantucket Pequot Indian Land Claims: Hearing on S. 2294 and S. 2719 Before the Senate Select Committee on Indian Affairs*, 97th Cong. 73 (1982).

263 **And Hayward volunteered:** *Settlement of Indian Land Claims in the States of Connecticut and Louisiana: Hearing on H.R. 5358 and H.R. 6612 Before the House Committee on interior and Insular Affairs*, 97th Cong. 48 (1982) [hereinafter "Pequot House Hearing"].

263 **In October, H.R. 6612:** 128 *Congressional Record* 27,396 (1982); 128 *Congressional Record* 31,610 (1982).

263 **Skip Hayward told:** "Veto of Mashantucket Land Bill Draws Ire," *New London Day*, April 6, 1983.

264 **When Representative Gejdenson:** Pequot House Hearing, at 40.

265 **In exchange for:** Benedict, 143.

265 **Less than three:** "Indians Look to Connecticut for Beano," *Bangor Daily News*, November 4, 1983.

265 **Skip Hayward told:** "Bingo Opens in Ledyard to Full, Very Smokey House," *New London Day*, July 6, 1986.

265 **Within a month:** "We're Expanding; Watch Out, AC," *Gaming & Wagering Business*, May 15–June 14, 1992.

265 **By 1994, the:** "Foxwoods, a Casino Success Story," *New York Times*, August 8, 1994.

266 **During the 2014:** State of Connecticut, Foxwoods Casino: Schedule of Selected Video Facsimile/Slot Machine Data for the Period Jan. 1, 1993 Through July 31, 2015, available at http://www.ct.gov/dcp/lib/dcp/pdf/gaming/fosltweb.pdf.

266 **In 2010, the:** "Butler Says He's Focused on Ensuring Mashantucket's Stability," *New London Day*, January 8, 2010.

266 **But as Bruce:** Fromson, 221.

266 *According to Casanova:* Ibid., 156–157.

266 *But until 2009:* "Reorder Priorities," *New London Day*, August 28, 2009; "Mashantuckets to End Incentive Payments," *New London Day*, July 10, 2010; "Gaming Tribes Facing Fresh Financial Scrutiny," *Gambling Compliance Ltd.*, July 16, 2010, available at http://www.gamblingcompliance.com /node/43614.

267 *While the teenager:* Sarris, 140–143; "The Invisible People," *Los Angeles Times*, June 16, 1996.

267 *Sarris says Reinette:* "Greg Sarris Tracing Family History," California State University, Sonoma, March 24, 2005, posted at http://www.youtube.com /watch?v =CFNhNYCeVZc.

267 *Sarris could take:* Ibid.

267 *In 1998, Sarris:* H.R. 4434, 105th Cong., August 6, 1998.

267 *In 2000 when:* H.R. 946, H.R. 4148—*To Make Technical Amendments to the Provisions of the Indian Self-Determination and Education Assistance Act Relating to Contract Support Costs, and for Other Purposes. "Tribal Contract Support Cost Technical Amendments of 2000": Oversight Hearing Before the House Committee on Resources*, 106th Cong. 72, 75 (2000) [hereinafter "H.R. 946 Hearing"].

267 *In 1904, the:* Memorial of the Northern California Indian Association, Praying That Lands Be Allotted to the Landless Indians of the Northern Part of the State of California, Senate Document No. 58–131 (1904).

268 *The Graton Rancheria:* House Report No. 85–1129, at 12–13 (1957).

268 *At the urging:* California Rancheria Act, Public Law No. 85–671, 72 Statutes 619 (1958).

268 *In 1966, the:* Notice of Termination of Federal Supervision Over Property and Individual Members, 31 *Federal Register* 2911 (1966).

268 *In 1992, the:* "Pomo Indians Eye Tomales Bay, *Press Democrat*, March 23, 1992; "Miwoks: 'Over Our Dead Bodies,'" *Press Democrat*, March 28, 1992.

268 *At the beginning:* "The Invisible People," *Los Angeles Times*, June 16, 1996.

268 *After interviewing Sarris:* "Coast Miwoks Fight for Recognition," *Indian Country Today*, August 2, 2000.

269 *The director concluded:* Memorandum from Director, BIA Office of Tribal Services, to Director, Office of Congressional and Legislative Affairs, September 8, 1998, available at http://www.stopthecasino101.com/gratonrancheria.html.

269 *Today, Greg Sarris:* "Graton Rancheria Tribe's Growth Likely Limited," *Press Democrat*, April 4, 2013.

269 *At the Committee:* H.R. 946 Hearing, at 78.

270 *She also reported:* Memorandum titled "Miwok Update" from SL to LW, August 28, 2000. LW.

270 *Another two months:* See 146 *Congressional Record* 25,037 and 26,572 (2000).

270 *What is known:* "Casino Proposed Near Sears Point," *Marin Independent Journal*, April 24, 2003.

271 *When I asked:* Lynn Woolsey interview.

271 *Woolsey was so:* H.R. 2656, 108th Cong., June 26, 2003.

271 *The land, which:* "Rohnert Park Casino Set to Open Nov. 5," *Press Democrat*, September 19, 2013.

271 *Station Casinos has:* "Graton Casino's Earnings Beat Expectations," *Press Democrat*, May 31, 2014; "California Indian Casino Built and Managed by Station Casinos Rising to Top of Class," *Casino City Times*, July 8, 2014.

272 *In 1891, Congress:* Chapter 65, 26 Statutes 712 (1891).

272 *Because the land:* Report of the Mission Indian Commissioners, at 48 (December 29, 1891), copy available at A.K. Smiley Public Library, Redlands, California.

272 *In 1906 L.A.:* Annual Report of Commissioner of Indian Affairs to the Secretary of the Interior (1906), at 205, 207.

272 *And prior to:* House Report No. 81–800, at 3 (1949).

272 *In 1947 a:* Letter from Margaret Andreas to Bureau of Indian Affairs, December 18, 1947. Records of the Southern California Agency, BIA.

272 *By 1972 there:* BIA, Sacramento, California, Roll of Augustine Band of Mission Indians Prepared in Accordance with the Provisions of the Act of August 25, 1950, January 20, 1956. Records of the Southern California Agency, BIA.

272 *She then met:* "Last in the Line," *Press-Enterprise*, January 4, 1998.

273 *During the hearing: Gaming Activities on Indian Reservations and Lands: Hearing on S. 555 and S. 1303 Before the Senate Committee on Indian Affairs,* 100th Cong. 93 (1987).

273 *According to Shull:* Letter from Robert J. Shull, California Indian Legal Services, to Assistant Secretary of the Interior for Indian Affairs, October 27, 1988. Records of the Southern California Agency, BIA.

274 *When the general:* See Augustine Band of Mission Indians Resolution Nos. 88–1 and 88–3 (July 29, 1988). Records of the Southern California Agency, BIA.

274 *They are seeking:* Letter from Timothy Sanford-Wachtel, California Indian Legal Services, to Virgil Townsend, Acting Superintendent, BIA Southern California Agency, August 15, 1990. Records of the Southern California Agency, BIA.

274 *That vouch accomplished:* Memorandum from Frances L. Muncy, Acting Superintendent, BIA Southern California Agency, to BIA Sacramento Area Director, June 6, 1991. Records of the Southern California Agency, BIA.

275 *Three weeks later:* Memorandum from Amy Dutschke, BIA Area Director, Sacramento Area Office, to Virgil Townsend, Superintendent, BIA Southern California Agency, June 24, 1991. Records of the Southern California Agency, BIA.

275 *Three years later, Mary:* See *People of State of California v. McKinnon,* 259 P.2d 1186 (Cal. 2011).

275 *Here is how:* EPA, Waste Management in Indian Country, Augustine Band of Cahuilla Mission Indians of the August Reservation, November 1, 1999. Although no longer available, was posted at http://www.epa.Gov/epaoswer/non-hw/tribal/augustine.htm.

276 *Three years later the Environmental:* Ibid.

276 *Five months later:* "Tiny Valley Tribe Near Deal on Coachella Casino," *Desert Sun*, August 8, 2000.

276 *The gaming floor:* "Intimate New Valley Casino Holds Big Opening Night," *Desert Sun*, July 19, 2002.

277 *The third member:* See Thomas N. Tureen, "Federal Recognition and the 'Passamaquoddy' Decision," reprinted in "Report of Task Force Ten: Terminated and Nonfederally Recognized Indian," at 1653–1674 (1976).

277 *At Task Force:* American Indian Policy Review Commission, Final Report, at 480 (1977).

278 *A year earlier:* Procedures Governing Determination That Indian Group Is a Federally Recognized Tribe, 42 *Federal Register* 30,647 (1977); Procedures for Establishing That an American Indian Group Exists as an Indian Tribe, 43 *Federal Register* 23,743 (1978).

278 *When Wyoming representative: Federal Recognition of Indian Tribes: Hearing on H.R. 13733 and Similar Bills Before the Subcommittee on Indian Affairs and Public Lands of the House Committee on Interior and Insular Affairs,* 95th Cong. 22 (1978).

278 *But two weeks:* 43 *Federal Register* 39,361 (1978).

278 *As of November:* Bureau of Indian Affairs, Office of Federal Acknowledgment, List of Petitioners by State (as of Nov. 12, 2013), available at http://www .bia.gov/cs /groups/xofa/documents/text/idc1–024418.pdf.

15: FAKE RESERVATIONS
page

280 *Just like real:* "Off the Reservation: Tribes Are Moving to Open More Casinos Far From Home," *Native Sun News,* July 18–24, 2012.

280 *In 1938, the:* Memorandum entitled "Lytton Rancheria," from Maurice Babby to Williams, Supervisory Program Officer, BIA, June 12, 1959. Record Group 75, BIA Sacramento Area Office, Tribal Group Files 1915–1972, National Archives—Pacific Region.

280 *After Bert Steele:* Property of California Rancherias and of Individual Members Thereof, Termination of Federal Supervision, 26 *Federal Register* 6875 (1961).

281 *A quarter of: Scotts Valley Band of Pomo Indians of the Sugar Bowl Rancheria v. United States,* U.S. District Court for the Northern District of California No. C-86–3660.

281 *In that agreement*: Stipulation for Entry of Judgment (March 14 and 21, 1991) and Order for Entry of Judgment and Judgment (August 30, 1991), *Scotts Valley Band of Pomo Indians of the Sugar Bowl Rancheria v. United States,* U.S. District Court for the Northern District of California No. C-86–3660.

281 *In 1993, the:* 58 *Federal Register* 54,364, 54,367 (1993).

281 *Sixteen months before:* Lytton-Sonoma Ventures, Inc., California Secretary of State Entity No. C1190658, available at http://kepler.sos.ca.gov/. And see also "Alexander Valley Upset by Proposal for Indian Bingo," *San Francisco Chronicle,* December 10, 1990.

281 *On August 6:* Grant Deed from Merrill Holmes to William Pedraza and George P. Vlassis, August 6, 1986. Instrument No. 1986099580, Book 82 of Maps, page 23, Sonoma County Records.

282 *On October 9:* Management and Economic Development Agreement, Oct. 9, 1988, copy attached to Affidavit of Carol J. Steele, September 17, 1990, *Scotts Valley Band of Pomo Indians of the Sugar Bowl Rancheria v. United States,* U.S. District Court for the Northern District of California No. C-86–3660.

282 *The business plan:* Business Plan, Lytton Station Bingo, October 1, 1988.

282 *Carol Joyce Steele later said:* "Documents for Indian Bingo Parlor Forged, Says D.A.," *Press Democrat,* May 1, 1991.

282 *He then began:* Sam Katz interview.

282   *But the sententious:* "AmCan Casino in the Spotlight," *Times Herald* (Vallejo), January 25, 1998; "AmCan Casino in Doubt, *Times Herald* (Vallejo), January 28, 1998; "Tribe Seeks Support for AmCan Casino," *Times Herald* (Vallejo), January 30, 1998.

283   *The city then:* Sharon Brown interview.

283   *Initially, the 100-table:* Ibid.

284   *Mejia did both:* "San Pablo Development Lifts Mood Amid Recession," *San Francisco Chronicle*, November 29, 2010.

284   *According to Katz:* Sam Katz interview.

285   *When the Indian:* 146 *Congressional Record* 25,058 (2000).

285   *In October 2003:* Proclaiming Certain Lands as Reservation for the Lytton Rancheria of California, 69 *Federal Register* 42,066 (2004).

285   *By 2008, the:* "Slot Machines Only 20 Minutes From S.F.," *San Francisco Examiner*, July 9, 2009.

285   *In 1990, Stephen:* Letter from Stephen Quesenberry, California Indian Legal Services, to Glen Goodsell, Attorney, U.S. Department of Justice, February 13, 1990.

285   *In 2005 Margie:* Lytton Rancheria of California: Hearing on S. 113 Before the Senate Committee on Indian Affairs, 109th Cong. 17 (2005).

286   *When Houle asked:* John Fedo interview.

286   *Fedo's first idea:* "Old Ore Boat May Harbor Bingo Parlor," *News-Tribune & Herald* (Duluth), January 26, 1984; "Indians Charge Developers Trying to Scuttle Bingo Plans," *News-Tribune & Herald* (Duluth), January 27, 1984.

286   *The profit would:* See *City of Duluth v. Fond du Lac Band of Lake Superior Chippewa*, 708 F. Supp.2d 890, 893–894 (D. Minn. 2010) (division of the profits described).

287   *Fedo and several:* "Cities League Meeting Ends Amid Gloom," *Los Angeles Times*, December 2, 1982.

287   *Members of the:* John Fedo interview.

287   *And because of:* Ibid.

287   *In June, Fritz:* Memorandum from Deputy Assistant Secretary—Indian Affairs, to Minneapolis Area Director, June 13, 1985. Author's Collection; "Former Sears Store in Duluth Approved for Indian Trust Land Bingo Venture," Bureau of Indian Affairs, Vol. 9, No. 24, *Indian News Notes*, reprinted in 131 *Congressional Record* 18926 (1985).

287   *On behalf of:* Addition of Certain Lands to the Fond du Lac Indian Reservation, 51 *Federal Register* 3263 (1986).

288   *In 1987, video:* "Authority Over Indian Casinos Remains Unclear," *News-Tribune & Herald* (Duluth), March 2, 1988.

288   *In 1994 real:* "Fond-du-Luth Marks 20 Years," *Duluth News-Tribune*, September 24, 2006.

288   *In 2003 the:* "Duluth, Minn., Casino Drops Bingo," *Knight Ridder/Tribune Business News*, March 19, 2003.

288   *And throughout his:* Ross Swimmer interview.

288   *But as a general:* "Interior Announces Policy on Taking Land Into Trust," *One Feather*, February 19, 1986.

288   *In February 1986:* Policy Decision on Implementation of Bureau of Indian Affairs Land Acquisition Regulations, 51 *Federal Register* 5993 (1986).

289 **Bereuter's bill gave:** H.R. 3130, 99th Cong. (July 31, 1985), reprinted in *Indian Gambling Control Act: Hearing on H.R. 1920 and H.R. 2404 Before the House Committee on Interior and Insular Affairs*, 99th Cong., Part II, 17 (1985).

289 **As Udall explained:** Ibid., 25.

289 **When the members:** H.R. 1920 Mark-up Transcript, December 4, 1985. USHR.

290 **But the prohibition:** Andrews Amendment No. 3226 to H.R. 1920, Sec. 4, 99th Cong., reprinted in 132 *Congressional Record* 29027 (1986).

290 In May 1988: S. 555 Mark-up Transcript, May 13, 1988. USS.

291 **Although no treaty:** Covington, 268–270; Kersey, *An Assumption of Sovereignty*, 184–189.

291 **In 1989, the:** *Tamiami Partners, Ltd. v. Miccosukee Tribe of Indians of Florida*, 22 *Indian Law Reporter* 2177 (11th Cir. 1995).

291 **One of Tamiami:** "White Man's Money," *Miami Herald*, October 31, 1993.

292 **And Ingenito purchased:** *Mandel v. Miccosukee Tribal Gaming Agency*, 22 *Indian Law Reporter* 6148 (Mickosukee Tribal Court 1994); Pennsylvania Crime Commission, Racketeering and Organized Crime in the Bingo Industry, at 19 (April 1992).

292 **When he disapproved:** Memorandum entitled "Guidance on Taking Off-Reservation Land into Trust for Gaming Purposes," from Carl Artman to Regional Directors, BIA, January 3, 2008. Author's collection. See also *Department of Interior's Recently Released Guidance on Taking Land Into Trust for Indian Tribes and Its Ramifications: Oversight Hearing Before the House Committee on Natural Resources*, 110th Cong. (2008) [hereinafter "Artman Oversight Hearing"].

292 **Leaders of tribes:** Memorandum entitled "Guidance for Processing Applications to Acquire Land in Trust for Gaming Purposes," from Assistant Secretary—Indian Affairs to Regional Directors, BIA, June 13, 2011. Author's collection.

293 **The reason was:** Artman Oversight Hearing, at 69.

293 **In 2012, the:** "$1 Million Each Year for All, as Long as Tribe's Luck Holds," *New York Times*, August 9, 2012.

293 **The casino's gaming:** "Ramos Turned Tax-Free Dollars Into a Political Empire," *San Bernardino Sun*, October 30, 2012.

293 **In 2012 the:** "Miccosukee Tribe Member Testifies She Didn't Pay Her Miami Lawyers in Perjury Hearing," *Miami Herald*, April 16, 2013.

294 **In the treaty:** Article 2, Treaty with the Sioux and Arapaho, 15 Statutes 635, 636 (1869).

294 **By 1875, more:** Robinson, 162–163.

294 **In 1889, Congress:** 25 Statutes 888 (1889).

295 **Housing on the:** "Clinton, Amid the Despair in a Reservation, Again Pledges Help," *New York Times*, July 8, 1999.

295 **And here is:** "Situation of Youth on Pine Ridge Reservation," *Medicine Wheel Hearing Community*, January 26, 2014, posted at http://www.medicinewhl.org/.

295 **According to Kristof:** "Poverty's Poster Child," *New York Times*, May 9, 2012.

296 **By October 1995:** "Proposed Cuts in Indian Programs Hit Those Who rely Most on Federal Aid," *New York Times*, October 15, 1995; "For Poorest Indians, Casinos Aren't Enough," *New York Times*, June 11, 1997.

296   **By 2006, the:** "Taking a Peek at the New Prairie Wind Casino," *Lakota Country Times*, Jan. 18–24, 2007.

296   **By then, the:** "Prairie Wind Casino Celebrates Opening With Generosity," *Lakota Country Times*, June 28–July 4, 2007.

296   **Less than a:** "OST Council Hires Management Team for Casino to Bring Up Revenue," *Lakota Country Times*, February 7–13, 2008.

296   **But according to:** Communication from Jeffrey Whalen to Author, November 23, 2014.

298   **And when I:** Jeffrey Whalen interview.

298   **So the council:** Ibid.

EPILOGUE
page

299   **Yes, in some:** "Economic Pulse: Indian Country; Economies Come to Life on Indian Reservations," *New York Times*, July 3, 1994.

299   **When the Foxwoods:** "Not a Grandma Moses Picture: Poker in the Woods," *New York Times*, February 16, 1992.

299   **In January 1993:** "Slot Machines Are Delayed; Weiker's Deal Is Hailed," *New York Times*, January 16, 1993.

299   **By June, Foxwoods:** "Report Suggests Ledyard Casino Is Among the Most Profitable," *New York Times*, July 16, 1993.

299   **Three casinos that:** "Two Trump Bankruptcies," *New York Times*, March 10, 1992.

299   **As Trump, with:** Transcript of WFAN-AM Broadcast, June 18, 1993, reprinted in 139 *Congressional Record* 14,508 (1993).

300   **To try to:** *Donald Trump v. Bruce Babbitt*, U.S. District Court for the District of New Jersey Civil Action No. 93–1882. And see also "Trump, in a Federal Lawsuit, Seeks to Block Indian Casinos," *New York Times*, May 4, 1993.

300   **Then he recruited:** H.R. 2287, 103d Cong., May 26, 1993. And see also "Nevada, N.J. Legislators Sponsor Indian Gaming Bills," *Gaming & Wagering Business*, July 15–August 14, 1993.

300   **In 1992, Caesars:** "Tribe, Caesars to Build Casino in Palm Springs," *Los Angeles Times*, November 18, 1992.

300   **When Donald Trump:** "The Donald Meets the Richard," *Desert Sun*, February 26, 1993.

300   **Trump flew to:** "Seminoles Say Trump Is Looking to Deal; Many Suitors Await Ruling on Casino Rights," *Sun-Sentinel*, March 15, 1996 ; "Seminole Gambling: A Trail of Millions," *St. Petersburg Times*, December 22, 1997.

300   **However, four years:** "When 'Have-Nots' Become 'Haves': Spotlight 29," *Desert Sun*, September 22, 1996.

300   **When the news:** "Las Vegas Glitz Is Set to Go West," *New York Times*, March 10, 2000.

301   **And it has:** See 2003 Annual Report, Station Casinos, Inc., at 72; "Notice of Intent to Prepare an Environmental Impact Statement for the North Fork Rancheria's Proposed Trust Acquisition and Hotel/Casino Project, Madera County, California," 69 *Federal Register* 62721 (2004).

301   **Billions of those:** Meister.

302 ***In 2000, the:*** "Casino Boom a Bust for Most Members of Indian Tribes," News-Gazette (Champaign, IL), September 2, 2000.

303 ***Here, for example:*** Oversight Hearing on *"Indian Gaming: The Next 25 Years" before the Senate Committee on Indian Affairs,* 113th Cong. (2014), available at http://www.indian.senate.gov/hearing/oversight-hearing-indian -gaming-next-25 years.

303 ***Also in 2012:*** Ibid.

304 ***Section 6 of:*** Section 6, H.R. 4566, 98th Cong., November 18, 1983.

305 ***In 1964, Charles:*** "The New Property," 73 *Yale Law Journal* 733 (1964).

BIBLIOGRAPHY

Abourezk, James G. *Advise & Dissent: Memoirs of South Dakota and the U.S. Senate.* Chicago: Lawrence Hill Books, 1989.

Allbritton, Orval E. *The Mob at the Spa: Organized Crime and Its Fascination with Hot Springs, Arkansas.* Hot Springs, Arkansas: Garland County Historical Society, 2011.

American Gaming Association. *2011 State of the States: The AGA Survey of Casino Entertainment.* Available at http://www.americangaming.org/files/aga/uploads/docs/sos/aga-sos-2011.pdf.

American Indian Policy Review Commission. *Final Report,* Washington, D.C.: U.S. Government Printing Office, 1977.

Ames, Florence. *Survey of Indian Reservations of Southern California.* Unpublished, 1927. Available at Shields Library, University of California, Davis.

Anderson, Gary Clayton, and Alan R. Woolworth. *Through Dakota Eyes: Narrative Accounts of the Minnesota Indian War of 1862.* St. Paul: Minnesota Historical Society Press, 1988.

Anderson, Martin. *Revolution: The Reagan Legacy.* Stanford, California: Hoover Institution Press, 1990.

Anderson, Paul. *Janet Reno: Doing the Right Thing.* New York: John Wiley & Sons, Inc., 1994.

Bailey, Garrick, and Roberta Glenn Bailey. *A History of the Navajos: The Reservation Years.* Santa Fe: School of American Research Press, 1986.

Baker, Bobby. *Wheeling and Dealing: Confessions of a Capitol Hill Operator.* New York: W.W. Norton & Company, Inc., 1978.

Beck, Warren A., and David A. Williams. *California: A History of the Golden State.* Garden City, New York: Doubleday & Company, Inc., 1972.

Benedict, Jeff. *Without Reservation: The Making of America's Most Powerful Indian Tribe and Foxwoods, the World's Largest Casino.* New York: HarperCollins, 2000.

Block, Allan. "IRS Intelligence Operations Under the Alexander Regime: A Commentary on Undercover Operations," reprinted in *Crime, Law, and Social Change,* at 76 (September 1992).

Boies, David. *Courting Justice.* New York: Hyperion, 2004.

Bourke, John G. *An Apache Campaign in the Sierra Madre.* New York: Charles Scribner's Sons, 1958.

Brewer, Suzette, ed. *Sovereign: An Oral History of Indian Gaming in America.* Albuquerque: Ipanema Literatures, 2009.

Brenkert, George, ed. *Corporate Integrity and Accountability.* Thousand Oaks, California: SAGE Publications, 2004.

Brodeur, Paul. "Annuals of Law: Restitution." *The New Yorker,* October 11, 1982.

Buchanan, John. *Jackson's Way: Andrew Jackson and the People of the Western Waters.* New York: John Wiley & Sons, 2001.

Buttes, Barbara Freezor. *Beyond Sovereignty: The Mdewakanton Identify Heist.* 2005. Available at http://www.mklaw. com/pdfs/027.pdf.

Cahill, William P., and Robert M. Jarvis. *Out of the Muck: A History of the Broward Sheriff's Office, 1915-2000*, Durham: Carolina Academic Press, 2010.

Cardano, Gerolamo, *The Book on Games of Chance.* New York: Holt, Rinehart & Winston, 1961.

Carr, Thomas P. *Suspension of the Rules in the House of Representatives.* The Library of Congress: Congressional Research Service, 2005.

Carrico, Richard, *Strangers in a Stolen Land: Indians of San Diego County from Prehistory to the New Deal*, San Diego: Sunbelt Publications, 2008.

Carson, Donald W., and James W. Johnson. *Mo: The Life & Times of Morris K. Udall*, Tucson: University of Arizona Press, 2001.

Cattelino, Jessica R. *High Stakes: Florida Seminole Gaming and Sovereignty.* Durham: Duke University Press, 2008.

Clinton, Bill. *My Life.* New York: Alfred A. Knopf, 2004.

Cohen, Felix S. *Handbook of Federal Indian Law.* Washington, D.C.: General Printing Office, 1942.

Collier, John. *From Every Zenith: A Memoir.* Denver: Sage Books, 1963.

Connolly, John. "Badlands: How Did a Former CIA Man Take Over a Tribe of Impoverished Indians Near Palm Springs." *Spy Magazine* (April 1992).

Cory, Charles B. *Hunting and Fishing in Florida, Including a Key to the Water Birds Known to Occur in the State.* Boston: Estes & Lauriat, 1896.

Covington, James W. *The Seminoles of Florida.* Gainesville: University Press of Florida, 1993.

Crooks, Norman. *Reminisences of Norman Crooks, Mdewakanton Community of Prior Lake, Minnesota.* Vermillion: American Indian Research Project, University of South Dakota, 1972.

Dana, Richard Henry Jr., *Two Years Before the Mast.* Boston: Houghton Mifflin Co., 1911.

Davis, Lanny J. *Truth to Tell.* New York: The Free Press, 1999.

De Forest, John W. *History of the Indians of Connecticut From the Earliest Known Period to 1850.* Hartford, Connecticut: William James Hamersley, 1851.

Deitche, Scott M. *Cigar City Mafia: A Complete History of the Tampa Underworld.* Fort Lee, New Jersey: Barricade, 2004.

Deloria, Vine, Jr., and Clifford Lytle. *The Nations Within: The Past and Future of American Indian Sovereignty.* New York: Pantheon Books, 1984.

Demaris, Ovid. *The Last Mafioso: The Treacherous World of Jimmy Fratianno.* New York: Times Books, 1981.

DeMichele, Matthew, and Gary Potter. "Sin City Revisited: A Case Study of the Official Sanctioning of Organized Crime in an 'Open City,'" available at http://www.rootsweb.ancestry.com/~kycampbe/newportgambling.htm.

de Tocqueville, Alexis. *Democracy in America.* New York: Alfred A. Knopf, 1985.

Dial, Adolph L., and David K. Eliades. *The Only Land I Know: A History of the Lumbee Indians.* San Francisco: The Indian Historian Press, 1975.

Doody, Louis Philip, and Betty Kikumi Meltzer. *Losing Ground: The Displacement of San Gorgonio Pass Cahuilla People in the 19th Century.* Banning, California: Malki-Ballena Press, 2007.

Ducheneaux, Franklin. "Legislative History of the Indian Gaming Regulatory Act of 1988," speech delivered at a symposium on Indian Gaming in Montana, University of Montana School of Law, April 26, 2006 ["Ducheneaux IGRA History"], available at http://www.umt.edu/law/library/IT/nalsa.htm.

_____. "The Indian Gaming Regulatory Act: Background and Legislative History." 42 *Arizona State Law Journal* 99 (2010).

Ducheneaux, Franklin, and Peter S. Taylor. *Tribal Sovereignty and the Powers of the National Indian Gaming Commission*. Washington, D.C.: National Indian Gaming Association and resources Center (2006), available at http://indiangaming.org/library/studies/1052-tribal_sovereignty.pdf.

Eadington, William R., ed. *Indian Gaming and the Law*. Reno: Institute for the Study of Gambling and Commercial Gaming, 1990.

Edmunds, David R., ed. *The New Warriors: Native American Leaders Since 1900*. Lincoln: University of Nebraska Press, 2001.

Eisenberg, Dennis, Uri Dan , and Eli Landau. *Meyer Lansky: Mogul of the Mob*. New York: Paddington Press Ltd, 1979.

Eisler, Kim Issac. *Revenge of the Pequots: How a Small Native American Tribe Created the World's Most Profitable Casino*. New York: Simon & Schuster, 2001.

English, T.J. *Havana Nocturne: How the Mob Owned Cuba—And Then Lost It to the Revolution*. New York: William Morrow, 2008.

Farrell, Ronald A., and Carol Case. *The Black Book and the Mob: The Untold Story of the Control of Nevada's Casinos*. Madison: University of Wisconsin Press, 1995.

Federal Bureau of Investigation. *Nevada Gambling Industry*. Las Vegas: Las Vegas Field Office, November 16, 1964.

Fey, Marshall. *Slot Machines: America's Favorite Gaming Device* Reno, Nevada: 6th ed. Liberty Belle Books, 2006.

Finger, John R. *Cherokee Americans: The Eastern Band of Cherokees in the Twentieth Century*. Lincoln: University of Nebraska Press, 1991.

Fitzpatrick, John, ed. *The Writings of George Washington from the Original Manuscript Sources, 1745–1799*. 39 vols. Washington, D.C.: Government Printing Office, 1931–1944.

Frank, Gelya, and Carole Goldberg. *Defying the Odds: The Tule River Tribe's Struggle for Sovereignty in Three Centuries*. New Haven: Yale University Press, 2010.

Fromson, Brett D. *Hitting the Jackpot: The Inside Story of the Richest Indian Tribe in History*. New York: Atlantic Monthly Press, 2003.

Getches, David H., Charles F. Wilkinson, and Robert A. Williams Jr. *Cases and Materials on Federal Indian Law* 5th ed. St. Paul: West Publishing Company, 2005.

Gosch, Martin A., and Richard Hammer. *The Last Testament of Lucky Luciano*. Boston: Little, Brown and Co., 1974.

Graves, Kathy Davis, and Elizabeth Ebbot. *Indians in Minnesota* 5th ed. Minneapolis: University of Minnesota Press, 2006.

Haas, Theodore H. "Ten Years of Tribal Government Under the I.R.A." United States Indian Service, 1947.

Hair, William Ivy. *The Kingfish and His Realm: The Life and Times of Huey P. Long*. Baton Rouge: Louisiana State University Press, 1991.

Harpster, Jack. *King of the Slots: William "Si" Redd*. Santa Barbara, California: Praeger, 2010.

Hauptman, Laurence M., and James D. Wherry (eds.). *The Pequots in Southern New England: The Fall and Rise of an American Indian Nation*. Norman: University of Oklahoma Press, 1990.

Heizer, Robert F., volume ed. *Handbook of North American Indians (California)*. Washington, D.C.: Smithsonian Institution, 1978.

_____. *Federal Concern About Conditions of California Indians 1853 to 1913: Eight Documents*. Socorro, New Mexico: Ballena Press, 1979.

Hoffman, Harlan Lanas. *In the Shadow of the Mountain: The Cahuilla, Serrano, and Cupeno People of the Morongo Indian Reservation, 1885-1934*. Riverside: Ph.D. Dissertation: University of California, 2006.

Hu-DeHart, Evelyn. *Yaqui Resistance and Survival: The Struggle for Land and Autonomy, 1821-1910*. Madison: University of Wisconsin Press, 1984.

Hughes, John C. *Slade Gorton: A Half Century in Politics*. Olympia, Washington: Washington State Heritage Center, 2011.

Hughes, Tom. *History of Banning and San Gorgonio Pass*. Banning, California: Banning Recod Print, 1937.

Hyer, Joel R. *"We Are Not Savages": Native Americans in Southern California and the Pala Reservation, 1840-1920*. East Lansing: Michigan State University Press, 2001.

Institute for Government Research. *The Problem of Indian Administration*. Baltimore: The Johns Hopkins Press, 1928.

Iverson, Peter. *The Navajo Nation*. Westport, Connecticut: Greenwood Press, 1981.

Jackson, Helen Hunt, and Abbot Kenney. *Report on the Condition and Needs of the Mission Indians*. reprinted at Senate Executive Document No. 49, 48th Congress, 1884.

James, Ralph C., and Estelle Dinerstein James. *Hoffa and the Teamsters: A Study of Union Power*. Princeton: D. Van Nostrand Company, Inc., 1965.

Johnson, Nelson. *Boardwalk Empire*. Medford, New Jersey: Plexus Publishing Inc., 2002.

Jumper, Betty Mae Tiger, and Patsy West. *A Seminole Legend: The Life of Betty Mae Tiger Jumper*. Gainesville: University Press of Florida, 2001.

Kappler, Charles J., ed. *Indian Affairs. Laws and Treaties*. Washington, D.C.: Government Printing Office, 1904.

Kaye, Marvin. *The Story of Monopoly, Silly Putty, Bingo, Twister, Frisbee, Scrabble, Et Cetera*. New York: Stein and Day, 1973.

Kelly, Lawrence C. *The Navao Indians and Federal Indian Policy*. Tucson: The University of Arizona Press, 1968.

Kersey, Harry A. *An Assumption of Sovereignty: Social and Political Transformation Amoing the Florida Seminoles, 1953–1979*. Lincoln: University of Nebraska Press, 1996.

_____. *The Florida Seminoles and the New Deal, 1933–1942*. Boca Raton: Florida Atlantic University Press, 1989.

_____. *The Stranahans of Fort Lauderdale: A Pioneer Family of New River*. Gainesville: University Press of Florida, 2003.

Kling, Dwayne. *The Rise of the Biggest Little City: An Encyclodic History of Reno Gaming, 1931–1981*. Reno: University of Nevada Press, 2000.

Kluger, Richard. *The Bitter Waters of Medicine Creek: A Tragic Clash Between White and Native America*. New York: Alfred A. Knopf, 2011.

Lacey, Robert. *Little Man: Meyer Lansky and the Gangster Life*. Boston: Little, Brown and Company, 1991.

Lamar, Howard, ed. *The New Encyclopedia of the American West*. New Haven: Yale University Press, 1998.

Land, Barbara and Myrick. *A Short History of Reno*. Reno: University of Nevada Press, 1995.

Lane, Ambrose I. *Return of the Buffalo: The Story Behind America's Indian Gaming Explosion*. Westport, Connecticut: Bergin & Garvey, 1995.

Lansky, Sandra, and William Stadiem. *Daughter of the King: Growing Up in Gangland*. New York: Weinstein Books, 2014.

La Perouse, Jean-Francois de Galaup *A Voyage Round the World Performed in the Years 1785, 1786, 1787, and 1788 by the Boussole and Astrolabe*. London: A. Hamilton, 1799.

Lazarus, Edward. *Black Hills White Justice*. New York: HarperCollins Publishers, 1991.

Lee, Gaylen D. *Walking Where We Lived: Memoirs of a Mono Indian Family*. Norman: University of Oklahoma Press, 1998.

Lewis, Richard S. *Appointment on the Moon: The Inside Story of America's Space Venture*. New York: Viking Press, 1968.

Lipscomb, Andrew A., and Albert E. Bergh, eds. *The Writings of Thomas Jefferson*. 12 vols. Washington, D.C.: Thomas Jefferson Memorial Association, 1904.

Littell, Norman M. *My Roosevelt Years*. Seattle: University of Washington Press, 1987.

Lord, Eliot. *Comstock Mining and Miners* reprinted in Department of the Interior, Vol. 4 *Monographs of the United States Geological Survey*. Washington, D.C.: GPO, 1883.

MacCauley, Clay. "Seminole Indians of Florida" *reprinted in Fifth Annual Report of the Bureau of Ethnology to the Secretary of the Smithsonian Institution, 1883–84*. Washington, D.C.: Government Printing Office, 1887.

Mahon, Gigi *The Company That Bought the Boardwalk*. New York: Random House, 1980.

Martin, Jill E. "A Year and a Spring of My Existence: Felix S. Cohen and the Handbook of Federal Indian Law." 8 *Western Legal History* 35 (1995).

McCain, John, with Mark Salter. *Worth the Fighting For*. New York: Random House, 2002.

Meese, Edwin. *With Reagan: The Inside Story*. Washington, D.C.: Regnery Gateway, 1992.

Meister, Alan. *Indian Gaming Industry Report*. Newton, Massachusetts: Casino City Press, 2014.

Meyer, John M., ed. *American Indians and U.S. Politics*. Westport, Connecticut: Praeger, 2002

Meyer, Roy W. *History of the Santee Sioux: United States Indian Policy on Trial*. Lincoln: University of Nebraska Press, 1967.

_____. Revised edition, 1993.

Mills, Earl, Sr., and Alicja Mann. *Son of Mashpee: Reflections of Chief Flying Eagle, a Wampanoag*. North Falmouth: Word Studio, 1996.

Mitchell, Donald Craig. *Sold American: The Story of Alaska Natives and Their Land, 1867–1959*. Fairbanks: University of Alaska Press, 2003.

Moody, Eric N. *The Early Years of Casino Gambling in Nevada, 1931–1945*. Ph.D. diss., Reno: University of Nevada, 1997.

Nash, Roy. *Report to the Commissioner of Indian Affairs Concerning Conditions Among the Seminole Indians of Florida*. Senate Document No. 314, 71st Cong., 1931.

National Institute of Law Enforcement and Criminal Justice. *The Development of the Law of Gambling: 1776–1976*. Washington, D.C.: Government Printing Office, 1977.

Nelli, Humbert S. *The Business of Crime: Italians and Syndicate Crime in the United States*. New York: Oxford University Press, 1976.

Nesteroff, Kliph. "The Comedians, The Mob and the American Supper Club," February 19, 2012, available at http://blog.wfmu.org/freeform/2012/02/the-mob-the-comedians.html.

O'Connor, Sandra Day, and H. Alan Day. *Lazy B: Growing Up on a Cattle Ranch in the American Southwest*. New York: Random House, 2002.

Parks, Douglas R. "Pawnee" 13 *Handbook of North American Indians*. Washington, D.C.: Smithsonian Institution, 2001.

Pemberton, William E. *Exit With Honor: The Life and Presidency of Ronald Reagan*. Armonk, New York: M.E. Sharpe, 1997.

Pennsylvania Crime Commission. *Racketeering and Organized Crime in the Bingo Industry*. Conshohocken, Pennsylvania: Commonwealth of Pennsylvania, 1992.

Perry, Richard J. *Apache Reservation: Indigenous Peoples and the American State*. Austin: University of Texas Press, 1993.

Piper, Harry M., and Jacquelyn G. Piper. *Archaeological Excavations at the Quad Block Site 8Hi-998 Located at the Site of the Old Fort Brooke Municipal Parking Garage, Tampa, Florida*. St. Petersburg: Piper Archaeological Research, Inc., 1982.

Pirtle, Robert L. *To Right the Unrightable Wrong*. Bloomington, Indiana: Xlibris Corporation, 2007.

Pistone, Joseph D., with Richard Woodley. *Donnie Brasco: My Undercover Life in the Mafia*. New York: New American Library, 1987.

Pennsylvania Crime Commission. *Racketeering and Organized Crime in the Bingo Industry*. St. Davids, Penn.: Commonwealth of Pennsylvania, 1992.

Prucha, Francis Paul. *American Indian Policy in the Formative Years*. Lincoln: University of Nebraska Press, 1962.

Quimby, Garfield M. *History of the Potrero Ranch and Its Neighbors*. Fresno: California History Books, 1975.

Raymond, C. Elizabeth. *George Wingfield: Owner and Operator of Nevada*. Reno: University of Nevada Press, 1993.

Reid, Harry, with Warren, Mark. *The Good Fight: Hard Lessons From Searchlight to Washington*. New York: G.P. Putnam's Sons, 2008.

Richardson, James D. *A Compilation of the Messages and Papers of the Presidents, 1789–1897*. Washington, D.C.: Government Printing Office, 1896–99.

Robinson, Charles M. *General Crook and the Western Frontier*. Norman: University of Oklahoma Press, 2001.

Roemer, William F., Jr. *War of the Godfathers*. New York: Ivy Books, 1990.

Rossum, Ralph A. *The Supreme Court and Tribal Gaming: California v. Cabazon*

Band of Mission Indians. Lawrence, Kansas: University Press of Kansas, 2011.

Sarris, Greg. *Mabel McKay: Weaving the Dream*. Berkeley: University of California Press, 1994.

Sattler, Richard A. "Seminole in the West," reprinted in 14 *Handbook of North American Indians*, edited by William C. Sturtevant. Washington, D.C.: Smithsonian Institution, 2004.

Schultz, Duane. *Over the Earth I Come: The Great Sioux Uprising of 1862*. New York: St. Martin's Press, 1992.

Schwartz, David G. *Roll the Bones: The History of Gambling*. New York: Gotham Books, 2006.

Scott, Steve, and Melissa Mikesell. "Following the Money." *California Journal*, October 1999.

Settles, Thomas M. *John Bankhead Magruder: A Military Reappraisal*. Baton Rouge: Louisiana State University Press, 2009.

Shaw, Benjamin Franklin. *Medicine Creek Treaty* (1903), reprinted in 1906 Proceedings of the Oregon Historical Society, Appendix C, at 24–32.

Sheehan, Jack, ed. *The Players: The Men Who Made Las Vegas*. Reno: University of Nevada Press, 1997.

Simmons, Charlene Wear. *California Tribal-State Gambling Compacts, 1999–2006*. Sacramento: California Research Bureau, 2007.

Skibine, Alex Tallchief. "Indian Gaming and Cooperative Federalism." 42 *Arizona State Law Journal* 253 (2010).

Slagle, Richard. "The Puyallup Indians and the Reservation Disestablishment Test." 54 *Washington Law Review* 653 (1979).

Smith, Adam. *An Inquiry Into the Nature and Causes of the Wealth of Nations*. Homewood, Illinois: Richard D. Irwin, Inc., 1963.

Smith, John L. *The Animal in Hollywood: Anthony Fiato's Life in the Mafia*. New York: Barricade Books, 1998.

Smiley, Albert K., Joseph B. Moore, and Charles C. Painter. *Report of the Mission Indian Commissioners*. reprinted in House Executive Document No. 96, 52d Congress, 1892.

Spencer, Donald D. *History of Gambling in Florida*. Ormond Beach: Camelot Publishing Company, 2007.

Starita, Joe. *The Dull Knifes of Pine Ridge*. New York: G.P. Putnam's Sons, 1995.

Sternlieb, George, and James W. Hughes. *The Atlantic City Gamble*. Cambridge: Harvard University Press, 1983.

Stewart, Kenneth M. "A Brief History of the Mohave Indians Since 1850." 34 *Kiva: The Journal of Southwestern Anthropology and History* 219–236, April 1969.

Spinale, Dominic. *G-Men and Gangsters: Partners in Crime*. Santa Ana, California: Seven Locks Press, 2004.

Strickland, Rennard, editor-in-chief. *Felix S. Cohen's Handbook of Federal Indian Law*. Charlottesville, Virginia: Michie Bobbs-Merrill, 1982.

Sturtevant, William C., and Jessica R. Cattelino. "Florida Seminole and Miccosukee." reprinted in 14 *Handbook of North American Indians*, edited by William C. Sturtevant. Washington, D.C.: Smithsonian Institution, 2004.

Thomas, Alfred Barnaby, ed. *After Coronado: Spanish Exploration Northeast of New Mexico, 1696–1727*. Norman: University of Oklahoma Press, 1935.

Thorne, Tanis C. "The Removal of the Indians of El Capitan to Viejas: Confrontation and Change in San Diego Indian Affairs in the 1930s." 56 *Journal of San Diego History* 43 (2010).

Thrapp, Dan L. *General Crook and the Sierra Madre Adventure.* Norman: University of Oklahoma Press, 1972.

Turdean, Cristina. "Computerizing Chance: The Digitization of the Slot Machine (1960–1985)," Occasional Paper No. 15, Center for Gaming Research, University of Nevada Las Vegas, March 2012.

Underhill, Ruth M. *The Navajos.* Norman: University of Oklahoma Press, 1956.

U.S. Department of the Interior. *Handbook of Federal Indian Law.* Washington, D.C.: General Printing Office (1941).

Utley, Robert M. *Frontier Regulars: The United States Army and the Indian, 1866–1890.* New York: Macmillan Publishing Co., Inc., 1973.

____. *The Indian Frontier of the American West 1846–1890.* Albuquerque: University of New Mexico Press, 1984.

Van Meter, Jonathan *The Last Good Time: Skinny D'Amato, the Notorious 500 Club & the Rise and Fall of Atlantic City.* New York: Crown Publishers, 2003.

Vaughan, Alden T. *New England Frontier: Puritans and Indians, 1620–1675.* Boston: Little, Brown & Company, 1965.

Wagoner, Jay J. *Arizona Territory 1863–1912: A Political History.* Tucson: University of Arizona Press, 1970.

Wakefield, Sarah F. *Six Weeks in the Sioux Tepees: A Narrative of Indian Captivity, edited by June Namias.* Norman: University of Oklahoma Press, 1997.

Wallace, Anthony F.C. *Jefferson and the Indians: The Tragic Fate of the First Americans.* Cambridge: The Belknap Press of Harvard University Press, 1999.

Washburn, Kevin K. "Agency Conflict and Culture: Federal Implementation of the Indian Gaming Regulatory Act by the National Indian Gaming Commission, the Bureau of Indian Affairs, and the Department of Justice." 42 *Arizona State Law Journal* 303 (2010).

West, Patsy. *The Enduring Seminoles: From Alligator Wrestling to Ecotourism.* Gainesville: University Press of Florida, 1998.

____. "From Hard Times to Hard Rock." Forum, Florida Humanities Council, Spring 2007.

Wilkinson, Charles. *Blood Struggle: The Rise of Modern Indian Nations.* New York: W.W. Norton & Company, 2005.

Williams, John. *Gambling in Minnesota: A Short History.* Research Department, Minnesota House of Representatives. March 2005.

Wolf, Marvin J. and Larry Attebery. *Family Blood: The True Story of the Yom Kippur Murders.* New York: HarperCollins, 1993.

Wykes, Alan *The Complete Illustrated Guide to Gambling.* New York: Doubleday & Company, Inc., 1964.

Zinn, Howard, and Anthony Arnove. *Voices of a People's History of the United States.* New York: Seven Stories Press, 2004.

Zuckerman, Michael J. *Vengeance Is Mine.* New York: Macmillan Publishing Co., 1987.

CONGRESSIONAL HEARINGS

Indian Gambling Control Act: Hearing on H.R. 4566 before the House Committee on Interior and Insular Affairs, 98th Congress (1984).

Indian Gambling Control Act: Hearings on H.R. 1920 and 2404 before the House Committee on Interior and Insular Affairs, 99th Congress (1985).

Gambling on Indian Reservations and Lands: Hearing on S. 902 before the Senate Select Committee on Indian Affairs, 99th Congress (1985).

Establish Federal Standards and Regulations for the Conduct of Gaming Activities within Indian Country: Hearing on S. 902 before the Senate Select Committee on Indian Affairs, 99th Congress (1986).

Gaming Activities on Indian Reservations and Lands: Hearing on S. 555 and 1303 before the Senate Select Committee on Indian Affairs, 100th Congress (1987).

Indian Gaming Regulatory Act: Hearing on H.R. 964 and H.R. 2507 before the House Committee on Interior and Insular Affairs, 100th Congress (1987).

Federal Government's Relationship with American Indians: Hearings before the Special Committee on Investigations of the Senate Select Committee on Indian Affairs, 101st Congress (1989).

MANUSCRIPT COLLECTIONS

Allen Library, University of Washington, Seattle Washington
   Norman M. Littell Papers (NML)
   Slade Gorton Papers (SG)
   Atlanta Records Center, National Archives and Records
Administration, Ellenwood, Georgia
   Bruce Todd Wheeland v. Seminole Management Associates, et al., U.S. District Court for the Southern District of Florida Case Nos. 93-2365 and 93-6956 (*Wheeland* file)

   Seminole Tribe of Florida v. Butterworth, U.S. District Court for the Southern District of Florida Case No. 79-6680 (*Butterworth* file)
Beinecke Library, Yale University, New Haven, Connecticut
   Felix S. Cohen Papers (FSC)
California State Archives, Sacramento, California
   Daniel Kolkey Papers (DK)
Pacific Region, National Archives and Records Administration, Laguna Nigel, California
   Record Group 75, Bureau of Indian Affairs, Mission Indian Agency (MIA)
Ronald Reagan Presidential Library, Simi Valley, California
   White House Files (RRWHF)
National Archives and Records Administration, San Bruno, California
   Record Group 75

Sacramento Area Office, Bureau of Indian Affairs
    Tribal Group Files, 1915 - 1972 (TGF)
    Records of *Scotts Valley Band of Pomo Indians v.*
    United States, District Court for the Northern District of California
    No. C-86-3360 (SVB)
National Archives and Records Administration,
 Washington, D.C.
  Record Group 46
  99th and 100th Congresses
  Select Committee on Indian Affairs
  United States Senate (USS)

  Record Group 233
  99th and 100th Congress
  Committee on Interior and Insular Affairs
  U.S. House of Representatives (USHR)
North Gila County Historical Society
 Payson, Arizona
  Doris Sturges Harger Papers (DSH)
Special Collections, University of Arizona Library,
 Tucson, Arizona
  Dennis DeConcini Papers (DD)
  Morris K. Udall Papers (MKU)
Special Collections, University Library, Sonoma State University
 Rohnert Park, California
  Lynn Woolsey Papers (LW)
Washington State Archives,
 Olympia, Washington
  Dan Evans Papers (DE)
William J. Clinton Presidential Library
 Little Rock, Arkansas
  White House Files (WCWHF)
  Digital Library (DL)

INTERVIEWS

Alvarez, Mikel, Las Vegas, Nevada, March 13, 2015 (telephone).
Anderberg, Myles, Port St. Lucie, Florida, April 5, 2009.
Avent, Loretta, Phoenix, Arizona, May 22, 2014 (telephone).
Baker, Bobby, St. Augustine, Florida, March 3, 2010.
Barlow, Earl, Spokane, Washington, January 4, 2012 (telephone).
Billie, James, Brighton Indian Reservation, January 25, 2011.
Bersin, Alan, Washington, D.C., May 15, 2014, June 7, 2014 (telephone).
Brown, Sharon, San Pablo, California, January 15, 2008.
Butterworth, Robert, Fort Lauderdale, Florida, April 10, 2009.
Christian, Cathy, Sacramento, California, February 28, 2014 (telephone)

Couso, Ray, Susanville, California, December 12, 2012 (telephone).

Cross, C.R. "Sam", Indio, California, January 29, 2009.

Drake, Wanda, Los Angeles, California, May 20, 2009.

Estrada, Alfred, Miami, Florida, January 16, 2012.

Fedo, John, Side Lake, Minnesota, October 9, 2014 (telephone).

Feldman, Glenn, Phoenix, Arizona, October 31, 2011.

Fisten, Michael, Davie, Florida, January 12, 2012 (telephone).

Forman, George, San Rafel, California, February 7, 2014.

Frechette, Michael, Medford, Massachusetts, April 25, 1913 (telephone), and May 2, 2013 (telephone).

Fried, Charles, Cambridge, Massachusetts, May 29, 2012 (telephone).

Gede, Thomas, Sacramento, California, September 23, 2014, and October 17, 2014 (telephone).

Gordon, Sam, Coconut Grove, Florida, June 14, 2013 (telephone), and October 16, 2013.

Gorton, Slade, Bellevue, Washington, October 4, 2013.

Hellman, Donald, Washington, D.C., October 9, 2013.

Homick, Steve, San Quentin, California, February 8 and 9, 2014.

Horenbein, Barry, Tallahassee, Florida, May 23, 2010, April 1, 2013 (telephone).

Katz, Sam, Philadelphia, Pennsylvania, April 2, 2008.

Kolkey, Daniel, San Francisco, California, February 8, 2014, and March 18, 2014 (telephone), June 8, 2014 (telephone).

Kupcha, Karen, Joshua Tree, California, July 31, 2014 (telephone).

Levy, Buddy, Miami, Florida, January 16, 2012.

Martinez, Bob, Tampa, Florida, January 11, 2012

MacNamara, Gary, Fairfield, Connecticut, May 27, 2011.

Ogden, David, Washington, D.C., March 12, 2014 (telephone).

Osceola, Marcellus, Hollywood, Florida, October 14, 2013, and June 12, 2014 (telephone).

Paskind, Steve, Davie, Florida, October 16, 2013, October 31, 2013, October 31, 2013 (telephone), May 27, 2014 (telephone), November 5, 2014 (telephone).

Passanante, Rocco, Los Angeles, California, May 20, 2009.

Rios, Stephen, San Juan Capistrano, California, February 13, 2013 (telephone).

Sarnoff, Marc, Miami, Florida, January 24, 2011, and May 10, 2011 (telephone).

Saunooke, Osley, Sarasota, Florida, June 17, 2010 (telephone), January 28, 2011, and January 14, 2012.

Schwartz, Fred, Boca Raton, Florida, January 30, 2012 (telephone).

Sertell, D. Robert, Vineland, New Jersey, May 2, 2011, May 10, 2011, July 30, 2013 (telephone).

Shailer, Phil, Fort Lauderdale, Florida, April 7, 2009.

Shulstad, Marina, Minneapolis, Minnesota, December 9, 2011 (telephone).

Skelding, Jack, Tallahassee, Florida, March 5, 2010.

Starr, Joel, Tulsa, Oklahoma, December 22, 2014 (telephone).

Suedel, Lynn Lamm, Henderson, Nevada, March 18, 2015.

Swimmer, Ross, Tulsa, Oklahoma, December 3, 2014 (telephone).
Taylor, Pete, Washington, D.C., October 9, 2013.
Toensing, Victoria, Washington, D.C., October 8, 2013
Tommie, Howard, Hollywood, Florida, March 16, 2013.
Turner, John, San Diego, California, November 5, 2013 (telephone).
Turnipseed, Bertha "BJ", Lakewood, Washington, January 22, 2011.
Walston, Roderick, Walnut Creek, California, January 17, 2013.
Whalen, Jeffrey, Pine Ridge, South Dakota, November 26, 2014 (telephone).
Wheeler, Tom, North Fork, California, September 25, 2014.
Whilden, Michael, Monterey, California, January 23, 2013.
Woolsey, Lynn, Petaluma, California, September 22, 2014.

INDEX